Sex, Thugs and Rock 'n' Roll

Monographs in German History

Volume 1
Osthandel and Ostpolitik: German Foreign Trade Policies in Eastern Europe from Bismarck to Adenauer
Mark Spaulding

Volume 2
A Question of Priorities: Democratic Reform and Economic Recovery in Postwar Germany
Rebecca Boehling

Volume 3
From Recovery to Catastrophe: Municipal Stabilization and Political Crisis in Weimar Germany
Ben Lieberman

Volume 4
Nazism in Central Germany: The Brownshirts in 'Red' Saxony
Christian W. Szejnmann

Volume 5
Citizens and Aliens: Foreigners and the Law in Britain and the German States 1789–1870
Andreas Fahrmeir

Volume 6
Poems in Steel: National Socialism and the Politics of Inventing from Weimar to Bonn
Kees Gispen

Volume 7
"Aryanization" in Hamburg:
Frank Bajohr

Volume 8
The Politics of Education: Teachers and School Reform in Weimar Germany
Marjorie Lamberti

Volume 9
The Ambivalent Alliance: Konrad Adenauer, the CDU/CSU, and the West, 1949–1966
Ronald J. Granieri

Volume 10
The Price of Exclusion: Ethnicity, National Identity, and the Decline of German Liberalism, 1898-1933
Eric Kurlander

Volume 11
Recasting West German Elites: Higher Civil Servants, Business Leaders and Physicians in Hesse between Nazism and Democracy, 1945–1955
Michael R. Hayse

Volume 12
The Creation of the Modern German Army: General Walther Reinhardt and the Weimar Republic, 1914–1930
William Mulligan

Volume 13
The Crisis of the German Left: The PDS, Stalinism and the Global Economy
Peter Thompson

Volume 14
The 'Conservative Revolutionaries': The Protestant and Catholic Churches in Germany after Radical Political Change in the 1990s
Barbara Thériault

Volume 15
Modernising Bavaria: The Politics of Franz Josef Strauss and the CSU, 1949–1969
Mark Milosch

Volume 16
Sex, Thugs and Rock 'n' Roll: Teenage Rebels in Cold-War East Germany
Mark Fenemore

Volume 17
Selling the Economic Miracle: Economic Reconstruction and Politics in West Germany, 1949–1957
Mark E. Spicka

Sex, Thugs and Rock 'n' Roll

Teenage Rebels in Cold-War East Germany

Mark Fenemore

Berghahn Books
New York • Oxford

First published in 2007 by
Berghahn Books

www.berghahnbooks.com
First paperback published in 2009

© 2007, 2009 Mark Fenemore

All rights reserved. Except for the quotation of short passages for the purposes of criticism and review, no part of this book may be reproduced in any form or by any means, electronic or mechanical, including photocopying, recording, or any information storage and retrieval system now known or to be invented, without written permission of the publisher.

Library of Congress Cataloging-in-Publication Data

Fenemore, Mark.
  Sex, thugs and rock 'n' roll : teenage rebels in cold-war East Germany / Mark Fenemore.
    p. cm. -- (Monographs in Germany history ; vol. 16)
  Includes bibliographical references and index.
  ISBN 978-1-57181-532-3 (hardback : alk. paper) -- ISBN 978-1-84545-718-1 (paperback : alk. paper)
  1. Teenage boys--Germany (East) 2. Subculture--Germany (East) I. Title.

HQ799.G5F45 2007
305.235'10943109045--dc22
                            2007012583

British Library Cataloguing in Publication Data

A catalogue record for this book is available from the British Library
Printed in the United States on acid-free paper.

ISBN 978-1-57181-532-3 (hardback)
ISBN 978-1-84545-718-1 (paperback)

Contents

List of Illustrations	vii
Preface	ix
Acknowledgements	xv
Abbreviations	xvii
1. Introduction	1
2. Gendering the GDR	19
3. Remasculinisation	43
4. Re-education	54
5. A Teenage 'Revolution'?	69
6. Street Culture	85
7. Sexing Up Socialism	100
8. Remilitarisation	118
9. Rock 'n' Roll	132
10. Manufacturing Consent	156
11. Making Men Out of Them	184
12. Predatory Males	206
13. Conclusion	237
Postscript: Where Are They Now?	243
Bibliography	245
Index	269

To My Son Tariq

List of Illustrations

1. Wild and uninhibited dancing to rock 'n' roll. Still from *Die Glatzkopfbande* — 134
2. Mugshot of one of the 'fascist cowboys' involved in the June 1953 uprising — 137
3. Still from *Berlin – Ecke Schönhauser* depicting a face-off between a People's Policeman and rowdy teenagers — 143
4. Mugshots used by the Leipzig police to portray the rockers as strange and other — 149
5. Forming a wall in Berlin (13 August 1961) — 156
6. Walter Ulbricht being influenced by stalwart members of the working class as a member of the *Leipzig* Gymnastic Association at the beginning of the century — 162
7. Man of action Walter Ulbricht demonstrating his continued vigour by playing volleyball with 'the youth' — 163
8. In creating a chronicle for their school, pupils captioned this picture 'That's the power of the working Class. Former pupils of, now teachers at our school'. — 166
9. Let's twist again like we did last summer. Proof of Walter Ulbricht's commitment to modern but safe youth activities — 171
10. Photographs of beat fans ('amateur or drop-outs') from Lichtenberg — 175
11. Caricature showing the negative effects of beat music — 191
12. Photograph allegedly 'proving the threat' posed by Western non-culture. The Beatles with guns — 201
13. A '*Gammler* troop' lounging on the stage of the NVA at the 1973 World Youth Festival — 207
14. 'Young revolutionaries, from our school follow with interest the account of a former concentration camp prisoner'. School chronicle — 211
15. Wild man tattoos. 'For the animal the love, for the woman the whip'. Tattoos found on the back of a rowdy arrested by the police — 220

16	Identification with the imperialist enemies. Tattoos depicting Paris, New York and the Iron Cross.	220
17	Still from *Die Glatzkopfbande* showing former Foreign Legionary and gang leader 'King' receiving a pedicure from a blond admirer	223
18	Still from *Die Glatzkopfbande* showing the gang after they had undergone a metamorphosis from annoying to evil by shaving their heads	223
19	Members of the real *Glatzkopfbande* at their show trial in 1961	224

Preface

What follows is a study of what happens when gender, sexuality, Nazism, communism and rock 'n' roll collide and interact. The original conception for the book was heavily influenced by Detlev Peukert's remarkable study of members of the *Leipziger Meuten* during the Third Reich.[1] As a consequence, it differs from the widely available, standard analyses of the German Democratic Republic (GDR) by focusing less on the institutions designed to establish conformity and more on the occasions when they failed to achieve their goal. In the course of what became nearly a decade spent contemplating youth in East Germany I became increasingly frustrated with the one-dimensional depiction of teenagers in the archival sources. The young people who appeared in official reports (particularly those produced by the official youth organisation, the FDJ) were class- and genderless. It was as if, in the minds of youth functionaries, no differences existed apart from those between believers and non-believers. 'The youth' depicted in such reports was often a largely imagined entity formed by ideology and propaganda. It was united in the goal of fulfilling the tasks set for it by the party but, in parts, it was lagging behind and was not yet fully 'on-message'. The actual make-up, interests, behaviour and opinions of the (in reality highly diverse) youth population were less important to report writers than that they gave the appearance of loyal support. The subcultures that they formed as a means of creating their own experiences and identities only became important as evidence of a failure to achieve uniformity.

My search for sources capable of revealing different perspectives, horizons and frames of reference led me increasingly to novels, films and articles in newspapers and magazines. Given the degree to which the Socialist Unity Party (SED) sought to use the media as a means of moulding attitudes and beliefs (and of combating harmful Western influences), East German discussions and arguments concerning real issues affecting youth often became sandwiched between and blurred by fictional representations and interpretations. Historians of Germany tend to focus on how images are used to manipulate and distort. But in certain circumstances they can also reflect and help to form perceptions and opinions. Novels and films in the GDR did not just serve as educational and propagandistic devices, but also as genuine and tangible attempts to develop new forms of meaning and identity. Despite the 'tense regulation of all DEFA activities by party and state', the East German cinema 'proved to be a site for negotiating more general changes in popular lifestyles and inter-gender and inter-generational relations'.[2] The study of films and other forms of popular culture can enrich our historical understanding of how it is that particular mentalities and collective identities are formed. In this perspective, representations do not replace realities, but they help to inform how meanings were created under complex political, economic and social conditions.

It was in the course of analysing representations of youth subcultures that I came across evidence for the ways in which gender, sexuality, class and race were interpreted and reproduced in the GDR. Such an approach owes a great deal to the work of historians of the everyday like Detlev Peukert, Dorothee Wierling and Thomas Lindenberger, but also to the cultural studies approach of historians like Erica Carter and Uta Poiger. Although the history of how class and gender have interacted can be traced back well beyond the industrial revolution (and the introduction of conscription) in Germany, when we try to examine the relationship between sexuality, race and the body, we tend to think first and foremost of the Third Reich. In identifying particular aspects of youth subcultural style and behaviour as alien and other, members of the SED were engaged in a complex process of memory manipulation and displacement. A difficult and morally ambivalent past (even for those defined as blamelessly antifascist and the 'victors of history') led to the creation and external projection of prejudices and stereotypes in an attempt at disguising and deflecting attention away from ideological fissures within. Unlike other people with guilty consciences, German communists did not just try to hide their skeletons (notably complicity in the purges, the Hitler-Stalin pact, mass rapes by the Soviet 'friends'). Rather they repeatedly tried to conjure them away by means of linguistic gymnastics, dialectical subterfuge and the notion that they were keeping the East German population (or rather the *Volk*) 'clean'. Just as conservatives in West Germany sought to muddy the waters of the past and to make out that they had been reluctant bystanders (or even victims) rather than willing supporters of National Socialism, so too in the East the production of 'heroes' served to disguise complicity and to downplay or erase alternative notions of victimhood.

The book begins with an introductory chapter setting out the methodology and sources and linking aspects of East German society and culture with wider debates about the nature of gender and sexuality in the cold war. The following chapter explores debates about the extent to which gender equality was achieved in the GDR and points to the implications of divisions and conflicts within the party for the ways in which issues of gender and sexuality were interpreted, discussed and reassessed. Subsequently, Chapter 3 explores how the longer history of National Socialism and communism influenced the development of notions of heroism and masculinity in the aftermath of the Second World War. In the East, 'remasculinisation' did not involve softening or disarming masculinity. Rather (after a brief period of pseudo-democratic demilitarisation) it meant trying to remould men for new struggles. Although the Holocaust and the chaos brought about by defeat were by no means denied in the GDR, blame for them was displaced and members of the population were encouraged to look ahead to the future rather than back to their former selves in the past.

Young people growing up in East Germany were subjected to competing and conflicting influences, particularly in relation to gender. Chapter 4 explores the ways in which, in parts, the education system undermined but, in others, reinforced traditional notions of gender. Chapter 5, in contrast, analyses the impact of the 'teenage revolution' brought about by international trends in youth culture. While East German teenagers shared many experiences (school, youth organisation and 'days in production') which were typically 'GDR', to a greater or lesser extent they also retained a sense of shared identity with teenagers in West Germany and in Western Europe as a whole. In seeking to pursue the question of what was specific about the East German youth experience, I was interested not just in similarities and differences but also in crossovers and reflections. Although it is true that the GDR lagged behind in pluralisation and possessed a much more socially and ethnically homogeneous population than the Federal Republic, it is important to recognise that urbanisation together with changes to the education system and the spread of mass media did foster the development of perspectives and outlooks more common in Western, 'individualistic' societies. In the East as in the West, young people increasingly expected to be valued as individuals and not just 'lumped together'. Like their contemporaries in the West, they expected to be free to make their own choices in their private lives. They placed increasing emphasis on intimacy in their personal relationships and on casualness in speech and style of dress.

Music and dancing served not only as means for negotiating, altering and 're-engendering' relations between the sexes, but also as sources of generational conflict and refusal to obey those in authority. A stubborn and macho working-class sense of self (which is examined in Chapter 6) combined with the opportunities for expression provided by rock 'n' roll to produce a potent, if inchoate, form of rebellious opposition (explored in Chapter 9). For a minority of East German youth, the desire to demonstrate masculine superiority became a source of competition and struggle with the state. In their attempts to regain authority and influence over wayward and disinterested groups of youth, the communist leaders resorted to a number of strategies. Some softened the contours of domination. Others hardened them until they were indistinguishable from those of previous German regimes (not least the Third Reich). These alternative attempts to cope with the changes occurring among youth are explored in Chapters 7 and 8 (for the 1950s) and 10 and 11 (for the 1960s).

Under Ulbricht, periods of quite radical reform were interspersed with periods of fairly reactionary repression (not least with the building of the

Berlin Wall). Fissures within the ruling party and differences over the balance between production and consumption, persuasion and compulsion, meant that the path of socialist development was far from smooth. Ideas that were in vogue as highly realistic solutions to concrete problems one week vanished overnight only to reappear in official discourse (as if they had not gone away) several years later. It is only by digging down deeper that it is possible to locate these underground streams of critical thinking. Although the short bursts of reforming zeal hardly made a dent in the impenetrable bedrock of Stalinist reaction, they did help to create pockets of more open-minded pragmatism within (psychologically more porous strata of) the intelligentsia. There were always groups and individuals in the GDR who were prepared to embrace Rosa Luxemburg's maxim that true freedom meant the freedom to think differently. In its efforts to harness youth as a modernising force, leading figures in the SED were willing, on occasion, to tolerate certain changes in social and cultural mores. Nevertheless, continuing ambivalence within the party resulted in a series of pendulum swings between reform and reaction, modernism and anti-modernism during the course of the 1950s and 1960s.[3] During periods of reform, leading SED figures appeared to recognise that the aspirations of youth had altered. Associating such changes with the onset of more modern relations, propagandists sought to present the changes that were occurring in society and culture as if they had been pre-planned and orchestrated by the party.

Periods of apparent understanding and reconciliation, however, were often disingenuous. They represented an attempt to outmanoeuvre enemies as well as to highlight problems. In each case they were followed by a rapid return to manipulation and coercion. In the latter mode, the regime sought to respond to the changes in youth culture and identity simply by blocking access to the West. State-sanctioned notions of masculinity played an important part in these attempts to re-establish control. Young men were encouraged to join paramilitary organisations, became subject to pre-military training and were exposed to official expectations during military service. Exaggerated notions (and performances of) masculinity were made to serve not just as a means of rebelling against SED rule, but also of upholding and conforming with it. Whether used by rebels or servants of the state, the ostentatious use of masculinity remained ambivalent and redolent with echoes from Germany's past. A stance in which all attention was focused on strength and superiority easily led to persecution of the weak and a pursuit of aggression for its own sake. Chapter 12 investigates the development of 'deviant' forms of machismo in the latter decades of the GDR.

A book manuscript is necessarily the product of a number of compromises: between scholarship and accessibility; general and more specific arguments; theory and historicity; short-term and long-term factors; specific, local issues and wide-ranging, international trends. A straightforward chronological approach would have been unable to make sense of the different, overlapping layers of 'GDR reality' and the disjointed nature of societal and political-ideological development. Instead I chose to focus on the ways in which particular themes developed or recurred over the years. As far as possible, I have sought to provide greater complexity to notions like the 'GDR', 'the party', 'the police', 'the press' and the 'youth organisation'. Their different perspectives influenced the way particular issues were experienced, perceived and depicted, but they rarely spoke with a single voice. While it is hard to get away from talking about 'young people', I have tried to make clear whether I am referring to schoolchildren, teenagers, apprentices, workers, FDJ members, music fans, mods or rockers, boys or girls. Likewise, I have sought to differentiate between SED members who were former Communists, Stalinists or Social Democrats and those who were would-be reformers, members of the armed forces or self-styled Stasi 'chekists'. While the book's thematic structure has allowed me to explore different identities and viewpoints in some depth, I have tried to preserve enough room to incorporate an understanding of the impact of particular events and how changes occurred across time.

It is probably too early to say what was comparable and what was unique about gender, sexuality and youth in the GDR. Research on similar issues elsewhere in Eastern Europe is slow to filter through to German- or English-language publications. Letters and diaries may one day provide a less mediated and contrived (though no doubt highly subjective) source for exploring contemporary personal–political perceptions and feelings. Despite the rush to strip-mine them after 1990, the archives are far from exhausted. Nevertheless, newspapers and magazines offer an additional, rich seam for exploring the relationship between representation and perception, which has barely been touched. Differences of opinion regarding the validity of different types of evidence often belie differences over what constitute valid subjects of historical enquiry. Many historians still refuse to contemplate issues of gender (let alone sexuality) because they are unable to recognise them as being relevant or 'serious'. And yet they have so much to tell us about subjects that can otherwise seem 'done and dusted'. In a highly polarised political climate, there has been less room than might otherwise have been the case for methodological experimentation.

In the decade after unification, a significant emphasis was placed on telling, rather than asking, East Germans how life in the GDR had been. Being on the losing side in the cold war meant giving up the right to define (or influence) how the history of their culture and society (with all its ambiguities and contradictions) should be written. Approaches that are neither overly judgemental nor uncritically exculpatory can help to point to issues, music, fashion and ideas that, in spite of the immense political and ideological divisions imposed by the Iron Curtain, nevertheless succeeded in uniting people in both East and West.

Washington, DC
March 2006

Notes

1. Detlev Peukert, *Inside Nazi Germany*, trans. Richard Deveson (London, 1993).
2. Thomas Lindenberger, 'Review of Joshua Feinstein, The Triumph of the Ordinary: Depictions of Daily Life in the East German Cinema, 1949–1989', H-Net Reviews (March, 2004), http://www.h-net.org/reviews/; Jennifer Evans, 'Constructing Borders: Image and Identity in Die Frau von Heute, 1946–1948' in Hilary Sy-Quia and Susanne Baackmann (eds), *Conquering Women: Women and War in the German Cultural Imagination* (Berkeley, 2000), 40–61, 51; Anton Kaes, 'German Cultural History and the Study of Film', *New German Critique* 65 (Spring/Summer 1995), 49–56.
3. Mario Stumpfe, 'DDR - Historische Gegenwart. Eine Reflexion' in Stadt Eisenhüttenstadt/Dokumentationszentrum Alltagskultur der DDR (ed.), *Tempolinsen und P2. Eine Sammlung zur Alltagskultur der DDR entsteht* (Berlin-Brandenburg, 1996), 142–45; see also Wolfgang Kühnel, 'Der Lebenszusammenhang DDR-Jugendlicher im Spannungsfeld von institutioneller Verregelung und alltagskultureller Modernisierung', *Zeitschrift für Sozialisationsforschung und Erziehungssoziologie* 1 (1990), 105–13.

Acknowledgements

Renting a spare room in a strange town is always a bit of a lottery. My 'housemates' varied from the former wife of a *Wehrmacht* general (who went on to become a leading functionary in the NDPD, the party for former Nazis) to a collective of committed Ostalgists from Halle, who refused to speak anything but their native dialect. I crossed paths with a former chess champion hopeful, found respite with some laid-back former Monday demonstrators (called Sascha and Ulrike) and stayed in the apartment of someone who once performed in a mid-1980s low-budget West German movie about life in a steamy, sexually charged East German women's prison (called, appropriately enough, *Red Heat*). My generous hosts allowed me to gatecrash their private functions, to share their food and to accompany them everywhere from rock concerts to nudist beaches and *louche* bars. In addition, I met a number of researchers from a variety of disciplines (notably Brigitte Hausstein, Peter Bischoff, Dieter Rink and Frank Schulz), who generously provided encouragement and assistance. The many hours of conversations, discussions and, on occasion, arguments unquestionably deepened and enriched my understanding of the multilayered, ambivalent and often conflicting nature of the GDR as well as making the time when I was not in the archives pass more quickly. Especial thanks go to Alan McDougall, Josie McLellan, Damian Mac con Uladh and Leon Quinn for providing their own amusing anecdotes and novel cures for archivitis.

My partner, Samia, continued to support the project despite several changes of country, frequent absences and occasional moments of financial and existential panic. Living in Nansen Village (an international 'communal living experiment' for overseas students set up by idealistic products of Weimar Germany) provided us both with friends from so many different places (geographically, spiritually and culturally). Thanks go to the Centre for Historical Research at Limerick University, Tony McElligott and the other 'stab city' regulars for providing me with a temporary home away from home. Precious time for revision and rewriting was made possible by an Isobel Thornley postdoctoral fellowship from the Institute for Historical Research. A John W. Kluge fellowship from the Library of Congress has proved to be an unforgettably enriching experience.

A number of people offered important suggestions on how to improve the manuscript. Particular thanks go to Mary Fulbrook, Mark Hewitson, Patrick Major, Nicholas Stargardt, Guy Thomas, Simon Potter, Josie McLellan and Corey Ross. Various libraries and archives provided access to resources, together with indispensable help: in Berlin: the Federal Archives, the *Bibliothek für Bildungsgeschichtliche Forschung*, the *Brandenburgisches Landeshauptarchiv* and the *Landesarchiv* Berlin; and in Leipzig: the Saxon State Archives, the Leipzig Town Archives, the Gauck *Behörde*, the Saxon School Museum, the *Deutsche Bücherei* and the German Youth Research Institute. Being able to travel to Germany to use these sources would have been impossible without financial assistance from the British Academy, University College London, the German Academic Exchange Service and the German Historical Institute.

Lastly, I would particularly like to thank those who allowed themselves to be interviewed by me. It was a rare and unusual experience to be given intimate glimpses of what it was like behind their masks of 'normality'. Many had only previously shared the details of their experiences with their families. The act of laying bare their emotions and insecurities, thinking back to their dreams and aspirations and balancing up how their lives had subsequently turned out was an unusual but I hope not overly unpleasant experience. Although there are undoubtedly many ways in which the book could be better, without their help it would certainly have been much poorer.

ABBREVIATIONS

ABV	Abschnittsbevollmächtigter ('Section Plenipotentiary' or voluntary policeman)
AFN	American Forces Network
BBC	British Broadcasting Corporation
BBF	Bibliothek für Bildungsgeschichtliche Forschung (Educational History Library)
BDVP	Bezirksverwaltung der Deutschen Volkspolizei (Regional Administration of the German People's Police)
BFC	Berliner Fußballclub (Berlin Football Club)
BStU	Bundesbeauftragter für die Unterlagen der Staatssicherheit (Federal Commissioner for the State Security Records)
Bt&RdB	Bezirkstag und Rat des Bezirkes (Regional Parliament and Council)
CCCS	Birmingham Centre for Contemporary Cultural Studies
DDR	Deutsche Demokratische Republik (German Democratic Republic)
DEFA	Deutsche Film-Aktiengesellschaft (East German Film Corporation)
FDGB	Freie Deutsche Gewerkschaftsbund (Free German Trade Union Association)
FDJ	Freie Deutsche Jugend (Free German Youth)
FRG	Federal Republic of Germany (West Germany)
GDR	German Democratic Republic (East Germany)
GST	Gesellschaft für Sport und Technik (Society for Sport and Technology)
HO	Handelsorganisation (state-run department stores)
KPD	Kommunistische Partei Deutschlands (Communist Party of Germany)
KVP	Kasernierte Volkspolizei (People's Police in Barracks)
LVZ	Leipziger Volkszeitung (Leipzig People's Newspaper)
MfS	Ministerium für Staatssicherheit (Ministry for State Security)
MMM	Messe von Meistern von Morgen (Showcase for the Masters of Tomorrow)
NKFD	Nationalkomitee 'Freies Deutschland' (National Committee of 'Free Germany')
NSDAP	Nationalsozialistische Deutsche Arbeiterpartei (Nazi Party)
NVA	Nationale Volksarmee (National People's Army)

NWDR	Nordwestdeutscher Rundfunk (North West German Radio)
RdB	Rat des Bezirkes (Regional Council)
RIAS	Radio in the American Sector
SA	Sturmabteilung (Nazi storm trooper organisation)
SAPMO	Stiftung Archiv der Parteien und Massenorganisationen der DDR (Archive Foundation of the Parties and Mass Organisations of the GDR)
SBZ	Sowjetische Besatzungszone (Soviet Occupation Zone)
SED	Sozialistische Einheitspartei Deutschlands (Socialist Unity Party of Germany)
SPD	Sozialdemokratische Partei Deutschlands (Social Democratic Party of Germany)
SS	Schutzstaffel (Protection unit of the NSDAP)
StAL	Sächsisches Staatsarchiv Leipzig (Saxon State Archive, Leipzig)
Stasi	Staatssicherheit (State Security Police)
Stv&RdSt	Stadtverordnetenversammlung und Rat der Stadt (Town Council)
VVN	Vereinigung der Verfolgten des Naziregimes (Association of the Victims of the Nazi Regime)
ZA	Zentralarchiv (Central Archive)
ZAIG	Zentrale Auswertungs- und Informationsgruppe (Central Evaluation and Information Group)
ZIJ	Zentralinstitut für Jugendforschung (Central Institute for Youth Research)
ZK	Zentralkomitee der SED (SED Central Committee)
ZPKK	Zentrale Parteikontrollkommission (Central Party Control Commission)

◈ Chapter 1 ◈

INTRODUCTION

In the West, historians have begun to explore the role played by gender in politicising the personal during the course of the cold war. One approach is to emphasise the ways in which 'powerful men' (with their fingers on the trigger) 'imagined masculinity'.[1] The language of brinkmanship, it is suggested, was dominated to a remarkable degree by themes of masculine toughness. Those with the power to obliterate hundreds of millions of people around the globe spoke as if they were settling a playground dispute.[2] Again and again the language used by American statesmen was straightforward, blunt and posited on a perceived shared understanding of 'what a man's gotta do'. From the U.S. perspective, the Cuban Missile Crisis (when the world came to the very brink of nuclear war) was going 'eyeball to eyeball and the other guy blinked'.[3] Khrushchev, meanwhile, is supposed to have stated, 'It's been a long time since you could spank us like a little boy – now we can swat your ass. So let's not talk about force; we are equally strong.'[4] Such was Lyndon Johnson's fear that Robert Kennedy (and others) would brand him a coward – 'An unmanly man. A man without a spine' – that some believe he took the fateful step of engaging the U.S.A. further in the Vietnam conflict.[5] Nixon's policy in escalating the bombing of North Vietnam was equated by one contemporary critic with gang warfare – this 'manly readiness to stand up against aggression, to face up to the test of will at whatever cost'. Condemning the 'machismo' rampant in Washington, I.F. Stone asked, 'How many must die in the smaller countries, how many millions elsewhere must be placed in jeopardy because a superpower suffers from an inferiority complex?'[6]

An alternative emphasis in gendered studies of the cold war is to focus on the role played by consumerism and images of the family in rhetoric and discourse. Joseph Stalin (himself no stranger to masculine posturing) once contemptuously remarked that America's primary weapons were 'stockings, cigarettes, and other merchandise'.[7] Each side competed with the determination to demonstrate moral and economic as well as military and technological superiority. The self-image of the Soviet Union was of a utopia in which everything was organised for the good of the collective. The people were, in principle, to be freed from material necessity and provided with access to education, medicine and services previously restricted to the middle and upper classes. While communist ideals portrayed the great advances that would be made by the collective, the American dream, meanwhile, emphasised the freedom and material possibilities available to the individual. Both sides condemned what they saw as the dangerous, degrading and inhuman features of the other: the sacrifice of individuality to the state and the collective; the dog-eat-dog characteristics of unrestrained capitalism.

In many ways, Germany became the battle- and showground in a war to prove which was the better system. On their own, the visibly greater prosperity and freedom that existed in the West acted as powerful arguments against communism. At the 1959 Moscow Fair an infamous 'kitchen debate' occurred between Nikita Khrushchev and then U.S. Vice President Richard M. Nixon.[8] 'The two leaders did not discuss missiles, bombs, or even modes of government. Rather, they argued over the relative merits of American and Soviet washing machines, televisions and electric ranges.'[9] Ulbricht echoed Khrushchev's boast that he would bury the West in a '1000 little things' with his own threats to disarm the allure of the West by overtaking it in consumption.[10] Even underwear could become a point of conflict in the struggle between capitalism and communism as each side tried to outdo the other in the production of synthetic stockings.[11] To be certain of winning the battle for hearts and minds, however, the U.S.A. (to Soviet eyes unfairly) deployed Marshall Aid, anticommunist propaganda, media penetration and CIA subterfuge.[12]

The cold war was, in part, waged using symbols and metaphors.[13] Rather than being fought on the ground and in the air, it was a war waged over the airwaves. Each side had its own particular techniques of publicity, propaganda and myth-making. The iconic heroes of the Soviet Union did battle with the legends of Hollywood.[14] Stars of stage and screen played a key role in a struggle that was as much about beliefs as it was about superiority in tanks and missiles. In East and West conflicts occurred not just over popular culture and consumption, but also over the gender stereotypes associated with them. Elaine Tyler May has argued that in the late 1940s and early 1950s, a symbolic connection was made in academic literature, anticommunist campaigns and popular culture in the U.S.A. between fears of out-of-control sexuality and the insecurities of the cold war era.[15] Frank Costigliola has emphasised the extent to which the language of George Kennan's Long Telegram of 1946 was both gendered and eroticised. 'Kennan portrayed the Soviet government as a rapist exerting "insistent, unceasing pressure for penetration and command" over Western societies.'[16] According to Kennan, the West was dangerously accessible to 'Communist penetration' via 'labor unions, youth leagues, women's organizations, racial societies, religious societies … liberal magazines'. He urged that the United States 'tighten' up, achieve greater 'cohesion, firmness and vigor' and approach the Soviet Union with a 'determination not to be emotionally provoked or unseated'.[17] Masculinity itself was under threat.

New research has shown the extent to which Senator Joseph McCarthy sought to whip up fear not only about 'reds' but also about homosexuals within government. Linking 'Communists and queers', McCarthy allegedly stated to reporters, 'If you want to be against McCarthy, boys, you've got to be either a Communist or a cocksucker.'[18] Homosexuals were depicted as particularly at risk to Communist 'infection' because of their 'softness', their 'instability' and their 'inability to deny themselves the pleasures of their "perverted" sexuality'.[19] In his book *The Vital Center*, Arthur Schlesinger argued that Communism perverted politics 'into something secret, sweaty and furtive'.[20] An excessive preoccupation with – and anxiety about – masculinity in early cold war American politics led to an exaggerated cult of masculine toughness and virility in political culture. Anything less was soft and feminine, in a word 'sissified'.[21] In popular culture (which the McCarthyites sought to exert control over), the solution to confusion about post-war male identities left behind by the Second World War was to emphasise hypermasculine figures like the cowboy and all-round action hero John Wayne.[22] Wayne not only served as an image of rugged manly individualism in countless Westerns, but also as a spokesman for anticommunism.[23]

While moral hygiene films designed to be shown in the classroom presented a domesticated image of American adolescent males as wimpy and easily led, Hollywood films depicting war, crime and juvenile delinquency painted men as both tough and brutal.[24] In advice books aimed at girls, middle-class masculinity was presented as 'an extremely fragile achievement that could crumble under prolonged exposure to any girl or woman who displayed ostensibly male characteristics, such as boldness, initiative, and intelligence'.[25] Meanwhile films directed at teenagers were 'full of he-men who fought, drank and swaggered through plots designed to flatter their masculinity in every scene, picking up and discarding, often with astounding sadism, the extravagantly beautified women who multiplied at the time in Hollywood'.[26] The internationalisation of the mass media carried these images throughout the Western world. Despite initial concern about the negative effects that Westerns might have on youth, Uta Poiger argues that West Germans managed to overcome their fears and came to embrace the strong, silent hero as the right kind of man.[27]

The Wild East

Hypermasculine posturing and fears about homosexuality, Jennifer Evans argues, were not confined to the West. In the East, too, a connection was made between physical strength and moral fortitude.[28] In the 'wild years' (beginning with the return of prisoners of war in 1948), a new type of masculine adventurer emerged, who came to dominate visual imagery and fiction. The heroic period of reconstruction (as opposed to the sacrifice of rubble women in the years immediately after the war) was often compared to the gold rush of America's Wild West.[29] The mining towns had a particular reputation for lawlessness. As the youth organisation's newspaper put it, 'The talk is of rowdies, who are always staging fights.'[30] This image of the early GDR as the Wild East, a frontier society fit for rough and ready adventurers, is also reflected in Brigitte Reimann's novels, *Ankunft im Alltag* and *Franziska Linkerhand*, and in the unfinished novel, *Rummelplatz*, by Werner Bräunig.[31] 'Wismut is a state within the state and vodka is its national drink ... Policemen rarely let themselves be seen after nightfall.'[32] Miners were reported to demonstrate their sense of invincibility by riding on the top of overcrowded trains and freeing colleagues unlucky enough to get themselves arrested.[33] Presenting male workers as pioneers at the frontier helped not only to make the struggle to build socialism more exciting, but also to combat the imagery and propaganda emanating from the West.

The GDR had its own superpotent, macho figure in the form of Balla. 'He had to remain hard. He could not let himself be afraid of anything.' The way he responded to problems was to 'ball his hands into fists'.[34] A carpenter and a local legend in Leuna, he became the protagonist of a novel by Erik Neutsch and was subsequently portrayed by Manfred Krug in the DEFA film *Spur der Steine*.[35] The head of a brigade of carpenters, who plied their trade on building sites up and down the Republic, Balla was part highwayman and part cowboy. Feared and respected in equal measure, he wore a hat 'bigger than the sombreros worn by the Mexicans'.[36] He had no trouble in imposing his will on other men. 'He just had to show them his fist or, if it really came to the crunch, his hammer.'[37] He was a daredevil ladykiller with a pearl ring in his ear – '*na eben Wild-West*'.[38] Only three things counted for Balla: women, money and to be respected on the building site. 'Every site is a conquest ... Ice-cold, he storms the dancehalls with his crowd ... probing the tables and their female occupants like a new cock strutting among the hens.'[39]

Possessed of enormous energy, talent and drive, but wild, furious and coarse, Balla epitomised everything the communists needed and, at the same time, everything they despised. A 'looter of the worst sort', an anarchist, he was 'the kind the fascists had made heroes of'. In the last days of the war, he had volunteered to serve in the navy. Filled with romantic dreams of adventure, he had been tricked by Hans Albers and the other stars of German wartime cinema into believing that they could be found in war. He had found himself piloting a 'human torpedo', as the one-man submarines of the North Atlantic were known.[40] The experience left him hard and unwilling to conform. 'Germany, Fatherland – what is that anyway? Ulbricht or Adenauer, the SED or the clerics (*Pfaffentum*), exploitation or pressure to believe. One is as bad as the other. If I had to choose, I'd choose neither.'⁴¹ Seeking his gold not in Nevada, but in 'the ripped apart then patched up' Wild East of Germany, he nevertheless behaved like an outlaw on the frontier. As a result, he came to act 'like an emigrant in his own country'.⁴²

The novel supposedly described Neutsch's first-hand experiences of life among the workers building the Bitterfeld chemical complex. With its 'raw customs' and 'obscene songs', the building site is painted like a frontier society. 'Here force rules ... only by means of brutal violence does anything get built.'⁴³ The utopian vision of socialism had no place for 'asocial elements, rowdies and adventurers'.⁴⁴ Nevertheless in the chaos of a post-war (re)construction lasting decades, it still needed men like Balla, who, when push came to shove, knew how to get the job done. Even after the collapse of socialism in the GDR, there was a powerful desire to hold onto the heroic vision conjured up in the *Spur der Steine* mythos. 'What would have become of the great historical attempt to build socialism on German soil without their elemental power – however spontaneous or conscious they might have been? Our country lay suspended on their shoulders.'⁴⁵

The film, which proved so controversial that it was banned for twenty-three years, opens with a scene that seems to come straight out of a Western. Balla's unruly brigade of carpenters come across 'like the Magnificent Seven'.⁴⁶ They are dressed in their traditional *Kluft* of black corduroy (with waistcoats and wide-bottomed trousers). Their wide-brimmed hats are set at a jaunty angle. Striding across the construction site, pushing other workers out of the way and grabbing and kissing any female within range, they raise their bottles of beer as if presenting arms and pop out the stoppers in unison. Played with supreme self-assurance and arrogance by Manfred Krug, Balla is both a raw muscleman and a suave dandy. With a pearl earring in his left ear and a back like a block of concrete, he alternates between breaking stools, deriding the party, threatening other workers and wooing the female engineer, Katrin Klee. Both the book and the film were products of the period immediately after the building of the wall, in which the party leadership was in search of a new beginning. It appeared to contemporaries as if 'a great historical chance' existed for a new 'relationship between the working class and its vanguard'.⁴⁷ By questioning and provoking people to think differently about their everyday lives ('in den Alltag hineinzuprovozieren') idealists believed that a new and genuinely more revolutionary beginning was possible.⁴⁸

Local, Oral and Everyday Histories

The setting for many of the incidents and events explored in this book is the West Saxon city of Leipzig. Described by Lessing as 'a place where one can see the whole world in microcosm', Leipzig's prominent role in the book trade and as an academic centre lent weight to its claims to openness to new ideas and outside influences.[49] The town's associations with Bach and Mendelssohn, Goethe and Schiller bolstered its claims to be a city of music and culture. Leipzigers were proud of their city's reputation for cosmopolitanism, noting that Goethe described it in *Faust* as being like a smaller version of Paris. Although severely damaged by Allied bombing, Leipzig strove to regain its reputation as a cultural and a trading centre as soon as the war was over.[50] By hosting the GDR's trade fairs, Leipzig came to act as a showcase for the regime as well as the backdrop to official celebrations and initiatives such as the MMM (*Messe von Meistern von Morgen*) movement, designed to show youth's ingenuity and commitment to the regime. Twice a year visitors poured into the town, described as the 'showcase of the world', bringing with them examples of the latest music, literature and fashions together with unorthodox ideas and hard currency.[51]

For all its claims to worldliness and cosmopolitanism, however, the outlooks of many of Leipzig's inhabitants stretched no further than their allotments.[52] Ties to local neighbourhoods remained strong, helped by the insulation they had provided against National Socialist penetration, and were the object of intense loyalty and local patriotism. 'In spite of the breaking of many traditions and the destruction of institutions by National Socialism, war and Stalinisation, milieu-specific elements of lifestyle, forms of community socialisation (*Vergemeinschaftungen*) and social moral norms remained.'[53] Leipzig had always been a divided city, both politically and geographically. Fanning out from the centre were its various different middle- and working-class milieux. For the middle classes and 'intelligentsia', there were the houses in the musicians' and theatrical quarters to the south, together with the villas in Gohlis to the north. For the working classes, there were the heavily industrialised districts of Reudnitz and Sellenhausen in the east, which produced printing presses, and Plagwitz in the west, producing cranes and other heavy machinery.[54] Although power had traditionally been exercised by middle-class liberals and conservatives, Leipzig was the birthplace and a major stronghold of Social Democracy. The working-class districts had also long played host to the communists. Leipzig received much attention in the 1950s and 1960s for being the birthplace of Walter Ulbricht, who was a frequent visitor.[55]

The archives offer access to a range of different organisations and perspectives of life in the GDR, but the files are heavily dominated by the ideal at the expense of reality. Qualitative material on (male-dominated) forms of youth nonconformity in the GDR is plentiful if patchy. Ranging from school inspectors' reports to letters from little girls to their teachers, such material can, on occasion, offer opportunities not just for analysing youth nonconformity from above or below but also from within. As historians, we are naturally drawn to the exceptions to the rule. These are often conveniently labelled 'unusual incidents (*besondere Vorkommnisse*)', but they come with their own set of problems and issues. Much of the evidence for nonconformity can be succinctly described as 'snapshots' and 'mugshots'. Overviews were provided by inspection teams, youth research surveys, reports in response to demands from the centre and policymaking initiatives. Descriptions and characterisations of 'offenders' emerged through the study of individual case histories, reports on nonconformist incidents and records of interrogations with participants.

In addition to the reports produced for internal consumption, newspaper articles provide concise summaries of the publicly expressed views of politicians, social commentators and other critics, together with hegemony-building condemnations of 'outrageous haircuts', wild music and sexually advanced young women. On the rare occasions when information about the thoughts, beliefs and aspirations of young people in the GDR reaches us through the written sources, it has almost always passed through a series of distorting viewpoints and intermediaries. It is obvious, from the formulaic nature of these reports, that style and technique were often more important than content. Party conferences, plans and world events come and go, but the frustratingly imprecise references to 'a few', 'some' and 'the vast majority' stay the same. The writers evidently seek a compromise between showing that things are going 'really quite well', but at the same time 'not everything is quite yet as it should be'. The 'evidence' marshalled to fit this picture of pessimistic over-optimism usually shows a mixture of wholehearted approval and support, cynicism and outright rejection and statements lying somewhere in between.

Local, biographical and oral history approaches allow a more complex and nuanced picture of life (in this case under communism) to emerge, one that renders the fate of the population more understandable and comparable. In Germany, research on the local, specific impact of National Socialism was driven forward under the name of *Alltagsgeschichte* or the history of everyday life.[56] Subscribers to this new movement believed in history influenced by anthropology. They were particularly attentive to the importance of cultural symbols and practices and the attempts, particularly of workers, to carve out spheres of autonomy in their daily lives.[57] Clifford Geertz writes that 'doing ethnography' is like trying to read 'a manuscript – foreign, faded, full of ellipses, incoherencies, suspicious emendations, and tendentious commentaries, but written not in conventionalised graphs of sound but in transient examples of shaped behaviour'.[58] In attempting to work out what the meanings of such texts are, one is forced to ask both what is going on in this precise incident of transient, shaped behaviour and what are the conventions that govern the way in which it has been selectively transcribed, codified and preserved. More often than not, one is confronted with overlapping frames of interpretation. These require analysis more akin to that of the literary critic, sorting out the structures of signification and determining their social ground and import. Through thick description one attempts to make intelligible the context in which events and symbols acquired meaning and without which remain meaningless.

More and more East Germans are penning their memoirs of life 'in the zone'.[59] But their writings are dwarfed by the mountain of files left behind by the SED and its sister organisations. In order to try and make up for this dearth, a series of oral interviews was carried out with people who were once participants in the various 'scenes' and 'incidents'. Although with one exception they were all male, they came from a range of backgrounds. Those I approached because of their involvement in youth subcultures tended to be working-class. Those I had come across because of their involvement in incidents involving high school pupils came from both middle- and working-class backgrounds. By allowing them to explain their perceptions and feelings in their own words, an attempt was made to bring back the subjective dimension left out in official reporting. In addition, I interviewed the writer Erich Loest, the rock musician Klaus Renft and the youth researcher Walter Friedrich.

Oral evidence is often criticised and sometimes completely rejected for offering overly subjective or even unrepresentative accounts, too vulnerable to the vagaries of memory, hindsight, wishful thinking and personal bias to be of any use. Elements of all of these factors did, on occasion, surface in the interviews conducted during research for this book (and even more so during informal conversations) as did other problems not described in the textbooks, such as an interviewee who halfway through the interview revealed himself to be a right-wing extremist in charge of a gun club. But, although people's memories do occasionally play tricks on them and there are always those who seek to exaggerate and embellish, interviews are also capable of providing insights and glimpses into the past that would otherwise be impossible to discover.[60] An important benefit of an oral history approach is the degree of self-reflexivity and humility it requires of the interviewer. Interviews were important not just as a counter to the often wildly exaggerated and inaccurate written sources on youth nonconformity, but in order to challenge my own notions and preconceptions.

Lutz Niethammer argues that, by approaching 'otherness' reflexively, we can reveal as much about our own self-perceptions and presumptions as observers as about those we are observing.[61] There is a danger for researchers of projecting onto people in the past ideas of how we would like them to have been. Reading a file, one can have an impression of them, an image of how they might have been. But it is a completely different experience to be sitting opposite them, to be able to ask questions about what happened and how they felt, but also to be questioned by them in turn about one's reasons and motivations for writing about their past. It is also useful for historians, concerned as they are with 'typifying' and categorising people and things, to be confronted by individuals determined not to be pigeonholed. As a general rule, even in old age, former youth nonconformists do not tend to be shrinking violets in expressing their views.

One area where the more vociferous and outspoken did tend to be more reticent was in discussing their sexuality. Although one or two interviewees did talk unselfconsciously about their sexual awakening, they tended to be the university-educated and introspective exception rather than the rule. Former 'rowdies' tended to shy away from questions about their inner life, their families and their feelings, blocking questions they regarded as too intimate or intrusive with blunt, but unequivocal answers along the lines that their experience in this regard had been fine, normal, unproblematic and unexceptional. On asking one interviewee how he had felt when he had been incarcerated, he replied, 'Oh lovely, what do you think?' At certain points I would have liked to ask more, but felt too reserved and intimidated or that it would be inappropriate and overly voyeuristic to do so. Although one explicitly outed himself as having been a Stasi informer and another seemed to give away that he had taken photographs for the police, extracting confessions was not something that I consciously strove for.

Oral history will always be an unsatisfactory but nevertheless powerful and useful tool for historical research. Of course, memories are fickle and easily clouded (particularly with regard to questions of personal responsibility), but for 'ordinary people' (as opposed to elderly statesmen and retired bureaucrats) interviews are the closest most people will ever come to recording what they remember of their own particular part in history. Germany's eventful past and often deeply divisive historical tradition mean that it is difficult to use terms like 'popular history' or 'ordinary Germans' with the same ease that might be the case in Britain, France or the U.S.A. (although non-Germans have their own family and national skeletons). Those who embarked on oral history projects exploring people's experiences during the Third Reich were right to be sceptical and unromantic in dealing with what they said. But while interviewees differ in what they reveal and what they try to keep hidden, interviews do shed important light on areas that archival evidence alone would leave invisible or shrouded in darkness.

Homages to Masculinity: the CCCS Approach

The pioneers of cultural studies were streetwise, theoretically aware, urban and multiracial. Even today their accounts of youth subcultures in 1960s and early 1970s Britain are redolent of the rush of exhilaration and bravado that comes from being let loose on an unsuspecting public armed with a cool pair of jeans and a tape recorder. But the hip and savvy young men of the Birmingham Centre for Contemporary Cultural Studies (CCCS) were hopelessly in the grip of a romanticism that blinded them to the negative effects of machismo and that led them to identify with the young men they were studying.[62] In a post-war world in which working-class (as opposed to student) radicalism was remarkable for its absence, they seized on the subcultures as offering a form of 'resistance'. Drawing on the recently translated works of Antonio Gramsci, researchers at the CCCS situated youth subcultures in a 'dialectic between a "hegemonic" dominant culture and the subordinate working-class "parent" culture'.[63] They ventured enthusiastically into cultural spaces where others feared to tread, 'immersing themselves in the culture they were studying', but in the process trampled on their own critical distance and, until it was too late, failed to heed the increasingly vocal arguments of feminism.[64] Writing about subcultures, Angela McRobbie argued, is not and should not be the same as being in one. Nevertheless, as a result of their shared appreciation of 'the liberating release of rock music, the thrill of speed, of alcohol or even of football', the CCCS male researchers managed to blind themselves to the more oppressive features of the subcultures.[65]

Subcultures were described as being 'resistant' to the ruling hegemony when, in reality, they were often racist, sexist and homophobic.[66] By winning space (both cultural and real), they argued, the different subcultures provided 'a section of working-class youth (mainly boys)' with strategies for negotiating their collective existence.[67]

> Thus, in the resurrection of an archetypal and 'symbolic' (but, in fact, anachronistic) form of working-class dress, in the displaced focussing on the football match and the 'occupation' of the football 'ends', Skinheads reassert, but 'imaginarily,' the values of a class, the essence of a style, a kind of 'fan-ship' to which few working-class adults any longer subscribe: they 're-present' a sense of territory and locality which the planners and speculators are rapidly destroying.[68]

The skinheads' appropriation of some of the more macho features of working-class identity, which CCCS researchers affirmed as representing latent class consciousness, was increasingly manipulated and whipped up into racial hatred by the extreme-right National Front. Nevertheless, the CCCS researchers did not subject the violence and physical assaults on outgroups ('queer-bashing', 'Paki-bashing') to thorough analysis and critique, but instead described them in terms of 'defence of their territory' (against intruders and 'speculators').[69] The skinheads' preoccupation with 'a particular type of masculinity' represented 'their magical recovery of community'.[70] Likewise, in his infatuation for the lads' rebellious creativity, Paul Willis neglected to comment on their hostility and contempt towards women.[71] He failed to confront the violence underpinning the 'language of aggressive masculinity' evident in one lad's description of sexual intercourse as having 'a good maul on her'.[72] Crucially, McRobbie pointed to the ways in which the shop-floor culture, with its emphasis on toughness and resilience, was not only used to deal with the brutality of capitalist productive relations, but also against 'women and girls in the form of both wife and girlfriend-battering'.[73]

Subcultures came to prominence within a triangle of identities formed by class, race and gender. In Britain, there was a marked tendency among those studying youth subcultures from a cultural studies perspective to prioritise class at the expense of gender and race.[74] Among the proponents of cultural studies in the U.S.A. who emerged in the late 1990s, in contrast, there has conversely been a shift in favour of gender and race at the expense of an appreciation of the importance of class.[75] Despite the great interest in and attention focused on post-war youth subcultures in many countries (from Europe to Australasia), the role played by girls remains largely shrouded in mystery. Though subcultures allowed both boys and girls important means of exploring their genders and sexualities, the recordings of subculture (official, autobiographical, visual, ethnographical) tend to present them as being uniquely male. Not only were researchers reluctant to investigate teenage girl culture, but female adolescence has proved remarkably resistant to academic attempts at probing. While boys sought out the adult gaze in order to provoke it, girls tended to frustrate voyeurism by erecting barriers, disguising their activities or retreating to the safety and privacy of their bedrooms.[76]

Gramsci and the Hegemony-less 'Zone'

While some would erect an impenetrable barrier between East and West – with right and justice on one side and illegality and injustice on the other – a cultural studies approach downplays the importance of the state in relation to the importance of hegemonies.[77] Such an approach displaces questions of conformity and opposition from the conventional institutional arena (of the state and its organisations) to a variety of settings previously regarded as 'non-political' – the workplace, the street, the deviant or criminal, subculture, recreation, the family and the home.[78] Originally associated with Antonio Gramsci, 'hegemony' implies structures of invisible, 'naturalised' domination that are not even seen by the oppressed. Rather than forcing themselves on the individuals of a society, hegemonies control them subtly through education and the media to the extent that people consent to their own domination.[79] But hegemony is always characterised by uncertainty, impermanence and contradiction. Questions of power, authority and control of the definitions of reality are constantly the subject of negotiations between men and women, parents and children, teachers and students, rulers and ruled.[80]

What is particularly interesting about East Germany in the 1950s and the 1960s is the absence of a dominant hegemony. Although the Socialist Unity Party (SED) was desperate to develop state-supportive notions as a means of gaining the population's support, or at least their acceptance, in contributing to the project of building socialism, these efforts to construct and impose a single, unifying vision stood in marked contrast to the diversity of ideologies and belief systems still active among the population. Young people growing up in East Germany found themselves sandwiched between the claims of two mutually exclusive ideological systems, both vying for their loyalty. Perceived as being idealistic, but malleable, they were bombarded from all sides by different interpretations and labels. As 'socialists' or 'bourgeois', as 'Christians' or atheists, or simply (but not unambiguously) labelled as 'Germans', they were forced to make choices about how to live their lives, what to do, what to believe, what to think, what to listen to, how to dress and how to behave.[81] The competing messages, claims and 'takes on reality' forced them to think more intensely about where they belonged and to pose more questions about their identity than other young people.[82] A cultural studies approach makes it possible to take account not just of the frontier of concrete and barbed wire surrounding the GDR, but of boundaries and borderlines that existed within East German society.

A major obstacle to regime attempts at influence was *Eigensinn*.[83] *Eigensinn* denotes 'wilfulness, spontaneous self-will, a kind of self-affirmation, an act of (re)appropriating alienated social relations on and off the shop floor'. In standard parlance, the word *Eigensinn* has pejorative overtones, referring to 'obstreperous, obstinate' behaviour, usually of children. A number of recent works have removed the term from its immediate associations with workers' pranks and used instead the 'discompounded' version of *Eigen-sinn* as a concept for explaining the behaviours of a wide range of social groups in the GDR.[84] The 'discompounding' of writing it as *Eigen-sinn* stresses its root signification of 'one's own sense, own meaning'.[85] In addition to the 'own sense' or *Eigen-sinn* provided for them by their sociocultural milieux, young people also acquired 'immunity' from influence by listening in to Western media. Not only was the GDR within broadcasting range of Western radio stations, but, until 13 August 1961, the 'dens of iniquity' in West Berlin were physically accessible to young people from the East.

Wrapped up in, and still scarred by, their own pathos-filled experiences of exile, imprisonment and resistance, communist leaders were initially taken aback by the development of a new, international youth culture spreading from America. Exposure to new forms of youth culture from the West not only offered young people alternative information and outlooks, but aided them in withdrawing from official incorporation strategies by submerging themselves into their own separate worlds of hobbies, youth-specific interests and subcultures.[86] In both Eastern and Western Europe, a series of 'moral panics' occurred in which garish images were projected onto youth.[87] In their hostility to subcultures, hardline communists in East Germany showed a remarkable similarity to the conservatives in the West. Both used racial and sexual stereotypes to construct young people in the subcultures as dangerous, deviant and other.

The struggles over youth that occurred in the GDR were similar in essence to those that were happening throughout the developed world during the

1950s and 1960s. This was the period in which the traditional gave way to the modern in relation to youth. Young people won for themselves a degree of freedom and autonomy in terms of sexuality and self-determination and expressed their growing difference from adults through clothing and haircuts. A culture in which parents were expected to act as autocratic dictators and their children obsequiously to obey gradually gave way to one in which children were seen more and more as equal partners in decisions affecting their future. In the West, one of the key features of post-war modernisation was 'the growth of individual options and of freedom in the sense of the loosening of ties'.[88] In the GDR, the SED sought to achieve modernisation 'objectively' from above by dictating 'what progress meant, what individual options should look like [and] what means should be used for what ends'. In contrast, the 'Western model' allowed greater opportunities for modernisation to occur 'from below', in the process giving it a more 'subjective' character.[89]

Although it may seem strange for some (particularly those writing institutional histories of political domination) to use terms like 'freedom' and 'self-determination' in relation to the GDR, East German youth did experience similar changes to their counterparts in the West. Young people in the subcultures were at the forefront of challenging and renegotiating the subjectivities and identities of youth. They acted as a visible manifestation of the pluralisation of values and lifestyles that, although given less discursive exposure, nevertheless did, to an extent, occur in the GDR. While the structures and techniques of influence and repression available to the state remained essentially static and unchanging, changes were afoot that made the state and its pathos-laden claims appear increasingly irrelevant to youth. Although they took place predominantly in the social and cultural rather than in the political sphere, these changes had a major impact on young people's outlooks and identities. Notions like self-realisation and self-expression, personal freedom and alternative lifestyles became important concepts, often with more importance and significance than the political issues presented by the party.

It is the personal–political nature of this struggle for a more modern outlook that explains how it was that young people could mount highly effective challenges to the regime and its attempts to control them and yet, in many cases, still consider themselves and their actions to be 'non-political'. As Klaus Renft put it, 'we didn't get out of bed in the morning thinking "Right, how are we going to bring down the state?"'.[90] Given the demands of his rock 'n' roll lifestyle, he frequently did not get out of bed at all. Although a few, isolated instances of explicit 'resistance' to the regime did occur, those in the subcultures mostly just got in the way of the SED's attempts to mould and influence young people. Anti-political in outlook, these groups nevertheless acted as an important source of opposition and protest. Having found themselves on the wrong side of boundaries of taste and behaviour imposed by the SED, pride, overexcitement, peer pressure, loss of self-control, a desire to impress the opposite sex, the search for popularity or the need to maintain 'image' or face could all lead to further transgressions, provocations and defiance. Once over the line, they rapidly challenged the regime's authority, thereby subverting its claims to legitimacy and undermining its professed ability to control societal development. Although the atmosphere in the cliques was heavily macho, these young men and the exceptional young women who 'marched' (or rather slouched) alongside them acted as living embodiments of the feminist slogan that 'the personal is political' long before it became a feminist slogan.

To truly understand the complexities of post-war Germany, we have to stop taking sides (at least along the classic geopolitical fault line). By finding our way beyond the East-West binary, we can explore and embrace the full range of different post-war 'German' experiences and identities. We need to recognise differences not just of politics and geography but of class, gender, education and culture. This is especially true of the period before the building of the Berlin Wall when it was possible (and over three million people did so) to change one's citizenship and alter one's identity.[91] A more productive approach is to explore the ways in which the two states often mirrored each other in their competition to prove which was the 'better' Germany (and in their desire to muddy the waters of the past). Internal police reports from the two Germanies reveal striking similarities as well as differences.[92] They point to the way in which those labelled as wayward youth (or loose women) ended up doubly damned, at home neither in the East nor in the West. While much of the literature emphasises separate paths of development (not least in terms of gender), there are also approaches that recognise the no-man's-land that existed in between the two states and explore the ways in which crossovers occurred between the two.[93]

Notes

1. Robert Dean, 'Masculinity as Ideology: John F. Kennedy and the Domestic Politics of Foreign Policy', *Diplomatic History* 22:1 (Winter 1998), 29–62, 30.
2. Within the hypermasculine culture of the military-industrial complex, more indirect modes of discourse were preferred. Carol Cohn, 'Sex and Death in the Rational World of Defense Intellectuals', *SIGNS* 12:4 (1987), 687–718.
3. Cynthia Enloe, *The Morning After: Sexual Politics at the End of the Cold War* (Berkeley, 1993); Robert Dean, *Imperial Brotherhood, Gender and the Making of Cold War Foreign Policy* (Amherst, 2001); Emily Rosenberg, '"Foreign Affairs" after World War II: Connecting Sexual and International Politics', *Diplomatic History* (Winter, 1994), 307–37; Carol Cohn, 'Wars, Wimps, and Women: Talking Gender and Thinking War' in Miriam Cooke and Angela Woolacott (eds), *Gendering War Talk* (Princeton, 1993), 227–46.
4. Stewart Udall's account of his meeting with Khrushchev as cited in Aleksandr Fursenko and Timothy Naftali, *'One Hell of a Gamble'. Khrushchev, Castro and Kennedy, 1958–1964* (New York, London, 1997), 209.
5. Dean, *Imperial Brotherhood*, 201.

6. I.F. Stone, 'Machismo in Washington', *New York Review of Books* (18 May 1972), 13–14.
7. Emily Rosenberg, 'Review Article', *Journal of American History* 84:4 (March 1998), 1576–78, 1576.
8. Walter Hixson, *Parting the Curtain: Propaganda, Culture, and the Cold War, 1945–1961* (New York, 1997), 151ff.
9. Elaine Tyler May, *Homeward Bound. American Families in the Cold War Era* (New York, 1988), 16ff.
10. Katherine Pence, 'The Myth of a Suspended Present: Prosperity's Painful Shadow in 1950s East Germany' in Paul Betts and Greg Eghigian (eds), *Pain and Prosperity. Reconsidering Twentieth-Century German History* (Stanford, 2003), 137–59, 157; Paul Betts, 'The Politics of Post-Fascist Aesthetics. 1950s West and East German Industrial Designs' in Richard Bessel and Dirk Schumann (eds), *Life after Death. Approaches to a Cultural and Social History of Europe during the 1940s and 1950s* (Washington, DC, Cambridge, 2003), 291–321.
11. On the 'battle of the stockings', see Erica Carter, *How German is She? Postwar West German Reconstruction and the Consuming Woman* (Ann Arbor, 1997), 164–70.
12. Scott Lucas, *Freedom's War. The US Crusade against the Soviet Union 1945–56* (Manchester, 1999), 35ff.; Hixson, *Parting the Curtain*, 16ff.
13. Rana Mitter and Patrick Major (eds), *Across the Blocs. Cold War Cultural and Social History* (London, Portland, 2004).
14. *Red Nightmare*, produced by Warner Bros. for the U.S. Department of Defence (USA, 1962). The film ends with the statement, 'To prevent Communism from consuming the entire world, there stands but one man. That man is you!'
15. Tyler May, *Homeward Bound*, 93; Geoffrey Smith, 'National Security and Personal Isolation: Sex, Gender, and Disease in the Cold-war United States', *International History Review* 14 (1992), 307–37.
16. Frank Costigliola, '"Unceasing Pressure for Penetration": Gender, Pathology, and Emotion in George Kennan's Formation of the Cold War', *Journal of American History* 83:4 (March 1997) 1309–39.
17. Ibid., 1333.
18. Robert Corber, *Homosexuality in Cold War America: Resistance and the Crisis of Masculinity* (Durham, 1997).
19. Dean, *Imperial Brotherhood*, 63ff.; John D'Emilio, 'The Homosexual Menace: The Politics of Sexuality in Cold War America' in John D'Emilio (ed.), *Making Trouble: Essays on Gay History, Politics and the University* (New York, 1992), 57–73; U.S. Senate, *Employment of Homosexuals and Other Sex Perverts in Government* (Washington, DC, 1950).
20. K.A. Cuordileone, '"Politics in an Age of Anxiety": Cold War Political Culture and the Crisis in American Masculinity, 1949–1960', *Journal of American History* 87:2 (September 2000), 515–45.
21. Ibid.; Michael Davidson, *Guys Like Us. Citing Masculinity in Cold War Poetics* (Chicago, 2003).
22. Suzanne Clark, *Cold Warriors. Manliness on Trial in the Rhetoric of the West* (Carbondale, Edwardsville, 2000); Steve Cohan, *Masked Men. Masculinity and the Movies in the Fifties* (Bloomington, Indianapolis, 1997); David Savran, *Communists, Cowboys and Queers. The Politics of Masculinity* (Minneapolis, 1992); Matthew Basso, Laura McCall and Dee Garceau (eds), *Across the Great Divide. Cultures of Manhood in the West* (New York, London, 2001).
23. *The Challenge of Ideas*, produced by the U.S. Army (U.S.A., 1961).
24. Ken Smith, *Mental Hygiene. Classroom Films, 1945–1970* (New York, 1999); James Gilbert, *A Cycle of Outrage. America's Reaction to the Juvenile Delinquent of the 1950s* (New York, Oxford, 1986).
25. Patricia McDaniel, 'Shrinking Violets and Caspar Milquetoasts: Shyness and Heterosexuality from the Roles of the Fifties to The Rules of the Nineties', *Journal of Social History* 34:3 (2001), 547–68, 549.
26. Dick Bradley, *Understanding Rock 'n' Roll. Popular Music in Britain 1955–1964* (Buckingham, 1992), 100.

27. Uta Poiger, 'A New, "Western" Hero? Reconstructing German Masculinity in the 1950s', *SIGNS* 24:1 (Autumn 1998), 147–69; Uta Poiger, 'Taming the Wild West: American Popular Culture and the Cold War Battles over East and West German Identities, 1949–1961' (Brown University: Ph.D. Thesis, 1995).
28. Jennifer Evans, 'The Moral State: Men, Mining, and Masculinity in the Early GDR', *German History* 23:3 (2005), 355–70.
29. Rob Roeling, 'Arbeiter im Uranbergbau: Zwang, Verlockungen und soziale Umstände (1945–1952)' in Rainer Karlsch and Harm Schröter (eds), *'Strahlende Vergangenheit'. Studien zur Geschichte des Uranbergbaus der Wismut* (St. Katharinen, 1996), 99–133, 118.
30. 'Das Maß ist voll. 900 jung Wismut-Kumpel warten auf die FDJ. Wie lange bestimmen noch die Rowdies?', *Junge Welt* (30 May 1956).
31. Brigitte Reimann, *Ankunft im Alltag* (Berlin, 1961), 27, 70ff., 124.
32. Werner Bräunig, 'Rummelplatz', *Neue Deutsche Literatur* 10 (1965), 7–29, 8.
33. Ibid., 15–16.
34. Erik Neutsch, *Spur der Steine* (Halle, 1964), 408.
35. *Spur der Steine*, directed by Frank Beyer (DEFA, 1966); Joshua Feinstein, *The Triumph of the Ordinary. Depictions of Daily Life in East German Cinema, 1949–1989* (Chapel Hill, London, 2002), 176ff.
36. Neutsch, *Spur der Steine*, 190.
37. Ibid., 126.
38. Ibid., 166, 190.
39. Ibid., 95; at the end of the film, however, Balla, the archetypal 'anarchic adventurer', becomes a working-class personality conscious of his societal responsibility.
40. Ibid., 99, 178.
41. Ibid., 234.
42. Ibid., 290.
43. Ibid., 60, 70.
44. Ibid., 179, 190.
45. Volker Müller, 'Wieder auf der "Spur der Steine" – Erstaunliches war zu entdecken. Endlich im Kino: Frank Beyers Film nach dem Roman von Erik Neutsch', *Neues Deutschland* (24 November 1989).
46. Karl Knietzsch, 'Die Spur der "Spur der Steine". Gedanken zur Wiederaufführung eines ehemals verfemten Films', *Die Union* (6 March 1990); 'Wohin die Spur der Steine führt … Verbotene DEFA-Filme kommen wieder', *Neue Zeit* (28 November 1989).
47. 'Wiederentdeckte Wirklichkeit nach 23 Jahren noch aktuell. Zur Neuaufführung des lange verbotenen Films "Spur der Steine" in Halle', *Freiheit Halle* (28 November 1989).
48. Müller, 'Wieder auf der "Spur der Steine"'.
49. Timothy Blanning, *The Culture of Power and the Power of Culture. Old Regime Europe 1660–1789* (Oxford, 2002), 169–70.
50. Ursula Oehme (ed.), *Alltag in Ruinen. Leipzig 1945–1949* (Altenburg, 1995), 44.
51. Reinhold Hennig, *Leipzig, Schaufenster der Welt* (Berlin, 1959).
52. Interview with Klaus Renft (2000).
53. Dieter Rink, 'Das Leipziger Alternativmilieu zwischen alten und neuen Eliten' in Michael Vester, Michael Hofmann and Irene Zierke (eds), *Soziale Milieus in Ostdeutschland. Gesellschaftliche Strukturen zwischen Zerfall und Neubildung* (Cologne, 1995), 193–229.
54. Michael Hofmann, 'Die Leipziger Metallarbeiter. Etappen sozialer Erfahrungsgeschichte. Milieubiographie eines Arbeitermilieus in Leipzig' in Vester, Hofmann and Zierke (eds), *Soziale Milieus in Ostdeutschland*, 136–92.
55. Michael Rudloff (ed.), *'Solche Schädlinge gibt es auch in Leipzig'. Sozialdemokraten und die SED* (Frankfurt am Main, 1997); Michael Rudloff and Thomas Adlam (eds), *Leipzig – Wiege der Deutschen Sozialdemokratie* (Berlin, 1996); Jürgen Tubbesing, *Nationalkomitee 'Freies Deutschland' – Antifaschistischer Block – Einheitspartei. Aspekte der Geschichte der antifaschistischen Bewegung in Leipzig* (Beucha, 1996).

56. For the best summary of this approach, see Alf Lüdtke (ed.), *The History of Everyday Life. Reconstructing Historical Experiences and Ways of Life* (Princeton, 1989).
57. David Barclay and Eric Weitz (eds), *Between Reform and Revolution. German Socialism and Communism from 1840 to 1990* (New York, Oxford, 1998), 18; Geoff Eley, 'Labor History, Social History, *Alltagsgeschichte*: Experience, Culture and the Politics of the Everyday – A New Direction for German Social History?', *Journal of Modern History* 61:2 (1989), 297–343; David Crew, '*Alltagsgeschichte*: A New Social History from Below?', *Central European History* 22:3/4 (1989), 394–407.
58. Clifford Geertz, *The Interpretation of Cultures* (London, 1993), 10.
59. Recent examples include Jana Hensel, *Zonenkinder* (Reinbek bei Hamburg, 2002); Claudia Rusch, *Meine Freie Deutsche Jugend* (Frankfurt am Main, 2003); Hans-Dieter Schütt (ed.), *Klaus Renft. Zwischen Liebe und Zorn* (Berlin, 1997).
60. For a romanticised view of the value of oral history as evidence, see Paul Thompson, *The Voice of the Past. Oral History* (Oxford, 3rd edn, 2000), ch. 4. For less positive views, see Ronald Grele, 'Movement without Aim. Methodological and Theoretical Problems in Oral History' in Robert Perks and Alistair Thomson (eds), *The Oral History Reader* (London, 1998), 38–52.
61. Lutz Niethammer, 'Zeroing In on Change – In Search of Popular Experience in the Industrial Province of the GDR' in Lüdtke (ed.), *History of Everyday Life*, 252–311.
62. Stuart Hall and Tony Jefferson (eds), *Resistance through Rituals. Youth Subcultures in Postwar Britain* (London, 1976).
63. John Clarke, Stuart Hall, Tony Jefferson and Brian Roberts, 'Subcultures, Cultures and Class' in Hall and Jefferson (eds), *Resistance through Rituals*, 9–74, 38.
64. Will Brooker, *Cultural Studies* (London, 1998), 60–69.
65. Angela McRobbie, 'Settling Accounts with Subcultures: A Feminist Critique' in Angela McRobbie, *Feminism and Youth Culture* (Houndsmills, London, 2nd edn, 2000), 26–43.
66. Angela McRobbie and Jenny Garber, 'Girls and Subcultures' in Hall and Jefferson (eds), *Resistance through Rituals*, 209–22.
67. Clarke et al., 'Subcultures, Cultures and Class', 45, 47.
68. Ibid., 48.
69. John Clarke, 'Style' in Hall and Jefferson (eds), *Resistance through Rituals* (London, 1976), 175–91, 181.
70. John Clarke, 'The Skinheads and the Magical Recovery of Community' in Hall and Jefferson (eds), *Resistance through Rituals*, 99–102, 99.
71. Brooker, *Cultural Studies*, 76.
72. McRobbie, 'Settling Accounts', 31.
73. Ibid., 32.
74. Ibid.
75. There has also been a concomitant shift towards what Stuart Hall describes as 'deconstructive ventriloquism' and, with it, a tendency to see 'power and politics as exclusively matters of language and textuality'. Stuart Hall, 'Cultural Studies and its Theoretical Legacies' in Simon During (ed.), *The Cultural Studies Reader* (London, New York, 2nd edn, 1999), 97–109, 108.
76. Erica Carter, 'Alice in Consumer Wonderland: West German Case Studies in Gender and Consumer Culture' in Angela McRobbie and Mica Nava (eds), *Gender and Generation* (London, Basingstoke, 1984), 185–214.
77. Thomas Lindenberger, 'Sonnenallee – ein Farbfilm über die Diktatur der Grenze(n)', *Werkstattgeschichte* 26 (2000), 87–96; Konrad Jarausch, *Dictatorship as Experience. Towards a Socio-cultural History of the GDR* (New York, Oxford, 1999).
78. Nicholas Dirks, Geoff Eley and Sherry Ortner, 'Introduction' to Nicholas Dirks, Geoff Eley and Sherry Ortner (eds), *Culture / Power / History. A Reader in Contemporary Social Theory* (Princeton, 1994), 3–45, 4.
79. Hall and Jefferson (eds), *Resistance through Rituals*, 38–39; Antonio Gramsci, *Selections from the Prison Notebooks* (London, 1971).

80. Dirks, Eley and Ortner (eds), *Culture / Power / History*, 4.
81. Walter Friedrich, *Flegeljahre? Zur Erziehung 13- bis 16jähriger Jungen* (Berlin, 1964), 28.
82. Siegfried Dübel, *Deutsche Jugend im Wirkungsfeld Sowjetischer Pädagogik* (Bonn, 1953), 5.
83. Alf Lüdtke, 'What Happened to the "Fiery Red Glow"? Workers' Experiences and German Fascism' in Lüdtke (ed.), *History of Everyday Life*, 198-251.
84. Thomas Lindenberger (ed.), *Herrschaft und Eigen-Sinn in der Diktatur. Studien zur Gesellschaftsgeschichte der DDR* (Cologne, 1999).
85. See the Glossary in Lüdtke (ed.), *History of Everyday Life*, 313-14.
86. Michael Rauhut, *Beat in der Grauzone. DDR-Rock 1964 bis 1972. Politik und Alltag* (Berlin, 1993); Michael Rauhut, 'DDR-Beatmusik zwischen Engagement und Repression' in Günter Agde (ed.), *Kahlschlag. Das 11. Plenum der SED 1965* (Berlin, 1991), 52-63; Dorothee Wierling, 'Die Jugend als innere Feind. Konflikte in der Erziehungsdiktatur der sechziger Jahre' in Hartmut Kaelbe, Jürgen Kocka and Hartmut Zwahr (eds), *Sozialgeschichte der DDR* (Stuttgart, 1994), 404-25; Uta Poiger, 'Rebels with a Cause? American Popular Culture, the 1956 Youth Riots and New Conceptions of Masculinity in East and West Germany' in Reiner Pommerhin (ed.), *The American Impact on Postwar Germany* (Providence, New York, 1995), 92-124; Uta Poiger, *Jazz, Rock and Rebels. Cold War Politics and American Culture in a Divided Germany* (Berkeley, 2000); Peter Wicke, 'Rock Around Socialism. Jugend und ihre Musik in einer gescheiterten Gesellschaft' in Dieter Baacke (ed.), *Handbuch Jugend und Musik* (Opladen, 1998), 293-305.
87. Hilary Pilkington, *Russia's Youth and its Culture: a Nation's Constructors and Constructed* (London, 1994); Mark Edele, 'Strange Young Men in Stalin's Moscow: The Birth and Life of the Stiliagi, 1945-1953', *Jahrbuch für Geschichte Osteuropas* 50:1 (2002), 37-61; Juliane Fürst, 'Prisoners of the Soviet Self? Political Youth Opposition in Late Stalinism', *Europe-Asia Studies* 54:3 (May 2002), 353-76; Sándor Horváth, 'Pubs and "Hooligans" in a Socialist City in Hungary: the Public Sphere and Youth in Stalintown' in Axel Schildt and Detlef Siegfried (eds), *European Cities, Youth and the Public Sphere in the Twentieth Century* (Aldershot, 2005), 80-89; Kristin Roth-Ey, '"Loose Girls" on the Loose? Sex, Propaganda and the 1957 Youth Festival' in Melanie Ilic, Susan Reid and Lynne Atwood (eds), *Women in the Khrushchev Era* (Houndsmills, New York, 2004), 75-95.
88. Stefan Hradil, 'Die "objektive" und die "subjektive" Modernisierung. Der Wandel der westdeutschen Sozialstruktur und die Wiedervereinigung', *Aus Politik und Zeitgeschichte* 29-30 (1992), 3-14, 4.
89. Ibid., 13.
90. Interview with Klaus Renft.
91. Patrick Major, 'Going West: the Open Border and the Problem of Republikflucht' in Patrick Major and Jonathan Osmond (eds), *Workers' and Peasants' State. Communism and Society in East Germany under Ulbricht, 1945-71* (Manchester, 2002), 190-208.
92. 'Erfahrungsbericht über den polizeilichen Einsatz anläßlich von Beat-Veranstaltungen in der "Neuen Welt" und im "Europa-Palast" (West Berlin, 23.12.1966)', Landesarchiv Berlin, B Rep 020, Nr. 7812.
93. Scholars who already examine the ways in which particular phenomena crossed over the border between East and West include Dorothee Wierling, Uta Poiger, Alfons Kenkmann and Volker Ackermann. Dorothee Wierling, 'Opposition und Generation in Nachkriegsdeutschland. Achtundsechziger in der DDR und in der Bundesrepublik' in Christoph Kleßmann, Hans Misselwitz and Günter Wichert (eds), *Deutsche Vergangenheiten - eine gemeinsame Herausforderung. Der schwierige Umgang mit der doppelten Nachkriegsgeschichte* (Berlin, 1999) 238-52; Poiger, *Jazz, Rock and Rebels*; Alfons Kenkmann, *Wilde Jugend. Lebenswelt großstädtischer Jugendlicher zwischen Weltwirtschaftskrise, Nationalsozialismus und Währungsreform* (Essen, 1996); Volker Ackermann, *Der 'echte' Flüchtling. Deutsche Vertriebene und Flüchtlinge aus der DDR 1945-1961* (Osnabrück, 1995).

◈ *Chapter 2* ◈

GENDERING THE GDR

*T*he first GDR constitution in 1949 granted women equality before the law, the right to work and the right to equal pay for equal work. The 1950 Law on the Protection of Mother and Child ended the previous right of the husband alone to make decisions on marital matters, cleared the ground for establishing a range of social services for working mothers (such as kindergartens) and 'dramatically expanded the opportunities for married women's employment outside the home'.[1] Yet, in spite of the SED's bold propaganda claims about the future of women in socialism and massive state support for women's involvement in the workplace, gender inequality proved highly resistant to 'quick fix' solutions. The principle of equality 'was not automatically implemented in everyday life'.[2]

There were many problems, contradictions and limitations in the SED's policy of early and widespread female employment. If, ultimately, socialism was to lead to the liberation of women, in reality women were often weighed down with the double burden of work and coping with a family.[3] As long as this double burden was not lifted, equality would remain a paper promise. Hilde Benjamin said as much in introducing the new laws.[4] Although they used the language of gender equality, in their behaviour the men heading the new socialist organisations often showed that they valued women as wives and mothers rather than as future leaders and fellow class warriors. 'The interwar KPD bequeathed a decidedly masculine political culture on the postwar East German SED, a party in which women – even veteran women communists – would have little influence.'[5]

Even before SED rule collapsed, historians and social scientists pointed to disparities between claims and reality. 'A long period was necessary to overcome traditional structures of expertise and gender-specific employment.'[6] The better-paid industrial workers (those involved in the most important jobs – mining, building, metalwork, mechanics and chemistry) were almost always male. Only a few branches, such as textiles and later electronics, were deemed to correspond to 'the feelings and nimble fingers of women'.[7] Top SED leaders were 'torn between' their determination to promote women in the factory and their connections to a trade union leadership that resisted the incursions of female outsiders into positions of competence.[8] Despite its emphasis on gender equality, the SED continued to emphasise the manly qualities associated with manual labour.[9] Even when women worked alongside men in such difficult and harsh environments as smelting plants, their male colleagues could not bring themselves to see their contribution as equal.[10] Men showed a remarkable ability not to take the work done by women seriously. 'For the most part, women work in offices whereas their men do back-breaking work', leaving them too exhausted for chores when they come home from work.[11]

Breakthroughs in some areas (like science and technology) were not accompanied by changes in the types of work done by the majority of women. The female dominance of many of the jobs at the lower end of the pay scale resulted in a lower earning potential for large numbers of women.[12] Ina Merkel estimates that women 'on average earned one-third less than men, partly as a result of their participation in so-called low-wage employment. Other studies reveal that on average women had forty per cent less leisure time than men.'[13] On balance, argues Mary Fulbrook, 'it has to be said that the GDR was not a female paradise. Despite a very real ideological commitment on the part of the regime to equality of men and women in career aspirations and participation in leadership positions ... East German women "advanced" only a little. They remained disproportionately employed in the lower levels of all professional hierarchies.'[14] The reality of everyday life in socialism taught women that 'everybody is equal, just some are more equal than others!'[15] Although the SED leadership consciously sought to define its citizens in relation to work rather than to the family, the West German model of the breadwinning husband and the dedicated, morally responsible housewife had their counterparts in the East German model of the hard-working, male physical labourer and the inventive, time- and budget-conscious female homemaker/employee.[16]

Family

While Robert Moeller argues that the family and women's status 'clearly emerged as symbols of the distance between the two Germanys', for many women in the East the reality of their experiences failed to live up to the ideal.[17] 'In the 1950s, West German warnings about the collapse of the family under Communism and East German declarations of the achievement of sexual equality were equally far-fetched.'[18] The lack of any explicit political or legal pressure to alter the division of labour within the home meant that raising the next generation would remain primarily women's work. Reform of laws governing the family served not so much to make women more free and equal, but rather to make the family function more effectively 'as an institution of the socialist state'.[19] Despite socialism's claim to liberate women from patriarchal gender roles, the GDR actually retained continuities in gendered divisions of labour. 'East German women continued to perform most of the household labour, including shopping, and the regime expected them to carry this burden alongside a new responsibility to participate in paid productive labour.'[20]

Double standards did not disappear overnight:

> At home many men who make themselves out to be progressive continue to behave in a medieval fashion towards their wives. They treat them as maids, demand absolute agreement when not obedience and allow them no independent opinion. Equal rights may be written in the laws, and are making more and more progress in the factories, but a lot of inequality remains in the relationships between the sexes. It is maintained and nurtured not only by men, but also by women and girls.[21]

The 1965 Family Code exhorted men as well as women to bear their share of the upbringing and care of children and household chores, but 'no serious re-evaluation of the role of men was attempted by the code's draftsmen'.[22] In 1974, Rudolf Neubert was still arguing that 'the redistribution of family burdens looms as one of the major tasks for the coming years'. Husbands still wanted to forbid their wives this or that. 'They forget that they are no longer superiors or "the board of directors on household matters".'[23] Many men found it hard to let go of the notion that fathers were for Sundays whereas mothers were there every day of the week.[24] Naturalised notions about what tasks were male and what were female proved highly resistant to outside pressure for change.

In 1968 the women's magazine *Für Dich* began to play a more vocal role in challenging outdated gender stereotypes.[25] But, as one of its key supporters conceded, the campaign succeeded only in addressing women. Men were able to continue the pretence that the organisation of domestic responsibilities was not a subject that related to them.[26] Although increased coverage meant that the process of trying to alter gender relations within the family received greater attention, it did not by any means act as a magic wand. In a letter to *Für Dich* from 1982, one woman stated that it had taken her nearly ten years of 'arduous and painstaking trouble' to get her husband to the stage he should already have been at by the time they got married. The failure of parents to teach their sons gender equality at an early age was responsible, she believed, for the later demise of many young marriages.[27] Several of the men interviewed by Christine Müller and Christine Lambrecht in the early 1980s were highly dismissive of the claims of 'so-called emancipated women'. One (an early volunteer for the East German armed forces) expressed hatred for the way such women's 'excessive self-certainty

... denies their own beautiful femininity and [yet] they are basically always in search of *him*'. Apart from in her job as a (highly qualified) chemical engineer, his wife was a 'blind hen' only good for cleaning up and cooking.[28] Another (a court-appointed medical expert) expressed the view (in all seriousness) that women were either 'stupid, great actresses or whores'.[29] Even those men who did more around the home felt that other men judged them to be weaker and henpecked (*unterm Pantoffel*) because they dared to change nappies.[30]

Sexuality

Dagmar Herzog argues that it was in the realm of sexuality (and not just in female employment or childcare provision) that the GDR truly excelled and demonstrated itself to be far more advanced than West Germany.[31] According to Herzog, East Germans were free from the shame to which women in West Germany were subject for deviation from conservative gender norms.[32] It is true that early on the GDR government took the stance that illegitimacy was no longer something to be ashamed about. However, the onset of a more tolerant attitude towards illegitimacy did not extend to other forms of behaviour traditionally interpreted as sexually transgressive. Women whose behaviour was not considered respectable were repeatedly subjected to public shaming. Rather than criticising the West German 'postwar campaign to clean up German sexual mores', the SED chose to compete with it.[33] An emphasis on cleanliness (*Sauberkeit*) may have been 'a core element in securing West German Christianity's antifascist moral authority'. But it also served the same purpose for the SED in the GDR.[34] Far from not using sex as a 'site for managing the legacies of Nazism', memories of postwar fraternisation (and the sense of defilement and degradation that these implied) were kept alive well into the 1950s. In 1954, for example, the *Ostsee-Zeitung* argued that 'The decadent contortions of the jazz dancer are like those of an African witch doctor ... Any girl who gives in to such revolting forms of dancing need not wonder when she is called "Veronika".[35] Veronika had been used in both East and West as a derogatory term for a woman who associated with an American GI.[36] Especial hostility had been reserved for those women whose GI lover happened to have been black.[37]

It is true that the SED did not idealise 'faithful, home-bound femininity' (in the way that conservatives and the law did in West Germany), but it still demanded that women make sacrifices as wives and mothers as well as by being workers.[38] The fact that the overwhelming majority of women went out to work did not prevent men from treating them in a sexist fashion or from seeing them either as beasts of burden, chaste paragons of virtue or depraved sex objects. Complaining about unreconstructed, adolescent male attitudes towards women, Rolf Borrmann argued that their 'overemphasis on masculinity' (*forcierten Männlichkeit*) easily deviated into a primitive, crude form of sexuality.[39] In Jürgen Lemke's fascinating book *Ganz normal anders*, several of his interviewees referred to their own difficulties, as gay men, in coping with and tolerating outward signs of effeminacy. Not only did they use machismo and muscle to hide their sexuality (and to conform with what they believed society expected of them), but they subsequently found it difficult to step outside that outlook.[40] 'I wanted to become like the men in Hemingway's novels – physically strong, taciturn, take action when it became necessary, at times slightly melancholic too,' stated one. 'I glorified "maleness" and despised everything that only remotely appeared gay.'[41] Another, who went from a children's home to a street gang and then in and out of prison, said that 'The more miserable things got, the sooner I punched somebody.'[42]

The SED may have had no need to use attitudes to sex in order to emphasise its antifascist credentials.[43] But, because of the need to deflect attention away from the rapacious Soviet occupiers, this is precisely what it did. The official guide to preparing young people for their 'youth oath' (*Jugendweihe*) suggested using literary examples based on the history of the working-class movement in order to show that there was nothing better than loyalty to one's friends (the term commonly used to describe the Soviets) and nothing worse than betrayal of the working class. It was hoped that this would somehow lead to 'an inwardly clean and steadfastly respectable [*charakterfeste*] relationship between boys and girls'.[44] Overt interest in Western music or fashion was enough to condemn young women as sexually promiscuous and young men as politically deviant. The police saw prostitution as the female equivalent of rowdyism – carried on by ineducable, work-shy elements who withdrew from the construction of socialism and who presented a threat to public safety and order (in their case by spreading disease).[45]

Female fans of bebop and rock 'n' roll were repeatedly and publicly accused of (and shamed by references to) sexual impropriety. Being 'cheeky, lazy and rebellious' was sufficient to condemn one girl as being 'in sexual danger'. The 'youth helper' at her firm helped to put her 'back on the right path' by organising 'discussions' with the firm's management, the FDJ Order Group and the first aid group to which she belonged.[46] Believing that listening to Western music was the same thing as decadence, SED officials and policemen frequently broke up parties in which young people flirted and danced with each other with the argument that what they were doing constituted 'indulging in an orgy'. 'The "Presley-Gang" organised get-togethers in apartments. Under the influence of "hot music" from Radio Luxembourg and alcohol, it came to orgies' was one of many such succinct, but highly ambiguous reports.[47] In the 1950s and 1960s, attempts at reforming gender and sexuality were hampered by the persistent belief among lower-level SED functionaries (intermittently supported and encouraged by those at the top) that the West was engaged in a campaign of 'moral subversion' designed to corrupt youth and undermine socialism in the GDR.[48]

While boys who liked Western music were painted as effeminate, girls who did so were portrayed as dangerous, contagious harlots.[49] This sense of girls being a source of contamination went beyond music and fashion. There was something about young women's bodies that made people in authority (but especially men) find them threatening. As Adolf Kossakowski sought to prove scientifically (using a panoply of new statistical questionnaire techniques), pubescent girls tended to be judged more than anything by their outward appearances.[50] Others felt that when girls 'came into bud', they posed a threat not just to themselves but also to society. In 1962, Armin Schmolling warned male teachers to be on their guard against (and to avoid being put in an awkward situation by) 'precociously sexual or morally corrupted girls'. 'A source of danger must be seen in the efforts of many adolescent girls to use the feminine forms of their bodies (notably the breasts) to try and arouse the attention of the teacher. Their preference is for poses that facilitate contacts of the tactile kind.'[51]

Although the SED perceived itself as anti-bourgeois and was, at times, overtly anti-Christian, this did not mean that it was free of petit bourgeois foibles and hang-ups or from a desire to divert attention away from the past. The SED's messages regarding normative gender roles were often contradictory and highly ambivalent. The image of women willingly supporting their husbands by creating the intimacy necessary to share their problems ('crass appeals to female masochism') was not simply, as Herzog suggests, a recurring trope in West German advice literature.[52] The appeals made in *Armee Rundschau* (a publication aimed at young men in the East German military and their wives) for women to 'stand by their men' were far more crass and persisted over several decades. Army wives (who saw their husbands so infrequently they might as well have been army widows) were encouraged to sacrifice themselves in order to enhance their husbands' performance. This meant 'disregard for their own achievements and individual needs as well as the acceptance of the role of mother as the central pillar of female identity'.[53]

Altered Images of Femininity

Even the woman-friendly propaganda images that the SED presented to the world were not free from repressive and sexist elements. Most images in socialist women's magazines, Jennifer Evans argues, depicted 'the domestic bliss reminiscent of at least two of the three K's' (Kinder, Küche, Kirche).[54] It was not until 1970 that an overhaul of children's picture books was considered. Prior to that point they had overwhelmingly depicted women in the kitchen while the father 'embodied the outside world of work'.[55] Irene Dölling argues that the photographs in *Für Dich*, the GDR's only women's magazine, continued to depict patriarchal stereotypes well into the 1980s.[56] Advice literature directed at GDR women not only suggested that they should 'stand by their men', but that they were to be seen and not heard. 'Bad moods and "troubles" should be kept for oneself. They cannot be got rid of by putting them on display. If she has real worries then there are state offices where she can receive guidance and get help.'[57] By the standards of early 1970s Western feminism, the GDR's officially authorised encyclopedia of women's issues (edited by Irene Uhlmann) was incredibly sexist, particularly in its use of 'amusing' cartoons depicting the right and wrong way for women to clothe and deport themselves.

With captions like 'Bending over in the right way can be learned' ('Richtiges Bücken will gelernt sein'), young women were taught to be decorous and respectable at all times. Casualness in speech, posture and dress was frowned upon. 'The woman in the workplace is a colleague with equal rights, but always still a woman! In the workplace, the woman should preserve her dignity and ignore the coarse humour of her male colleagues rather than joining in with them.'[58] Instead of beating men at their own games, women were encouraged to help create a good working atmosphere by decorating their workstations with 'pleasant paintings, pretty curtains or easily looked-after plants'.[59] In the street and on public transport they were encouraged to prioritise femininity and respectability over independence. 'Only a demure glance towards a strong, masculine fellow passenger helps with heavy luggage.'[60] The continued uncritical (and non-ironic) use of such stereotypes did little to challenge remnants of male chauvinism that allowed husbands to dole out criticisms of their wives' bodies while maintaining their own 'pasha'-like round bellies.[61]

Rudolf Neubert played an important role in creating the outlines for how sexuality (and 'socialist sexual pedagogy') would be approached in the GDR.[62] His books helped to shape the measured secular-rational (but also bold and visionary) tone of the language used to describe sexuality in GDR advice literature. Although he demonstrated a remarkable degree of openness when he preached empathy for the needs and desires of young East Germans in the mid-1950s, his autobiography (published in 1974) shows that he struggled to gain insights into his own life choices. His candour in discussing his prior membership of the NSDAP and the comfortable and prosperous life he led in the pre-war Third Reich is not matched by critical distance or self-awareness.[63] From his tales about visiting the brothel quarter of Cairo (as a representative of the Dresden Hygiene Museum) in the 1920s and his business dealings with Zionists in Palestine (they were too mean to make him a decent offer) to his later comments about Israel and 'open dancing' with a girl who looked like Queen Nefertiti, Neubert showed that he found it difficult not to think in terms of race, essentialism and 'orientalising' the other.[64] Such an outlook probably did not constitute the best prerequisite for a self-proclaimed 'social hygienist'.[65]

There again, through hard work (teaching anatomy and 'human types' to post-war art students) and the demonstration of unswerving loyalty to his new political masters (and their shibboleths), Neubert had 'made good' (by the standards of the early GDR) his previous misdemeanours (which not only included membership of the NSDAP, but taking over the medical practice of a Jewish doctor who 'went away').[66] In his autobiography, Neubert makes clear that he faced an uphill struggle in trying to challenge the 'old male dominance' of the 1950s and 1960s. He received much criticism from functionaries who (paradoxically) accused him of being a petit bourgeois for wanting to explore issues of 'domestic living arrangements, the distribution of burdens in the household or even techniques of loving' that they considered to be 'beneath' what a socialist should be striving for.[67]

Gender, Sexuality and Inner-party Conflict

Although trumpeted as ending the long-standing and harmful division of the working class, the forced merger of the KPD and SPD in the new Socialist Unity Party (SED) in April 1946 brought only a brief honeymoon period before the real business of creating a 'party of a new type' began. Despite the outward show of unity, sectarian hostilities still lingered about the 'social fascist' Weimar SPD. Social Democrats continued to be accused of indiscipline and lack of fighting spirit (in other words of not being sufficiently manly).[68] Although they had greater claims to butchness, veteran communist members of the SED were no less problematic. The large and influential Saxon SED, in particular, was rent by all kinds of divisions. 'According to Fritz Grosse, there were "Muscovites, Spaniards, Buchenwalders, Sachsenhausers, Mauthauseners, Waldheimers, and Auschwitzers – [there were] groups of the National Committee [NKFD], front school veterans, and old underground [activists], and also English emigrants".'[69] The one thing they had in common was that they were overwhelmingly male. Senior women in the SED faced enormous difficulties (and not a little sexism) in trying to influence (let alone transform) gender relations. Not only were they considered to be 'naturally suited' to discussing issues affecting youth, education and the family but they were also deprived of resources and opportunities for influencing policy.

Facing opposition within the party from both the left and the right, Ulbricht embarked on a Stalinist course of reorganisation and party purges in order to achieve discipline and ideological uniformity. One of the fundamental characteristics of the 'party of the new type' (announced at the Third Party Congress in July 1950) was 'that no one could get things quite right except for the leadership'.[70] Although he effectively held the most powerful position within the SED, Ulbricht's authority was far from firmly established in the period 1945-58. Ulbricht's key supporters were those who had either been in Moscow exile with him or those who had been imprisoned in Germany – Wilhelm Pieck, Erich Honecker, Horst Sindermann and Hermann Axen. Ulbricht's goal was a mass party in the image of the Communist Party of the Soviet Union. The troublesome and divisive independent-minded veterans of the past would be 'watered down with an influx of new, more pliable young Germans'.[71] Critics feared that the majority of these newly recruited functionaries 'had learned to think and act under fascism' and believed that by 'bossing people about' they could secure the success of whatever it was they were aiming at.[72] Although far less charismatic than Stalin, Ulbricht strove to develop his own cult of personality.

As head of the Central Party Commission, Hermann Matern supervised the expulsion of former Social Democrats who were believed to be connected to the Eastern Bureau of the Western SPD and veteran communists accused of association with Tito, Trotsky or Western intelligence agencies.[73] Particularly suspect were those who had been exiles in the West or members of the Association for Victims of the Nazi Regime (VVN), which at times had demonstrated considerable hostility to the SED leadership.[74] The result, Jeffrey Herf argues, was a marginalisation of the Holocaust and the suspicion that Jews and others who had been in the West might have picked up potentially subversive ideas about democracy and freedom.[75] Following the Slansky trial in Prague in 1952, preparations were made for similar show trials in the GDR involving the leading 'Western exile' communists Paul Merker and Franz Dahlem.[76] Although he could hardly be accused of Western contamination or an incomplete grasp of the communist vision, Anton Ackermann acted as a persistent thorn and potential rival to Ulbricht. In his February 1946 article 'Is There a Special German Road to Socialism?' Ackermann had set out an alternative vision of non-Soviet, peaceful transformation along national lines.[77]

Within the leadership, division arose over how central German unity was in plans for political development. Ulbricht, Pieck and Dahlem were more interested in socialism than unity, whereas for Ackermann unity was central.[78] The controversy surrounding Tito's defiance of Stalin forced Ackermann to recant and the special path was abandoned as being too nationalistic. Nevertheless Ackermann continued to act as the spokesman for opposition to Ulbricht's leadership within the Politbüro. His supporters included Rudolf Herrnstadt, Wilhelm Zaisser, Heinrich Rau and Elli Schmidt (head of the Central Committee department for women). Ulbricht pressed ahead with the construction of socialism, heightening the division between East and West and alienating large parts of the population. Soviet intervention forced a new course, but the lack of provision for workers exacerbated discontent and sparked a major uprising.[79] The Politbüro was forced to flee to safety in Karlshorst.⁸⁰ The tensions within the SED leadership came to a head in the aftermath of the June 1953 uprising, with a number of leading figures directly voicing criticism of Ulbricht. Schirdewan, in particular, criticised the 'sergeant-major tone' with which Ulbricht had handed out orders and dealt with objections. By his own account, he gave the older man such a piece of his own medicine that he broke down and cried.⁸¹ Despite the fact that the massive popular unrest was a direct consequence of his failings as leader, the uprising paradoxically strengthened Ulbricht's hand with the Moscow leadership. Herrnstadt and Zaisser lost their positions.⁸² For Herrnstadt, the worst thing was having to bear the 'hate-filled stares of honest old workers' who had been convinced that he was a traitor.⁸³

Erich Honecker had caused a great deal of unnecessary discontent in the lead-up to the 1953 uprising, particularly in the countryside, by embarking on a campaign to 'liquidate' the young Christian *Junge Gemeinde*. His naked ambition and clumsy heavy-handedness as head of the FDJ had made him highly unpopular not just with large sections of youth, but also within the Politbüro. Elli Schmidt was particularly critical of Ulbricht's 'pet' (*das liebe Kind*). Ulbricht responded by saying that Honecker had been dealt with. He would be going back to school.⁸⁴ Nevertheless, Ulbricht had to do something in order to demonstrate to the Soviets, his Politbüro colleagues and the population at large that he had come to terms with and learned the lessons of the uprising. The continuing divisions within the Politbüro produced highly contradictory policies with regard to gender and sexuality. On the one hand, the SED leadership authorised the publication of *Das Magazin* (a highly popular and difficult-to-obtain monthly containing travel reports on foreign countries, fashion and photographs of demure female nudes).⁸⁵ Not only did *Das Magazin* commission articles on 'Love and Marriage in Socialism', but in the summer of 1954 *Neues Deutschland* printed an article referring back to left-wing experts on sex from the 1920s like Max Hodann.⁸⁶ On the other hand, renewed importance was placed on family values and persecution of homosexuals in the name of the 'healthful mores of the working people'.⁸⁷ 'The SED initiated a series of pronatalist policies designed to spark early marriages and child rearing to help control the population decline and counteract the effect of mass exodus of GDR citizens.'⁸⁸

Although the party continued to strive to present an image of unity to the outside, behind the scenes important power struggles raged back and forth during the period 1954–56. In 1955, Ulbricht finally fulfilled his promise to remove Honecker as head of the FDJ.⁸⁹ Under his leadership, the need to recruit young men for the armed police units had become the youth organization's sole focus. That such attempts met with 'deep disquiet (hesitation and reservations)' among a large part of male youth significantly undermined the FDJ's popularity.⁹⁰ The change of leadership had unexpected and far-reaching consequences for the newspaper *Junge Welt*. Overnight the monotonous calls for male youths to demonstrate their loyalty and patriotism by volunteering to serve in the KVP (People's Police units housed in barracks) gave way to frank discussions about issues of gender and sexuality. The editorial tone shifted from authoritarian, male and militaristic to fresh, cheeky, girl- and sexuality-friendly. Within the Politbüro, Albert Norden called for more lively leisure opportunities for youth, arguing that 'A ponytail is not in any way a sign of opposition to socialism.'[91] Likewise, Fred Oelssner pointed to the failure of East German industry to meet consumer demands (not only in terms of the quantity of consumer durables, but in the quality of textiles and clothing).[92] Hilde Benjamin announced a new, more understanding approach to illegitimacy.[93] Nevertheless, in a consistent demonstration of the party leadership's inconsistency, the period 1954–55 simultaneously witnessed high-profile and increasingly futile attempts to suppress nudism by force. The reason why the communist leaders were so determined to repress nudism was that they viewed it as a dangerous (and contagious) form of Social Democratic immunity (or 'resistance' to ideological persuasion).[94] They also felt that young people corrupted by the West were using nudism 'as a cover for mischief'.[95] As late as 1960, policemen were sent onto the beaches to repress nudist subculture armed with machine guns. Nevertheless, during the course of the early 1960s, it went from a suspect, minority activity to a largely unpolitical mass-participation, mass-spectator sport.

    The zigzag policies in relation to gender, youth and sexuality can be seen as resulting from the ongoing rifts and arguments within the SED. The need to improve relations with the population had been given further support by Khrushchev's denunciation of Stalin at the Twentieth Party Congress in February 1956. Opponents of Ulbricht were sufficiently emboldened to begin criticising his policies and style of rule with a view to removing him. Ernst Bloch and Robert Havemann called for a more humanistic, third-way socialism with greater emphasis on justice, freedom and emancipation.[96] During the spring and summer of 1956, an opposition grouping emerged within the party and called with increasing emphasis for liberalisation of policy. A number of 'revisionists' (Wolfgang Harich, Walter Janka, Karl Schirdewan, Ernst Wollweber, Gerhart Ziller, Fred Oelssner, Fritz Selbmann) began to advocate more wholehearted de-Stalinisation and the removal of Ulbricht.[97] The desperate urge of so many young people to leave the GDR, it was argued, could not be overlooked. Neither could the opportunities for creating a genuinely popular form of socialism in the GDR continue to be squandered through lip service to Ulbricht's party line. Schirdewan came to symbolise a more modern, democratic, humane variant of socialism.[98] Wollweber's participation in the 'revisionist conspiracy' was paradoxical because, as head of the MfS, he was also responsible for heightening cold war tensions by orchestrating a campaign of kidnapping opponents and critics of SED rule based in West Berlin. Nevertheless, his ruthlessness was nothing to that of his deputy, Erich Mielke.[99]

The period of questioning, negotiation and reform was brought to an end by the Hungarian Uprising in the autumn of 1956.[100] Wolfgang Harich was arrested on the 29 November 1956.[101] Despite protests at the Humboldt and other universities, which were repressed by the paramilitary 'fighting groups' (*Kampfgruppen*), he was condemned to ten years in prison.[102] Ulbricht and his supporters began a long, but effective, counter-attack, determined to reduce and eventually completely remove the influence of their critics.[103] The dictatorship of the proletariat, Ulbricht believed, could not afford to be humane. On the contrary, it had to be brutal and ruthless.[104] In the spring of 1957 Schirdewan was appointed to a special commission for improving the party's work with youth.[105] But, when he went on holiday to the USSR, Honecker succeeded in getting the decisions reversed, thereby reinstalling his own doctrinaire youth policy.[106] Ulbricht had 'stomped on progress' with his militaristic jackboot (*Husarentritt*).[107]

Although the wave of trials and imprisonments effectively killed off reform-minded opposition within the party leadership, would-be reformers at lower levels remained remarkably resilient and paradoxically optimistic that one day their ideas would find support and favour with the party's leaders. Since the party archives were opened up for outside scrutiny following German unification, historians have tended to focus their attentions on the weight with which SED mass organisations crushed innovation and stifled debate by dominating what passed for a public sphere, silencing dissidents and engaging in all kinds of behind-the-scenes manipulation and intrigue. But, because these examples do not fit easily into black-or-white accounts of SED rule, they have tended to overlook those cases where eccentric would-be reformers persisted in arguing for highly novel changes to society, culture, gender and sexual life in the GDR. The period 1953–56 saw the emergence of all kinds of creative and utopian suggestions and ideas about how to reform socialism. Ranging from the sublime to the ridiculous, some of the most outspoken reformers in the early years thought well and truly 'outside of the box'. While Reginald Rudorf argued that the need existed for harmonisation between the values of jazz and those of socialism, Heinz Bachmann suggested that the health benefits of nudism warranted not only its legalisation but the creation of a nudist mass organisation.

Bachmann wanted to call his mass organisation the Pavlov Association (*Pavlov-Bund*) after the pioneering Russian scientist famed for conditioning dogs to salivate at the sound of bells. The link apparently was that nakedness helped to 'deconstruct old conditioned reflexes and to construct new ones in their place'.[108] Both of these eccentric, left-wing Leipzigers were able to use their membership of the SED to gain a public platform for their ideas. Although Bachmann eventually got the message after various members of the SED leadership (and several other branches of government that he corresponded with) failed to take up his ideas, Rudorf needed more 'gentle persuasion' to desist (by having one of his talks picketed by regime loyalists, some of whom held him down and kicked his teeth in).[109] Because SED leaders could not be seen to announce that they had just abandoned the reform agenda that they had spent the previous months triumphantly promoting, going back on their promises was never a totally successful endeavour.

Anomalous pockets (and the hopes that they would one day spread and join with others to create wider changes) were allowed to persist. Decades of state-sponsored secularism and female employment did eventually give rise to more matter-of-fact attitudes to sexuality.[110] Reformers who lobbied for the acceptance of sex education within the education system gradually saw their ideas receive official approval. So too (later and more abruptly) did those advocating the repeal of legislation outlawing homosexuality and abortion.[111] Having spent the previous twenty years upholding the status quo, regime leaders nimbly performed a series of somersaults to argue that they had always been in favour of reform. As the regime continued to zig and zag erratically from the mid-1950s through to the late 1960s, reformers were careful to push their ideas only when there was a window of reform and to hold (or turn) back when the regime's weathervane swung from thaw to freeze. More open-minded, sex-friendly commentators mingled with those prepared to argue that visible signs of 'a decline into sexual depravity' were caused by the 'negative influence of the West'.[112]

Regarded by many 'as a drab junior Ulbricht, devoid of imagination, absolutely loyal to the Soviet Union and unsympathetic to liberal trends in culture', Erich Honecker became increasingly involved in security affairs following his return from re-education in the Soviet Union in 1957. Taking a leading role in strengthening the 'fighting spirit' of the *Kampfgruppen*, he played a crucial part in planning and preparing the building of the Berlin Wall.[113] With the introduction of conscription in the GDR in January 1962, the SED leadership renewed its attempts to develop a new (old) conception of the male citizen as a man who was able to defend himself and his fatherland.[114] Although it was primarily presented as enabling a crackdown on rebellious and disobedient male youth, the building of the wall also provided Ulbricht with the firm boundaries he needed in order to experiment. Unveiling his New Economic System (NES) at the Sixth Party Congress in January 1963, Ulbricht outlined a technocratic vision of socialism in which science was raised to the status of a main production force. Condemning bureaucratisation and overcentralisation of the economic system, he announced that party functionaries would be retrained and that there would be a general upgrading of technical and professional skills. Technical innovation, greater openness and creativity and expert know-how were all 'hailed as the keys to unlocking the full potential of the people and, ultimately, realizing socialism'.[115]

Ulbricht's attempts at reform from above resulted in the Family Code and the Law on the Integrated System of Education (both of which came into force in 1965). Alarm at developments in popular culture (notably the spread of Beatle mania to the GDR) became the subject of a counter-attack by political and moral conservatives. Liberalisation was brought to an abrupt end at the Central Committee's Eleventh Plenum in December 1965. Once again Erich Honecker played a key role in undermining Ulbricht's reform agenda by spearheading the attack on creative intellectuals and condemning writers, film-makers and musicians for corrupting the minds of youth.[116] Although what obviously pained conservatives more was open discussion of party hypocrisy, creatives and artists were actually vilified for their uninhibited discussions of sexuality. In the process, the 'angry young men from Babelsberg' were neutered.[117] Honecker's claims that gang rape was caused by 'American-inspired immorality and decadence' were echoed by Dr Josef Streit, the GDR's Attorney General. He, in turn, argued that a NATO conspiracy existed to undermine the GDR by manipulating young people's desires and urges (carrying out, in effect, *Triebpropaganda*).[118] Prosecutors were encouraged to crack down on any perceived signs of deviance or decadence.[119]

During the 1950s and 1960s, Honecker had shown a remarkable degree of consistency in pursuing an authoritarian, militaristic agenda and in undermining the possibility of alternatives. After he had succeeded in usurping Ulbricht in early 1971, however, he performed an equally remarkable about-face. Going from 'bad cop' to 'good cop', he succeeded in stealing what was left of Ulbricht's thunder by reintroducing the very same language of reform and liberalisation, but surreptitiously stripping it of any real sense of openness or creativity. Above all what he offered the population was improved consumption. 'The satisfaction of everyday needs requires supplying the population [with products] that in their value to the consumer and in their stylish flair [*modischen Pfiff*] provide ever more pleasure.'[120] What the humiliations of the 1950s had taught Honecker was the need to deploy greater stealth. It is true that Honecker was a lot more generous with regard to welfare, consumerism and housing. He was also prepared to turn a benevolent blind eye to certain changes in the realm of gender and sexuality. Under his rule, publications encouraging the mutual and equal pursuit of sexual pleasure (thereby presenting the GDR as an idyll of relaxed and humane hedonism) proliferated.[121] Nothing that was sexual was considered too unimportant for discussion. Even topics like 'group sex' were not too risqué for the new 'no taboos' approach of rational discussion.[122]

Paradoxically, it became easier for the Central Institute for Youth Research to publish sex surveys than it was for them to report on political attitudes. These studies showed that 'there were a large number of single mothers, an early start to sexual activity by young people, nearly as many sexual partners on the part of women as of men, and a more casual attitude to the body'.[123] Nevertheless there were limits to what was considered appropriate or tolerable. Walter Friedrich, in particular, found the message of the *Hite Report* offensive.[124] It suggested, he argued, that 'Women should deploy their sexuality as a weapon in their fight for equal rights. Orgasm should be striven for, but less in cooperation with the man. Masturbation and women gaining satisfaction from one another is more valuable. If heterosexual intercourse cannot entirely be avoided, then the woman should rule from above and in this way oppress the man.'[125] Hite might have responded that 'liberated' conceptions of sex in the GDR (and the research carried out by Starke and Friedrich) were problematic because they still revolved around 'male erection, male penetration, and male orgasm'.[126] Similarly, sex advice writers in the GDR had little wish to explore topics like sadomasochism, fantasy or role play. Having freed themselves from the yoke of capitalist oppression, socialists had no need to play at domination – although this was something engaged in by nonconformist youth cliques (as documented by photographs seized by the secret police) and did crop up as a symbol of inappropriate homoerotic male bonding in fantasy literature aimed at soldiers.[127]

By 1979, the atmosphere was sufficiently relaxed and open with regard to sexuality for East German academics to be able openly to ask, 'In view of sexuality, is socialism a tolerant and liberal societal order?' The answer Peter Klemm came up with was, 'As far as codified law is concerned, the question is without any doubt to be affirmed. A lot harder to answer, however, is the question of how far there exists a certain "public" tolerance for sexuality.'[128] He noted the widespread popularity of nudism, not just at the coast, but at lakes throughout the GDR. Nevertheless people still referred to homosexuals as 'inverted' and avoided pubs where they were known to meet. Klemm pointed to what he saw as a dismantling of taboos surrounding sexuality in the mass media, notably in magazines. 'Peculiar contradictions persist however. For example when a magazine aimed at 12- to 18-year-olds presents and discusses intimate sexual problems in the text, it nevertheless carefully avoids referring to the existence of gender differences in its pictures.'[129]

Between 1968 and the mid-1970s, East German society had undergone a seismic shift in relation to sexuality. Having long since been capable of being economically independent of men, women increasingly began to take advantage of opportunities for divorce if they no longer felt that their relationships were working for them.[130] The reasons why this occurred were complex and multifaceted. What had changed was not the state (or its attitudes) but society (and the social stigma attached to divorced women and their children). The high-profile discussions about sexuality that dominated the media in West Germany undoubtedly played an important role. They seeped into discussions in the East German press (albeit in filtered form). With the emergence of groups in the West claiming to be left-wing because they were pursuing sexual liberation, it became important for East German sexperts to prove that sexuality in the GDR was more liberated and humane.[131]

East German men and women followed the debates provoked by the student movement and second-wave feminism in the West. They began to question the ways in which their own relationships were structured. The new East German literature on sexual fulfilment emerged to cope with these questions (and in turn provoked new ones). The turn towards the body coincided with a renewed upsurge in impromptu nude sunbathing. Even Leipzig's Clara Zetkin Park ceased to be out of bounds to young Germans wishing to bare flesh.[132] Echoes of Woodstock filtered into the East German rock music scene. The term 'flower power' became shorthand for uncomplicated, hedonistic sexual relations – a less politicised version of the slogan 'peace and love'.[133] According to the musician (and former member of the Butlers) Peter Gläser, 'A real longing for freedom and permissiveness emerged. Things like group sex were tried, tolerance in living together was practised … People tore their clothes from their bodies during concerts, and drank like crazy.'[134] Although the state generally sought to avoid high-profile overreactions, it instead sought pre-emptively to target those groups and individuals it suspected were most likely to cause trouble. The shame that had once accompanied infidelity did not entirely disappear. Women characterised as having 'frequent changes of partner' or 'unsettled family relations' continued to be viewed with disdain. Their children attracted increased attention from the authorities, who believed that, if not closely watched, they were more at risk from political and other forms of deviation.[135]

The difficulties faced by women in trying to balance their own needs with those of their partners and children while holding down full-time jobs became a recurring theme in the highly popular and influential *Kinder von Golzow* series. This remarkable documentary chronicled the lives of young people from a particular school class in Golzow from 1961 through (in some cases) to the (re)unification of Germany and after. The long span of the project and the degree of familiarity they developed with its protagonists allowed the authors Barbara and Winfried Junge fascinating insights not just into the social history of the GDR, but also into the nature of relationships, longing and love.[136] Two other important documents charting the changing nature of relationships in the GDR are the interview-based (but reinterpreted and retold) story collections by Christine Müller and Christine Lambrecht.[137] Christine Müller's interview literature suggests that in the East (as in the West) the outlook and strategies that people took into relationships were consciously or unconsciously learned from their parents in childhood. Although for some couples it was possible to find a new, more equal relationship to each other, the path to 'East German men's domesticity' was not simple, straightforward or easy.[138] Ironically, although men's share in household activities began to grow at the start of the 1970s, this did not reduce the burden on women because the time needed to maintain the household also increased.[139] With both partners finding their time swallowed by chores around the home, frustration and tension were inevitable.

The autobiography Erich Honecker produced for Robert Maxwell's 'Great Men' (or 'Leaders of the World') series did much to endorse the trend towards greater openness in discussion of sexual matters that came to characterise 'his' GDR. In his willingness to demonstrate both his sexual liberality and his potency, Honecker went out of his way to talk frankly about his pre-Margot (hetero)sexual experiences:

> I was neither a saint nor a 'wet blanket'. I did like a glass of beer then even though money was short and I knew that alcohol could be a dangerous enemy of the working man. Later on I also smoked but at a more advanced age gave it up on medical advice. My activity in the workers' sports and the 'Spruce' athletics club contributed to a healthy way of life. I took part in gymnastics and played handball. I was also closely associated with the Young Friends of Nature.[140]

His sexual development was caught between the 'six sisters' he had spent his adolescent summers with in Pomerania and the 'free love' scene of 1920s Moscow that he claimed to have gained personal insights into.[141] This was a topic he referred back to even after he was no longer a 'great man' and had fallen from power. 'Under the then existing conditions, a registration was all that was needed to be married or unmarried. That, so to speak, was free love. But societal life did not suffer as a result. I could notice that in the enthusiasm for work.'[142]

Photographs of Honecker as an eighteen-year-old do portray a handsome, sexually charged young man, his wide-open eyes filled with naive, hopeful curiosity about the world. But after his ideological training in Moscow and the years he spent in prison during the Third Reich, Honecker became irrevocably bitter and cynical. Although he was ready in public to give his approval to signs of social and cultural change (in 1987 he famously bestowed his regal sign of approval by waving to a carnival float of nudists as they passed by his podium during celebrations marking Berlin's 750th anniversary), behind the scenes he was still both prudish and repressive. As well as encouraging increased Stasi penetration of society, the bankrupting of the GDR economy and the repression of minority groups that threatened to disrupt the utopian (and largely chimeric) image of 'real existing socialism', Honecker and his key collaborator Erich Mielke were instrumental in deploying arbitrary incarceration in psychiatric institutions as a means of dealing with prostitutes and other alleged 'asocials' who might disrupt (or tarnish) the 'clean and orderly' image of the 1973 World Games.[143]

The surface appearance of a sex-friendly utopia belied deeper problems and inconsistencies. Party authorities continued to police not just prostitution but 'asocial' behaviour. 'Milieu-damaged', recalcitrant people who were unwilling or unable to pursue 'regular', 'normal', respectable, conformist, non-messy lives were closely watched by teachers, children's home employees, employers, probation officers, social workers, the police and the Stasi. At the same time as recruiting vulnerable people like these as informers, the Stasi was also willing to disrupt the marriages of its opponents either by encouraging one partner to spy on the other or by sending letters to their neighbours implying infidelity or outlandish forms sexual depravity.[144] The 'emperor's new clothes' (or Potemkin village) characteristics of Honecker's rule relied on the population being too scared or sated to question how consumerism could continue (or by the mid-1980s be revived) without sharp increases in productivity.[145] The SED ruler sought to divert attention by ploughing state resources into pronatalist policies and housing initiatives designed to benefit young couples. As Ursula Sillge suggests, 'The sociopolitical measures characterised the increasingly feudal sides of GDR society. The generous maternity leave [Babyjahr] and the forty-hour week for mothers with several children were gifts from the father of the nation and the old men of the Politbüro. Young women were kindly expected to be grateful.'[146] From the mid-1980s, however, young people from both sexes began to demand that they be treated 'fully as equal partners'.[147]

Notes

1. Robert Moeller, *Protecting Motherhood. Women and the Family in the Politics of Postwar West Germany* (Berkeley, Los Angeles, London, 1993), 71; Hilde Benjamin, *Vorschläge zum neuen deutschen Familienrecht* (Berlin, 1949); Horst Barthel, 'Die Sozialpolitik bei der Schaffung der Grundlagen des Sozialismus (1949 bis 1960)' in Gunnar Winkler (ed.), *Geschichte der Sozialpolitik der DDR, 1945-1985* (Berlin, 1989), 70-101, 79-80; Irene Uhlmann (ed.), *Die Frau* (Leipzig, 9th edn., 1973), 91f., 279.
2. Barbara Bertram, Walter Friedrich and Otmar Kabat vel Job, *Adam und Eva heute* (Leipzig, 1988), 7-8.
3. Jeanette Madarász, *Conflict and Compromise in East Germany, 1971-1989* (Basingstoke, 2003), 12f., 37ff.
4. Benjamin, *Vorschläge zum neuen deutschen Familienrecht*, 17.
5. Catherine Epstein, *The Last Revolutionaries. German Communists and their Century* (Cambridge, MA, London, 2003), 33.
6. Gerhard Tietze, 'Die Sozialpolitik beim umfassenden Aufbau des Sozialismus (1961 bis 1970)' in Winkler (ed.), *Geschichte der Sozialpolitik der DDR, 1945-1985*, 102-52, 122.
7. Hildegard Maria Nickel, 'Ein perfektes Drehbuch. Geschlechtertrennung durch Arbeit und Sozialisation' in Gislinde Schwarz and Christine Zenner (eds), *Wir wollen mehr als ein 'Vaterland'!* (Hamburg, 1990), 73-89.
8. Donna Harsch, 'Approach/Avoidance: Communists and Women in East Germany, 1945-9', *Social History*, 25:2 (May 2000), 156-82, 171.
9. Zentralrat der FDJ (ed.), *Handbuch des FDJ-Gruppenleiters* (Berlin, 1956), 143-45.
10. Lutz Niethammer, Alexander von Plato and Dorothee Wierling (eds), *Die Volkseigene Erfahrung. Eine Archäologie des Lebens in der Industrieprovinz der DDR* (Berlin, 1991), 118ff.
11. Christine Müller, *Männerprotokolle* (Berlin, 1985), 235.
12. Peter Hübner, 'Arbeiterklasse als Inszenierung? Arbeiter und Gesellschaftspolitik in der SBZ/DDR' in Richard Bessel and Ralph Jessen (eds), *Die Grenzen der Diktatur: Staat und Gesellschaft in der DDR* (Göttingen, 1996), 199-223, 210.
13. Ina Merkel, 'Working People and Consumption under Really-existing Socialism:

Perspectives from the German Democratic Republic', *International Labor and Working-Class History* 55 (Spring 1999), 92–111, 105.
14. Mary Fulbrook, *Interpretations of the Two Germanies* (Basingstoke, 2000), 60.
15. Ursula Sillge, *Un-Sichtbare Frauen. Lesben und ihre Emanzipation in der DDR* (Berlin, 1991), 112.
16. Katherine Pence, 'Labours of Consumption: Gendered Consumers in Post-War East and West German Reconstruction' in Lynn Abrams and Elizabeth Harvey (eds), *Gender Relations in German History: Power, Agency and Experience from the Sixteenth to the Twentieth Century* (Durham, NC, 1997), 211–38.
17. Moeller, *Protecting Motherhood*, 71.
18. Elizabeth Heineman, *What Difference does a Husband Make? Women and Marital Status in Nazi and Postwar Germany* (Berkeley, Los Angeles, London, 1999), 207.
19. Ute Gerhard, 'Die staatlich institutionalisierte "Lösung" der Frauenfrage. Zur Geschichte der Geschlechterverhältnisse in der DDR' in Hartmut Kaelbe, Jürgen Kocka and Hartmut Zwahr (eds), *Sozialgeschichte der DDR* (Stuttgart, 1994), 383–403, 390.
20. Katherine Pence, '"You as a Woman Will Understand": Consumption, Gender and the Relationship between State and Citizenry in the GDR's Crisis of 17 June 1953', *German History* 19:2 (February 2001), 218–52, 226.
21. Rudolf Neubert, 'Gedanken zum Problem der Sexualpädagogik' in Rudolf Neubert and Rudolf Weise, *Das Sexuelle Problem in der Jugenderziehung* (Rudolstadt,1956), 7–38, 18.
22. Mike Dennis, *German Democratic Republic. Politics, Economics and Society* (London, New York, 1988), 57.
23. Rudolf Neubert, *Mein Arztleben. Erinnerungen* (Rudolstadt, 1974), 151.
24. Müller, *Männerprotokolle*, 192.
25. 'Das tut ein Mädchen nicht …', *Für Dich* 25 (1968). For criticism of men's continued belief in their 'breadwinner position', see *Für Dich* 36 and 38 (1967); 21 and 32 (1968).
26. Karlheinz Otto, *Disziplin bei Mädchen und Jungen. Ein Beitrag zur Gleichberechtigung der Geschlechter aus psychologischer, pädagogischer, soziologischer und historischer Sicht* (Berlin, 1970), Note 11, 239.
27. 'Cornelie Z., Güstrow', *Für Dich* 28 (1982).
28. Müller, *Männerprotokolle*, 185.
29. Ibid., 80.
30. Ibid., 164.
31. Dagmar Herzog, *Sex after Fascism. Memory and Morality in Twentieth-Century Germany* (Princeton, 2005), 194–95.
32. Ibid., 194
33. Ibid.
34. 'Helfen nur Verbote? Die Berliner Zeitung diskutierte mit ihren Lesern über Jugendliteratur', *Junge Welt* (10 April 1956).
35. 'Veronikas', *Ostsee-Zeitung* (2 September 1954).
36. Maria Höhn, *GIs and Fräuleins. The German-American Encounter in 1950s West Germany* (Chapel Hill, London, 2002), 126ff.
37. Heide Fehrenbach, *Race after Hitler. Black Occupation Children in Postwar Germany and America* (Princeton, 2005).
38. Herzog, *Sex after Fascism*, 192.
39. Rolf Borrmann, *Jugend und Liebe. Die Beziehungen der Jugendlichen zum anderen Geschlecht* (Leipzig, 1966), 91, 94.
40. Jürgen Lemke, *Ganz normal anders. Auskünfte schwuler Männer aus der DDR* (Berlin, Weimar, 1989). For English translations, see John Borneman (ed.), *Gay Voices from East Germany. Interviews by Jürgen Lemke* (Bloomington, Indianapolis, 1991).
41. Borneman (ed.), *Gay Voices*, 132.
42. Ibid., 115.
43. Herzog, *Sex after Fascism*, 194.

44. Zentralen Ausschuß für Jugendweihe in der DDR (ed.), *Jugendstunde. Themenplan zur Vorbereitung auf die Jugendweihe* (Berlin, 1955/56), 35. The texts specifically mentioned for doing this were *Soja und Schura* by Ljubov Kosmodemjanskaja, *Die Junge Garde* by Alexander Fadejew and *Die Patrioten* by Bodo Uhse.
45. 'Schreiben der U-Abteilung' (24 September 1957), Sächsisches Staatsarchiv Leipzig (henceforth StAL), Bezirksverwaltung der Deutschen Volkspolizei (henceforth BDVP) 24/113, 279.
46. 'Bekämpfung des Rowdytums (March 1961)', Bundesarchiv Berlin (henceforth BArch.) DO1/11.0/785, 59.
47. 'Auftreten der "Presley-Bande" an der erweiterten Oberschule Pößneck' (c. November 1959), BArch. DR2/4814; see also 'Sammlung von Nachrichten – Rowdytum' (c. October 1950), StAL BDVP 24/71, 96; 'Politisch-ideologisch und Pädagogische Arbeit an Schulen, 1960', StAL, Rat des Bezirkes (henceforth RdB) Volksbildung 4140, 2; 'Kreisleitung Hoyerswerda: Feindinformation' (6 February 1961), Stiftung Archiv der Parteien und Massenorganisationen der DDR (henceforth BArch. SAPMO), DY24/3727; 'SED-Stadtleitung Leipzig: Teilbericht zur Analyse über Jugendarbeit in der Stadt Leipzig - gefährdete Jugendliche' (11 January 1965), StAL IVA-5/01/269, 9ff.; for Honecker's claims during the Kahlschlag plenum, see 'Bericht des Politbüros an die 11. Tagung des Zentralkomitees der SED (15–18 December 1965)', BArch. SAPMO DY30/2067, 163; for a literary mention of SED views on 'orgies', see Brigitte Reimann, *Ankunft im Alltag* (Berlin, 1961), 200; see also Thomas Lindenberger, *Volkspolizei. Herrschaftspraxis und öffentliche Ordnung im SED-Staat 1952-1968* (Cologne, Weimar, Vienna, 2003), 405, 409ff.
48. Zentralen Ausschüß fur Jugendweiche in der DDR (ed.), *Jugendstunde*, 36.
49. Benno Pludra, *Haik und Paul* (Berlin, 1957), 41, 82.
50. Adolf Kossakowski, *Über die psychischen Veränderungen in der Pubertät. Bedingungsanalyse* (Berlin, 1965), 114.
51. Armin Schmolling, 'Zur Frage der sittlichen Gefährdung des Lehrers', *Pädagogik Beiheft* 2 (1962), 34–35.
52. Herzog, *Sex after Fascism*, 119.
53. Christine Eifler, '"Ewig unreif". Geschlechtsrollenklischees in der Armeerundschau' in Simone Barck, Martina Langermann and Siegfried Lokatis (eds), *Zwischen 'Mosaik' und 'Einheit'. Zeitschriften in der DDR* (Berlin, 1999), 180–88, 187.
54. Jennifer Evans, 'Constructing Borders: Image and Identity in Die Frau von Heute, 1946-1948' in Hilary Sy-Quia and Susanne Baackmann (eds), *Conquering Women: Women and War in the German Cultural Imagination* (Berkeley, 2000), 40–61, 50; Ina Merkel, 'Leitbilder und Lebenswesen von Frauen in der DDR' in Kaelbe, Kocka and Zwahr (eds), *Sozialgeschichte der DDR*, 359–62, 362; Annette Kuhn, 'Der Refamilialisierungsdiskurs nach '45', *Beiträge zur Geschichte der Arbeiterbewegung* 33:5 (1991), 593–606; Robin Ostow, 'Die volkseigene Familienromanze. Arbeitende Mütter und entrechtete Väter in der Deutschen Demokratischen Republik, 1949–1989' in Dagmar Reese, Eve Rosenhaft, Carola Sachse and Tilla Siegel (eds), *Rationale Beziehungen? Geschlechterverhältnisse im Rationalisierungsprozeß* (Frankfurt am Main, 1993), 344–62.
55. Gisela Helwig, *Jugend und Familie in der DDR. Leitbild und Alltag im Widerspruch* (Cologne, 1984), 44–45.
56. Irene Dölling, 'Gespaltenes Bewußtsein. Frauen- und Männerbilder in der DDR' in Hildegard Maria Nickel and Gisela Helwig (eds), *Frauen in Deutschland, 1945–1992* (Bonn, 1993), 23–52.
57. Uhlmann (ed.), *Die Frau*, 743.
58. Ibid., 741.
59. Ibid., 742.
60. Ibid., 744.
61. Neubert, *Mein Arztleben*, 146.
62. Ibid., 148ff.

63. Ibid., 80.
64. Ibid., 59–63.
65. In 1952 Neubert was deemed to be fully rehabilitated and was made Professor of Social Hygiene at the University of Jena. Neubert, *Mein Arztleben*, 133.
66. Ibid., 119–25, 79.
67. Ibid., 155.
68. Norman Naimark, *The Russians in Germany. A History of the Soviet Zone of Occupation, 1945–1949* (Cambridge, MA, 1995), 309.
69. 'Shikin to Zhdanov' (3 August 1946), cited in Naimark, *Russians in Germany*, 295.
70. Naimark, *Russians in Germany*, 310.
71. Ibid., 271, 313.
72. Rudolf Herrnstadt, *Das Herrnstadt-Dokument. Das Politbüro der SED und die Geschichte des 17. Juni 1953*, edited by Nadja Stulz-Herrnstadt (Reinbek bei Hamburg, 1991), 109–10; Karl Schirdewan, *Aufstand gegen Ulbricht. Im Kampf um politische Kurskorrektur, gegen stalinistische, dogmatische Politik* (Berlin, 1994), 11.
73. Hermann Weber, *Die DDR 1945–1990* (Munich, 1993), 32.
74. Naimark, *Russians in Germany*, 286; 'Außerordentliche Sitzung des Politbüros am 2. Jan. 1953: Verschwörerzentrum Schlansky', BArch. SAPMO DY30/JIV2/2/255.
75. 'Purging "Cosmopolitanism": the Jewish Question in East Germany, 1949–1956' in Jeffrey Herf, *Divided Memory. The Nazi Past in the Two Germanys* (Cambridge, MA, London, 1997), 106–61.
76. Josie McLellan, *Antifascism and Memory in East Germany. Remembering the International Brigades 1945–1989* (Oxford, 2004), 59f.; Peter Grieder, *The East German leadership, 1946–1973. Conflict and Crisis* (Manchester, 1999).
77. Anton Ackermann, 'Gibt es einen besonderen deutschen Weg zum Sozialismus?' *Einheit* 1 (February 1946), 23–42.
78. Naimark, *Russians in Germany*, 302.
79. Christian Ostermann, 'This is not a Politburo, but a Madhouse: the Post-Stalin Succession Struggle, Soviet Deutschlandpolitik and the SED. New Evidence from Russian, German and Hungarian Archives', *CWIHP Bulletin* 10 (March 1998), 61–110.
80. Herrnstadt, *Das Herrnstadt-Dokument*, 82.
81. Karl Schirdewan, *Ein Jahrhundert Leben. Erinnerungen und Visionen. Autobiographie* (Berlin, 1998), 268.
82. 'Politbüro Sitzung' (5 January 1954), BArch. SAPMO DY30/JIV2/2/341.
83. Herrnstadt, *Das Herrnstadt-Dokument*, 109–10.
84. Ibid., 128.
85. Josie McLellan, based at the University of Bristol, is set to publish a number of important and groundbreaking articles on the topic of erotica and nude photography in the GDR, including *Das Magazin*.
86. Neubert, *Mein Arztleben*, 149.
87. Jennifer Evans, 'The Moral State: Men, Mining, and Masculinity in the Early GDR', *German History* 23:3 (2005), 355–70, 360.
88. Jennifer Evans, 'Bahnhof Boys: Policing Male Prostitution in Post-Nazi Berlin', *Journal of the History of Sexuality* 12:4 (2003), 605–36, 636.
89. *Junge Welt* (18–19 June 55); Alan McDougall, *Youth Politics in East Germany. The Free German Youth Movement 1946–1968* (Oxford, 2004), 69.
90. Richard Bessel, 'Was bleibt vom Krieg? Deutsche Nachkriegsgeschichte(n) aus geschlechtergeschichtlicher Perspektive – Eine Einführung', *Militärgeschichtliche Zeitschrift* 60:2 (2001), 297–305, 298; 'Kurze Analyse der Stimmungen und Meinungen zum Gesetz über die Schaffung der Nationalen Volksarmee in der DDR' (Berlin, 1 January 1956), BArch. Berlin, DO-1-11, Nr. 210, 71f.; Mary Fulbrook, *Anatomy of a Dictatorship. Inside the GDR. 1949–1989* (Oxford, 1995), 135f.
91. Schirdewan, *Aufstand gegen Ulbricht*, 110.

92. Mark Landsman, 'The Consumer Supply Lobby – Did it Exist? State and Consumption in East Germany in the 1950s', *Central European History* 35:4 (2002), 477–512, 506.
93. Hilde Benjamin, 'Familie und Familienrecht in der Deutschen Demokratischen Republik', *Einheit* 10 (1955), 448–57.
94. See Josie McLellan's forthcoming article in *Journal of Modern History* on the SED's attempts to grapple with nudism in the GDR.
95. Letter from the Ministry of the Interior to local organs (c. spring 1954), BArch. Berlin, DO1/10.0/174/4, 90.
96. Weber, *Die DDR 1945–1990*, 47.
97. 'Politbüro Sitzung: Maßnahmen zur Durchführung des Vorschlags der 3. Parteikonferenz zur breiteren Entfaltung der Demokratie in der DDR' (17 April 1956), BArch. SAPMO DY30/JIV2/2/462.
98. Schirdewan, *Ein Jahrhundert Leben*, 258, 267.
99. Jan von Flocken and Michael Scholz, *Ernst Wollweber: Saboteur - Minister - Unperson* (Berlin, 1994), 142f.; for West Berlin police and newspaper reports on the kidnapping wave, see Landesarchiv Berlin, B Rep 020, Nr. 8161–8163.
100. Wolfgang Harich, *Keine Schwierigkeiten mit der Wahrheit. Zur national-kommunistischen Opposition 1956 in der DDR* (Berlin, 1993); Schirdewan, *Aufstand gegen Ulbricht*; Schirdewan, *Ein Jahrhundert Leben*.
101. 'Politbüro Sitzungen: Tätigkeit des konterrevolutionären Zentrums Harich und andere' (18–20 December 1956), BArch. SAPMO DY/JIV2/2/519.
102. Honecker was the main proponent of deploying the *Kampfgruppen* to truncheon the children of working-class fathers. Schirdewan, *Aufstand gegen Ulbricht*, 116.
103. The Thirtieth Party Conference (30 January – 1 February 1957) revealed the alleged plans of the 'Harich Group' to depose Ulbricht. The leadership struggle ended at the Thirty-Fifth Party Conference (3–5 February 1958) with the exclusion of the 'Schirdewan/Wollweber Group'. Norbert Podewin, *Albert Norden. Der Rabiner-Sohn im Politbüro* (Berlin, 2001), Note 9, 294; Weber, *Die DDR 1945–1990*, 47, 184; Manfred Hertwig, 'Deformationen. Die Rebellion der Intellektuellen in der DDR' in Reinhard Crusius and Manfred Wilke (eds), *Entstalinisierung. Der XX. Parteitag der KPdSU und seine Folgen* (Frankfurt, 1977), 477–84, 477ff.; Brigitte Hoeft (ed.), *Der Prozeß gegen Walter Janka und andere. Eine Dokumentation* (Reinbek bei Hamburg, 1990); Ernst Wollweber, 'Aus Erinnerungen. Ein Porträt Walter Ulbrichts', *Beiträge zur Geschichte der Arbeiterbewegung* 32:3 (1990), 350–78.
104. Schirdewan, *Ein Jahrhundert Leben*, 268.
105. 'Bericht über die Lage der FDJ sowie ihren Einfluß in verschiedenen Schichten der Jugend (6.4.1957)', BArch. SAPMO DY30/JIV2/2J/350.
106. Schirdewan, *Aufstand gegen Ulbricht*, 123.
107. Schirdewan, *Ein Jahrhundert Leben*, 264.
108. 'Ministerium des Innern, Hauptabteilung Schutzpolizei: Freikörperkultur und Freikörperkulturbund, 1953–1957', BArch. DO1 10.0 174/4; see, in particular, the letter from Dr. med. Heinz Bachmann to the MdI (17 February 1953) in which he outlines his vision for the Pavlov-Bund.
109. Reginald Rudorf, *Jazz in der Zone* (Cologne, Berlin, 1964), 102–3.
110. Ina Merkel, 'Sex and Gender in the Divided Germany: Approaches to History from a Cultural Point of View' in Christoph Kleßmann (ed.), *The Divided Past. Rewriting Post-War German History* (Oxford, New York, 2001), 91–104, 92.
111. Letter from Dr. med Rudolf Klimmer (Leitender Arzt der Nervenabteilung, Abteilung für Ehe- und Sexualberatung, Poliklinik Löbtau, Dresden) to the Fraktion der Freien Deutschen Jugend in der Volkskammer (18 October 1952), BArch. SAPMO, DY 24/11962 II; Karl-Heinz Mehlan, *Wunschkinder? Familienplanung, Antikonzeption und Abortbekämpfung in unserer Zeit* (Rudolstadt, 1970); Donna Harsch, 'Society, the State, and Abortion in East Germany, 1950–1972', *American Historical Review* 102:1 (February 1997), 53–84; Günter Grau, 'Return to the Past: the Policy of the SED and the Laws Against Homosexuality in Eastern Germany between 1946 and 1968', *Journal of Homosexuality* 37 (1999), 1–21.

112. Walter Friedrich and Adolf Kossakowski, *Zur Psychologie des Jugendalters* (Berlin, 1962), 171.
113. Dennis, *German Democratic Republic*, 36; 'Redemanuskript von Erich Honecker auf einer Parteiversammlung in Berlin-Köpernick am 29. Nov. 1957', BArch. SAPMO, DY30/2183.
114. Bessel, 'Was bleibt vom Krieg?', 305.
115. Greg Eghigian, 'Psychologization of the Socialist Self: East German Forensic Psychology and its Deviants, 1945–1973', *German History* 22:2 (2004), 181–205, 193; Jeffrey Kopstein, *The Politics of Economic Decline in East Germany, 1945–1989* (Chapel Hill, London, 1997), 41ff.
116. 'Rede E.H. in Auswertung der 11. Tagung des ZK der SED und Vorbereitung des 20. Jahrestages der DDR' (31 January 1966), BArch. SAPMO DY30/2150.
117. Klaus Wischnewski, 'Die zornigen jungen Männer von Babelsberg' in Günter Agde (ed.), *Kahlschlag. Das 11. Plenum der SED 1965* (Berlin, 1991), 171–88; 'Diskussionsbeitrag des Genossen Frank Beyer ... in Auswertung des 11. Plenums des ZK' (May 1966), BArch. SAPMO DY30/JIV2/2J/1669; 'Stellungnahme des Genossen Konrad Wolf ... zum Film "Spur der Steine" (15.9.1966)', BArch. SAPMO DY30/JIV2/2J/1766; 'Bericht des Politbüros an die 11. Tagung des Zentralkomitees der SED (15.-18.12.1965)', BArch. SAPMO, DY30/2067.
118. Heinz Ahlborg, 'Zu einigen Fragen der Sexualerziehung in der Schule. Pädagogische Lesung', Brandenburg, 1967 (Unpublished MS in the Bibliothek für Bildungsgeschichtliche Forschung Berlin, henceforth BBF), 7, 12; Josef Streit, 'Die nächsten Aufgaben der Staatsanwaltschaft', *Neue Justiz* (1966), 65.
119. Dieter Plath, 'Über Kriminalität und innere Sicherheit' in Agde (ed.), *Kahlschlag*, 32–38, 35.
120. Erich Honecker, *Unsere Kampfkraft stärken und sicher vorwärtsschreiten zum Wohl des ganzen Volkes* (Berlin, 1973), 33. After his fall from power, Honecker blamed the popular discontent that arose against him on the 'one-sided overemphasis on consumerism' that had focused attention on shortages, notably of bananas, rather than on achievements, such as widespread childcare provision. Erich Honecker, *Zu dramatischen Ereignissen* (Hamburg, 1992), 42–43. See Kopstein, *Politics of Economic Decline*, 80ff.; see also Merkel, 'Working People and Consumption'.
121. Siegfried Schnabl, *Mann und Frau Intim: Fragen des gesunden und des gestörten Geschlechtslebens* (Rudolstadt, 1969); Siegfried Schnabl, *Plädoyer für die Liebe* (Leipzig, 1978); Siegfried Schnabl, *Intimverhalten, Sexualstörungen, Persönlichkeit* (Berlin, 1973); Peter Hesse (ed.), *Sexuologie*, 3 vols (Leipzig, 1979); Kurt Starke, *Junge Partner. Tatsachen über Liebesbeziehungen im Jugendalter* (Leipzig, Jena, Berlin, 1980).
122. Starke, *Junge Partner*, 83.
123. Merkel, 'Sex and Gender in the Divided Germany', 99.
124. Shere Hite, *The Hite Report. A Nationwide Study on Female Sexuality* (New York, 1976).
125. Kurt Starke and Walter Friedrich (eds), *Liebe und Sexualität bis 30* (Berlin, 1984), 41.
126. Hite, *Hite Report*, 366ff.
127. Heinz Kruschel, *Der rote Antares* (Berlin, 1979), 53–54; 'Hauptabteilung Kriminalpolizei: Bilddokumentation zu Verkommnissen mit negativen Jugendlichen (1964–1969)', BArch. Berlin DO1/38215.
128. Peter Klemm, 'Sexualität im Sozialismus' in Hesse (eds), *Sexuologie*, vol. 3, 200–13, 210.
129. Ibid., 212.
130. Beate Schuster and Angelika Traub, 'Single Mothers in East Germany' in Eva Kolinsky and Hildegard Maria Nickel (eds), *Reinventing Gender. Women in Eastern Germany since Unification* (London, Portland, 2003), 151–71, 153f.; Norbert Schneider, *Familie und private Lebensführung in West- und Ostdeutschland. Eine vergleichende Analyse des Familienlebens 1970 bis 1992* (Stuttgart, 1994), 192f.
131. Walter Hollitscher, *Der überanstrengte Sexus. Die sogenannte sexuelle Emanzipation im heutigen Kapitalismus* (Berlin, 1975); Rolf Borrmann, 'Sozialistische Persönlichkeitsentwicklung und Sexualerziehung', *Pädagogik Beiheft* 30:1 (1975), 1–6.
132. Kurt Starke, '... ein romantisches Ideal' in Ute Kolano, *Nackter Osten. Erotik zwischen Oben und Unten* (Frankfurt an der Oder, 1995), 77–104, 87–88.

133. Thomas Kochan, *Den Blues haben. Momente einer jugendlichen Subkultur in der DDR* (Münster, Hamburg, Berlin, London, 2002); 'Woodstock des Ostens', *Der Spiegel* (26 August 1996), 68–69; Hans-Dieter Schütt (ed.), *Klaus Renft. Zwischen Liebe und Zorn* (Berlin, 1997).
134. Peter Gläser in an interview with Michael Rauhut, *Beat in der Grauzone. DDR-Rock 1964 bis 1972. Politik und Alltag* (Berlin, 1993), 235. Gläser apparently rolled up his trouser leg to show Rauhut the scar where an ecstatic girl had bitten him during a concert.
135. Thomas Lindenberger, 'Das Fremde im Eigenen des Staatssozialismus. Klassendiskurs und Exklusion am Beispiel der Konstruktion des "asozialen Verhaltens"' in Jan Behrends, Thomas Lindenberger and Patrice Poutrus (eds), *Fremd-Sein in der DDR. Zu historischen Ursachen der Fremdenfeindlichkeit in Ostdeutschland* (Berlin, 2003), 179–91, 181–82; BDVP, Abteilung K: 'Ermittlungsverfahren wegen Grenzverletzungen' (24 May 1966), StAL BDVP 24.1/435, 99f.
136. One of the best films in the series is *Da habt ihr mein Leben/Marieluise – Kind von Golzow*, directed by Barbara Junge and Winfried Junge (Germany, 1996).
137. Müller, *Männerprotokolle*; published in West Germany as *James Dean lernt kochen: Männer in der DDR, Protokolle* (Darmstadt, 1986); Christine Lambrecht, *Männerbekanntschaften. Freimütige Protokolle* (Leipzig, 1986).
138. See Herzog, *Sex after Fascism*, 218. Pride in the hard-won achievement of domestic equality definitely exists among a section East German men (particularly those with confident, university-educated wives). Several of the men I interviewed were as much concerned to show off the support they gave to their wives as they were to emphasise their own personal achievements. Reversing gender clichés, male victims of post-unification job cuts could take pride and solace in the fact that they were still married and that (with their help and support at home) their wives were still working.
139. Merkel, 'Working People and Consumption', 106.
140. Erich Honecker, *From My Life* (Oxford, New York, 1981), 27.
141. Ibid., 28, 45.
142. Reinhold Andert and Wolfgang Herzberg, *Der Sturz. Erich Honecker im Kreuzverhör* (Berlin, Weimar, 1990), 143; for an account of the other women in his life, see Reimer Hinrichs, 'Krankheit ohne Leidensdruck. Psychogramm des Angeklagten', *Kursbuch* 111 (February 1993), 71–86, 77–78.
143. See Sonja Süß, *Politisch mißbraucht? Psychiatrie und Staatssicherheit in der DDR* (Berlin, 1998), 523–34, for the orchestrated covert campaign to 'clean up' the streets; see also 'Bekämpfung der Asozialität' (c. 1973), BArch. DO1/050/43168.
144. Irena Kukutz and Katja Havemann, *Geschützte Quelle: Gespräche mit Monika H., alias Karin Lenz* (Berlin, 1990); Reiner Kunze, *Deckname 'Lyrik'. Eine Dokumentation* (Frankfurt am Main, 1990); Fulbrook, *Anatomy of a Dictatorship*, Note 47, 50; the best thing to blackmail church leaders with, of course, was photographic evidence of one of their prominent members engaging in 'sodomy' with underage boys. Details withheld to preserve anonymity.
145. Stefan Wolle, *Die heile Welt der Diktatur. Alltag und Herrschaft in der DDR 1971–1989* (Berlin, 1998), 163ff.
146. Sillge, *Un-Sichtbare Frauen*, 110.
147. Walter Friedrich to Egon Krenz: 'Einige Reflexionen über geistig-kulturelle Prozesse in der DDR' (21 November 1988), BArch. SAPMO DY30/IV2/2.039/246.

~ Chapter 3 ~

Remasculinisation

Germany's catastrophic defeat in the Second World War, numerous commentators (contemporaries and historians) have argued, caused a deep crisis in conceptions of masculinity.[1] Far from returning from the war as all-conquering heroes, German men (when they came back at all) returned humiliated, defeated and dejected, having failed in their 'historic mission'. They came home to find how easily they could be replaced by women in the workplace and by other men in the bedroom. 'German men felt cheated, hurt, and humiliated. For the returning soldiers, women's independence and autonomy (including sexual autonomy) became a huge problem.'[2] The two post-war German states inherited what was left of a society ruined by war, one in which men were remarkable by their absence. At the war's end there were seven million more women than men in occupied Germany and the surplus was greater in East than in West Germany.[3] Responsible for the devastation of large parts of Europe, together with the destruction of their own society, German men had been revealed as hollow heroes. Far from fulfilling their function as male protectors, their absence left their women and children defenceless and unprotected against the hunger and mass rapes that stalked post-war Germany.[4]

Many returning soldiers sought to compensate by throwing themselves wholly into the work of reconstruction as a way both of rebuilding the country and of providing materially for their families.[5] This absence from home due to work added to the distance created by the time they had spent away from home during the early, formative years of their children's upbringing and education, which had left their sons feeling alienated and abandoned.[6] Many boys felt ambivalent about their fathers' return. Years of separation had made them strangers to one another and the father's position as head of household could only be restored by reducing and downgrading the increased freedom and responsibility their sons had enjoyed in their absence.[7] Many fathers sought to bridge the divide (and to reinstate their dominant position within the family) by overcompensating and overcontrolling their children.[8] In many cases, this urge to restore weakened authority involved violence.[9] The consequence of fathers who were unapproachably distant or entirely absent, Alexander Mitscherlich suggested, was rebellion on the part of their sons.[10]

Both post-war Germanies embarked on processes of 'remasculinisation', beginning in the late 1940s and early 1950s. Whereas Robert Moeller argues that a demilitarisation took place in West Germany and that defeated men were reintegrated through civilian models of masculinity, Frank Biess argues that in East Germany reintegration of returning POWs was conceived as taking place through politics and work in production rather than through a restoration of family values.[11] 'Remasculinisation' for Moeller means softening the hard edges created in the Third Reich and creating an image of men who could be both soldiers and family men. In West Germany, he argues, Adenauer's key adviser Theodor Blank sought to identify 'military virtues based on German not National Socialist lines of tradition' in order to demonstrate the compatibility of democracy and remilitarisation. The martial ethos of earlier soldiery was to be replaced with a more positive image of 'citizens in uniform' whose values were closer to those of the family.[12] 'These men were strong, but they were definitely not silent. Theirs was a "gentle strength," expressed in tears and testimony, the strength of sons, fathers, and husbands overcome by the need to share their emotions with mothers, children, and wives.'[13] The returnees from the Soviet Union 'represented a chastened, wiser masculinity … a man whose strong arms could carry a gun but could also embrace a wife and child'.[14]

Moving as these images no doubt were, they represented a conscious attempt at spin rather than real changes in the outlook of men. Although Moeller contrasts this benign image of returning POWs, transformed and reconfigured as family men, with a statement by Gisela Bock about fatherhood in the Third Reich beginning and ending 'with ejaculation', even in the 'militarized system of male supremacy' created by the Nazis masculinity was more complex than this reductive image. Studies of the Holocaust suggest that male perpetrators were able to compartmentalise their feelings, doing the job of killing while out in the field and then returning home to be tender and loving with those closest to them.[15] Although some soldiers became squeamish at the prospect of exterminating women and children, those who worked in the death camps found that the domesticity of family life helped them to relax and forget about work.[16] Claudia Koonz controversially argued that this domestic distraction was a conscious endeavour on the part of Nazi women to facilitate their husbands' important work. While 'Nazi men brutally murdered their political, racial, and national enemies, Nazi women organized motherliness so the world would appear normal and virtuous to average German citizens and to the most murderous SS men'.[17]

Far from being radical and new, the emotive post-war images of men joyfully returning to 'the domesticity of a healthy family' can be seen as a redeployment of earlier motifs of Nazi propaganda. As Amy Beth Carney suggests, the SS tabloid *Das Schwarze Korps* linked SS men with images of healthy families and promoted fatherhood (rather than just fathering) as a responsible and natural duty.[18] The newspaper even printed photographs of SS men pushing prams, changing nappies and bottle-feeding their babies with the caption 'Why shouldn't the father also provide for his child ...? He loses nothing of his masculinity by doing so, but shows that his love for his wife and child is not only lip service.' An SS man, the paper suggested, could be 'a proper bloke and a real man' ('ein echter Kerl und ein richtiger Mann').[19] As GDR propaganda frequently sought to emphasise, older traditions of masculinity and militarism were vocally kept alive by veteran groups and organisations for those displaced from territories in the East. Magazines aimed at adolescents (such as the *Landser*) continued to glorify war and to describe German soldiers as virtuous and brave.[20]

What was remarkable, Richard Bessel argues, was not the attempt to find new heroes, but the difficulties both post-war German states had (as a consequence of the Third Reich) in 'finding new heroes and a new relationship to the German "nation"' that proved popular and acceptable with male youth.[21] In 1945, the Allied occupiers could count on little in the way of 'natural social authority'. Young people had borne the brunt of Nazi attempts at indoctrination. Large numbers of men had died fighting for National Socialist ideals. Many felt a deep, instinctive rejection of anything associated with militarism or ideology.[22] Their attitudes to post-war attempts at re-education and re-indoctrination were often described as *'ohne mich'* ('count me out').[23]

> My father had told me that war was a wonderful adventure ... War was bloody lunacy ... For at least two years I had terrible nightmares and horrific memories of the night in which two of my classmates were killed. I had to tell myself again and again that their deaths were completely pointless. I knew who was really to blame for this senselessness: men like my father.[24]

Remasculinisation East German Style

In East Germany, the communist leadership foresaw great upheaval in pursuit of a better future. The workplace and not the family was to be the key site for reconfiguring citizenship.[25] The SED's conception of its new, antifascist soldiers had little in common with the 'citizens in uniform' image put out by what it called the 'militarists in Bonn'. Men had to sacrifice their domestic and patriarchal role in order to build and defend socialism. The long-term threat posed by the capitalist armies massed just over the border merged with a very real fear (post-1953) of communists being lynched in the event of another mass uprising. The duty of every GDR soldier and policeman was, first and foremost, to serve and protect the SED regime. Families and fellow citizens were very much a secondary consideration. As a result, East German depictions of masculinity 'revealed greater continuity with Prussian-German traditions than did West German ones'.[26]

Whatever else was in short supply in the GDR, there was no shortage of heroes. Antifascist heroes, heroes of labour, sporting heroes, space heroes – collectively and individually – were held up as examples. They were fêted in literature, films, the press, schools and factories and at party congresses. They made their mark on public space with new monuments, statues and street names. Living or dead, they personified ideals cherished by the party and acted as strong points of identification and veneration for those willing to believe. By far the strongest influence was exercised by the heroic martyrs of the antifascist resistance. Whether imprisoned in concentration camps or trying to continue the struggle underground and in exile, the communists had endured immense suffering and had held fast to their ideals in spite of the fruitlessness of resistance. During the dark days of imprisonment, the sense that they were the better men, warriors in a just cause, sustained them through all their hardships and sacrifices.[27] Ernst Thälmann demonstrated the virtues of a communist soldier in remaining loyal until death at the hands of the Nazis. To be a 'soldier of the revolution', he is supposed to have told a fellow inmate, 'means remaining steadfast and faithful, a loyalty that proves itself through life and death. It means showing absolute dependability, confidence, courage and drive in all situations. The flame that surrounds us, that glows in our hearts, that fills our spirits, will accompany us like a guiding light on the battlefields of our lives.'[28] These heroic acts were capable of generating a profound sense of respect among some, if not all, young people.

The antifascist fighters were joined by the 'heroes of labour'. Drawing their inspiration from the Stakhanovite movement in the USSR, the role of the heroes of labour was to bridge the gap between the necessity of substantially increased industrial production and the absence of real incentives.[29] According to Erich Honecker, 'It was a matter of life and death for socialism. During those harsh years of accelerated industrialisation and complete collectivisation, when there was much to do and little to eat, the foundation stone was laid with unrivalled heroism for the later victory of the Soviet people over the fascist intruders.'[30] In the 1930s, these 'shock workers' had become a substantial grass-roots movement in the Soviet Union, creating a new layer of privileged workers at the expense of managerial authority and productive efficiency. Quality and preservation of machinery were sacrificed in favour of the quantitative improvements theoretically spurred by short bursts of excess production. Stakhanovism played a significant role in laying the ground (with tensions, hostility and suspicious breakdowns in production) for the purges that subsequently gripped party cadres in the Soviet Union. Fortunately, the movement never took off to the same extent in the GDR. Instead, attempts to raise work norms while increasing prices and lowering wages resulted in the 1953 workers' uprising.[31]

The heroization of individual workers was essentially a bid to reverse the century-old logic of *Eigensinn*. It continued a trend started by the National Socialists in seeking to break down workers' solidarity by introducing individual and performance-related pay.[32] In the name of collectivism and the working class, individuals were now encouraged to undermine their implicit sense of collective identity and solidarity. However the SED tried to dress it up, workers knew that what they were being asked to do went against their class interests and the tradition of the working-class movement. But, in 1953 at least, East German workers defended their tradition of independent working-class organisations and joined together to defend their collective interests.[33] They sent the 'slave-drivers' (*Antreiber*), 'shoe cleaners' (*Schuhputzer*) and 'bone knackers' (*Knochenschinder*) packing.[34] By embarking on a bold experiment without the support of the population, the GDR's leaders left themselves no alternative but to keep forcing the pace along a route marked 'the planned economy'. To stop and pause to think, Stalinists feared, would lead to a loss of momentum. Instead, they sought to use hero worship as a means of lending their claims moral authority.[35] By invoking important sacrifices made on their behalf, they sought to create the idea that the population owed them a debt. Heroes added a strongly emotional, subjective and personal touch to demands for self-sacrifice and self-denial. In creating a 'heroics of antifascism', the German communists drew on their own experiences not only during the Third Reich, but also in the Weimar Republic. This led them to champion 'an aggressive, powerful masculinity'.[36]

The first hero of labour to emerge blinking into the public spotlight was the miner Adolf Hennecke. Hennecke 'represented the model of the class-conscious proletarian, who has thrown off his old lords and has now become his own boss'.[37] He was quickly followed by a series of others – proclaimed 'Hennecke of the rails' and 'Hennecke of agriculture' for their struggles to beat records and to raise work norms.[38] The heroes of labour were remarkable not just for their superhuman feats of strength and endurance, but for their ordinariness. In the most famous picture of Adolf Hennecke, he seems dwarfed by his pneumatic drill. The pose is heroic, but the man behind the tool looks old, skinny and worn-out. What made men like miners, railway workers, policemen and construction workers heroic was not just their physical toughness, but their preparedness to make sacrifices for their work and to spend long hours away from family and home.[39]

The creation of heroes of labour marked a new phase in the cold war. Male workers were to be at the forefront of an abrupt and radical break with the past, a struggle of new against old. The language was correspondingly militant, reminiscent of the all too recent war. The workplace became a field of class conflict:

> Once again battles were fought, this time in production. They took place above all in the coal mines, in the production of steel and during the harvest in the fields. These were all proving grounds for true masculinity, for physical strength and

courage. Men need no longer prove their race, but had instead to prove their class ... The sphere of work was systematically politicised. Activists and Innovators, Heroes of Socialist Work: these are the ideological formulas cultivated in answer to the Cold War waged by the other side. And they too, once again, centred on men. Men were the protagonists of this war, the fighters, the heroes and naturally also the victors. They decided the content and the rules of engagement. Man was not only architect of the new world but epitomised the 'new person'.[40]

The emphasis on production as combat ensured that the concept of the bright new socialist future was dominated by and replicated old male sensibilities. The emphasis the new regime placed on the 'heroes of labour' (exclusively involved in inherently male occupations) ensured that men continued to represent the vanguard of the struggle to build socialism. The slogan 'I am a miner – who is more?' ('Ich bin Bergmann – wer ist mehr?') summed up 'the respect shown for the job of the miner in the workers-and-peasants' state'.[41]

The 'new person' (*neue Mensch*) was actually the old man writ large. In spite of the much weakened demographic position of men as a result of the war, the image of masculine heroes served to replace and erase the image of the *Trümmerfrau* as the saviour of society.[42] The 'heroes of labour' functioned to reassert masculinity after the emasculating effects of the war. By presenting the myth of hero workers, the SED allowed all men in East Germany the chance not only to express pride in their manhood, but also to make up for having fought on the wrong side before 1945. Men who had proved themselves as 'activists in socialist construction' were placed on the same pedestal as 'those who had already demonstrated their courage in the class struggles of the German proletariat, who received their baptism of fire in the International Brigades of the Spanish Civil War and who came through the prisons of the fascist regime unbroken and upstanding'.[43] Heroic leaders, it was hoped, would pass on the torch of antifascism to youth.[44] The younger generation was encouraged to see the antifascist heroes as role models that they should emulate. Hans Beimler, for example, lent his name to competitions in militarised sport. By joining the People's Police or the NVA, young East Germans were offered the possibility of making up for their failure to act before 1945 and to regain their honour by following in the footsteps of the antifascists.[45]

In the immediate aftermath of the Second World War, the communist leadership had declared itself completely and irrevocably opposed to militarism. SED propagandists recognised the role that even apparently innocent activities such as playing with toy soldiers could have in developing a sense that the military way of life was right and proper for German men.[46] Nevertheless, the communists in the SED soon revived their Weimar 'cult of militarism'.[47] The language and rhetoric of the dictatorship of the proletariat came to be characterised by a 'might is right' ethos. The communist leadership increasingly began to use masculinity as a means of generating support among the working class. To maintain and strengthen the state, the communist leaders encouraged the cult of communist 'machismo' that in the late 1920s and early 1930s had found expression in the Red Front fighting associations. Written by and for workers, the red one-mark novel series had depicted the red worker-warriors as heroic and virtuous. Rather than challenging the existing gender order, they had reflected a normative masculinity with astounding consistency. Women had appeared in the novels more as a nuisance and a hindrance than as true equals of men.[48] With Johannes R. Becher as Minister of Culture, the proletarian novels were reissued, but revised for a new, young audience.[49] Hans Marchwitza's classic, *The Storming of Essen*, now contained a critique of young men who stood around lazily on street corners when they were urgently needed in the important battle taking place elsewhere.[50]

Josie McLellan argues that the heroes of the antifascist resistance (notably those who had fought in the Spanish Civil War) had to be shorn of their individual characteristics and idiosyncrasies in order to fit into the regime's heroic mould. 'The very characteristics that made them fully rounded people were removed in the name of heroism, producing flawless, but ultimately unattainable standards of behaviour.'[51] A major part of this reworking was the excision of anything that suggested unmanliness.[52] Being dead, Ernst Thälmann was unable to criticise those who had succeeded him as party leaders. This made him invaluable to his erstwhile comrades as a malleable symbol of resistance. In death he became the charismatic leader the Communist Party never had, achieving a popularity that had eluded him in his own lifetime: 'this powerful figure with the impressive head, the shining eyes, the energetic fists, the volcanic passion'.[53] His murder at the hands of the Nazis ensured that he became stylised as *the* ultimate antifascist martyr by the SED.[54] Depicted in pictures with strong features and powerful, hypnotic, penetrating eyes, he served as a shining moral example and symbolic leader for the young pioneers. 'Wherever the struggle was most intense and most difficult there Thälmann could also be found. It was as if he had a thousand arms and a thousand eyes.'[55] Thälmann had been primarily responsible for the militarisation of the KPD. As the figurehead of the pioneer organisation, his image became omnipresent. As soon as they were old enough to talk and wear a uniform, young East Germans pledged their allegiance to the dead hero. To make him more child-friendly, Thälmann was renamed Teddy. But even as a fairy-tale figure, Teddy's message was simple: that 'five fingers make a fist'.[56] So important was Thälmann to the SED that entire Politbüro meetings were taken up discussing how to turn his life into a film.[57]

Conclusion

The SED clearly believed that heroes could reach parts of the population that its other symbols, statements and policies could not reach. Heroes added a strongly emotional, subjective and personal touch to the regime's otherwise heavy-handed attempts to influence people. If they could not be completely won over by the system, they could at least be inspired by (and identify with) its heroes. It was hoped that the accounts of revolutionary struggle and underground resistance as thrilling adventures would help to form a bridge between the world of the party and the world of young men.[58] For many, the antifascist heroes were a point of redemptive virtue that, in spite of itself, the SED could not completely sully or destroy. Heroes functioned to emphasise the moral debt owed by the population to their leaders. Even strong critics of the regime found it very difficult to counteract the power exercised over them by its instrumentalisation of heroes. A sense of solidarity with the 'victims of fascism' was deeply tied to a sense of 'hereditary guilt'.[59] Christa Wolf felt that her own past involvement in the League of German Girls burdened her with a deep sense of inferiority vis-à-vis those who were legitimised by their past. 'Because as young people we grew up under fascism, we were filled with guilt and were thankful to those who saved us from it ... We felt strongly inhibited in opposing people who had sat in concentration camps during the Nazi period.'[60] Even today many of the regime's heroes have a stronger resonance than the regime that pushed them to prominence. The cycling hero, Gustav-Adolf 'Täve' Schur, and the first German in space, Siegfried Jähn, were still attracting large crowds in the 1990s.[61] The film *Goodbye Lenin* ends by imagining how much more popular and successful the GDR might have been if Erich Honecker had been replaced by Jähn and not Egon Krenz.[62]

Notes

1. For a summary, see Uta Poiger, 'A New, "Western" Hero? Reconstructing German Masculinity in the 1950s' in Hanna Schissler (ed.), *The Miracle Years. A Cultural History of West Germany, 1949–1968* (Princeton, Oxford, 2001), 412–27, Note 3, 423–24.
2. Hanna Schissler, '"Normalization" as Project. Some Thoughts on Gender Relations in West Germany during the 1950s' in Schissler (ed.), *Miracle Years*, 359–75, 361.
3. Elizabeth Heineman, *What Difference does a Husband Make? Women and Marital Status in Nazi and Postwar Germany* (Berkeley, Los Angeles, London, 1999), 9.
4. Heide Fehrenbach, *Cinema in Democratizing Germany. Reconstructing National Identity after Hitler* (Chapel Hill, 1995), 95–98; Although subsequently ignored and denied by the communist authorities, large numbers of incidents of rape were documented in the Soviet archives. Norman Naimark, *The Russians in Germany. A History of the Soviet Zone of Occupation, 1945–1949* (Cambridge, MA, 1995); in conditions of stark deprivation, women were also subjected to objectification and sexual violence by the other occupying powers.
5. Klaus-Michael Bogdal, 'Hard-Cold-Fast. Imagining Masculinity in the German Academy, Literature and the Media' in Roy Jerome (ed.), *Conceptions of Postwar German Masculinity* (Albany, 2001), 13–42, 36.
6. In Brigitte Reimann's novel, it is the son of an antifascist functionary whose father lives only for his work, leaving his spoilt son to go rotten. Brigitte Reimann, *Ankunft im Alltag* (Berlin, 1961), 25.
7. Christoph Meckel, *Image for Investigation. About My Father* (London, 1987), 64–65. See also Elaine Tyler May, *Homeward Bound. American Families in the Cold War Era* (New York, 1988), 88.
8. Pierre Bourdieu, *Masculine Domination*, trans. Richard Nice (Cambridge, 2001), 69–72.
9. Hans-Jürgen von Wensierski, '"Die anderen nannten uns Halbstarke" – Jugendsubkultur in

den 50er Jahren' in Heinz-Hermann Krüger (ed.), 'Die Elvis-Tolle, die hatte ich mir unauffällig wachsen lassen'. Lebensgeschichte und jugendliche Alltagskultur in den fünfziger Jahren (Opladen, 1985), 103–28, 115.

10. Robert Moeller, 'Heimkehr ins Vaterland: Die Remaskulinisierung Westdeutschlands in den fünfziger Jahren', Militärgeschichtliche Zeitschrift 60:2 (2001), 403–36, 426; Alexander Mitscherlich, 'Der geteilte Vater: Generationskonflikte in der modernen Welt', Der Tagesspiegel (13 November 1955); Alexander Mitscherlich, 'Der unsichtbare Vater: Ein Problem für Psychoanalyse und Soziologie', Kölner Zeitschrift für Soziologie und Sozialpsychologie 7 (1955), 188–201; Dorothee Wierling, 'Mission to Happiness. The Cohort of 1949 and the Making of East and West Germans' in Schissler (ed.), Miracle Years, 110–125, 115–16.

11. Frank Biess, 'Männer des Wiederaufbaus – Wiederaufbau der Männer. Kriegsheimkehrer in Ost- und Westdeutschland, 1945-1955' in Karen Hagemann and Stefanie Schüler-Springorum (eds), Heimat-Front. Militär und Geschlechterverhältnisse im Zeitalter der Weltkriege (Frankfurt, New York, 2002), 345–65, 355f.; Frank Biess, '"Pioneers of a New Germany". Returning POWs from the Soviet Union and the Making of East German Citizens 1945-1950', Central European History 32 (1999), 143–80.

12. Moeller, 'Heimkehr ins Vaterland', 428ff.; Thomas Kühne, 'Kameradschaft – "das Beste im Leben des Mannes": Die deutschen Soldaten des Zweiten Weltkrieges in erfahrungs- und geschlechtergeschichtlicher Perspektive', Geschichte und Gesellschaft 22 (1996), 504–29, 525f. As far as SED propagandists were concerned, 'Blank sucht Kanonenfutter. Wer die DDR verläßt, kommt geradenwegs in die Kaserne', Junge Welt (17 April 1956).

13. Robert Moeller, War Stories. The Search for a Usable Past in the Federal Republic of Germany (Berkeley, Los Angeles, London, 2003), 118.

14. Ibid., 119.

15. Christopher Browning, Ordinary Men: Reserve Police Battalion 101 and the Final Solution in Poland (New York, 1992); on compartmentalisation and the Holocaust, see Zygmunt Bauman, Modernity and the Holocaust (Ithaca, 1989), 98ff. Professional detachment was not just a male prerogative – see Götz Aly and Susanne Heim, Architects of Annihilation. Auschwitz and the Logic of Destruction, trans. A.G. Blunden (London, 2002), 122ff.

16. Mark Mazower, 'Military Violence and the National Socialist Consensus: the Wehrmacht in Greece, 1941-44' in Hannes Heer and Klaus Naumann (eds), War of Extermination: The German Military in World War II, 1941-1944 (New York, 2000), 146–74; Gitta Sereny, Into that Darkness. From Mercy Killing to Mass Murder (London, 1974), 131–39.

17. Claudia Koonz, 'Competition for Women's Lebensraum, 1928-1934' in Renate Bridenthal, Atina Grossmann and Marion Kaplan (eds), When Biology Became Destiny: Women in Weimar and Nazi Germany (New York, 1984), 199–236, 228.

18. Amy Beth Carney, '"As Blond as Hitler": Positive Eugenics and Fatherhood in the Third Reich' (Florida State University: MA Dissertation, 2005), 74ff.

19. 'Ist das unmännlich?', Das Schwarze Korps (10 August 1939) cited in Carney, 'As Blond as Hitler', 86. See also William Combs, The Voice of the SS: A History of the SS Journal "Das Schwarze Korps" (New York, 1986). Till van Rahden argues that an intensive debate occurred in the late 1930s about the role of fathers. Till van Rahden, 'Die Politik der Vaterschaft in West- und Ost-Deutschland von 1945 bis 1980' (Unpublished MS), http://www.ruendal.de/aim/pdfs/Rahden.pdf (accessed 21 November 2005), 6.

20. Kühne, 'Kameradschaft', 523ff.

21. Richard Bessel, 'Was bleibt vom Krieg? Deutsche Nachkriegsgeschichte(n) aus geschlechtergeschichtlicher Perspektive – Eine Einführung', Militärgeschichtliche Zeitschrift 60:2 (2001), 297–305, 299.

22. Frederik Hetmann, Enteignete Jahre. Junge Leute berichten von drüben (Munich, 1961), 36.

23. Michael Buddrus, 'A Generation Twice Betrayed: Youth Policy in the Transition from the Third Reich to the Soviet Zone of Occupation (1945-1946)' in Mark Roseman (ed.), Generations in Conflict: Youth Revolt and Generation Formation in Germany, 1770-1968 (Cambridge, 1995), 247–68.

24. Hetmann, *Enteignete Jahre*, 38-39.
25. Thomas Lindenberger, 'Everyday History: New Approaches to the History of the Post-War Germanies' in Christoph Kleßmann (ed.), *Divided Past: Rewriting Post-War German History* (Oxford, New York, 2001), 43-67, 63.
26. Biess, 'Männer des Wiederaufbaus', 355-56.
27. Divisive Social Democrats, meanwhile, were apparently 'sentimental like old women'. Willi Bredel, *Die Prüfung* (Berlin, 1950), 82ff.
28. Ernst Thälmann cited in Klaus Herde and Wilfried Weidner (eds), *Pioniere voran* (Berlin, 1961), 38-39.
29. Stephen Kotkin, *Magnetic Mountain. Stalinism as a Civilisation* (Berkeley, London, 1995).
30. Erich Honecker, *From My Life* (Oxford, New York, 1981), 42.
31. 'Konterrevolutionärer Putschversuch 17.6.1953', StAL, BDVP 24/42, 63.
32. Detlev Peukert, *Inside Nazi Germany*, trans. Richard Deveson (London, 1993), 108, 117.
33. 'Analyse über die Entstehung des Ausbruches des faschistischen Abenteuers vom 17.6.1953 im Bezirk Leipzig', StAL IV-2/12/588.
34. Erik Neutsch, *Spur der Steine* (Halle, 1964), 280.
35. Jeffrey Brooks, *Thank you, Comrade Stalin! Soviet Public Culture from Revolution to Cold War* (Princeton, 2000), 85.
36. George Mosse, *The Image of Man. The Creation of Modern Masculinity* (New York, Oxford, 1996), 126.
37. Ina Merkel, *... und Du, Frau an der Werkbank. Die DDR in den 50er Jahren* (Berlin, 1990), 106-16.
38. Newsreels, *Kinder, Kader, Kommandeure*, directed by Wolfgang Kissel and C. Cay Wesnigk (Germany, 1992).
39. Heinz Kruschel, *Der Rote Antares* (Berlin, 1979), 211; Erik Neutsch, *Helden-Berichte* (Berlin, 1976).
40. Merkel, *... und Du, Frau an der Werkbank*, 113.
41. 'Walter Ulbricht, Zehn Jahre Kampf um ein einiges, friedliebendes, demokratisches Deutschland', *Junge Welt* (7/8 May 1955).
42. Merkel, *... und Du, Frau an der Werkbank*, 111.
43. 'Aufgebot der FDJ vom 16.8.1961: "Das Vaterland ruft! Schützt die Republik!"', BArch. SAPMO, DY24/3753-1.
44. Young and old were united by a 'glowing hatred for the exploiters'. 'Erich Honecker: Zum 20. Jahrestag der Gründung der Deutschen Volkspolizei (5.6.1965)', BArch. SAPMO DY30/2512.
45. Josie McLellan, 'Remembering Spain. The Contested History of the International Brigades in the GDR' (Oxford University: D.Phil, 2001), 81.
46. Newsreels, *Kinder, Kader, Kommandeure* (1992).
47. Eric Weitz, *Creating German Communism 1890-1990. From Popular Protests to Socialist State* (Princeton, 1997), 379; Hildegard Nickel, 'Geschlechtertrennung durch Arbeitsteilung', *Feministische Studien* 8 (1990), 10-19, 10ff.; Julia Hell, 'At the Center an Absence. Foundationalist Narratives of the GDR and the Legitimatory Discourse of Antifascism', *Monatshefte* 84:1 (1992), 23-25; Mark Thompson, 'Reluctant Revolutionaries: Anti-Fascism and the East German Opposition', *German Politics* 8:1 (1999), 40-65; David Bathrick, *The Powers of Speech. The Politics of Culture in the GDR* (Lincoln, 1995), 10-13.
48. Mosse, *Image of Man*, 129.
49. Hans Marchwitza, *Sturm auf Essen* (Berlin, 1931/1953), 361.
50. Ibid., 15.
51. McLellan, 'Remembering Spain', 85ff., 235.
52. Ibid., 81.
53. Julia Hell, *Post-Fascist Fantasies. Psychoanalysis, History and the Literature of East Germany* (Durham, NC, 1997), 46; Willi Bredel, *Ernst Thälmann. Sohn seiner Klasse* (Berlin, 1954).
54. Zentralleitung der Pionierorganisation Ernst Thälmann, *Thälmann ist niemals gefallen. Geschichten und Berichte* (Berlin, 1961).

55. Max Zimmering, *Buttje Peter und sein Held* (Berlin, 1951), 157.
56. 'Der Rote Oktober und die jungen Revolutionäre unserer Heimat. Schulschrift der Oberschule Ehrenburg, 1969', Leipzig School Museum B8-143-2900.
57. 'Sitzung 13 Jan. 1953: Einsatz des Genossen Bredel zur Fertigstellung des Thälmann-Filmes', BArch. SAPMO DY30/JIV2/2/257; 'Sitzung 21. Apr. 1953: Thälmannfilm', BArch. SAPMO DY30/JIV2/2/276.
58. Hetmann, *Enteignete Jahre*, 24.
59. Hell, *Post-Fascist Fantasies*, 60; Annette Simon, 'Ich und sie: Versuch, mir und anderen über meine ostdeutsche Moral zu erklären,' *Kursbuch* 111 (February 1993), 27.
60. Christa Wolf, *Im Dialog: Aktuelle Texte* (Berlin, Weimar, 1990), 136.
61. Silke Satjukow and Rainer Gries (eds), *Sozialistische Helden. Ein Kulturgeschichte von Propagandafiguren in Osteuropa und der DDR* (Berlin, 2002), 9, 23.
62. *Goodbye Lenin!*, directed by Wolfgang Becker (Germany, 2003).

◌ॐ *Chapter 4* ॐ◌

RE-EDUCATION

*T*he SED inherited a population severely damaged by war and an education system polluted by National Socialism. Its leaders viewed education as the key to restoring what had been lost and to creating new, more equal relationships between men and women. This chapter explores the SED's attempts to re-educate society and argues that they contained mixed messages. On the one hand, its leaders undertook a massive transformation of the education system in the hope of removing the historic inequalities of class and gender.[1] On the other, the educational message itself contained an inherent gender bias. Although quick to challenge class privilege in education, the SED was slower to challenge gender privilege and disadvantageous stereotypes. It was optimistically hoped that boys and girls would learn to overcome gender inequalities by interacting with each other in the classroom and by following the (chaste) example set for them by the heroes and heroines of the revolutionary working-class movement. The continued existence of alternative influences overlapping with (and, in part, contradicting) the regime's official educational message undermined its efficacy. Boys and girls acquired gendered ideas about correct and appropriate behaviour from a number of different sources – including the home, school, peer groups, mass media, the street, sports and the workplace.

Class, Gender, Upbringing and Education

The SED aimed to use the education system to combat the structural causes of social inequality by removing discrimination against working-class children and allowing them the same opportunities to obtain education and qualifications as had once exclusively been enjoyed by the children of the middle class. At the same time, however, it was important for the regime to produce as many young cadres as possible to take over positions in industry, the economy, public service and the administration. The decade and a half after the communists took power saw a significant amount of flux as large numbers of hastily recruited and rudimentarily trained young adults were brought into schools to cope with the dearth of teachers caused by extensive denazification.[2]

For generations, boys and girls had been brought up differently. The specific messages they received about gender were influenced by the culture and outlook of their particular milieu. The National Socialist vision of 'national community' had promised to supersede differences of class, religion and locality by emphasising strong divisions of gender and race.[3] But despite the brutal violence meted out to political opponents, a range of different progressive and humanistic currents persisted in Germany (and even more so in exile). These began to reassert themselves vocally after the regime's collapse. An important (but largely unheeded) argument made by some progressive educational reformers during the Weimar Republic had been the need to remove the gender segregation of education.[4] In the aftermath of National Socialism, which had taken the idea of 'separate spheres' to new and deadly extremes, both communists and Social Democrats saw the dismantling of gender segregation as an essential component of reform. One of the earliest and most important changes the communist-backed reformers made to the education system was to introduce co-education as part of the Law for the Democratisation of German Schools (1946).[5] It guaranteed boys and girls (whatever their social background or milieu) 'an equal right to education' and equal chances of going to grammar school and university. 'Without doubt this was an essential contribution to freeing women from exploitation ... A thousand-year-old injustice to the female sex was revoked; girls now received the same possibilities as boys to train themselves to develop a conscious personality.'[6]

Although education ministry officials (in the various *Länder* governments) clearly hoped that teaching boys and girls together would gradually lead to the erosion of gender inequality, co-education was increasingly taken for granted. In West Germany, in contrast, discussions for and against co-education continued for over two decades. In the immediate post-war period education officials there refused to abandon gender separation in spite of the limitations on space created by bomb damage to school buildings.[7] An unseen problem with the early granting of formal equality of educational opportunity in the GDR was that very little discussion about the ongoing implications of gender for schooling occurred either at this time or in later decades.[8]

> All the same one can by no means assume that distinct psychological features, which historically originated from the unequal societal positions of the sexes and which were passed down from generation to generation, are going to automatically disappear now that objectively equal possibilities of development have been created for both sexes. This mechanistic conclusion is nevertheless frequently made and in our view encourages the underestimation of the problems caused by gender differences in mentality.[9]

Both leaders and rank-and-file members of the SED believed that male youth possessed an enormous (and almost magical) reservoir of malleable energy and strength (*Kraft*). They assumed the characteristics of 'the working class' to be essentially male – strong, physical, macho.[10] Thus, when SED leaders talked about youth as the helpers and 'fighting reserve' of the party, they were really talking about working-class young men.[11] Eager to enlist the support of this 'vanguard of youth' in the building of the new Germany, SED leaders consistently tailored their message to make it attractive (*schmackhaft*) for the perceived interests of this particular constituency. Ending the middle-class monopoly on education was presented as an economic necessity in order to harness and educate young workers for specialist technical positions within the new economy. In return for hard work and acceptance of the new authorities, they were promised rapid promotion to positions of leadership and responsibility. But, in many ways, their attempt to loosen the middle-class stranglehold on academic success resulted in a none too subtle gendering of education (with the emphasis on the hard sciences, physics and technology).

The struggle to defeat 'imperialism' (a catch-all term that conveniently referred both to the Nazis and to the Western powers, which had fought Nazi Germany) would be waged by means of technical know-how and efficiency. Economic and political priorities meant that increasing female participation in higher education took a 'back seat' to the 1950s mass incorporation of (largely male) workers and peasants into university-level education. Women were only discovered as a further educational reserve ten years later, in the 1960s.[12] Although great emphasis was placed on the new society being equal, little thought was given to how to combat the gender stereotypes and differential treatment that continued to exist within the education system. The failure to combat traditional stereotypes meant that the education system followed a 'hidden curriculum' that permitted continued gender inequality. Questioned in 1963, boys and girls explained their attraction for different subjects in terms of gender. 'Physics is more for the boys.' 'Physics, that's more technical things. It doesn't really interest girls.'[13] Teachers themselves, Helga Hörz argued, helped to reproduce gender stereotypes.[14] Although the politicisation of the school system in the GDR was glaringly obvious, the gendering of education was much more difficult for participants and observers to see, conditioned and accustomed as they were to seeing it as something natural and normal.[15]

Although repeatedly berated for allowing their children to watch Western television, parents did not receive much in the way of guidance about how to avoid reproducing gender stereotypes until the late 1960s. Writing in 1970, Karlheinz Otto emphasised the extent to which parents were prone to overlook boys and to let them grow up 'wilder'. Brazenness and daredevil behaviour were even accepted as 'typically boyish'. Girls, in contrast, were educated from a very young age to be more conformist and ready to subordinate themselves, to be 'nicer' and more polite.[16] Parents, feeling worried if their child did not manifest the expected gendered behaviour, were liable to comment 'He's almost too quiet and good for a boy!' or 'Don't cry, you're not a girl after all!' Girls meanwhile were admonished that 'Really, a girl does not charge about!' or 'Little girls do not fight with each other and pull one another's hair!'[17] While girls were expected to form little cliques in which they could be 'spiteful, garrulous, silly and pert', boys were almost encouraged to be 'untidy, rebellious, impolite and impudent'.[18] The wide variety of different names that existed for undisciplined behaviour on the part of boys (*Flegel, Rüpel, Grobian, Bengel, Lausbub, Raufbold, Schlingel, Rowdy, Frechdachs, Rabauke, Klassenclown, Lümmel*) stood in stark contrast to the lack of names for girls who misbehaved (apart from those referring to them as flirtatious or sexually 'loose').[19]

Co-education failed to extend to all subjects or to act as a panacea for gender stereotyping. Although believed to be especially important in building character, physical education and work in production nevertheless continued to be divided along gender lines.[20] Writing in 1962, the educationalist Kurt Bach felt that the day each week that all school pupils were obliged to spend in production was being underutilised as a means of improving gender relations because it was not organised according to the principles of co-education. This meant lost opportunities for boys to 'prove their helpfulness to girls' by 'carrying heavy burdens and handling heavy machinery' for them. If only boys and girls worked in the same space, then the boys could stand next to the girls and give them the benefit of 'their richer and more in-depth technical know-how'.[21] Although it was the one subject area in which schools might have been expected to address the issue of gender specifically, biology teachers remained aloof from the thorny issue of human sexuality for most of the 1950s.

Rolf Borrmann argued that the immensity of the political transformation of the education system had left little time to consider sex education.[22] Many teachers were scared of burning their fingers by broaching questions of sexuality. They did not possess the necessary general knowledge or the ability to speak freely and openly about sex.[23] 'Far from being correctly educated, it is a fact that around 80 per cent of our children and young people are not enlightened at the right time. And yet our ministry hushes this up.'[24] Even when it did become part of the curriculum in 1959, teachers remained in two minds about whether to broach the difficult subject of 'reproduction' with the whole class or to inform boys and girls about it separately.[25] In a private letter to Heinz Ahlborg, Rudolf Neubert revealed, 'In the last few years I have come to the belief that it is not youth that we should be sexually enlightening, but the parents and teachers. Without a thorough enlightenment of the teaching profession we will not take a step further towards teaching the correct way for boys to behave towards girls and vice versa.'[26]

Although more modern 'scientific' theories were developed about the role played by sport in personality development, the emphasis on the perfect body can be traced back to Weimar. In 1952 (with shades of Nietzsche), Johannes R. Becher had optimistically proclaimed, 'The sportsman's way of life: his training, his hard work on himself and his bodily discipline – we are strongly convinced of this – will largely decide the lifestyle of a new generation, in which the dream of the unity of body and soul, and of the beauty and omnipotence of the human being, will be fulfilled.'[27] Boys were encouraged to engage in rough and tumble sports that would help them in their tough, manly professions. They were to gain 'courage, self-confidence and stamina through sport'.[28] Exceptional sportsmen were awarded a badge declaring them 'Ready for work and for the defence of the *Heimat*'.[29] Preparing young men for the day when they might have to defend the republic by force of arms required the creation of a deep sense of love for the GDR and hatred of its imperialist enemies.[30] 'You should love your fatherland and always be ready to apply your whole strength and ability to defend the workers' and peasants' state.'[31] Girls, meanwhile, were expected to become adept and nimble for their future work. The goal for the boys was a strong body and for the girls 'a sporty figure'.[32] Although girls were strongly encouraged to be active in the new youth organisation (and in other educational and ancillary positions), they were largely assigned a supportive role in the wider scheme of things.[33] In the 1950s, girls were encouraged to develop their needlework skills in order to create 'fashionable blouses and skirts'. Failing that, they could produce clothing that could be sent to 'the family members of imprisoned freedom fighters'.[34]

Learning to be a Lad: Acquiring Traditional Machismo

'Deteriorating school results, improper behaviour, booze-ups, sexual dissipations, criminal offences':[35] this list marked the stages (accompanied by comics, pornography, cigarettes and beer) that marked out the slippery slope that threatened to take a schoolboy from a potentially useful socialist personality to a dangerous and decadent '*Rowdy*'. Although the exact opposite of the picture of orderly, committed young socialists that the regime sought to project for its young people, the figure of the 'rowdy' crops up frequently both in 'shock, horror' reports in the socialist press and in educational literature, particularly in parental-guidance pamphlets.[36]

> Many grown-ups claim that youngsters are thoughtless and cheeky; that they do not have any respect for older people; that they don't give up their seats on trams; that they deliberately disturb people's sleep during the night in the same way as they annoy people at the beach [by kicking sand in their faces]; that they disregard warnings and are more likely to greet them with pitying smiles or snotty answers. They feel particularly 'strong' when they are in a like-minded group.[37]

Parents, grandparents and party officials struggled to understand the 'youth of today' and saw the aggressive behaviour of young males as characteristic of a wider problem of loss of respect for wisdom and authority. While many argued that 'conspicuous and loud behaviour, opposition and acting important in front of peers or girls' were signs of degeneration or hormonal imbalance, those with more of a sense of history or a more advanced understanding of science argued that the causes were to be found in changes taking place in society and culture.[38] A 1963 study asked pupils to produce diaries recording how they spent their free time during a typical week. The results were correlated against their marks, revealing striking differences between 'good' and 'bad' pupils.[39] The latter spent four times less time on household chores and more than twice as much watching television or going to the cinema. While the good pupils spent seventy minutes a week reading and no time on the street, the bad ones, in contrast, did not read at all and spent an estimated 130 minutes (by far their most important activity besides sleep) on the street.[40]

Described by Paul Willis as 'learning to labour' and by Alf Lüdtke as *Eigensinn*, the process of acculturation both allude to was about adopting specific attributes of working-class masculinity in order to pass muster with fellow workers.[41] Both depict a factory environment in which 'getting one over' on the foreman and the bosses was an important collective endeavour. Unwritten rules were more important than the official order. As well as the skills and abilities necessary to engage in hard and demanding physical work, employees needed to be able to stand up for themselves and to fit in. Weakness in the face of authority or of work tasks led to marginalisation and exclusion. Practical jokes and other forms of intimidation provided a form of initiation. Those youngsters who passed muster were allowed to become members of the factory community and were afforded assistance. Weaklings or individualists who threatened to undermine the unofficial status quo were undermined by having 'spanners thrown in the works'. Being provided with unsatisfactory work tools or items that constantly went missing ensured that they never advanced below the bottom rung of the hierarchy. When women workers entered previously exclusively male domains, they found that these bullying tactics were deployed against them with especial vindictiveness.[42] Nevertheless, the few who managed to survive in such a hostile environment took on the outlook of their male colleagues and deployed the same tricks against the generation of young women who (in the late 1960s) began to assume positions of responsibility over them.[43]

Many industries gave rise to worker dynasties as working-class patriarchs found jobs for their sons and nephews. For young men who came from working-class backgrounds, a major part of growing up was about learning the skills essential for survival in the factory environment. Already in their adolescence, those who expected to go on to manual labour began acting out the features of a laddish masculinity. Being teased by parents or older siblings for being a clumsy or 'feeble fellow' (*schlapper Kerl*) was a way of preparing the adolescent for what to expect when he entered the world of work.[44] Developing adroitness and a thicker skin would provide them with the means of being accepted and of fitting in. Manual work not only emphasised the necessity of physicality and toughness, but demanded particular ways of thinking and talking as signs of membership of the otherwise closed world of factory life. Thanks to the day in production, youngsters from all backgrounds could also experience shop-floor masculinity at first hand. 'With clichés like "You only live once", "You have to enjoy it while you can" disreputable friends and even older colleagues encourage them to have premarital sex particularly by making their "manliness [Mannbarkeit]" dependent upon it.'[45]

It was easier to make institutional changes than to alter tastes and sensibilities.[46] Many working-class parents continued to see longer and more advanced education as a waste of time for their children.[47] The parent culture they had grown up in emphasised macho activist values that put them in contradiction with the perceived passive and feminine ethos of formal education (or 'book learning' as opposed to 'real learning'). Although officials strove to make the education system more open and accessible to pupils from the working class, the latter often struggled to cope in an alien and intimidating environment. While education officials continued to counter and condemn 'bourgeois' arguments about 'ability', they could not deny that working-class parents, in particular, expressed the opinion that their children could not reach the goal of the *Oberschule*.[48] 'The grounds for such doubts lie in the bad experiences that these parents had during their own time at school. [They lie] in the worry that they cannot help their children in the same way as those who, in their own youth, were not excluded from a better education.'[49] Instead of seeing school and formal qualifications as a means of enlightenment and emancipation, many young people from the proletariat feared that education would alienate and estrange them from their family and surroundings.

For young men from working-class neighbourhoods, academic qualifications and anything that smacked of formal education or organisational control appeared much less important than the process of becoming and proving oneself to be a man (expressing their new-found maturity through clothes, body language and adult tastes).[50] Already at school, youngsters who wanted to become workers started exhibiting the coarse humour, sexism, horseplay and badinage that would help them to stand up to authority and to the pressures from other workers.[51]

> On 17.3.64, pupils from class 10c of the 26th *Oberschule* consumed onions and garlic during the day in production in order to make the atmosphere of the lesson completely impossible. Discussions in the youth organisation and with the teachers concerning their behaviour revealed that they were of the opinion that because they all now had their contracts to become apprentices, they could lark about [Fez machen] in the last months of school.[52]

Even within a single school class a range of different personalities, modes and models of performing gender existed. These differences became most apparent during breaks in teaching and on school trips. For many boys, school seemed like one long popularity contest. Masculine capital (or credit) was gained through sporting prowess, reputation for rebelliousness and knowledge of things that mattered (mainly topics not covered in the school curriculum, such as street life, music and the West).[53] Those who were most popular and admired tended to be stronger, quicker, smarter, wittier, bolder and more handsome. A lot of 'bragging, boasting and showing off' went on.[54] They knew who won which match, who sang what song and who had done what with whom behind the bike sheds. Boys rivalled and competed with each other, often in an attempt to gain the respect of other boys.[55] What was said and done was often less important than who did it and how they told it. Some boys had an explicit advantage over others. They came from outwardly successful, privileged homes or had fathers involved in manly types of work. Their clothes, accents and confident manner set them apart and made them easier to admire than to pick on.

Others struggled harder. 'Swots' who were good at chess or who won maths competitions generally were not viewed as manly unless they also happened to be sporty. The status of amateur dramatics was ambivalent, depending on the handsomeness of the actors and the modernity of the performances. Joiners, doers and go-getters were not necessarily frowned upon as long as they retained a certain implicit sense of irony, critical distance and tongue-in-cheek humour. The children of church preachers or SED functionaries (which amounted in many eyes to the same thing) found it much harder to fit in. Knowing that someone was not allowed to watch Western television at home or was forced to have a portrait of Ulbricht, a crucifix of Jesus or a bust of Lenin on their wall made them a target for mockery. As expressed by one particular middle-class interviewee, the son of a professor, it was a constant struggle not to stand out at school – or rather to stand out only in ways validated and approved by the peer culture.

> You had to pretend that you knew what was what. I didn't want to stand out ... I placed a lot of value on having this image because, in the circles I wanted to belong to, it was important ... Perhaps [I pretended] in order to belong to that image. As a good socialist, I couldn't get any image among my fellow pupils – only through sport or [by being] 'oppositional'.[56]

Whatever plans the education ministry had for schools in the GDR, education was dominated by a herd instinct, which had an uncanny consistency in identifying anything remotely 'sissy' as a weakness.

In their struggle to come to terms with 'loutish behaviour' (*flegelhaftes Benehmen*), which they interpreted as 'false romanticism', SED leaders sought to emphasise the pure, wholesome (and self-sacrificing) traditions of the German working-class movement.[57] Nevertheless, functionaries were forced to admit that 'a series of pupils who act the goat in class are often those who stand out as future boxers, wrestlers and other types of sportsmen. Spoilt by trainers, "idolised" by their parents, they have become arrogant and think they can get through life with boxing.'[58] For many workers, old and young, drinking was an important expression of manliness, as well as an enjoyable way of socialising and letting off steam. Pubs remained important centres of working-class socialisation and leisure. 'Drinking, fights, moral excesses and bad work discipline are the consequences.'[59] However, the occasional drink-fuelled excess was considered by many working-class youths (and some of their parents) as a normal part of growing up.

> Parents do not pay enough attention to this problem. Time and time again, one can observe adults ordering drinks for children and youths. If they are reminded by the bar staff of the observance of youth protection prescriptions, this often leads to unpleasant disagreements. But young people themselves show no understanding for these measures. Many youths deride and laugh at serving staff if they offer them non-alcoholic drinks.[60]

Many boys continued to belong to communities in which an unruly sense of working-class culture and identity survived and which, in certain areas, could be seen to prevail. 'The custom, for example, of celebrating starting a new job [der Brauch des Einstand gebens] is still widespread. Young people who work in breweries receive their free beer [Deputat] in the same way as adults. The same is the case for young people in the coal mines.' As far as SED functionaries were concerned, there was 'a lack of clarity among working-class youth about the sensible use of free time', together with 'a lagging behind in the area of ideology'. Instead of growing up free from the 'morality and way of life under capitalism', working-class boys inherited from older generations a disrespectful attitude to socialist property, in which minor pilfering was seen as acceptable. 'So, for example, tools, wood and other things are taken home and nothing is seen as being wrong with it. Other appearances such as skiving off work [Krankfeiern], drinking during work, celebrating starting and stopping jobs, frequent changing of workplace and the organised exchange of trash literature are equally expressions of an underdeveloped consciousness.'[61]

The Effectiveness of the Educational Claim

Although pupils were increasingly able to repeat the appropriate formulas and phrases, this did not mean that they had internalised the regime's message. As one headmaster reported in 1962, they were quite capable of shutting their ears to attempts at manipulation and manifesting their scepticism to one another through 'deliberate and malicious' smiles and winks.[62] When nobody was looking they demonstrated the regime's failure to influence them by attacking the symbols of state control adorning their classrooms. Wall newspapers were defaced. Comments were added to desks, textbooks and membership cards. Portraits of regime leaders were attacked with compasses, ink and occasionally used as targets for shooting practice (an unintended consequence of issuing the FDJ with air rifles). Although a minority of pupils were prepared to act as policers and enforcers for the party, informing on their classmates, even when they held functions in the youth organisation many found it difficult to escape or ignore the implicit irony and pressure exerted by their peers (described in official reports as 'false comradeship').[63]

Youth researchers estimated that the proportion of young people with a 'generally negative attitude' was between 12 and 15 per cent – made up almost exclusively of working-class males.[64] Far from demonstrating the uniform application of political influence and control as the leaders of the SED would have hoped, youth research surveys revealed significant disparities between different types of school and different areas. In fact, so damaging were the results of the '1969 Survey' for the reputation of the education ministry that Margot Honecker, the minister responsible for education, banned youth researchers from carrying out any further surveys on the pupils in her schools.[65] Significant disparities existed as a result of age, school type, gender and milieu.[66] Contrary to expectations, the youth organisation appears to have been more popular with country than town dwellers, girls rather than boys and middle-class as opposed to working-class youth. Urban working-class boys were consistently by far the most disengaged.[67] In spite of the SED's emphasis on the positive virtues possessed by members of the working class, young men who were on the verge of taking up working-class jobs showed significantly more negative responses than pupils studying for their A levels (or *Abitur*).[68] Educational officials were forced to concede that, 'Even though we [have] put a stop to the discrimination of workers' and peasants' children by opening up the same educational possibilities for them as for other children, we still have not managed to eliminate completely the consequences of educational privilege.'[69] The children of professionals often performed better than their working-class classmates in tests designed to assess the development of socialist consciousness.[70]

Most alarming of all, the longer they spent in the education system and the older they were, instead of becoming more susceptible to the party's influence, the less willing young people became to give the answers expected of them.[71] As adolescents grew more independent and mature, both teachers and youth researchers recorded a growing reluctance and resistance to accept the debt the SED claimed they owed it. As one inspection noted, 'The pupils in the lower forms are easiest to enthuse whereas in the upper forms it often comes to discussions and disputes.'[72] Another inspection report stated that 'with pupils in the sixth class, their knowledge and convictions still reflect a certain belief in the opinion of the teacher. There then begins a period of highly critical evaluation.'[73] While Karlheinz Otto's findings in part reflected this trend, he emphasised that the increase in critical distance was heavily influenced by gender. Arguing that the attitudes pupils exhibited in school were directly related to the gendered messages they received at home – in particular to the degree to which they were involved in household chores – he argued that a radical shake-up was needed. He went as far as to suggest that a greater problem than adolescent male indiscipline was the willingness of girls to subjugate themselves uncritically.[74]

Conclusion

In spite of their attempts to broaden the education system and to make it more accessible, SED leaders were surprised to find that many working-class youths rejected the rubric of self-development, improvement and qualification and instead voluntarily embraced unqualified, unskilled labour. Contrary to their own expectations and experiences, later generations of young people from the working class did not have a 'natural' interest in educating themselves. Instead of seeing education as a means of emancipation, they could see it as a threat.[75] Underlying their rejection of formal education lay an implicit sense that it was impossible to embrace schooling without rejecting the culture and milieu of their upbringing, 'the distinctive styles of speech, thought and behaviour characteristic of working-class culture'.[76] An unwritten and often unspoken rule of working-class life was the need to maintain the solidarity and respect of their peers.[77] It was difficult for young people from this background to conceive of being successful at education without leaving behind or turning their backs on their family and friends.

Although significant numbers of young proletarians did take advantage of the opportunities made available to them and were thereby able to enjoy educational advancement from which previous generations had been excluded, many others remained unmoved and uninterested by the changes in education. School remained an unwanted imposition that they did their best to leave at the earliest possible opportunity. 'There are many young people who don't particularly want to learn and who disrupt lessons for the whole class,' noted Walter Ulbricht in a speech to the youth of East Berlin in 1963.[78] Ulbricht criticised the tendency of certain parents not to realise that a 'modern person' needed at least ten years of schooling.[79] Although the SED had declared that it was in the interests both of workers and of the regime for young people from working-class backgrounds to succeed in education and to gain qualifications that would enable them to take on positions of responsibility, it struggled to convince working-class parents 'that their children are in a position to achieve the same results as those of other classes'.[80] For many working-class parents, there remained a basic incompatibility between being workers and being educated: 'We're workers and our children should also be workers – why do they have to go to school for ten years?'[81]

Notes

1. Günter Wilms, 'Gleiche Bildungsmöglichkeiten für alle: Bildung in der DDR' in Günter Manz, Ekkehard Sachse and Gunnar Winkler (eds), *Sozialpolitik in der DDR. Ziele und Wirklichkeit* (Berlin, 2001), 243–62; Christa Uhlig, 'Gleichheit als Bildungsanspruch. Gedanken zum Bildungssystem der DDR' in Klaus Himmelstein and Wolfgang Keim (eds), *Gleichheit und Ungleichheit in der Pädagogik* (Frankfurt am Main, 2001), 149–67.
2. Gert Geißler and Ulrich Wiegmann, *Schule und Erziehung in der DDR. Studien und Dokumente* (Neuwied, Berlin, 1995), 289f.
3. Renate Strien (ed.), *Mädchenerziehung und -sozialisation in der Zeit des Nationalsozialismus und ihre lebensgeschichtliche Bedeutung* (Opladen, 2000), 135ff.
4. Wolfgang Scheibe, *Die reformpädagogische Bewegung, 1900–1932* (Weinheim, 1977), 125ff., 304; Wolfgang Ellerbrock, *Paul Oestreich. Porträt eines politische Pädagogen* (Weinheim, Munich, 1992), 88.
5. Gert Geißler, 'Zäsuren in der Schulpolitik der SBZ und der DDR 1945–1965' in Dietrich Hoffmann and Karl Neumann (eds), *Erziehung und Erziehungswissenschaft in der BRD und der DDR*, vol. I, *Die Teilung der Pädagogik, 1945–1965* (Weinheim, 1994), 41–55, 42.
6. Karlheinz Otto, *Disziplin bei Mädchen und Jungen. Ein Beitrag zur Gleichberechtigung der Geschlechter aus psychologischer, pädagogischer, soziologischer und historischer Sicht* (Berlin, 1970), 32.
7. Wilfried Breyvogel and Inge Seemann, 'Aus der Not keine Tugend. Jungen und Mädchen zusammen und doch getrennt 1945–1957' in Wilfried Breyvogel (ed.), *Mädchenbildung in Deutschland* (Essen, 1996), 175–88.
8. Gerd Reinhold, Guido Pallak and Helmut Heim (eds), *Pädagogik-Lexikon* (Munich, Vienna, 1999), 298.
9. Otto, *Disziplin bei Mädchen und Jungen*, 32–33.
10. Nicholas Dirks, Geoff Eley and Sherry Ortner (eds), *Culture/Power/History. A Reader in Contemporary Social Theory* (Princeton, 1994), 34.
11. Sixteenth Conference of the Central Council of the FDJ (25 April 1957) cited in Karl Heinz Jahnke (ed.), *Geschichte der Freien Deutschen Jugend* (Berlin, 1976), 5, 131.
12. Gunilla-Friederike Budde, 'Wettkampf um Gerechtigkeit. Frauenförderung und Arbeiterkinder in den Hochschulreformdebatten in Ost und West', *Jahrbuch für Universitätsgeschichte* 8 (2005), 123–42.
13. Helga Hörz, *Die Frau als Persönlichkeit* (Berlin, 1968), 105.
14. Ibid., 106f.
15. Otto, *Disziplin bei Mädchen und Jungen*, 34, 185ff.
16. Ibid., 187.
17. Ibid., 187ff.; B. Wagner, 'Geschlechtsspezifische Verhaltensweisen über Rollenspiele' (Jena Institute for Psychology: Diplomarbeit, 1967); U. Siegel, 'Junge Mädchen'. Unpublished MS (Leipzig, Institut für Jugendforschung, 1969).
18. Otto, *Disziplin bei Mädchen und Jungen*, 186, 191.
19. Ibid., 184. The German terms for naughty boys translate loosely as 'lout, boor, rascal, scamp, ruffian, rogue, hooligan, cheeky little so-and-so, roughneck and class clown'.
20. Paul Marschner, 'Die Körpererziehung als Faktor sozialistischer Persönlichkeitsentwicklung' in Akademie der Pädagogischen Wissenschaften (ed.), *Erziehung sozialistischer Persönlichkeiten* (Berlin, 1976), 241–46.

21. Kurt Bach, 'Erfahrungen aus den Zusammenarbeit von Schule, Elternhaus, Betrieb und Jugendorganisation bei der geschlechtlichen Erziehung', *Pädagogik Beiheft* 2 (1962), 57-59, 59.
22. Rolf Borrmann, 'Die mittelbare, indirekte Teilnahme des Lehrers an der sexuellen Bildung und Erziehung', *Pädagogik Beiheft* 2 (1962), 24-28, 25; Heinz Ahlborg, 'Zu einigen Fragen der Sexualerziehung in der Schule. Pädagogische Lesung', Brandenburg, 1967 (Unpublished MS, BBF Berlin), 11.
23. Heinz Grassel, 'Stand und Probleme der Sexualerziehung' in Heinz Grassel (ed.), *Psychologische und pädagogische Probleme der sexuellen Bildung und Erziehung* (Rostock, 1972), 12-50, 43.
24. Kurt Bach, 'Meine Erfahrungen bei der systematischen sexuellen Bildung und Erziehung unserer Kinder und Jugendlichen. Pädagogische Lesung', Hohenmölsen, 1964 (Unpublished MS, BBF Berlin), 2.
25. C. Neutsch, 'Zur Zusammenarbeit von Jugendarzt und Schule auf dem Gebiet der sexuellen Aufklärung und Erziehung', *Pädagogik Beiheft* 2 (1962), 30-31.
26. Cited in Ahlborg, 'Zu einigen Fragen der Sexualerziehung', 24.
27. Johannes R. Becher, *Verteidigung der Poesie* (Berlin, 1952), 402, as cited in Marschner, 'Die Körpererziehung', 246.
28. 'Der Jugend Vertrauen und Verantwortung' in Zentralkomitee der SED, *Jugend von heute. Hausherren von Morgen. Kommuniqué des Politbüros des ZK der SED zu Problemen der Jugend in der DDR* (Berlin, 1963), 1-34, 16.
29. Ibid., 29.
30. 'Analyse der Unterrichtsstunde des Koll. R. (17.3.55)', BArch. Berlin DR2/3410, 154, 166.
31. Walter Ulbricht presented his ten commandments at the Fifth Party Conference (10-16 July 1958). Cited in Rolf Borrmann, *Jugend und Liebe. Die Beziehungen der Jugendlichen zum anderen Geschlecht* (Leipzig, 1966), 56.
32. 'Der Jugend Vertrauen und Verantwortung', 28.
33. Christa Wolf, *Im Dialog* (Berlin, Weimar, 1990), 157.
34. Zentralrat der FDJ (ed.), *Handbuch des FDJ-Gruppenleiters* (Berlin, 1956), 302.
35. Walter Friedrich, *Flegeljahre? Zur Erziehung 13- bis 16jähriger Jungen* (Berlin, 1964), 41.
36. 'Rowdietum = Heldentum?', *Junge Welt* (29 December 1955); 'Zwei Halbstarke - vier blutige Schlägereien', *Junge Welt* (7-8 January 1956).
37. Friedrich, *Flegeljahre?*, 14.
38. Ibid., 2ff.
39. Ibid., 43.
40. Ibid., 42-43.
41. Alf Lüdtke, 'What Happened to the "Fiery Red Glow"? Workers' Experiences and German Fascism' in Alf Lüdtke (ed.), *The History of Everyday Life. Reconstructing Historical Experiences and Ways of Life* (Princeton, 1989), 198-251, 226-28; Alf Lüdtke, 'Cash, Coffee-Breaks, Horseplay: *Eigensinn* and Politics among Factory Workers in Germany circa 1900' in Michael Hanagan and Charles Stephenson (eds), *Confrontation, Class Consciousness and the Labour Process* (New York, 1986), 65-95; Alf Lüdtke, *Eigen-Sinn. Fabrikalltag, Arbeitererfahrungen und Politik vom Kaiserreich bis in den Faschismus* (Hamburg, 1993); for examples of generational conflict between workers in the factories, see 'SED Betriebsparteiorganisation des Werkes für Schwermaschinenbau S.M. Kirow' (2 May 1968), StAL IV B-7/177/08.
42. Lutz Niethammer, Alexander von Plato and Dorothee Wierling (eds), *Die Volkseigene Erfahrung. Eine Archäologie des Lebens in der Industrieprovinz der DDR* (Berlin, 1991), 118ff.
43. Ibid.
44. Friedrich, *Flegeljahre?*, 34.
45. Ibid., 38-39.
46. Dieter Rink, 'Das Leipziger Alternativmilieu zwischen alten und neuen Eliten' in Michael Vester, Michael Hofmann and Irene Zierke (eds), *Soziale Milieus in Ostdeutschland. Gesellschaftliche Strukturen zwischen Zerfall und Neubildung* (Cologne, 1995), 193-229, 197.

47. 'Warum zehn Jahre "Schulbank drücken"?', *Junge Welt* (5 April 1956)
48. 'Durchsetzung der sozialistischen Oberschule' (6 May 1959), BArch SAPMO DY 6/3939; 'Material über wichtige Probleme der Volksbildung' (8 March 1963), BArch SAPMO DY30/IVA2/2.024/6.
49. 'Durchsetzung der sozialistischen Oberschule'.
50. Paul Willis, *Learning to Labour. How Working Class Kids Get Working Class Jobs* (Farnborough, 1977), 15, 18; for GDR examples of such behaviour, see 'Protokoll über einen Erfahrungsaustausch über die Arbeit der Jugendklubs in der DDR' (1960), BArch. SAPMO DY24/6724; 'Für Ordnung und Sauberkeit: Prozeß gegen junge Aufrührer auf der Leipziger Kleinmesse', *LVZ* (24 October 1965); for the powers of seduction and potency vested in workers' boots, see Erich Loest, *Es geht seinen Gang oder Mühen in unserer Ebene* (Halle, 1977).
51. Willis, *Learning to Labour*, 55.
52. 'Bemerkungen zu den Fragen der Disziplin und Ordnung (Leipzig, 21.3.1964)', StAL IV A-2/9.02/353, 56–64.
53. Interviews with Herbert O., Dieter J., Wolfgang V., Hans-Peter D. and Franz P. (1999–2000).
54. Friedrich, *Flegeljahre?*, 11.
55. Friedrich mentions 'unhealthy competition' in tasteless clothing and exaggerated haircuts. Ibid., 11, 13.
56. Interview with Herbert O.
57. 'Die Aufgaben der weiteren Einschränkung von Jugendkriminalität und Rowdytum' (c. 1960), BArch. DY6/3937; 'Lage an den allgemeinbildenden polytechnischen Oberschulen (Leipzig, 8.10.1963)', StAL, IV A-2/9.02/353, 50.
58. 'Bemerkungen zu den Fragen ...'
59. 'Fragen der Jugenderziehung im Zusammenhang mit der Bekämpfung des Rowdytums und der Jugendkriminalität (Berlin, 14.5.60)', BArch. SAPMO DY30/IV2/16/230.
60. 'Ratsinformation über die Kontrolltätigkeit zur Einhaltung der Verordnung zum Schutze der Jugend (Leipzig, 18.8.66)', StAL, IV A2/16/464, 263.
61. 'Fragen der Jugenderziehung ...'
62. 'Vertraulich! Argumente zum Nationalen Dokument (5.6.1962)', BArch. DR2/6298, 13.
63. 'Kriminalpolizei: Rowdytum (26.4.1973)', StAL, BDVP 24.1/420, 332.
64. Zentralinstitut für Jugendforschung (henceforth, ZIJ): 'Umfrage '69'. Unpublished MS (Leipzig, 1969), 70.
65. Walter Friedrich, (Geschichte des Zentralinstituts für Jugendforschung) in Walter Friedrich, Peter Förster and Kurt Starke (eds), *Das Zentralinstitut für Jugendforschung Leipzig 1966–1990. Geschichte, Methoden, Erkenntnisse* (Berlin, 1999), 13–69, 26–27.
66. 'Umfrage '69', 2, 16.
67. 'Umfrage (69), 32; ZIJ: (Jugendstudie zur Effektivität der Jugendweihe) (1968), StAL, IV B-2/16/706, 15–63; F82/41 Dr. Helfried Schmidt, ZIJ: (Ausgewählte Einstellungen und Verhaltensweisen Jugendlicher in Abhängigkeit von der Wohnortgröße - Teilbericht zur Komplexstudie U 79). Unpublished research report (Leipzig, July 1982).
68. 'Umfrage '69', 2, 68.
69. Untitled discussion material (c. 1959), BArch. Berlin DY6/3939, 14.
70. 'Gutachtung zu der Habilitationsschrift von Herrn Walter Friedrich "Zum Problem der Verhaltensdetermination im Jugendalter" (27.2.1965)', BArch. SAPMO DY30/IVA-2/16/159.
71. 'Umfrage '69', 2.
72. 'Informationsbericht (24.10.1961)', Stadtarchiv Leipzig, Stadtverordnetenversammlung und Rat der Stadt (henceforth Stv&RdSt) (1), Nr. 2311, 27–29.
73. 'Bericht über den Stand des politisch-moralischen Bewußtseins von Schülern und Lehrlingen (7.9.1963)', StAL, IVA2/16/461.
74. Otto, *Disziplin bei Mädchen und Jungen*, 191.
75. Sonja Häder, 'Mytholigisierung der "Arbeiterkinder"? Mentalitäten – Handlungsmuster –

Bildungswege von Kinder aus einem traditionellen Ost-Berliner Arbeiterbezirk (1945–1958)' in Peter Hübner and Klaus Tenfelde (eds), *Arbeiter in der SBZ-DDR* (Essen, 1999), 691–708.
76. Stephen Humphries, *Hooligans or Rebels? An Oral History of Working-class Childhood and Youth 1889–1939* (Oxford, 1981), 54.
77. Lüdtke, 'What Happened to the "Fiery Red Glow"?', 226.
78. 'Ihr seid die Schmiede der deutschen Zukunft. Rede des Genossen Walter Ulbricht auf der Großkundgebung der Berliner Jugend (23.9.1963)' in Zentralkomitee der SED, *Jugend von Heute. Hausherren von Morgen*, 35–70, 57.
79. Ibid., 62.
80. Ibid.
81. Ibid.

◌̃ Chapter 5 ◌̃

A Teenage 'Revolution'?

*U*nfortunately for the SED, its attempts to mould the younger generation according to its own notions of what was good for them were undermined not only by gendered forms of inherited immunity, but also by the development of new forms of teenage identity. It proved impossible for the state to prevent 'its' youth from becoming subject to alternative, competing influences. The most important of these was Western media, which offered young East Germans alternative interpretations together with up-to-the-minute news about the latest music, ideas and fashions. The modernisation the regime so desperately strove for and sought to impose from above proved more complex and equivocal than it had hoped. In the West, the 1950s saw changes in culture and identity that increasingly identified youth as a separate social category with its own interests and ideals.[1] These changes, fostered by the increasingly international mass media, attacked the 'traditional padding' and authority of school and parents by bringing into question previously unchallenged moral systems and world views. They also had an impact on the party-state's ability to mould and to steer the transformation of society.

SED leaders were encouraged by the fact that more and more young people were drifting away from Christianity, particularly in urban areas. But they were slow to realise that they too were caught up in a process of 'desacralisation' that undermined the symbolic and 'spiritual' effects of their ideological claims. Although the SED strove to create a society in which individuals sacrificed their interests for the good of the collective ('the step from "I" to "We"'), by extending horizons and providing access to new ideas and outlooks, changes in education and the media fostered the growth of subjectivity and individualism. Technological changes, themselves encouraged by the party, meant that young people had access to a far greater range of sources of information than ever before and were able to tap into the Zeitgeist that existed among their peers elsewhere on the globe. The world in which they were growing up was very different (technologically, culturally, intellectually) from that experienced by their parents and grandparents.[2] The influence of the much more varied means of mass communication was making them 'more expert, more independent, more widely informed and more interested in technology ... in mentality and character [they are] actually "prematurely mature [*frühreif*]"'.[3]

Teenage Culture

When Ulbricht and his colleagues took power in East Germany, they were thoroughly unprepared for the changes in teenage culture and identity that began spreading from the West in the early 1950s. Standing in direct opposition to the attempt to appropriate and functionalise youth in the service of the regime, new forms of youth culture and identity emerged that contradicted the SED's message. The communists had difficulty making out (to them) alien cultural forms and often blurred the boundaries between different groups and trends.[4] As far as members of the SED were concerned, the important thing about the teenagers was that 'they read Western trash literature and make fun of everything about our GDR'.[5] In sharp contrast to the uniform blue shirts of the FDJ, dissident youth wore bright, mass-produced checked shirts.[6] It was only during the course of the 1953 uprising that the leadership was able to find names for them, describing them as 'samba boys', 'tango youths' and 'Bubis'.[7] In reality, those targeted during the crackdown were fans of bebop.[8]

The SED's struggle to impose its own norms on society took place during a period in which 'teenagers' throughout the developed world were discovering new ways of rebelling against adult-imposed norms. The reasons why adolescents increasingly began to reject authority – the desire for autonomy, for self-experimentation, the wish to escape the feeling of being controlled – were similar in both East and West. As they neared maturity, they began chafing at the restrictions imposed on them and demanded appropriate recognition of their changing status. News about what teenagers were doing elsewhere in the world provided young people in the GDR with alternative images and models. They began to search for and to test the limits – seeing what reactions were provoked by the adoption of an attitude of opposition and nonconformity. Experimentation with clothes, haircuts and identity allowed the teenager opportunities to explore and express what kind of person he or she wanted to be. The culture they embraced shocked their elders by challenging existing societal mores and promising liberation and escape from the drudgery and constraints of everyday life.

In the U.S.A., post-war affluence encouraged the development of a separate 'youth culture' as a growing range of media products were targeted directly at youth.[9] Perceiving 'teenagers' as a lucrative and previously untapped consumer group, publishers bombarded them with magazines and comics, trash literature and books. The ready accessibility of mass-produced consumer items made it possible for teenagers to begin experimenting with their look and identity thereby expressing their difference from their parent culture. The media helped to transmit ideas and fashions to new audiences, whetting their appetites, inflating their aspirations and encouraging them to redefine themselves. Getting the 'pose' of casual nonchalance and effortless cool right brought them standing and approval from their peers. In the West, the youth culture 'revolution' transformed German teenagers for the first time into fully fledged consumers. Films, music shows and, later, television fostered the growth of interest in pop music and Anglo-American culture.

In West Germany, the 'economic miracle' allowed the emergence of teenagers with extravagant tastes at odds with the previous period of post-war gloom. Their pocket money could buy them records, magazines, chewing gum, Coca Cola and jeans.[10] Advertisers, interested in their disposable income, began marketing products specifically for teenagers. This provoked concern among adults about the dangers of them turning into passive consumers. Young Germans no longer saw themselves as belonging just to a narrow, tradition-bound community. Instead they were part of a new and increasingly important age group whose interests and tastes now spanned the globe. The increasing internationalisation of mass media and youth culture provided an alternative set of values and encouraged changes in self-perception. Mass media and entertainment opened up another world and gave them new, alternative models for how and what to think. Their increased importance as consumers in turn provided teenagers with an acknowledgement of their changing status. They began developing their own (often provocative) forms of style and manner, erecting barriers of fashion and custom around adolescence.[11]

Symbolising the altered balance between work and leisure, the 'showbiz' (or entertainment) industry played a very important role in articulating, spreading and standardising youthful feelings. American movies provided German youth with models for juvenile fashions, dances and postures. Films like *The Wild One* (1953) and *Rebel Without A Cause* (1955) highlighted changes and, at the same time, created their own iconic symbols of teenagers' growing frustration with adult restrictions. Marlon Brando and James Dean symbolised potent, sexually charged anti-heroes rebelling against adult society and its restrictive mores. In the famous line in *The Wild One* when Marlon Brando's character, Johnny, is asked 'What are you rebelling against?', he replies 'What have you got?'[12] Later in the 1950s, movies introduced Western audiences to rock 'n' roll. In several countries, *The Blackboard Jungle* (1955) and *Rock Around The Clock* (1956) sparked 'moral panics' as the wild and raucous new music sent young people dancing into the aisles.[13] To adults, rock 'n' roll appeared hostile and aggressive – heralding a dangerous breakdown of order and obedience. Riots occurred as the police attempted to maintain control and to prevent what they saw as disorderly conduct.[14] At home, differences of opinion regarding music and clothing frequently became the source of confrontations between parents and their adolescent children.

Fashion and music allowed young people to express difference from their parents' generation while at the same time staking a claim to adulthood in their own right. In the West, niche markets (in advertising and the print media) developed for articulating and explaining the growing generation gap, for providing advice and tips on what it was and how to be a teenager. The mass media encouraged teens to feel that they had a share in the creation of fame and glamour, thereby offering them alternative dreams and aspirations. Identification with pop stars and film icons allowed teenagers to imagine themselves in different situations and at the same time to affirm things about who they were. Television and radio, comic books and magazines offered an outlet for escapist fantasy. Elvis and Norma Jean were powerful figures of identification, not least because they had succeeded in escaping the poverty and humbleness of their beginnings.

In the U.S.A. itself fears about the new forms of youth culture led to Senate hearings in Washington.[15] In other countries, the new attitudes and behaviour associated with teenagers led to debates about the harmful effects of Americanisation. Liberating and occupying U.S. servicemen brought with them new mass-produced styles of clothing, 'hot' music and radio stations as well as an abundance of chewing gum and chocolate. America appeared as the paradigm for the future, threatening the economies and traditional cultures of every advanced industrial democracy in the Western world.[16] Germany's defeat in the Second World War seemed to mark the victory of American ideals and lifestyles in Central Europe, which had long resisted the encroachments of Western, 'urban-rational' ideas.[17] To the extent that America appeared to represent the future of Europe, adopting American manners and dress was interpreted as being modern.[18] The American model promised a future in which consumption and leisure would be much more important.[19] Nevertheless, Germans in both East and West were concerned about the role played by American music and films in shaping post-war German personalities.

If, for teens, America seemed the epitome of all things 'cool', for teachers and middle-class parents, American cultural imports were often perceived as invasive and a dangerous lowering of standards. What commentators feared was not just 'Americanisation', but 'Americanisation from below'.[20] Fear of America as an image of modernity overlapped with fears about the new popular culture imbuing youth with lower-class values. 'It was the novel and unsolicited ingression of new tastes coming from "below", and their evident powers to challenge and redraw some of the traditional maps of cultural habits, that generated many an acid but apprehensive rebuttal.'[21] A youth culture was developing that not only crossed geographical boundaries, but threatened to blur social distinctions. West German social commentators noticed signs that the changes in consumption associated with the development of a mass market were not only creating a growing distance between the generations, but also a decline in political interest, particularly among younger workers. Work and production were becoming less important in forming identity than consumption and leisure.

Karl Bednarik, in particular, remarked that the 'political' type of working-class youth formed by a tight network of organisations, associations and clubs of parties had effectively disappeared and had been replaced by the 'sceptical type', who viewed political organisations with mistrust and placed more value on individual experiences. Young workers no longer expressed membership of the working class through proletarian dress so much as through 'primitive', vulgar ways of talking. While the First of May could only attract a few small groups of youngsters in the West, every evening groups of young people could be seen clustered on particular street corners, especially in the vicinity of cinemas and fairgrounds.[22] For those on the Left, these changes in identity were particularly dangerous because they threatened to radiate false consciousness from below. The collapse of interest in traditional German culture in the face of the American imports amounted to the 'Coca-colonisation' of Germany.[23]

The increased social and cultural power of the Western marketplace and mass media also impacted on East German parents' ability to communicate with and to control their children. But a much greater threat was posed to the SED and to its attempts to influence youth politically. To the SED, teenage culture was just a new form of false consciousness. The romantic dreams of escape and the fairy-tale stories of rags-to-riches success had nothing to do with the self-sacrifice and hard work that was needed if socialism was to be built from scratch. The development of commercialised youth culture was a clear sign that capitalism was seeking to blind young people in the West (in particular young workers) to their status at the bottom of society. The class enemy needed to divert youth's innate desire for revolution into disorganised and non-political forms of behaviour that posed no fundamental challenge to the political and economic system.[24]

> In West Germany and West Berlin, those in power try to keep young people away from societal life because they know that, if politicised, young people would find out about their *volksfeindliche* plans to destroy the population ... They try to dull the minds of as many young people as possible in the Democratic Sector and our Republic in order to keep them away from societal construction.[25]

Access to Western programmes gave Eastern teenagers an important means of immunising themselves from the effects of official propaganda. It provided them with other ways of assessing, judging and making sense of the reality that they were experiencing. On certain issues they were much better informed than their teachers. This knowledge gave them power, if not to resist the demands made on them by the state, then at least to resist internalising its messages. Even when they turned a deaf ear to the anticommunist messages broadcast from the West, they could not help but get the impression that things were brighter, freer and more fun in the outside world.[26] What was worse, there was evidence that exposure to Western media made them immune to certain forms of ideological influence.

> Particularly problematic is the following tendency: young people who frequently tune in to Western stations already rate our programmes and films (e.g. political news in our media, GDR television commentators, TV films like the *Der Sonne Glut* and *Arthur Becker*, but also contemporary DEFA films) according to the content and form of bourgeois mass communication. Their expectations as well as their criteria of assessment are already influenced by phenomena that are alien to our socialist ideology.[27]

Not only were Western radio and television providing alternative messages, but they were increasingly shaping the way in which young people perceived attempts to influence and control them by schools, the youth organisation and even their own parents.

If youth was distracted by Western media from the task of building socialism, then given the emphasis the SED had placed on youth acting as the vanguard and harbinger of future relations, this did not augur well for the future. By focusing attention on problems of consumption in the GDR, the new consumer culture threatened to undermine the great progress that was being made, under the leadership of the SED, in transforming the means of production. The spending power of teenagers in the West contrasted sharply with the difficulties faced by adults in the East not only in purchasing expensive consumer durables, but in obtaining reliable supplies of essentials like coal and potatoes.

'Psychological Warfare'

The experimentation and diversification of lifestyles fostered by access to the mass media posed a serious threat to the regime's attempts to form its teens into uniformly dutiful and committed socialist personalities. SED propagandists and functionaries presented the disruption in simian terms. 'By spreading American ape culture, they hope to demoralise youth and to create the conditions necessary for the recruitment of willing tools for spying and subversion work within the GDR.'[28] Although the state was able to assert control over the education system and to develop its own network of organised leisure, it could exert little control over the airwaves and the flood of information and radio programmes coming from the West. Prior to the building of the Berlin Wall, the still open border with West Berlin acted as the main conduit for the tangible artefacts of Westernised youth culture to enter the GDR. Every day thousands of young East Germans crossed over the border to West Berlin in search of entertainment and amusement.[29]

> Because our Democratic Berlin has an open border to West Berlin, it is not surprising that, here and there, certain phenomena that actually only belong to an imperialist societal order, spread to particular, especially susceptible groups of young people here. So, unfortunately, there are still cases of young people who are driven to commit crimes by the *Gangsterromantik* coming from West Berlin.[30]

The undisguised popularity of Western media products for large numbers of young East Germans not only revealed the extent to which the regime was failing to win over teenagers, but posed a serious threat of contamination. For the police and the party, the mass culture that was so attractive to their own citizens was an assault on the GDR. The music and images transmitted from the West contained within them the 'virus of subversion'.[31] In order to combat this threat, the regime sought, on the one hand, to make clear the danger posed by Western manipulation and, on the other, to provide youngsters with safe alternatives. Propagandists' attempts to emphasise the corrupting effects of Western media were easiest with regard to the trash literature, comics and teenage films, which became a source of public fear and moral panic in both West Germany and the U.S.A. in the 1950s.[32] Detective stories and gangster novels, it was argued, led susceptible young men to commit crime. Similar assertions were used in relation to films depicting violence. Although such arguments may have made good copy for newspapers, they seem to have convinced few parents of the need to change their children's viewing habits. Nor did such rhetoric prevent forbidden literature passing from hand to hand among groups of teenagers.[33]

In reports that often drew on sensationalist articles in the capitalist tabloid press, East German journalists sought to juxtapose the 'clean and healthy' culture provided in schools and the officially controlled youth organisation with the dirt and disease, corruption and decay inherent in Western trash culture. Examples of the 'trash and smut literature' confiscated included such titles as *Micky Maus, Der 30 Pfennig Roman, Stella Roman* and the *Illustrierte Kriminal-Bücherei*.[34] While official culture would raise youth to new heights of consciousness and productivity, exposure to Western '*Unkultur*' was said to numb their minds and have degrading effects.[35] 'The West German militarists need heartless killers who are ready without hesitation to shoot at their own workers or to attack another people in the name of "freedom".'[36]

At the height of the cold war, mass media was clearly an important tool in the battle for ideological superiority. Gregory Mitrovich and Scott Lucas have each used declassified intelligence files to argue that the Americans did use non-military methods, psychological warfare and covert action to promote instability in the Soviet bloc.[37] An early CIA plan involved dropping Mickey Mouse watches and candy bars into East Germany tied to balloons.[38] The

West German political establishment (together with other western powers) was undoubtedly interested in using the popularity of Western media among East German youth as a means of influencing its listeners and viewers in the East and of presenting them with an alternative to the news and information transmitted by officially controlled GDR media outlets.[39] By tuning in to Western media, they would realise that the FRG represented not only a freer society but a superior social and economic system.

To encourage youngsters from the GDR to visit cinemas in West Berlin, the West German government sponsored reduced ticket prices for border crossers (*Grenzgänger*). 'With an *HO* bag as proof that I was from the East, I could get into the cinema for 25 West Pfennigs.'[40] Visitors to West Berlin were able to bring back with them records, shoes and articles of clothing (albeit at prohibitive rates of exchange). Comics were frequently added to food parcels sent by relatives. Even after the Berlin Wall was built, West Berlin acted as an island of Western culture located deep within the GDR. American and West German radio stations spread awareness of the latest fashions, music and items of consumption. The increasing availability of television sets in the GDR (itself trumpeted as an achievement of socialism) brought pictures of what East Germans were missing out on right into their living rooms. The images of commercialised youth culture were far slicker and more attractively packaged than the SED's attempts to popularise its own policies and provisions for youth. In contrast to the dull repetitions and grey sameness of many of the SED's political and educational offerings, Western media promised endless variety and entertainment at minimal cost.

SED propagandists chose to present commercialised youth culture as a new and entirely alien influence on youth ('eine niedere Bastardkunst').[41] Nevertheless, consistency being less important than dialectics, they were also able to see these new forms as a recrudescence of fascist methods of exploitation. If anything, it was the SED's attempts to prevent the spread of Western media influence that represented a continuation of Nazi manipulation. As far as many young people (and adults) were concerned, there was not much to distinguish the two regimes in their attempts to stop the population listening to 'enemy broadcasts'. In West Germany, commercial pressure and attempts at more enlightened press reporting gradually served to defuse the tension surrounding American imports and accommodate the new trends. SED attempts to accommodate and control the new youth culture were a lot less subtle and successful. In 1956 Marilyn Monroe's relationship with 'the progressive playwright' (and critic of McCarthyism) Arthur Miller led *Junge Welt* to reassess a 'young woman whose body measurements do more to excite U.S. newspapers than world politics'. It declared that she was also a woman who, knowing the 'law of the capitalist jungle', 'dared to leave the gutter and, through hard work, to become an actress'.[42] Attempts to co-opt 'progressive parts' of Western popular culture were marred by a continued need to emphasise the sinister relationship between Western-inspired culture and crime. Journalists did little to convince the population by exaggerating and misrepresenting the threat. Members of the FDJ refused to accept that pop songs caused crime or that Western 'lifestyles' led to murder.[43]

Western news broadcasts with their 'lies and misinformation' were interpreted as only one component in a much larger and more all-encompassing attempt to influence East German youth. Seeing Western intelligence agencies as a mirror image of their own, the GDR authorities saw a network of deliberate and co-ordinated ideological subversion encompassing not just radio and television stations, but youth magazines, fan clubs and even penfriend exchanges.[44]

> The class enemy works with the most diverse methods. There are a series of covert espionage organisations, such as the film and music clubs and so-called parties. Through the influence of [Radio] Luxembourg many young people are in contact with this broadcasting station and receive direct instructions about club work. With the help of the so-called hit parades and the show 'Top of the Pops' [*Schlager der Woche*], RIAS [Radio in the American Sector], NWDR [North West German Radio] and *Freies Berlin* [Free Berlin] make contact with the youth of our Republic. As a result of their temptations and enticements, a part of our youth continues to commit [the crime of] flight from the Republic ... The sending of trash literature is systematically organised. In addition, clear indications are given for their sale and transmission inside the GDR.[45]

The party-controlled press repeatedly argued that Western media influence was part of a covert, psychological war. 'The enemy seeks to hinder the process of education and development of socialist consciousness, to provoke mistrust between youth and the state, to manufacture disbelief about our societal development as well as to spread decadent and amoral conceptions. Thereby the enemy seeks to create bases for itself among youth ... in preparation for the covert war.'[46] RIAS was accused of mixing 'the dehumanised bawling of a Presley with covert reception'. It not only supplied 'slushy tear-jerkers', but also 'spying tips'.[47]

> The goal of the enemy consists of carrying out ideological subversion, particularly among youth; to develop licentiousness and anarchy, in order to stir up parts of youth against their own Workers-and-Peasants' State and to incite them to riot. They carry this out by means of their radio and television stations, particularly Radio Germany [*Deutschlandfunk*], through the infiltration of trashy literature and inflammatory material, but also very cleverly by means of the non-culture of music and dance, the Beatles ideology and the ideology of bumming around [*Gammlertum*], inciting them to skive off work [*Arbeitsbummelei*]. In West Germany itself, they need this lifestyle to contaminate youth psychologically, and using all means of brutalisation, to stir up the lowest interests to prepare them ideologically for their criminal war plans.[48]

Psychological warfare was a hidden but deadly menace, insidiously creeping in to pollute teenagers' consciousness and to poison them from within. 'Drop by drop the youngster absorbed the poison of psychological warfare ...' until he was ready to undertake subversive activity 'for the Judas-pay of ten West marks'.[49] By presenting popular culture in the West as a form of warfare, spokesmen for the SED were able to present teenagers who were interested in (or 'seduced by') it as potential and real fifth columnists. For the SED leaders, 'psychological warfare' designed to undermine and sap youth's defences was a serious and dangerous threat.[50] White House strategists, meanwhile, believed that 'unsettling the reds' (by stoking their paranoia) was an important means of 'keeping the Soviet Bear so busy scratching its own fleas that he has little time for molesting others'.[51] For East German teens, their media links to the West were essential for learning the latest about what was modern, glamorous, stylish, 'chic' and 'cool'. Reading such 'texts' against the backdrop of life in the GDR provided them with an additional subversive thrill.

Although they did not have the same opportunities for consumption, teenagers in the East were nevertheless affected by and took part in the changes that were taking place in youth identities and aspirations. By guaranteeing youth improvements in wages and limitations on the length of the working week, the SED deliberately created time for leisure activities. But the persistent failure of the youth organisation to provide teens with activities that interested them left a vacuum. The Politbüro was shocked to find that, instead of using these opportunities to become better young socialists, they filled the space by embracing the commercialised youth culture imported from the West. What was less apparent was that the misspending of youth was also gendered. As they grew older, the boys spent disproportionately less time on housework than girls.[52] They were more likely to spend this 'stolen' free time watching television or listening to the radio.

After the construction of the wall, on 13 August 1961, young people no longer had any opportunity to experience the reality of the West for themselves. For those who did not believe what they were told in school, the West acquired the nebulous quality of a world without borders, a place where dreams could be realised, another world to escape to. Difficulties in acquiring magazines, records and movies were offset by the availability of radio and, later, television, allowing a 'pop media culture' also to develop in the East. Youth research surveys found that, during the 1960s, the proportion of young people surveyed who were absolutely against tuning in to Western media shrank to 4 percent. In contrast 67 per cent of those surveyed listed either Radio Luxembourg or Radio Germany (or both) as their favourite stations.[53] Although the construction of the wall imposed a physical barrier between East and West, contraband items continued to arrive in parcels from the West or were smuggled across the border by foreigners. The packet from the West with its own distinctive smell – a mixture of chocolate, coffee and soap – left many an East German with the bittersweet taste of only partially fulfilled longing.[54] Later, when travel restrictions for pensioners were eased, grandparents became the major carriers for records and tapes from West Germany.

Birmingham School theorist John Clarke used Claude Lévi-Strauss's concept of *bricolage* (which translates both as 'sticking together' and 'do-it-yourself') to argue that, by using objects and symbols in youth subculture, participants were able to reorder and recontextualise them to communicate fresh meanings.[55] In a process described by Dick Hebdige as 'semiotic guerrilla warfare', a transformation and rearrangement of meanings occurs as a result of placing old objects in a new context.[56] In the GDR, the difficulties in obtaining items of teenage consumption heightened the need for 'DIY solutions'. In spite of unfavourable exchange rates, restrictions on supply only served to increase demand. The subjective value teenage consumers placed on scarce fashion items from the West ensured that they traded in the East for many times their real market value.[57] Teenagers in East Germany had to expend far more effort to achieve an authentic look. The result, however, was that they were much more deeply tied up in the creation of symbolic importance and meaning. Each item of clothing told its own story, the story of the obstacles that had been overcome in order for it eventually to have been acquired. Informal channels, networks and contacts were essential for acquiring anything from a genuine pair of jeans to comics and fan-club addresses. The extra effort and sacrifices they had to make brought rewards in the form of envy and approval from their peers.[58]

By making such items contraband, the SED turned large parts of the population (including some party members) into smugglers and accomplices. If, for their parents, the unavailability of fruit and vegetables was a source of irritation, for teenagers the added difficulties involved in participation in commercialised youth culture served to surround it with an atmosphere of excitement and adventure. The SED struggled against the fact that the more forbidden the fruit, the sweeter it tasted. The lengths to which teens had to go to access Western media or to conceal their consumption of it heightened the experience.[59] For many young people, acquiring coveted items of youth fashion or symbols to mark out their difference involved genuine cases of *bricolage* (or DIY). Clothes that were otherwise impossible to obtain in the East were sewn together by girls themselves.[60] Young metalworkers used the opportunities available for them at work to manufacture badges, in some cases even knuckledusters.[61]

Encounters with their relatives from West Germany may have convinced young East Germans that they were very much the poor relations, dependent on their Western aunts and uncles for cast-offs and scraps.[62] On the other hand, with the right shirt or the right pair of jeans, the degree of attention they could draw to themselves (with its concomitant prestige and peer approval) was much greater. As Edgar Wibeau, the protagonist in Ulrich Plenzdorf's cult GDR-youth novel, stated, 'Jeans are a state of mind, not a pair of trousers.'⁶³ As Klaus Renft put it, 'Ripped and washed out, the jeans were often covered in holes and sewed and scrawled on until they took on a completely different form ... it was an attitude and it was great because it was against this annoying petit bourgeois mentality. Jeans were this rebellion.'⁶⁴ The SED struggled against the fact that adopting a 'modern', Western look was intimately bound up with sex appeal. Exercising control over and experimenting with their own outward appearance were the means by which both boys and girls could demonstrate their increasing sexual maturity and exploit the sense of power that attractiveness with the opposite sex brought them.

In 1961, a group of head teachers had come to the same conclusion: 'the general overstimulation plays an [important] role. That begins with television. The pupils are trained only for sensation, which we can't always offer them in lessons.'⁶⁵ The short attention span and unwillingness to read of the 'television generation' was much talked about in both East and West, as was their apparent inability to cope with lessons that required them to think and listen rather than passively absorbing audio-visual information. The effects of televisual 'overstimulation' also undermined the work of the FDJ. In many ways, the regime's politicisation of Western media and youth culture had a counterproductive effect. The at times rabid hostility shown towards their otherwise harmless pursuit of entertainment and amusement made young East Germans more ready to identify with the radio stations condemned by the SED. Their presenters seemed to have a much closer and more realistic understanding of their listeners' interests and needs. They presented a common challenge to outdated attitudes and authoritarian conceptions that continued to persist in both East and West.⁶⁶ Their breezy unorthodoxy served to undermine the stuffy and elitist conservatism of the establishment stations, which were forced to copy them so as not to lose their audiences.

The crateloads of letters and record requests to Western stations intercepted and seized by the Stasi testify to a pervasive desire not to be left out in the cold and instead to be part of the changes in music and fashion that were putting youthful lifestyles and experiences centre stage.⁶⁷ In August 1959, the Stasi intercepted a letter to Margaret D., in Rostock, from the Elvis Presley Club in Munich. The club secretary, Judy, thanked her for her recent letter, expressed hopes that her cold was better and accepted her into the club.

> I'm sorry that you can't listen to Elvis often. Especially as here in the club, we have all the records by Elvis (about 130 songs) and can dance rock 'n' roll in our dance parties as often as we want. Besides that, we listen to AFN [American Forces Network] every day, which of course also exists in Munich and the great sensation at the moment is Elvis's newest disc, 'A Big Hunk o' Lovin'' with 'My Wish Came True' [*Auf Deutsch 'Ich brauche Dich dazu'*] on the B-side. 'I Need Your Love Tonight' is naturally really cool. As far as Elvis himself is concerned, he was born on 8 January '35 and is therefore now 24 years old ... Greetings to your fellow Elvis fans and, if you have any other questions, just ask me.⁶⁸

Conclusion

The SED sought to combat the challenge to its cultural hegemony posed by Western youth culture by exacerbating adult fears about the dangerous effects of Americanisation. Although the population was subjected to repeated bouts of intimidation and persuasion in an effort to prevent them from receiving Western media, it was difficult for the state to determine what went on behind closed doors. A gulf continued to exist between the teenage view of Western youth culture and that presented by the regime. The SED's refusal to tolerate even music broadcasts acted as an important breach between it and sections of the youth population. The combined effect of being bombarded from all sides with competing and conflicting messages was often to produce a state of ambivalence and confusion. Although their heads may have 'always been turned to the West', in their hearts young people often felt a deep sense of attachment to their families, friends and immediate surroundings in the East – to their *Heimat*.[69] State attempts at control were dogged by scepticism, disbelief, inner conflict (*Zwiespalt*), passive resistance, self-segregation, escapism and evasion. Teenagers responded to attempts at control by switching off, retreating and embarking on 'inner emigration'.

Notes

1. Paolo Capuzzo, 'Youth Cultures and Consumption in Contemporary Europe', *Contemporary European History* 10:1 (2001), 155–70.
2. Walter Friedrich, *Flegeljahre? Zur Erziehung 13– bis 16jähriger Jungen* (Berlin, 1964), 4ff.
3. Ibid., 6–7.
4. For visual propaganda on negative youth cultures merging stereotypes of effeminate men and overly masculine young women, see 'Wahlaufklärung' (1958), Landesarchiv Berlin, C Rep 101–02, Nr. 14.
5. Kreis Partei Kontrollkommission: 'Untersuchungsberichte' (2 August 1951), StAL IV/5/01/273.
6. SED propagandists and lower-level functionaries continued to believe that it was possible to recognise Western agents from their telltale 'checked shirts' well into the 1960s. 'Materialdokumentation über die konterrevolutionäre Entwicklung in der CSSR (Sept. 1968)', Bundesbeauftragter für die Unterlagen der Staatssicherheit (henceforth BStU), ZA, HA IX 5118.
7. 'Tagesbericht' (27.6.1953), BArch. SAPMO, DY 24/2301.
8. Mark Fenemore, 'Saints and Devils: Youth in the SBZ/GDR, 1945–1953' in Eleonore Breuning, Jill Lewis and Gareth Pritchard (eds), *Power and the People. A Social History of Central European Politics, 1945–1953* (Manchester, 2005), 168–81.
9. Arne Andersen, *Der Traum vom guten Leben. Alltags- und Konsumgeschichte vom Wirtschaftswunder bis heute* (Frankfurt am Main, 1997).
10. The new consumer culture was depicted as having a highly negative influence on youth in the West German film *Die Halbstarken*, directed by Goerg Tressler (BRD, 1956).
11. James Gilbert, *A Cycle of Outrage. America's Reaction to the Juvenile Delinquent of the 1950s* (New York, Oxford, 1986), 14; for West German examples of this response, see Hans-

Jürgen von Wensierski, '"Die anderen nannten uns Halbstarke" – Jugendsubkultur in den 50er Jahren' in Heinz-Hermann Krüger (ed.), *'Die Elvis-Tolle, die hatte ich mir unauffällig wachsen lassen'. Lebensgeschichte und jugendliche Alltagskultur in den fünfziger Jahren* (Opladen, 1985), 103-28, 118ff.; Axel Schildt, 'Von der Not der Jugend zur Teenager-Kultur: Aufwachsen in den 50er Jahren' in Axel Schildt and Arnold Sywottek (eds), *Modernisierung im Wiederaufbau. Die westdeutsche Gesellschaft der 50er Jahren* (Bonn, 1993), 335-48.
12. *The Wild One*, directed by Laslo Benedek (USA, 1953).
13. Linda Martin and Kerry Seagrave, *Anti-Rock. The Opposition to Rock 'n' Roll* (Hamden, 1988), 8.
14. Uta Poiger, *Jazz, Rock & Rebels. Cold War Politics and American Culture in a Divided Germany* (Berkeley, 2000), 94.
15. The report's authors revealed that the need to act was, in part, a response to communist propaganda coming from East Germany. U.S. Congress, Senate Committee on the Judiciary, *Comic Books and Juvenile Delinquency* (Washington, DC, 1955), 21.
16. 'Towards a cartography of taste, 1935-1962' in Dick Hebdige, *Hiding in the Light. On Images and Things* (London, 1988), 45-76, 52-53.
17. Alf Lüdtke, Inge Marssolek and Adelheid von Saldern (eds), *Amerikanisierung: Traum und Alptraum im Deutschland des 20. Jahrhunderts* (Stuttgart, 1996); on the 'alarming modernity of Americanism', see Adolf Halfeld, *Amerika und Amerikanismus* (Jena, 1927).
18. Axel Schildt, *Moderne Zeiten. Freizeit, Massenmedien und 'Zeitgeist' in der Bundesrepublik der 50er Jahre* (Hamburg, 1995), 398-423.
19. Arnold Sywottek, 'The Americanization of Everyday Life? Early Trends in Consumer and Leisure-time Behaviour' in Michael Ermarth (ed.), *America and the Shaping of German Society, 1945-1955* (Providence, Oxford, 1993), 132-52.
20. Kaspar Maase, *Bravo Amerika. Erkundungen zur Jugendkultur der Bundesrepublik in den fünfziger Jahren* (Hanover, 1992), 19.
21. Ian Chambers, *Urban Rhythms. Pop Music and Popular Culture* (Basingstoke, 1985), 4.
22. Karl Bednarik, *Der junge Arbeiter von heute: Ein neuer Typ* (Stuttgart, 1953), 17; Schildt, *Moderne Zeiten*, 174-75.
23. Reinhold Wagnleitner, *Coca-Colonization and the Cold War: The Cultural Mission of the United States in Austria after the Second World War* (Chapel Hill, London, 1994); Mark Pendergrast, *For God, Country and Coca-Cola* (Oxford, 1993); C.W.E. Bigsby (ed.), *Superculture: American Popular Culture and Europe* (London, 1975), 1-27.
24. 'Eine "Industrie", die der Jugend schadet', *Junge Welt* (13 June 1956).
25. 'Streng Vertraulich! Bericht über die Jugendkriminalität' (c. 1957), Landesarchiv Berlin, STA Rep. 303/26, Nr. 137, 139ff.
26. ZIJ: 'Funktion und Zusammenwirken der Massenmedien bei der ideologischen Erziehung der Jugend' (Leipzig, 1971), BArch. SAPMO, DY 30/21420.
27. Ibid.
28. Nationalrat der Nationalen Front, Arbeit mit der Jugend, 'Die Aufgaben zur weiteren Einschränkung von Jugendkriminalität und Rowdytum' (c. 1958), BArch. DY6/3937.
29. Poiger, *Jazz, Rock & Rebels*, 84-85.
30. 'Streng Vertraulich! Bericht über die Jugendkriminalität'; 'Die grausame Tat eines 14jährigen klagt an. Er braucht Geld fürs Westkino', *Junge Welt* (25 January 1956); 'Freibrief für Mörder. Ein Killer-Film und seine Folgen', *Junge Welt* (10 February 1956).
31. Michael Rauhut, *Beat in der Grauzone. DDR-Rock 1964 bis 1972. Politik und Alltag* (Berlin, 1993), 56.
32. Peter Kuhnert and Ute Ackermann, 'Jenseits von Lust und Liebe? Jugendsexualität in den 50er Jahren' in Krüger (ed.), *'Die Elvis-Tolle'*, 43-83, 47; Gilbert, *A Cycle of Outrage*, 3ff.
33. '52. Oberschule: Rechenschaftsbericht, 1960/61', Leipzig Stadtarchiv, Stv&RdSt (1), Nr. 2312.
34. 'Bilddokumentation zu Vorkommnissen mit negativen Jugendlichen' (1964-69), BArch. DO1/38215.

35. Alan Nothnagle, *Building the East German Myth. Historical Mythology and Youth Propaganda in the German Democratic Republic, 1945–1989* (Ann Arbor, 1999), 48–60.
36. 'Entwurf für den Leitartikel des Oberbürgermeisters in die LVZ: Die Stadtverordneten beraten Probleme der Jugend' (c. 1961), Stadtarchiv Leipzig, Stv&RdSt (1), Nr. 2311, 78.
37. Gregory Mitrovich, *Undermining the Kremlin: America's Strategy to Subvert the Soviet Bloc, 1947–1956* (Ithaca, London, 2000); Scott Lucas, *Freedom's War. The US Crusade against the Soviet Union 1945–56* (Manchester, 1999); Walter Hixson, *Parting the Curtain: Propaganda, Culture, and the Cold War* (New York, 1997); Christopher Simpson, *Blowback. America's Recruitment of Nazis and its Effects on the Cold War* (New York, 1988); Peter Grose, *Operation Rollback. America's Secret War behind the Iron Curtain* (Boston, 2000).
38. Lucas, *Freedom's War*, 60.
39. RIAS broadcasters William Heimlich and Christine Olsen explain their methodology in the BBC *Cold War* series (1998), produced by Jeremy Isaacs and Pat Mitchell; Günter Neumann was a popular RIAS performer who did his best to tease the East Germans with sketches like 'Der Funzionär und die Säuberung'. Günter Neumann, *Die Insulaner* (Berlin, 1955), 16–20. For the East German view, see Verband der Deutschen Journalisten (ed.), *RIAS und SFB im Spionageschungel Westberlin* (East Berlin, 1962).
40. Interview with Dieter S. (1999). HO stood for *Handelsorganisation*, the GDR's state-owned retail outlet.
41. 'Eine "Industrie", die der Jugend schadet', *Junge Welt* (13 June 1956).
42. *Junge Welt* (19 July 1956).
43. In February 1962, the *Leipziger Volkszeitung* reported on a murder by a 'returnee' from West Germany under the headline 'Für 45DM westliche Freiheit in Aktion', *LVZ* (14 February 1962). Discussions about the article can be found in StAL, FDJ Bezirksleitung Leipzig 82 (Kiste Nr. 79).
44. Erich Mielke, 'Dienstanweisung Nr. 4/66, Verschlusssache Nr. 365/66 "Zur politisch-operativen Bekämpfung der politisch-ideologischen Diversion und Untergrundtätigkeit unter jugendlichen Personenkreisen in der DDR" (15.5.1966)', cited in Armin Huttenlocher, 'Zurück oder vorwärts, du mußt dich entschließen ...' in Klaus Behnke and Jürgen Wolf (eds), *Stasi auf dem Schulhof. Der Mißbrauch von Kindern und Jugendlichen durch das Ministerium für Staatssicherheit* (Berlin, 1998), 78–102, 79f.
45. 'Die Aufgaben zur weiteren Einschränkung von Jugendkriminalität'.
46. Ibid.
47. 'Schulen des Verbrechens: Hetzsender und Westberlin', *LVZ* (14 October 1960).
48. SED Bezirksleitung Leipzig: 'Zu einigen Fragen der Jugendarbeit und dem Auftreten der Rowdygruppen (12.10.1965)', StAL, SED IV A2/16/464.
49. 'Schulen des Verbrechens ...'.
50. 'Der Jugend Vertrauen und Verantwortung' in Zentralkomitee der SED, *Jugend von heute. Hausherren von Morgen. Kommuniqué des Politbüros des ZK der SED zu Problemen der Jugend in der DDR* (Berlin, 1963), 1–34, 27.
51. Lucas, *Freedom's War*, 86.
52. Karlheinz Otto, *Disziplin bei Mädchen und Jungen. Ein Beitrag zur Gleichberechtigung der Geschlechter aus psychologischer, pädagogischer, soziologischer und historischer Sicht* (Berlin, 1970), 194.
53. ZIJ, 'Umfrage '69'. Unpublished MS (Leipzig, 1969), 25, 75.
54. Christian Härtel and Petra Kabus, 'Zwischen Gummibärchen und "Playboy". Ein innerdeutscher Dialog' in Christian Härtel and Petra Kabus (eds), *Das Westpaket. Geschenksendung, keine Handelsware* (Berlin, 2000) 9–22.
55. John Clarke, 'Style' in Stuart Hall and Tony Jefferson (eds), *Resistance through Rituals. Youth Subcultures in Postwar Britain* (London, 1976), 175–91.
56. Dick Hebdige, *Subculture: The Meaning of Style* (London, 1979).
57. On the lengths to which young people went to get the right 'look', see Poiger, *Jazz, Rock & Rebels*, 81, and Dorothee Wierling, 'Die Jugend als innere Feind. Konflikte in der

Erziehungsdiktatur der sechziger Jahre' in Hartmut Kaelbe, Jürgen Kocka and Hartmut Zwahr (eds.), *Sozialgeschichte der DDR* (Stuttgart, 1994), 404-25, 410.
58. Interviews with Klaus Renft and Franz P. (1999-2000).
59. See Klaus Renft's memories of image creation in Hans-Dieter Schütt (ed.), *Klaus Renft. Zwischen Liebe und Zorn* (Berlin, 1997), 47-48.
60. Gerlinde Irmscher, 'Der Westen im Ost-Alltag' in Ina Merkel and Felix Mühlberg (eds), *Wunderwirtschaft. DDR-Konsumkultur in den 60er Jahren* (Cologne, 1996), 185-93; 'Bericht über die Tätigkeit im Wahlkreis 8 (innere Neustadt) Stadtbezirksleitung Nord Dresden in der Zeit vom 19.4-29.4.1961', BArch. SAPMO, DY24/3844.
61. 'Information über das Auftreten der "Presley-Bande" an der erweiterten Oberschule Pößneck' (c. November 1959), BArch. DR2/4814; 'Bezirksbehörde Deutsche Volkspolizei: Bericht' (1 November 1965), BDVP 24.1/348, 94.
62. Ina Dietzsch, 'Deutsch-deutscher Gabentausch' in Ina Merkel and Felix Mühlberg (eds), *Wunderwirtschaft*, 204-13.
63. Ulrich Plenzdorf, *Die neuen Leiden des jungen W.* (Frankfurt am Main, 1976), 27.
64. Interview with Klaus Renft.
65. 'Diskussion um die Probleme der 13-16jährigen (Zusammenfassung einer Diskussion mit 30 Direktoren und stellv. Direktoren in Berlin-Weissensee)' (14 April 1961), BArch. DR2/6956.
66. In Britain, generations of disc jockeys undermined the monopolistic hold of the BBC by working first for Radio Luxembourg and later for the floating pirate radio station Radio Caroline.
67. Intercepted letters are on show in the exhibition, 'STASI-Macht und Banalität' in the Museum der 'Runden Ecke' in Leipzig. Reports relating to such letters can also be found in the 'special incident' files for the Ministry of Education held at the Leipzig Stadtarchiv.
68. 'Anlagekarte zur Argumentation über westdeutsche "Film- und Schlager-Star-Clubs"', BArch. DO1/38215.
69. Interviews with Manfred S., Hans-Peter D. and Dieter L. (1999).

◈ *Chapter 6* ◈

STREET CULTURE

An emphasis on physical toughness, territoriality and standing up for oneself and the group to which one belonged had long been part of the self-understandings of adolescent, working-class males. The arrival of American-influenced youth culture allowed the blending of old and new forms of masculinity to form a novel and potent masculine self-image. For the politically disinterested and educationally disengaged, becoming a worker and a man were the be-all and end-all of existence, a black-and-white stance unsullied by grey, a *raison d'être* that owed nothing to the SED regime. Although their emphasis on outward appearance appeared new and strange to many adults, underneath it they still valued physicality, territorialism and machismo. In the conflicts that occurred on the street, it was the gangs, predominantly composed of working-class boys (and 'their' girls), which demonstrated allegiance to Western culture in the face of state hostility and police harassment. Without ambitious career aims or qualms about respectability to hold them back, they had the greatest freedom to defy and rebel against the regime's restrictions. They continued to be motivated by a macho sense of working-class habitus emphasising physicality and the ability to 'look after oneself' (the characteristics Alf Lüdtke originally described as *Eigensinn*).[1] Throughout the 1950s and 1960s, local festivals provided opportunities for rebellion and disorder.[2]

For many young men, free time was centred around the street, the park and the gang.[3] Gangs continued to form in the GDR's large urban centres, in the historically separate and distinct proletarian neighbourhoods with traditions of marginality and hostility to outside interference. In Leipzig, there was a long tradition of young men joining gangs called 'packs' (*Meuten*), which were territorially associated with a particular part of town.[4] By the late 1950s, the three *Meuten* (Reeperbahn, Hundestart and Lille) that had given the Hitler Youth patrols so much trouble during the Third Reich had grown to five:

To the North, the Wahrener *Meute*, which had been meeting up outside the town hall in Wahren since at least 1953.

To the East, the Thälmann-Str. *Meute*, which met in front of a cinema on the Thälmann Straße (today the Eisenbahn-Str.) running through Reudnitz.

To the South, the Adler *Meute*, which met in front of the Adler cinema.

To the West, the Lindenfels *Meute*, which met in front of the Lindenfels cinema.

And, in the centre of Leipzig, the Capitol *Meute*, which got its name from the Capitol cinema on the Petersstraße.

Those in the gangs were naturally drawn to the in-between (or liminal) space offered by the silver screen. It did not matter that East German picture houses were not allowed to show gangster movies, Westerns, horrors or films about juvenile delinquents. Standing outside them, the boys could act like their idols. The medium itself challenged and pushed back the boundaries of respectability. Street gangs had always been in favour of cigarettes and alcohol, raucous music and clothing frowned on by older generations. But the development of consumer opportunities within the reach of ordinary working-class youth created an additional barrier between them and their elders.

Interactions on the street allowed masculinity to be performed, evaluated and tested. Asserting confidence and self-assurance, confrontations allowed the men to be separated from the boys. Potential adversaries were ranked according to their physical and verbal dexterity, their macho ability to conceal ignorance, weakness and other inadequacies. Young men became familiar with the 'rules' of the street, a place that for respectable people conjured up visions of violence and danger. The wisdom alluded to in the term 'streetwise' refers not to learnedness and erudition, but to a person's perceived adroitness in dealing with the potential dangers of being involved in street situations and interactions. The danger comes from the fact that the street is also inhabited by criminals (thieves, con men, pimps, prostitutes, rapists and muggers) and other unsavoury, disreputable people, who are more than ready to hustle and prey upon the naive. Street knowledge is gained through familiarity and ability to navigate the 'urban jungle'. Stripping away the advantages and defences provided by privilege and education, the street forces people from different backgrounds to share the same space and to come into contact with one another. The logic and culture of the street obliges urban dwellers to be on their guard and ready to defend themselves. By putting everyone on the same level and imposing very different criteria from those recognised in the world beyond, the street increases the vulnerability of those who are least capable of verbally and (if necessary) physically defending themselves. The continued existence of violence and street crime reveals a much more primitive set of relations beneath the city's veneer of civilisation.

The gangs provoked respectable society through a combination of their presence, dress and demeanour. Prizing toughness and physicality, they sought to defend 'their' space, their territory and their girls from potential intrusions by other marauding gangs. Their territoriality and sense of mischief brought the gangs into conflict not only with one another, but frequently also with the authorities. Members accepted violence as a means of resolving conflicts. Aggressive posturing represented a ritualised form of self-representation and mutual entertainment. Street corners and the entrances to cinemas offered opportunities for the symbolic occupying of space and the jostling and jeering of passers-by (usually of the same age).[5] Often, violence appeared as a 'means of enforcing the right of the clique to some form of entertainment – where fighting itself or the aggressively maintained freedom to intrude on other people's amusements could [itself] be construed as entertainment.'[6] In the GDR, gang members thought nothing of 'kicking up a stink' (*Rabatz machen*) during film showings by means of loud interruptions and catcalls or abusing people as they went into the cinema.[7]

The boys in the gangs cultivated a 'meaningful taciturnity' while taking delight in the fact that they struck others as being deviant. A contradictory mixture of cultures and identities, old and new, they demanded the right to privacy and self-determination, at the same time as physically occupying public spaces and annoying other people. Regarding these spaces as 'their' territory, they sought to defend them against intrusion by outsiders. Fights between rival gangs were a sporadic but recurrent feature of street life. Such conflicts were nevertheless 'ritual-bound' and 'not as serious' in essence as they could outwardly appear.[8] Contrary to popular perceptions, violence was not indiscriminate. Rather there was a certain amount of choreography to it. The goal was to prove their manhood, not to kill one another. 'In working-class cultures, recognition is always of a difference – either one that is shared or one that isn't … For working-class kids the paradigm of recognition takes the form of ritual insult', with a repertoire ranging from staring or repartee to 'taking the piss' and practical jokes.[9] 'Preliminary rituals of eye contact, verbal abuse, weapon brandishing and pushing and shoving' were as important as the actual encounter. 'Many conflicts did not progress beyond this ritualistic expression of aggressive masculinity.'[10]

The Communist Party was not a complete stranger to the phenomenon of juvenile street gangs. In her book *Beating the Fascists*, Eve Rosenhaft studied attempts by the KPD to take over and utilise the cliques as a means of community defence against the Nazis in the early 1930s.[11] During this time, the *Meuten* had sung songs of wandering and adventure and shown 'lively interest in every news broadcast about the civil war between the Spanish workers and the fascists'.[12] Ironically, East German historiography showed no awareness of or interest in the opposition of the *Meuten* or the Edelweiß Pirates, despite the fact that both subcultures drew their participants almost exclusively from the working class.[13] Rosenhaft shows that the communists' attitudes to what they saw as lumpen elements were highly ambivalent. While recognising the gangs' 'spontaneous antifascism' as a potent means of defending working-class neighbourhoods, at the same time, the communists showed unease about their indiscipline and unruliness together with their lack of interest in politics. They were unsure whether to consider the street as a reservoir for potentially revolutionary working-class recruits or to see it as a cesspool of un-proletarian, pre-political, lumpen elements.[14]

Communist antipathy for what they saw as the sub- or 'lumpenproletariat' had a long history stretching back to Marx himself. Although the venerable father of communism had taken part in his fair share of drunken student brawls and physical confrontations with Prussian officer cadets and had even smashed street lanterns while he was in exile in London, he viewed the lumpenproletariat with nothing but contempt. They were 'the "dangerous class", the social scum, that passively rotting mass thrown off by the lowest layers of the old society'. Although they could be swept into the movement by a proletarian revolution, they were far more likely to act as the 'bribed tool of reactionary intrigue'.[15] The history of the working-class movement can be seen as a history of attempts to domesticate and hegemonise lower-class identity, 'to order it into a strong programmatic statement'.[16] It can also be seen as a history of exclusion. Women, teenagers, the unskilled and immigrants were often 'excluded from a movement which claimed to represent them, which tried to uplift them at the same time as it depended on their general sympathy and support'.[17]

> The positivity of the working class presumed the negativity of others – and not just other classes, but also other kinds of workers (for example, the unorganised, the rough and unrespectable, the criminal, the frivolous, the religiously devout, the ethnically different, and of course the female), and of other elements of subjectivity – in effect all those aspects of identity that could not be disciplined into a highly centered notion of class-political agency.[18]

Hawkers, traders and petty criminals may have lived in working-class communities, but, for the workers' movement and its political representatives, they were not 'real' members of the working class. Even though they continued to condemn the Social Democrats for being petit bourgeois, when it came to the lumpen, the SED shared many of their prejudices.[19] There was no place in the SED's modern, scientific, technocratic vision for survivals of a more anarchic, pre-industrial, plebeian past. Such survivals were blamed for the betrayal perpetrated by the thousands of young men from working-class backgrounds who had joined and fought for the SA and the SS.[20] The suspicion felt by those in the party for disorganised elements of the working class easily bordered on contempt. The lumpen 'other' served to emphasise everything that a disciplined comrade was not. When one FDJ functionary criticised another with the words, 'His position is not that of a comrade but of a washerwoman,' he revealed a gender dimension to this hostility.[21] Only ideologically aware, disciplined and organised proletarians, the communists suggested, could claim to be real men.

Seemingly unaware that they were following in others' footsteps, youngsters from working-class neighbourhoods continued to behave in a boisterous and disorderly manner.[22] Although the gangs continued to engage in street culture throughout the 1950s and 1960s, their haircuts and clothing changed in response to Western fashions. The earliest 'cliques' and *Meuten* shared certain *Bündische* stylistic features with the gangs that had gone before them. Gang members wore neckerchiefs and checked shirts as a means of distinguishing group members from outsiders.[23] As in the 1920s and 1930s, knives and knuckledusters represented important fashion accessories for urban street gangs. With the rise in importance of commercialised youth culture in West Germany, the gangs and *Meuten* in the East gradually lost their trappings of *Bündische* style – swapping checked shirts and shorts for jeans, T-shirts and leather jackets.[24] But, although their outward appearance changed substantially, the gangs still exhibited similar styles of behaviour to those that had gone before them. Youth subculture developed as an extension of gang activities and as a response to changes in male youth identity and the growing feeling of restlessness and rebellion against adult restrictions and controls.

Through their loud, intimidating and unruly presence, the *Meuten* generated a name for themselves among the local population and the police. In January 1958, for instance, it was reported that there was 'increasing disquiet in the population, above all among residents of the Ernst-Thälmann-Straße about the public nuisance and the ganging together of young people in the streets'.[25] One of the 'bad things' they were reported as doing was throwing 'jumping jacks' (*Knallfröschen*) in front of passers-by.[26] The younger gang members tended to get their inspiration from comics, giving themselves names like 'Revolver-Jimmy, Texas-Bill, *Grey der Gangsterschreck*, Messer-Joe'.[27] The older, more important gangs, composed of fifteen- to seventeen-year-olds, made themselves noticeable with 'impoliteness, crude, overfamiliar remarks and arrogance'.[28] According to Klaus Renft, their leading members became 'infamous local celebrities'.[29] A number of those in the *Meuten* were said to have been young men who had gone over to West Germany in the mid-1950s, but who had come back home to the East to escape being conscripted into the West German army. Although the regime was officially proud that they had decided to return home, unofficially they were also accused of importing 'Wild West methods' (*Wildwest-Methoden*) that they had picked up in West Germany.[30]

Hostility to Working-class Popular Culture

Within working-class communities, attitudes to the gangs (and to other forms of rough, non-respectable popular culture) had always been contradictory and ambivalent.[31] Although their macho attitudes and unruly behaviour emulated and stemmed from attitudes prevalent within their parent community, there were also many within that same community who perceived such behaviour as lumpen and non-respectable. The fault lines between respectable and non-respectable culture ran not above or below but right through the middle of the working class. Therefore, while some were prepared to defend or excuse certain forms of behaviour as being a long-running feature of working-class life, others simply attacked what they saw as a lowering of standards and morals that would not have happened when they were young.[32] In 1960, youth club leaders in Karl-Marx-Stadt organised a cultural event to highlight the continuities in youth culture. Among the songs played were 'In her truss my grandma packs a six-shooter' ('*Meine Oma hat am Bruchband 'nen Revolver*') and 'Show me your birthmark wherever it may be' ('*Zeig mir Dein Muttermal, egal wo's hängt*'). 'This is what our grandfathers and grandmothers danced to and now they don't want to let young people dance apart!'[33] As Brigitte, a pupil at the *Oberschule* in Friedrichshain suggested, 'Many old people seem to have forgotten that they were once young too.'[34]

The development of the GDR as a workers' and peasants' state had a complex and contradictory impact on the status of the working class. The dictatorship of the proletariat removed the social stigma attached to being born a proletarian as well as opening up opportunities for training and development previously restricted to higher social classes. There was no longer any shame attached to doing manual labour and certainly no reason to feel inferior for wearing overalls or working men's boots. But at the same time the SED presented a conception of working-class life that was solidly sober and respectable, shorn of reckless and unruly features, pasteurised and homogenised to fit in with the requirements of socialism. Continuing differences in education and status were concealed behind a general appearance of mateyness (deliberately fostered by party functionaries, who addressed everyone around them with the informal *Du*).[35] Yet, in terms of self-identity, the difference between skilled and 'manual workers' remained a culturally significant division. The decline in power and privilege of the bourgeoisie meant that workers ceased to have a common enemy and allowed inequalities of opportunity and interest to open up within the working class itself. At times when the community was subject to official hostility or external threats, the barriers between it and the outside world served to increase the sense of solidarity and toleration of the gangs. As these barriers disappeared (or became submerged), as was the case from the late 1950s onwards in the GDR, the divisions, particularly between respectable and non-respectable sections of the working class, increased. 'The same historical process which pushed the parent culture inwards on itself pushed working-class youth to its periphery as the residual legatees of street culture.'[36]

SED propagandists were much more interested in exposing the alien influence of the West than in exploring potential sources of continuity with older patterns of working-class behaviour. Any behaviours that threatened attempts to create order and authority were criticised and condemned, frequently using bourgeois notions of 'decency' and 'respectability'.[37] Culture was seen as an antidote that all young people needed to imbibe if they were to inoculate themselves against Western imperialism.[38] What was held up as traditional, working-class culture (such as folk dancing and political singing) was often very different from what young men from the working class actually enjoyed doing. On 8 April 1956, a cultural ensemble from Dresden visited the nearby mining town of Wismut.

> Already in the first minutes of their performance the boys and girls were subjected to a chorus of verbal abuse from the drunken youths. Every part of the programme was met with a concert of whistling. On the stage working-class children sang for children of the working class. In the room itself young hooligans rampaged, throwing cigarettes to each other and played skittles with beer glasses.[39]

The state may have taken over the folk culture (*Volkskultur*) movement, believing that it was acting as a shield for Social Democratic immunity.[40] But the patchwork of local working-class groups, associations and societies that were incorporated by the FDGB (the official trade union) and the National Front struggled to find a youth audience.

Although they claimed to represent 'the people', party leaders also maintained that workers needed to be educated, improved and disciplined.[41] As old men they had clearly lost any sense of what it was to be rebellious and defiant of the established order. The main arguments used for harrying and persecuting the gangs (known officially as 'liquidating' them) were that they were misspending time that could have been used for educating themselves and acquiring culture. Not only were they ignorant and vulgar, but they were wasting energy that could have been better spent on the reconstruction of society. The *Bitterfelder Weg*, launched in 1959 with the catchy slogan 'Grab your pen mate', was supposed to dismantle the wall between the masses and high culture.[42] 'Intellectual workers' (*Kopfarbeiter*) were encouraged to go into the factories and to write about the lives of workers, while 'manual workers' (*Handarbeiter*) were to craft artistic adaptations of their everyday life and thereby 'storm the heights of culture'. Although the *Bitterfelder Weg* did create more realistic depictions of working-class life in the work of Christa Wolf, Brigitte Reimann and Erik Neutsch, SED leaders continued to maintain a reductive conception of working-class culture, disavowing those elements that could not be politically managed and controlled in support of the state.[43] There was a contradiction between official conceptions of culture as a weapon or as a tool for the advancement of the working class and popular culture as it was experienced as a way of life inextricably bound up with people's sense of self.[44]

While SED propagandists emphasised the foreign and alien character of Western youth culture, smuggled into the GDR as part of a deliberate effort to undermine socialism, what the police actually attacked was the continued existence of lower-class street culture under the label of 'rowdyism'. In this way, the party succeeded in turning itself against young people from the very class it claimed to represent. By attempting to take 'their' spaces away from them, communist leaders alienated young workers and called forth their stubborn resistance. The refusal to recognise gang members' use of the street as a space for recreation and socialisation led the police to embark on an attempt to remove them from public view. Ever since the end of the nineteenth century, would-be social reformers had been trying to get *eigensinnig* working-class youths off the streets.[45] As a result, although much of the power of the bourgeoisie had been removed and middle-class groups had been made to serve as scapegoats and reminders of the injustice of the past, SED leaders implicitly took over the bourgeois 'mission' to reform working-class youth.[46] In Gramscian terms, the hegemonic processes of cultural domination continued to work against working-class youth even though radical steps had been taken to equalise social relations and to redistribute societal resources.[47] In effect, the SED became responsible for policing and enforcing conformity with bourgeois norms.

Tag X, 17 June 1953

Fans of bebop were the first groups of adolescent males to challenge respectability in post-war society. In both East and West, a class split continued to exist between middle-class fans of 'serious', 'authentic', high-art jazz and working-class fans of the more edgy and vulgar, 'down and dirty' bebop.[48] With their striped socks and long haircuts, the 'Bubis' acted as inheritors to the working-class traditions of rebellious youth subculture. Both the communist authorities and respectable society were shocked by their pursuit of hedonism through 'wild' music and dancing. Journalists found further evidence for the threat posed by such developments in the 1953 uprising. Labelling it as *Tag X*, 'the attempted fascist putsch', propagandists sought to show that the revolt was not the result of widespread hostility to SED rule centred around workers' grievances, but part of a cynical plan of disruption and disorder orchestrated by Western intelligence agencies. To bolster such claims, the party-controlled press highlighted the prominent role played by young men in the uprising and targeted those with identifiable signs of interest in Western youth culture as hired agents of Western imperialism.

Under the headline 'the knights of Western culture', both the national and local press sought to demonstrate that, because of their contamination with Western youth culture, the youngsters involved had acted against the interests of the working class.[49] Carriers of the alien disease were scapegoated. *Neues Deutschland* – the 'organ of the SED' – printed pictures of the 'sorts of people' involved in the disturbances. One purportedly showed a young worker wearing 'samba socks' and brothel creepers underneath his overalls. 'The crepe sole shoes and the Samba socks don't easily fit with a building worker coming straight from work. The real Berlin construction workers want nothing to do with these fascist bandits.'[50] Leipzig's local newspaper, the *Leipziger Volkszeitung*, also printed pictures of young workers who had participated in the uprising. In a report by Erich Loest, 'Bubis' with striped socks and 'Ami' haircuts were described as flying through the streets on shiny chrome bicycles.[51]

For Jakob Kaiser, the West German Minister for All-German affairs (*Gesamtdeutsche Frage*), those young East Germans who had taken part in the rising had shown that they were 'tuned in to freedom', not 'infected with communism'.[52] In the years that followed, youth culture became increasingly politicised as both sides in the cold war tried to use it as a means to demonise and demonstrate the inferiority of the other. The overreaction to youth culture shown by the East German authorities provided West German politicians and other commentators with a potent means of demonstrating the repressiveness and intolerance of communism. They interpreted young East Germans' interest in Western youth culture as a sign of opposition to 'totalitarian indoctrination'. SED propagandists, meanwhile, identified such an outlook with support for National Socialism. They were part of the 'fascist mob that sneaked its way between our ranks and sprayed its poison, part of the same mob that had destroyed the pavilion of the National Front, where the Waterworks Choir used to sing old folk songs – our good old folk songs … Such were the people the workers allowed to lead them astray.'[53]

Resistance through Riot: Carnival and Misrule

The gangs' pleasure in spoiling and disrupting other people's amusements had historical antecedents in the traditional practice of charivari and rough music.[54] Upsurges of misrule tended to occur at particular times of the year, often following the celebration of traditional events. In the 1950s FDJ members were encouraged to celebrate a wide range of different festivals, from commemorations of key socialist events (like the October Revolution or the First of May) to more joyful parts of the traditional calendar like new year, carnival, Easter and harvest time. Many towns and villages maintained their own traditional festivals (like the lantern festival in Halle) or annual fairs (*Kirmes*).[55] Traditionally, these had permitted a temporary break from routine and order and a chance to engage in ritualised excess. Shrovetide (*Fasching*) and new year, in particular, provided opportunities for dressing up and engaging in boisterous merriment. Leipzig's own special festival of misrule came in September. Just as *Fasching* traditionally implied the temporary suspension of order, so had the Tauchscher traditionally been marked by running battles between students and apprentices. The festival dated back to the Middle Ages and marked Leipzig's ascendancy over its neighbour and rival, Taucha. Ever since the 1890s, when Barnum's circus had visited the town, it had been customary for children to dress up as Red Indians for the Tauchscher.[56] Walter Ulbricht had himself taken part as a young brave at the turn of the century.[57]

Whereas at one time such events had been considered an important part of the life of the community, as society gradually became more 'civilised', bourgeois and self-controlling, the local authorities took a much dimmer view of such periodic releases of 'high spirits'.[58] Nevertheless, in the 1920s and 1930s, the Tauchscher continued to provide an occasion for 'letting go' and for fights between rival gangs. In 1929, it was reported that 'in a few parts of town large fights have taken place, in which participants set about one another with fencing slats, cudgels and other implements'.[59] During the Third Reich, the Nazis appropriated the festival and used it in support of their notions of German 'national community'. After the war, the festival returned to some of its former glory with a procession of the town inhabitants dressed up once again as Red Indians.

Writing in the Soviet Union, Mikhail Bakhtin contrasted the unconstrained vitality of the carnivalesque with the sterile modernising programme and rhetoric of Soviet communism.[60] 'For Bakhtin, carnival contained a utopian urge: it displaced, even inverted, the normal social hierarchies. Carnival was also a time which encouraged bodily needs and pleasures different from those called upon by the ordinary rhythm of labour and leisure.'[61] Unfortunately for the SED, both the Tauchscher and *Fasching* provided young workers with an irresistible excuse for misrule. As was the nature of such events, the normal reign of order and authority was temporarily suspended, providing opportunities for ridicule and mischief that the GDR's political authorities could ill afford to tolerate.[62] In February 1962, 'friends' from the FDJ organisation of the People's Own High-Current Equipment Works organised a *Fasching* party. People's Policemen were called when a person or persons unknown turned out the lights, let off a tear gas canister and threw lighted rolls of film into the overcrowded room. During the pandemonium and confusion that ensued, someone put a burning roll of film into the apron pocket of one of the sales assistants, thereby singeing both her garment and her underwear. The police seized several 'revolvers of West German production' and a dagger. A youth wearing a shirt with Presley pictures, pictures of naked girls and corresponding labels such as 'Elvis' and 'rock 'n' roll' was made to take it off. Questioned afterwards, the FDJ organisers failed to produce a political conception for the carnival. Instead, it was reported, they had opened the door to anarchy and licentiousness by printing invitations with the formulation 'Everything Upside Down' (*Alles steht Kopf*).[63]

FDJ theorists believed that popular festivals and other large-scale events helped to 'create a friendly connection to the broad mass of young people, to the whole population and help us to win new forces'.[64] The 'many lovely traditions and jolly customs' symbolised 'expressions of the struggles of the repressed classes'.[65] But, in spite of official attempts to control them, popular festivals continued to keep alive traditions of opposition. In the GDR, the ritual character of carnival and misrule easily lent itself to expressions of symbolic opposition to the regime in the form of chants and oppositional choruses. Misrule was exciting and contagious and could easily lead young men to do things that they might later have regretted. They got swept up in a group dynamic that caused them to lose their inhibitions and behave in an uncharacteristically bold way. Attempts by the police to arrest the 'ringleaders' (even though heavily outnumbered) often provoked the crowd into challenging their fragile authority. Thomas Lindenberger argues that the police's heavy-handedness in such situations resulted from their practice of viewing all such incidents as potential preludes to mass insurrection. The police had to counter every incident as if it were the real thing in order to show that they were capable of dealing with such an eventuality if the need were to arise.[66]

One unusual feature of such 'fairground disorders' was the tendency of participants to evoke the language of Westerns. In the 1970s and 1980s the GDR famously identified itself with the Red Indians by producing its own series of socialist Westerns. In the late 1950s and early 1960s, however, the rhetoric of the frontier was frequently used by both the regime and its rowdy opponents in their struggles over Western culture. The heroic John Wayne cowboy figure stood for rugged individualism, independence and manly virtue. For communist spokesmen, Westerns represented a prime example of the insidious psychological warfare techniques used to undermine the GDR and represented the lawlessness that awaited if the frontier with the West were not rigidly controlled. For those who identified with Western culture, however, the regime's stance left them with little alternative but to embrace the negative stereotype (of the outlaw) developed by communist propaganda. But, with their calls for the 'sheriff' to give up their friends, the groups of rebellious youths pointed to the fact that the GDR was itself a frontier society with an authority that was far from unquestioned. Such calls also served to remind the 'People's Police' of the fate that awaited them if ever the tables were turned.

> 'Sheriff gibt den Klaus heraus, sonst machen wir dir den Garaus.' – Sheriff let our Klaus out, or we'll do you in.[67]

> 'Sheriff gib die Kumpel frei, sonst haue ich Dir die Knochen ein.' – Sheriff let our mate go free or I'll come and break your legs.[68]

SED functionaries repeatedly criticised the failure of older workers to intervene or to exercise a more positive influence over rebellious youth. In March 1951 older workers not only failed to intervene but actively applauded and joined in with the unruly ringleaders.

The many visitors to the fair, who wanted to go home, stayed in front of the police guardpost and were deliberately misled about the incident by the 'checked shirts' [Buntkarierten] ... As a result of this false information, working-class elements also took up a completely false position against the People's Police ... A section of our comrades, particularly those colleagues from the factories, did not fully recognise the political implications of this organised provocation. They are of the opinion that it was only a childish prank [Dumme-Junge-Streiche] and that there have always been fights at the 'Tauchscher' and that they're only horseplay [Rüpeleien].[69]

The reactions of older workers to events that occurred during the 1951 Tauchscher showed the extent to which they were still aware of and ready to defend older traditions of misrule. At this stage, young workers could still rely on a sense of reciprocal support and solidarity based on common working-class understandings and experience.

Conclusion

Significant sections of the working class in both East and West Germany were anticommunist. Distrust of the communists came not only from above, from older and more established workers who had been members of the SPD, but also from below, from those who were classed by the organised labour movement as the lumpenproletariat for their failure to share class consciousness and political awareness. The disorganisation of the street was the antithesis of the communist ideal of rigid discipline and control. Those in the gangs fell foul of the efforts of the SED leadership to assert the respectability of communism by arguing that true proletarian consciousness could only develop through exposure to education, hard work and 'clean' (sauber) German culture (which happened to be controlled by the state). Although arguably part of a long-standing tradition of working-class street behaviour and culture, street culture and other forms of uncontrolled popular culture became increasingly viewed with suspicion and hostility.

Notes

1. Alf Lüdtke, 'What Happened to the "Fiery Red Glow"? Workers' experiences and German fascism' in Alf Lüdtke (ed.), *The History of Everyday Life. Reconstructing Historical Experiences and Ways of Life* (Princeton, 1989), 198–251, 226–27; Alf Lüdtke, '"Deutsche Qualitätsarbeit", "Spielereien" am Arbeitsplatz und "Fliehen" aus der Fabrik: Industrielle Arbeitsprozesse und Arbeitsverhalten in den 1920er Jahren – Aspekte eines offenen Forschungsfeldes' in Friedhelm Boll (ed.), *Arbeiterkulturen zwischen Alltag und Politik* (Vienna, 1986), 155–97.
2. 'Zusammenrottung von 500 Jugendlichen in Wismar gegen Volkspolizei' (January 1958), StAL RdB Bildung, Kultur und Sport: 1723; 'Zusammenrottung lärmender Jugendlicher am Capitol (26.7.58)', StAL BDVP 24/65; 'Zusammenrottung von Jugendlichen in

Hohenmölsen (28.11.59)', BArch. SAPMO DY30/IV2/16/230; 'Provokation und den Aufruhr jugendlicher Rowdys anläßlich der Eröffnung des Herbstfestes in Dresden am 17.9.1960', BArch. DO1 11.0 HVDVP 729; 'Randalierende Jugendliche in der Innenstadt (Leipzig, 4.9.1961)', StAL BDVP 24.1/420; 'Aufruhr auf dem Leipziger Weihnachtsmarkt am 29.11.1964', StAL IVA-5/01/269, IV A-2/12/411; 'Landenfriedensbruch beim Volksfest am 7. Oktober durch Beat-Anhänger in der Karl-Marx-Allee', Landesarchiv Berlin, STA Rep. 303/26.1, 490, C Rep 902, 2085; 'Zusammenrottung von "Rolling Stones" Fans (7.10.69)', BArch. DO1/38215 'Zusammenrottung jugendlicher Rowdys am 21.3.73 in Döbeln', StAL BDVP 24.1/226; 'Zusammenrottungen von Trampern' anläßlich Pfefferbergfest Schmölln und 1000-Jahr-Feier in Altenburg (Leipzig, 27 July 1976), BStU, Ast. Lpz., Abt. IX 00133.

3. 'Jahresanalyses der Kreise auf dem Gebiete des Jugendschutzes (27.1.58)', StAL RdB Bildung, Kultur und Sport 1723, 15; Hans-Jürgen von Wensierski, '"Die anderen nannten uns Halbstarke" – Jugendsubkultur in den 50er Jahren' in Heinz-Hermann Krüger (ed.), 'Die Elvis-Tolle, die hatte ich mir unauffällig wachsen lassen'. Lebensgeschichte und jugendliche Alltagskultur in den fünfziger Jahren (Opladen, 1985), 103-28, 103ff.
4. Detlev Peukert, Inside Nazi Germany. Conformity, Opposition and Racism, trans. Richard Deveson (London, 1993), 145ff.; Arno Klönne, Jugend im Dritten Reich: die Hitler-Jugend und ihre Gegner (Cologne, 1999).
5. 'Jahresanalyses der Kreise ... (27.1.58)'.
6. Eve Rosenhaft, 'Organising the "Lumpenproletariat": Cliques and Communists in Berlin during the Weimar Republic' in Richard J. Evans (ed.), German Working Class 1888-1933. The Politics of Everyday Life (London, 1982), 174-219, 186.
7. See, for instance, the case that occurred in April 1967, BStU, Ast. Lpz., AU 762/67, Band I, 125-27.
8. Interview with Klaus Renft (2000).
9. Philip Cohen and David Robins, Knuckle Sandwich. Growing Up in the Working-class City (Harmondsworth, 1978), 78.
10. Stephen Humphries, Hooligans or Rebels? An Oral History of Working-class Childhood and Youth 1889-1939 (Oxford, 1981), 190.
11. Eve Rosenhaft, Beating the Fascists? The German Communists and Political Violence, 1929-1933 (Cambridge, 1983); Eve Rosenhaft, 'Working-class Life and Working-class Politics: Communists, Nazis and the State in the Battle for the Streets, Berlin 1928-1932' in Richard Bessel and E.J. Feuchtwanger (eds), Social Change and Political Development in Weimar Germany (London, 1981), 207-40.
12. Peukert, Inside Nazi Germany, 165, 157.
13. Fritz Petrick, Zur sozialen Lage der Arbeiterjugend im Deutschland 1933 bis 1939 (East Berlin, 1974). Detlev Peukert's work did begin to have an impact in the 1980s. Hermann Langer, 'Wollt ihr den totalen Tanz?' Streiflichter zur imperialistischen Manipulierung der Jugend (Berlin, 1985), 187f.
14. Rosenhaft, Beating the Fascists?, 136.
15. Francis Wheen, Karl Marx (London, 1999), 16, 257; Karl Marx and Frederick Engels, 'Manifesto of the Communist Party' in Marx and Engels Selected Works (London, 1968), 35-62, 44.
16. Nicholas Dirks, Geoff Eley and Sherry Ortner (eds), Culture/Power/History. A Reader in Contemporary Social Theory (Princeton, 1994), 32.
17. Nicholas Stargardt, 'Male Bonding and the Class Struggle in Imperial Germany', Historical Journal 38:1 (March 1995), 175-93, 176.
18. Dirks, Eley and Ortner (eds), Culture/Power/History, 32.
19. 'Erich Honecker: "Wer seine Hand gegen die Arbeiter-und-Bauern-Macht erhebt, wird vernichtet". Eröffnungsvorlesung des 7. zentralen Lehrganges für Kampfgruppen-Kommandeure am 20.4.1959 in Schmerwitz', BArch. SAPMO DY30/2513, 45-78, 66.
20. Omer Bartov, 'The Missing Years: German Workers, German Soldiers', German History 8:1 (1990), 49-65; Alf Lüdtke, 'The Appeal of Exterminating "Others": German Workers and

the Limits of Resistance', *Journal of Modern History* 64 (December 1992), 46–67; Alfons Kenkmann, *Wilde Jugend. Lebenswelt großstädtischer Jugendlicher zwischen Weltwirtschaftskrise, Nationalsozialismus und Währungsreform* (Essen, 1996), 255ff.

21. 'Kampfpläne, Entlarvung feindlicher Agenten und Provokateure' (July-August 1953), StAL, SED IV5/01/483.
22. On the relationship between Edelweiß pirates from the 1940s and those from the Weimar Republic, see Detlev Peukert, 'Die "Wilden Cliquen" in den zwanziger Jahren' in Wilfried Breyvogel (ed.), *Autonomie und Widerstand. Zur Theorie und Geschichte des Jugendprotestes* (Essen, 1983), 66–77, 74.
23. The use of the the term 'brightly checked (*Buntkarierte*)' as a label for gang members in Leipzig in the 1950s suggests continued associations with the '*buntkarierte Skihemden*' worn by members of the *Meuten* in the late 1930s. See Lothar Gruchmann, 'Jugendopposition und Justiz im Dritten Reich. Die Probleme bei der Verfolgung der "Leipziger Meuten" durch die Gerichte' in Wolfgang Benz (ed.), *Miscellanea. Festschrift für Helmut Krausnick zum 75. Geburtstag* (Stuttgart, 1980), 103–30, 105; for a report on gangs in Berlin wearing neckerchiefs, see 'Cliquenbildung' (c. 1952), Landesarchiv Berlin, STA Rep. 303/26, 137.
24. Arno Klönne, *Umerziehung, Aufbau und Kulturkonflikt: Zur Geschichte der Jugend im geteilten Deutschland von 1945 bis in die fünfziger Jahre* (Hagen, 1998), 77–78.
25. 'Der Kampf gegen Jugendkriminalität und Rowdytum im Bezirk Leipzig (ca. 1960–61)', StAL, BDVP 24/113, 215.
26. 'Rat des Kreises Delitzsch: Kreisanalyse Jugendschutz' (1957), StAL RdB Bildung, Kultur und Sport: 1723, 75.
27. 'Rat des Landkreises Döbeln: Jugendhilfe (4.1.55)', StAL RdB Bildung, Kultur und Sport: 1723, 90.
28. 'Jahresanalyses der Kreise ... (27.1.58)'.
29. Hans-Dieter Schütt (ed.), *Klaus Renft. Zwischen Liebe und Zorn* (Berlin, 1997), 48; their nicknames were *Der Weiße*, Elvis, Locke, *Banane*, Klotz, Knut, Khrushchev and *Der Lange*.
30. 'Jahresanalyses der Kreise ... (27.1.58)'.
31. Richard J. Evans, *Proletarians and Politics. Socialism, Protest and the Working Class in Germany before the First World War* (New York, 1990).
32. Walter Friedrich, *Flegeljahre? Zur Erziehung 13– bis 16jähriger Jungen* (Berlin, 1964), 3ff.
33. 'Erfahrungsaustausch über die Arbeit der Jugendklubs in der DDR' (1960), BArch. SAPMO DY24/6724.
34. 'Befragung von Schülern' (19.11.64), BArch. DY6/3944.
35. Günter de Bruyn, *Vierzig Jahre* (Frankfurt am Main, 1996), 13.
36. Cohen and Robins, *Knuckle Sandwich*, 29, 36–37, 74.
37. Promoting socialism as 'a decent (*anständiges*) life rich in culture' was, Walter Ulbricht argued, the key to winning over the middle class, the intelligentsia and many farmers to the regime. Speech by Walter Ulbricht, *LVZ* (24 June 1958).
38. Alan Nothnagle, *Building the East German Myth. Historical Mythology and Youth Propaganda in the German Democratic Republic, 1945–1989* (Ann Arbor, 1999), 48–60.
39. 'Das Maß ist voll. 900 jung Wismut-Kumpel warten auf die FDJ. Wie lange bestimmen noch die Rowdies?', *Junge Welt* (30 May 1956).
40. Horst Groschopp, 'Herkommen, Struktur und Verständnis' in Hildegard Bockhorst, Brigitte Prautzsch and Carla Rimbach (eds), *Woher – Wohin? Kinder- und Jugendkulturarbeit in Ostdeutschland* (Remscheid, 1993), 14–30, 15.
41. Ibid., 14, 16; Anna-Sabine Ernst, 'The Politics of Culture and the Culture of Daily Life in the DDR in the 1950s' in David Barclay and Eric Weitz (eds), *Between Reform and Revolution. German Socialism and Communism from 1840 to 1990* (New York, Oxford, 1998), 489–506.
42. Lieselotte Thoms, Hans Vieillard and Wolfgang Berger, *Walter Ulbricht. Arbeiter, Revolutionär, Staatsmann* (Berlin, 1968), 193.
43. Christa Wolf, *Der geteilte Himmel* (Halle, 1963). The book tempered its realistic depiction of economic and other problems with an optimistic account of people finding their place in socialism.

44. Dirks, Eley and Ortner (eds), *Culture/Power/History*, 5.
45. Alf Lüdtke, 'Introduction: What is the History of Everyday Life and Who Are its Practitioners?' in Lüdtke (ed.), *The History of Everyday Life*, 3–40, 9; Detlev Peukert, *Jugend zwischen Krieg und Krise. Lebenswelten von Arbeiterjungen in der Weimarer Republik* (Cologne, 1987), 246f.; Detlev Peukert, *Grenzen der Sozial-Disziplinierung. Aufstieg und Krise der Deutschen Jugendfürsorge, 1878–1932* (Cologne, 1986).
46. Some of the best work on bourgeois attempts to control working-class behaviour has, in recent years, been carried out in Australia. See Lynette Finch, 'On the Streets: Working Class Youth Culture in the Nineteenth Century' in Rob White (ed.), *Youth Subcultures. Theory, History and the Australian Experience* (Hobart, 1993), 75–79.
47. Joanna Wyn and Rob White, *Rethinking Youth* (London, 1997), 83.
48. 'Jazz and German Respectability' in Uta Poiger, *Jazz, Rock & Rebels. Cold War Politics and American Culture in a Divided Germany* (Berkeley, 2000), 137–67.
49. 'Diebe, Straßenräuber, Brandstifter – das sind die "Ritter der abendländischen Kultur"', *Neues Deutschland* (1 July 1953).
50. *Neues Deutschland* (25 June 1953).
51. 'Der Tag X von Erich Loest', *LVZ* (23 June 1953), 4.
52. Bundesministerium für gesamtdeutsche Fragen, *Der Volksaufstand vom 17. Juni 1953 in der sowjetischen Besatzungszone und in Ostberlin* (Bonn, 1953), prefacing citation.
53. 'Nicht wahr, Arbeiter, das warst du nicht, das da drüben?' *LVZ* (24 June 1953).
54. Natalie Zemon Davis, 'The Reason of Misrule: Youth Groups and Charivaris in Sixteenth Century France', *Past and Present* 50 (February 1971), 41–75; Norbert Schindler, 'Guardians of Disorder: Rituals of Youthful Culture at the Dawn of the Modern Age' in Giovanni Levi and Jean-Claude Schmitt (eds), *Stormy Evolution. A History of Young People in the West* (Cambridge, MA, 1997), vol. I, 240–82.
55. Zentralrat der FDJ (ed.), *Handbuch des FDJ-Gruppenleiters* (Berlin, 1956), 261–62.
56. Susanne Schottke, 'Zur Entstehung und Entwicklung des Tauchscher. Ein Volksfest und seine Wandlungen' in Katrin Keller (ed.), *Feste und Feiern. Zum Wandel Städtischer Festkultur in Leipzig* (Leipzig, 1994), 103–16, 110.
57. Thoms, Vieillard and Berger, *Walter Ulbricht*, 7.
58. Lynn Abrams, *Workers' Culture in Imperial Germany* (London, New York, 1992), 37ff.
59. 'Der Tauchscher. Die Polizei warnt vor Ausschreitungen' (Zeitungsauschnitt, 28 August 1929), StAL, Stadt Taucha, Nr. 1390.
60. Mikhail Bakhtin, *The Dialogic Imagination* (Austin, 1981); Mikhail Bakhtin, *Rabelais and his World* (Bloomington, 1987).
61. Peter Stallybrass and Allon White, 'Bourgeois Hysteria and the Carnivalesque' in Simon During (ed.), *The Cultural Studies Reader* (London, New York, 2nd edn, 1999), 382–88, 382.
62. Schottke, 'Zur Entstehung und Entwicklung des Tauchscher', 115.
63. 'Information über die Faschingsveranstaltung im HO-Warenhaus in Leipzig (13.2.1962)', BArch. SAPMO DY24/3726.
64. Zentralrat der FDJ (ed.), *Handbuch des FDJ-Gruppenleiters*, 233.
65. Ibid., 264.
66. Thomas Lindenberger, *Volkspolizei: Herschaftspraxis und öffentliche Ordnung im SED-Staat, 1952–1968* (Cologne, Weimar, Vienna, 2003), 370f.
67. 'Vorkommnis auf dem Weihnachtsmarkt' (Leipzig, 30 November 1964), StAL, IV A-5/01/247, 35–40.
68. 'SED Kreisleitung Eilenburg an Paul Fröhlich (19.6.1967)', StAL IVA-2/9.02/353, 248.
69. 'Bericht über die provokatorischen Vorfälle zum Volksfest "Tauchscher" am 10.9.51 auf der Kleinmesse in Leipzig', StAL IV/5/01/273, 51–59.

~ Chapter 7 ~

SEXING UP SOCIALISM

*E*quating their own brand of state socialism with the best interests of youth, SED leaders sought to monopolise and control the free time of 'their' teenagers. Expropriation of time for relaxation and unforced interaction took place under the cloak of ensuring that young people used their time 'sensibly'. As a result their own sense (*Eigen-sinn*) was denied. The consequence was an official youth policy that was out of touch with young people's interests and needs and a youth organisation that proved repeatedly incapable of competing with alternative forms of leisure and culture. A major survey carried out in 1969 found that less than half of young people found membership of the FDJ interesting and varied. 'It is clearly difficult for many leaderships to organise meetings that are effective and suitable for youngsters.'[1] On paper, the FDJ appeared to be highly successful. In reality, it was frequently dull and unimaginative. 'As many as 85 per cent said that they found spontaneous, informal groups a more fulfilling source of leisure than the FDJ.'[2] The FDJ was criticised for failing, not only to attract and keep committed members but to keep youth off the streets or clear of juvenile crime.[3]

In part, the FDJ's lack of effectiveness resulted from too much emphasis being placed on harking back to the traditions of the German *Wandervogel*. This had been a popular move in the immediate aftermath of the war, attracting young working-class men who wanted to take part in reconstruction and, at the same time, build themselves a better life. As the population in both parts of Germany struggled to come to terms with what had happened and how they had allowed themselves to become caught up as part of it, the FDJ offered a potent and optimistic message of societal renewal through personal engagement in the cause of democracy and socialism.[4] While it later became clear to many of these early converts that they had been duped by a cynical manoeuvre on the part of the Communist Party – to take over and then increasingly marginalise rival influences on youth – many remained firmly committed to the ideal conveyed by the slogan 'Never again fascism, never again war'.[5] They felt guilty for their part in the Third Reich and incapable of arguing with the antifascists, who had been prepared to accept them and declare them as their own. The problem for the SED leadership was that, once they had channelled this generation of idealistic converts (for the most part former members of the Hitler Youth) into responsible positions in the bloc parties and mass organisations tasked with 'democratic-socialist renewal', they bequeathed a youth organisation that was increasingly hollow, bureaucratic and inert.[6] The 'pioneers of the first hour' took with them the skills they had gained in getting people organised and motivated, making contacts, finding resources and getting things done. They left behind a youth organisation composed of people who, for the most part, did not have anything better or more important to do.

Contrary to the communists' claims to modernity, they continued to emphasise hiking, camping and singing as the best ways for youth to find happiness (*fröhlich sein*).[7] The emphasis on leisure being 'sensible' and beneficial to both youth and society was a major barrier to providing activities that teenagers might actually find enjoyable and worth their while doing. Reports on what really went on in local communities showed an alarming lack of initiative on the part of local organisers and functionaries and widespread disinterest on the part of youth.[8] Certain aspects of the regime's social and educational provisions were more attractive and worthwhile than others. One in two teenagers was a member of a leisure club or society, with most belonging to a sports organisation, a music club or an amateur dramatics society. During class harvesting expeditions and FDJ-sponsored youth construction projects, young people could genuinely experience feelings of responsibility and confidence in their own abilities. Being left to carry out activities on their own initiative without overt adult control was much more important in creating the sorts of positive feelings the regime wanted to generate.[9] Unfortunately, the activities of the youth organisation were so bound by routine that there was very little opportunity of incorporating such experiences into everyday life.[10]

A major disparity continued to persist between the SED's conception of politics as the single most important influence on young people's lives and their own conception of politics as boring and irrelevant. Despite its claim to be a leisure organisation, the FDJ was also tasked with politically influencing them. 'As soon as teachers start talking about political questions, then many in the class start yawning.'[11] Asked by the regional SED secretary whether he had considered organising a course on the classics of Marxism-Leninism, the local FDJ organiser replied that he could hardly expect anyone to come to that because it was 'too boring'. Other 'youth friends' (the name applied to members of the FDJ) said that they would never be able to grasp Marxism-Leninism and that it was 'all too dry'.[12] Nevertheless, the regime continued to push members to join political discussion circles despite the fact that there was next to no interest in them.[13] Only one in five FDJ members said that they had joined the youth organisation out of political conviction. Nearly a third said that they had joined the FDJ only because everyone was carried over automatically from the Young Pioneers.[14] The competing imperatives of ensuring that youth was sufficiently exposed to political demands and, at the same time, providing teenagers with interesting and enjoyable leisure activities were difficult to fulfil. The urge to fill up all of their time with political influence clashed with the desire of most young people to escape the influence of the SED at least in their free time. Far from mobilising young people, the youth organisation seems to have actively repelled them.

Unfortunately for the SED, the changes that had occurred in society and culture made large-scale, centrally planned, heavily regimented youth organisations like the FDJ appear increasingly outdated and irrelevant. As a result of the internationalisation of youth culture, teenagers were graduating from short pants to long trousers and correspondingly gaining a new sense of maturity and worldliness. They no longer needed to be led by the hand. They were quite capable of amusing themselves. Increasingly the songs they wanted to sing had English lyrics and an alternative rhythm to the marching songs and *Kampflieder* favoured by veterans of the communist youth movement. While teenagers became increasingly interested in and caught up by the changes taking place in media, youth culture and fashion, the youth organisation remained wedded to notions of 'the happy youthful life' that saw hiking and campfire songs as the most important and exciting form of youth recreational activity.[15]

The increasing accessibility of consumer items like transistor radios, TVs, bicycles and mopeds made the leisure opportunities provided by the FDJ appear unnecessary and redundant. As early as 1960, it was noticed that 'Many young people today possess bicycles, motorbikes, boats, tents, etc.'[16] By 1969, 93 per cent of young people had access to a TV at home. Fifty per cent had transistor radios. Forty-nine per cent had their own rooms. One in four apprentices and one in three young villagers possessed his or her own moped.[17] Although it was very difficult for young bachelors to find a place of their own, in other respects they enjoyed a good level of disposable income. Having bought a motorbike, camping gear, a transistor radio and a camera, one young man felt that he had already accomplished his most important material ambitions.[18] With the independence they gave him, he no longer had much need for a youth organisation.

Not only were young people more independent materially, but their aspirations were often set on other goals than those the youth organisation could provide.[19] Once they had reached their late teens, many wanted to make their own decisions about what to watch and listen to, what to wear, how to behave and where to go. 'If I spend the whole day working in the factory, then that's not very meaningful (*sinnvoll*). The main thing is that my "dough" [*Piepen*] is correct. In my free-time I do what I want and won't let myself be dictated to.'[20] As young workers became more prosperous and independent (in relative terms), the youth organisation lost much of its appeal as a source and coordinator of leisure.

> Many functionaries don't take account of the altered standard of living of our youth in the activities [they organise] in the neighbourhood ... They try to win young people for the work with old approaches and methods. There are a few functionaries who go on and on about the good old days of the FDJ and don't understand that life has become a lot richer and brighter since then.[21]

Despite outward appearances, neither the FDJ nor the SED was a monolithic, conflict-free organisation in which everyone thought alike. In the mid-1950s reform currents emerged (pre-empting and subsequently coalescing with Khrushchev's revelations about Stalin) that linked senior Politbüro members like Karl Schirdewan to idealistic students and academics in the universities. Although their ability to articulate ideas and coordinate with each other remained limited, a shared desire emerged for a newer and more humane form of socialism based on modern values. Turning their critical gaze on the organisation that was failing to serve young people's interests or to meet their needs, senior SED politicians sought to find a way of bringing in those 'standing on the sidelines', frustrated, bored and turned off by the previous youth policy.[22] As Ernst Wollweber, the former head of the MfS, put it: the natural inclination of the SED apparatus was to '"kneel on people's souls", to give them all kinds of orders about how they should dress, what haircuts they can have, how they should dance, how they may amuse themselves and how they ought to go on holiday'.[23]

Impatience at Ulbricht's intransigence together with hostility to Honecker's continued influence came to a head in the Politbüro in October 1955. Albert Norden, in particular, used the alarming levels of *Republikflucht* among young people to highlight problems with the youth organisation. This was an issue, he suggested, that should be keeping all functionaries awake at night. The problem was how to captivate young people so that they would stay in the republic. The phrase he used was 'Wie fesseln wir die Jugendlichen?' This was an interesting choice of words because *fesseln* can mean both gripping (as in providing gripping entertainment) and, more literally, tying down. Norden was uncompromisingly frank in his criticism of the FDJ, describing its structure as being 'far too similar' to that of the party. 'We read in an FDJ circular that young people must be won for hiking. That's a joke. We don't need to convince young people to go for a wander. They're quite capable of wandering without us.' Arguing that bureaucracy was stifling initiative and isolating the youth organisation from 'a large part of youth', he called for 'a shake-up of our youth work'.[24]

As a bureaucratic, top-down mass organisation, the FDJ was simply ill-suited to responding to grass-roots needs. 'If young people want to experience something, then they have to organise it themselves.' There was,

Norden complained, 'no trust between members and the FDJ hierarchy'. Most were convinced that they could exercise no influence on the activity of the FDJ because everything was 'decided from above' and because anyone who thought differently was viewed and treated with distrust. In any case, there was little point in having original ideas because they never received an answer from the youth leader. Norden referred to a youth secretary in Magdeburg as an example of what FDJ work should not be. 'This secretary revealed that he has no idea what young people do in the evenings because he is not there. And how can he be? He must read all the circulars that come from the Central Council of the FDJ and must take part in numerous meetings.'[25]

If the Central Council of the FDJ was to win over youth, then it had to show young people that it had their interests at heart. The way to do this, Norden argued, was by addressing: 'questions of fashion ... personal hygiene ... marriage ... technology and science ... music ... literature ... board games'.[26] Even when they were trying to appeal directly to youth, regime leaders could not refrain from lecturing them. The reference to personal hygiene rather than beauty and cosmetic products revealed that even those arguing for a new approach were incapable of seeing young people as fully fledged consumers. Instead of being capable of making their own choices, they still had to be taught the correct way. The aversion to fashion (and other forms of consumerism) gained in socialist youth groups of the 1920s proved difficult to shake off even during the 'shake-up' of youth policy. Alan McDougall argues that Schirdewan's views on the need to counter 'the penetration of bourgeois ideology' in relation to youth differed little from those of Ulbricht.[27] The would-be reformers did not have a fully worked out programme for what to do with the FDJ. Their real contribution was in removing (albeit temporarily) Honecker's retrograde influence and in spurring Ulbricht to become bolder in an attempt to recapture the moral high ground.

Walter Ulbricht appears to have been caught out by Norden's determination to push through what amounted to a powerful and controversial, but highly original and persuasive, reform programme.[28] Outflanked by Norden and other supporters of 'more humane, reform socialism' within the Politbüro, Ulbricht added a passage to his own speech that surprised many in his audience at the Fifth FDJ Parliament (25–27 May 1955).[29] In it, not only did he appear to embrace the ideal of reform, but his words marked a radical break from existing policy in relation to youth. Adding his own support to the criticisms of FDJ micromanagement, an exasperated Walter Ulbricht asked, 'Must the Politbüro organise kite-flying?'[30] Given that 'evening after evening the greater part of young people in towns up and down our Republic are in search of some kind of variety or another that they don't find here in the GDR', the question Ulbricht wanted answered was, 'Why then do we pay for this huge apparatus?'[31]

With a still open border to West Berlin the consequences of the youth organisation's failings were clear. 'Young people in Berlin have nothing else to do other than to go to a pub or to the cinema in West Berlin.' The latest craze sweeping Berlin teenagers was roller skating. The problem with the FDJ, Ulbricht quipped, was that it was not mobile enough to keep up with them.[32] In a process that became known as 'having a heart for youth', functionaries were encouraged to take responsibility and to be critical about their own failings. In addition, they were urged to take urgent measures to stop the rot and to renew their efforts in order to regain young people's trust. 'Having a heart for youth' entailed temporarily renouncing the prejudices against those who clustered on street corners and admitting that, as well as the pernicious influence of Western media, they might have more prosaic reasons for their behaviour like boredom or not having anywhere else to go.

Female Sexuality

Although it claimed to interpret the scientific laws of historical development, the SED could not alter the laws of sexual chemistry. 'A pretty young thing is besieged from all sides. In the morning she is a schoolgirl. As soon as she is out of school, all [men] between the ages of fifteen and eighty dance a courtship display around her.'[33] For girls, the implications of the changes produced by Western youth culture were particularly explosive because they coincided with and ran counter to a revival of traditional ideas about how young women should behave. In both East and West Germany, the early 1950s were marked by attempts to 'restore ordered relations after the chaos of wartime'.[34] In both German states, girls were expected to be pretty and chaste, their grace, charm and elegance only betraying innocence and virtuousness. Plaits and sensible shoes (both hangovers from the *Wandervogel*) dominated the ideal image of the adolescent girl in the early 1950s.[35] Whatever the government might have said about work, their family upbringing also prepared them for a future as housewives and mothers. To preserve their 'freshness and purity', impulses and desires had to be controlled and repressed.

With the onset of puberty, a girl's comings and goings became strictly regulated. Parents worried about their daughter's reputation and sought to ensure that at all times she was 'smart, orderly and clean'.[36] Erica Carter has emphasised the importance of the bedroom for girls in providing them with the space in which they could overcome feelings of homeliness and awkwardness to experiment with sexuality in the form of make-up, dressing up and dreaming of unattainable, inaccessible pop stars.[37] It was here, long before they felt confident in overtly challenging their parents or society, that girls privately engaged in deviation from gender norms. The problem for historians is that in and of itself such a culture leaves very little in the way of tangible traces.

Instead of a positive sense of what young women were doing, all we are left with are the negative images left by those who sought to influence and control them. The street, the arena in which most subcultural activity took place, remained in many ways 'taboo for women', associated as it was with danger and shame.[38] Girls had more to lose by failing to conform to rigid gender norms. For seventeen-year-old Brigitte Reimann, the options in the event of an unplanned pregnancy were limited to using 'a household product that one of my classmates suggested (the efficacy of which I am not entirely sure about) and yes, the second option would be to go over to the other side'.[39] By the 'other side', Reimann meant taking her own life. But, for many girls, the best way out of an unplanned pregnancy was to escape over the border in the hope of being accepted as a political refugee in the West. Various humiliations awaited them in the reception camps, which were often run by Christian charitable organisations keen to impose their own values on the new arrivals.[40] Nevertheless, for some even this inhospitable reception was preferable to the reaction they were likely to receive at home. 'You see we can't marry yet, the doctors are not allowed to operate and I could not stand the shame.'[41]

By the time Reimann emerged as a bright (and, by her own account, very attractive) young aspiring author at the beginning of the 1960s, she had managed to lose her ('petit bourgeois') sense of shame. Frequently branded as a brazen harlot by her elderly (male and female) rivals in the SED, her diaries reveal that she had found her own very personal and subjective way of exploring East German society 'from the bottom up'. Reimann's skill as a precociously talented young writer was in making everyday, mundane GDR reality sound dramatic and exciting. Other East German teenagers were more prosaic. They complained of violent, overbearing parents who sought to control every aspect of their lives.[42] Nosy neighbours, who kept a close watch and who reported back any suspicious activities, were another source of displeasure. New opportunities for education, employment and interaction with the opposite sex were tempered by continued pressure not to gain a reputation as a 'loose' woman. At stake was the family's standing in the community.

From the mid-1950s in West Germany, Erica Carter argues, girls began to challenge parental restrictions on clothing, hairstyles and make-up. For young women, consumption 'simultaneously and paradoxically offered itself as a route to micropolitical resistance'.[43] Much of their protest was aesthetic, not political. As the advertisers of Triumph underwear proclaimed in *Bravo* magazine, 'We teenagers have our own style. And that's just what makes so many people see red.'[44] The 'American' fashion for lipstick, high heels and capri pants became a source of conflict in many West German households.[45] Hedonistic consumption was associated with sexual transgression. School authorities tried to ban girls from wearing indecent 'drainpipe' trousers.[46] For many girls, escaping from the family and its pressures to act like a 'nice girl' represented their first political experience. In the context of post-war Germany, Carter argues, 'to don the accoutrements of an American female ideal ... was in part to register a public disavowal of the fascist images of femininity: scrubbed faces shining with health, sturdy child-bearing hips sporting seamed stockings and sensible shoes'.[47]

In East Germany the party-state's claim to represent but also to educate youth put it in an ambivalent position in relation to such changes in identities and fashion. At times, SED propagandists berated teenagers as if they were their surrogate parents. On other occasions, spokespeople took on the role of concerned bystanders and sought to educate parents about the need for more understanding of the changes their daughters were undergoing. The SED was strongly in favour of girls escaping from the confines of the domestic sphere, but opposed to anything that smacked too much of sassy independence or Western decadence. Honecker's removal as head of the FDJ (in May 1955) coincided with a changed outlook towards adolescent sexuality within the highest reaches of the party. Honecker was proclaimed as belonging 'to the type of youth movement functionaries, who were brought up in the hard struggle, the hard class warfare of the party of Ernst Thälmann'.[48] Under his leadership, the focus on militarisation had been such that the only time female members of the FDJ appeared to speak was when they condemned those young men who were not brave enough to volunteer to serve in the armed forces. Dismissing young women's fears that their boyfriends would be unfaithful during their military service, a leading FDJ woman proclaimed, 'I would be ashamed if I were a boy and older comrades came and said to me: we fought when we were young and achieved a great deal and now you don't want to join the ranks of the KVP?'[49] Nevertheless, having thanked Honecker for his contribution to the creation of the FDJ, Walter Ulbricht went on to suggest that it was time for a new, more modern approach.

Almost overnight *Junge Welt*, the daily newspaper aimed at members of the FDJ, replaced the language of intolerance and distrust with a rhetoric of dialogue and understanding. Ulbricht had asked the editors what was stopping them from broaching issues of sexuality. 'Are you scared of it or what? You can't argue that most young people are unconcerned by these issues. Why don't you talk about specific problems in your articles? You need not just talk about production.'[50] The editors responded by encouraging readers to write in with comments in response to the question 'May an apprentice have a girlfriend?'[51] The answer was apparently 'Why not?' One FDJler from Schwerin (who provided his full name) proclaimed that 'what me and my girlfriend do has nothing to do with anyone else'.[52] The change in editorial focus allowed greater discussion of the issues affecting girls. It coincided with a critique of the bureaucratism that was turning FDJ clubhouses into mausoleums staffed by mummy-like functionaries.[53] Rank-and-file members of the FDJ were urged to bring the functionaries back down to earth when 'phrases rain down from above'. After all, 'The Fifth Parliament of the FDJ called for bureaucrats to be swept out with an unyielding broom [*mit eisernem Besen*]'.[54] Nevertheless, the reformers were concerned to emphasise that the more modern stance was not to be confused with acceptance of Western youth culture. 'Stupid bodily contortions' should not be mistaken for dancing.[55]

In its more gender-aware and women-friendly guise, *Junge Welt* began to address issues concerning relationships and sex in its advice column. The articles followed a trend set by Hans Modrow, who had been organising highly successful and popular youth forums for young people from both East and West Berlin. The forums invited teenagers to ask any questions they felt like asking, however impertinent. Straightforward answers were provided by more worldly representatives of the SED leadership. Thus Professor Hanns Eisler was brought in to make comments like 'A good dress has nothing to do with capitalism. The important thing is that it has a pretty woman in it.'[56] The caption of a photograph showing girls from Berlin learning to cook emphasised that this was 'because, for men in particular, love begins in the stomach'.[57]

Although its tone and editorial focus continued to be dominated by a gaze that was decidedly male, a recognition emerged that girls also had their own interests and issues.[58] The newspaper sought to cater to their interest in fashion with articles about synthetic fabrics.[59] Readers, meanwhile, raised the issue of capri pants. A consensus emerged that what mattered was what was modern and tasteful, not where the fashion came from. 'Three-quarter-length trousers' were declared to be acceptable. 'Yellow shirts with palm trees [*Affenpalmen*] and cowboys' were not.[60] Formal dancing appears to have constituted a considerable bone of contention between the sexes. Girls with plaits complained that no boys asked them to dance.[61] Other girls complained bitterly about the boys' manners. They shouted abuse at girls who did not want to dance with drunken men or who withdrew from their clumsy caresses, threatened other boys with violence for dancing with 'their' girls or devoted the whole evening to getting drunk without dancing with the girl they had invited. Boys meanwhile responded that in that case the girls should pick up the tab, take the boys home afterwards and later also make the proposals of marriage.[62]

In many respects this new emphasis on gender and sexuality was a shrewd move because it created a renewed appreciation of one of the organisation's early strengths. In the very beginning, its mixed intake (and the possibilities this provided for interacting with the opposite sex) had been a significant selling point for the FDJ. It broke with the forced segregation that had existed in the *Bündische* movement and in the Third Reich. While youth organisations in the Western Zones continued to separate girls and boys, the FDJ allowed them to intermingle freely. In the early years at least, membership of the FDJ had provided girls with more autonomy and opportunities for fraternising and socialising not only with each other, but also with boys. *Junge Welt* was so keen to emphasise that co-education in the FDJ was clean and healthy that in the summer of 1956 it encouraged a debate among its readers about whether girls and boys should share the same tents.[63]

Hilde Benjamin used *Junge Welt* to announce changes in family law that gave women a more equal say in the upbringing of children, and declared that it was no longer a disgrace for a child to be born out of wedlock.[64] Professor Rudolf Neubert, meanwhile, launched a campaign of 'enlightenment' about sexuality and raised the question, 'Is it utopian, is it whimsy to expect and to demand a higher form of love life?'[65] Yet, remarkable though these changes were, gender relations remained far from transformed. Addressing girls as the 'women of tomorrow', the Central Council of the FDJ also emphasised that they were the 'wives and mothers of tomorrow' who should continue to 'stand by their men' there where they lived and worked.[66] Toleration of coupledom did not extend to those still at school. Officially at least, sixth-formers continued to be discouraged from forming relationships with members of the opposite sex on the grounds that it weakened the collective spirit and lowered group morale.[67]

The SED's new-found interest in gender found reflection in Hans Marchwitza's industrial novel, *Roheisen* (raw iron). Where before his work had been marked by a one-sided emphasis on masculine heroism, his new novel stressed that the 'violent struggle' to exceed norms in building an iron-smelting works was one in which both men and women were engaged.[68] Some of the heroic old men he depicted continued to believe that political correctness, which demanded that women take a leading role in the struggle, was hampering reconstruction. 'I made the suggestion that they should send half the ignorant young women back where they came from and to take on more men – and now they even send me a female as shaft overseer? Outrageous!'[69] Nevertheless, while remaining suitably feminine, chaste and motherly, skilled women workers were presented as having acquired sufficient knowledge of the masculine world to become part of it. Marchwitza stressed that they had one man in particular to thank for this conversion. 'The women, who stood there with their children in their Sunday best, pointed joyously to the bearded man on the grandstand who spoke of their work, of the improvements to the building plan for the suburbs and of a new, beautiful future. "That is Comrade Walter Ulbricht!"'[70]

Youth Clubs: a Masculine Alternative?

In *A History of Youth*, Michael Mitterauer describes youth clubs as the most important development in the collective life of young people since the Second

World War. In contrast to the old-style regimented youth organisations, the decade after the war saw the development of a new type of 'club' that was characterised by 'unforced social interaction created principally by the sharing of space' rather than hierarchical organisation based on a shared commitment to common ideals. The principle of the club was that it was egalitarian and open to all. 'Friends can be brought along. A loose network of informal contacts forms around a nucleus ... A person can fall in with this or that activity as the mood dictates.'[71]

Although the Hungarian Uprising and the attacks on the 'Schirdewan group' brought discussions of reform to an abrupt end, the thaw had lasted long enough for networks of specialists to form. They continued to discuss new ideas for how to reorganise work with disenfranchised and disengaged young people. During a renewed period of reform in 1959/60 (and then again in 1963), these discussions re-emerged into the public sphere, bringing with them implications for how to respond to modern haircuts, clothing and behaviour.[72] Youth clubs, in particular, seemed to offer a means of redressing the imbalances that were occurring in youth provision and of addressing the divergent culture and needs of young, working-class men. 'Without a doubt these methods will allow us not only to win over the many youngsters who still stand on the sidelines, but also to contribute to overcoming the boredom that the enemy uses as a means of distraction.'[73]

For some officials, the club ethos appeared to represent the key to solving the problems of youth disaffection and uncontrolled street culture by providing an intermediate step between the youth organisation and informal groupings. Instead of having a uniform, a membership list and set times for meeting, they would take anyone, however they were dressed, and allow their clients to drop in as and when they chose. The aim of the youth clubs was to provide a more informal and less restrictive atmosphere than that provided by the FDJ. For the youths who attended, fewer rules and less regimentation provided an atmosphere that was both more fun and more grown-up. A tension remained, however, between those who understood that the clubs could only be effective if they allowed an opportunity to let off steam, to relax, to switch off and to have fun and those who persisted in seeing free time as something to be 'filled up' with culture, ideas and politics.[74]

The youth clubs had emerged in a grey area between individual firms, the official trade union (FDGB), local municipal authorities, the National Front and the movements for amateur performances (*Laienkunst*) and traditional culture (*Volkskunst*). Firms with over three hundred employees were obliged by law to create a venue for cultural events.[75] Space was given over to youth activities on an ad hoc or a permanent basis (with and without the support of the FDJ). Despite attempts to exert greater central control, the clubs remained tangled in a spaghetti-like jumble of overlapping jurisdictions. At the Fifth Parliament of the FDJ, Walter Ulbricht had tactically signalled his support for the idea of greater autonomy and self-help. 'You can decide for yourselves whether you listen to a talk in the culture park or go to a concert or to the dance floor. You should do what you want.'[76] Although in the aftermath of the Hungarian Uprising he rapidly reneged on the promise not to interfere, the notion that youth clubs could offer a space for recreation (rather than just additional re-education) persisted and gained supporters at the grass roots. The idea of the youth clubs providing a space for creative energy and self-constructed cultural activities (rather than passive absorption of notions of culture disseminated centrally from above) was given renewed emphasis during the Bitterfeld Conference of 1959.[77]

Between 1956 and 1960, Hans Szewczyk, later distinguished as the person responsible for developing psychological profiling in the GDR, carried out a study of 'several hundred young people in the streets, squares, ice-cream parlours, youth clubs and other spaces where they congregated in Friedrichshain, Prenzlauer Berg and Pankow'.[78] Influenced by Trasher's 1927 study of gangs in Chicago and by their own experiences in trying to establish contact with the gang members, Szewczyk's researchers took on certain (for the GDR unusual and unorthodox) ethnographical aspects in their research approach.

> We did not present ourselves to the youths as if we were criminal policemen, asking a lot of questions. Instead, we just stood with them at first, not doing anything on the corner and 'shooting the breeze [blödeln]'. A prerequisite for this was a knowledge of the slang or the vocabulary of these youths, which cannot be translated into high German without losing something of its atmospheric character.[79]

Only when they had established a relationship of trust did they start to ask questions. 'This work is not easy because, particularly among the more behaviourally damaged, this [deep-seated] mistrust is hard to overcome.'[80] Those involved in trying to work with 'problem youth' knew what a difficult job it was to win their trust. If society at large was deeply hostile to their dress and demeanour, the young men who roamed the streets were very suspicious of any attempt to try to impose order and control on them. Those who favoured the formation of youth clubs recognised that young people could not be won over by prescription and organisation alone. It was necessary instead to acknowledge their desire for independence and autonomy by giving them a greater say in how local youth clubs were run. The goal was to entice teenagers back off the streets and into an environment that was safer and more controlled, but less overtly top-down and controlling. In the summer of 1958, the authorities in Leipzig had considered employing a youth worker (*eine Art Betreuer*) to befriend and help young people who gathered on the streets and who had received a poor upbringing at home.[81]

Local initiatives showed that, with the right people in charge, youth clubs could become popular venues for the sorts of young people who shied away from the youth organisation with its blatantly officially orchestrated and regimented activities. One such 'rough diamond' was Klaus-Dieter Z., the former 'chief' of the Adler gang (named after the Adler district in south-west Leipzig), who had become involved in running a youth club for former gang members. Klaus-Dieter, or Zammo as he was known, had an instinctive feel for what 'the kids on the streets' would accept and how to make it interesting or attractive for them.

> There's no point if someone says to a youngster, 'You've been noisy, you're out' ... You can't just say 'meaningful free-time activities', particularly when they're in a group. With a big group of youngsters it's a lot more difficult to get them interested. You might be able to interest one young lad on his own in going to an art gallery. But, when there's a group of twenty of them, they already have other interests. If they say, 'We want to listen to music!', then they want to hear music, they want to have their own way [wollen sich darin durchsetzen]. That's the main problem that has to be solved ... All I want to say is that getting young people interested in something is a problem in itself.[82]

The problem with this logic (based on an implicit understanding of street youth psychology) was that it went completely against the grain of SED organisational principles. Although lip service was often paid to encouraging local initiative, in reality, endeavours that were not explicitly orchestrated by the party or the education authorities rarely received proper recognition and could easily come to be viewed with suspicion.

As a long-term strategy for dealing with wayward youth and preventing them from falling into criminal or disruptive behaviour, the youth clubs had much to offer. But, without a genuine relaxation and liberalisation of the way in which East German society was dictatorially run, they could never compete with the immediate and highly visible 'quick fixes' offered by the coercive organs. Walter Ulbricht had himself suggested that a way to overcome the mistrust that existed in relation to the youth organisation was to co-opt 'young people who have authority in the neighbourhood'.[83] It was often the case, however, that figures who had credibility on the street (such as Zammo) were precisely those who had already themselves been in trouble with the authorities.[84] Such 'poachers turned gamekeepers' had an implicit and intuitive understanding of how to talk to and get on with youngsters in a way in which both sides could maintain 'respect'. The problem was that as soon as they succeeded in attracting the right kind of clientele (i.e. those who were genuinely disruptive and at risk of becoming criminal), the youth clubs quickly gained a reputation as 'dens' inhabited by delinquents and repeat offenders.[85]

Although youth clubs were brought into the front line of the struggle against juvenile delinquency and disaffection, they were not given the backing necessary to succeed in their mission. An immense gulf separated the self-understood aims and purpose of the police from the position of youth club leaders, whose job it was to build bridges to young people. To outside authorities like the People's Police, the decision to place 'former criminals' in positions of authority seemed like irresponsibility bordering on madness. The police often suspected (not entirely without reason) that the youth clubs were harbouring rather than transforming young miscreants and troublemakers. Faced by hostile and aggressive police authorities, on the one hand, and suspicious and distrustful youngsters, on the other, it was very difficult for youth club organisers to know what was the right thing to do. Although their stated purpose was to get gang members off the streets, they received very little in the way of concrete guidance about how to do this or what to do with them once they had. The education authorities complained that 'the young friends involved in youth clubs often receive insufficient support from experienced cultural functionaries ... Those currently employed in the clubhouses are mostly very young and have little experience in cultural work and in how to lead people. Yet it is precisely of them that such great demands are made.'[86]

While the police had fairly straightforward and clear-cut definitions and notions about what to do with troublesome youth (locking them up and beating them up), those involved in 'soft policing' functions like the youth club leaders had a much more difficult path to tread.[87] If they got it wrong, they could find themselves hopelessly out of their depth. Physically intimidated, without any authority or backup, unable to deal effectively with misbehaviour and criticised by police, parents and teachers for being too lenient, being a 'soft policeman' was not an enviable task. Tasked with controlling and regulating behaviour, but without effective coercive means of enforcement, they could easily be seen as pushovers. Apart from refusing them admission, there was very little that they could concretely do to make troublemakers behave. Youth workers had to become more 'streetwise' in order to cope with the culture of the young people they were dealing with and to try and gain their respect. If, for the authorities, political reliability was an important prerequisite for working with youth, for those 'on the streets' the efficacy of a particular youth worker was intimately connected to his or her openness, directness and tolerance of alternative viewpoints.

As far as those in the gangs were concerned, youth clubs were much more attractive when it was cold and raining, when they could offer a warm, dry place in which they could be with others of a similar mind. 'They are mainly in search of space where they can go and be undisturbed after work. They openly express their desire to have nothing to do with the FDJ, but instead want to listen to their music and play *Skat* in their free time after work.'[88] The more 'streetwise' youth workers knew that nothing was more likely to send young people fleeing out of the door than 'sensible' activities or a lecture on the 'virtues of socialism'. Those at the cutting edge, working in the no-man's-land between the regime and the street, also knew that their authority over their young clientele was never more than fragile and that they were still highly prone to misrule. Deciding where to draw the boundaries was very demanding. If his or her regime was too strict or stuffy, then nobody would come. If they loosened up too much, then the kids would walk all over them and they would then be accused of complicity. It is not surprising that the authorities had so much difficulty in recruiting staff for the youth clubs who were both suitably able and 'politically qualified'.[89]

Conclusion

The SED had promised to be more pragmatic in its dealings with youth and had thereby raised hopes that tolerance and realism would prevail. Socialism should not just be about control, but also about understanding. But the continued emphasis placed on 'sensible' leisure activities (and fear of Western-inspired alternatives) prevented the SED leadership from genuinely seeking to address youthful desires. The SED continued to insist on providing young people with what it thought they should want rather than what they themselves actually enjoyed doing. Unfortunately, the period of experimentation and optimism, which began in 1955 and was given added momentum by Khrushchev's policy of de-Stalinisation, was brief. It was brought to an end within a year by the Hungarian Uprising in the autumn of 1956. Reform ideas began to re-emerge in 1960 with a Politbüro communiqué directed specifically at youth, but this was halted a year later on 13 August 1961 by the building of the wall.

Notes

1. ZIJ: 'Umfrage '69'. Unpublished MS (Leipzig, 1969), 16.
2. Ibid., 20, 84.
3. 'Besondere Vorkommnisse' (1960–62), BArch. SAPMO DY 24/3727.
4. Hermann Weber was at one time an eager FDJ member. Hermann Weber, 'Die Jugendpolitik der SED 1945 bis 1989. Forschungsfragen, Quellenlage und wissenschaftliche Erwartungen' in Helga Gotschlich (ed.), *'Links und links und Schritt gehalten …'. Die FDJ: Konzepte – Abläufe – Grenzen* (Berlin, 1994), 20–31.
5. Helga Gotschlich, 'Die Gründung der FDJ in der SBZ' in Helga Gotschlich, Katharina Lange and Edeltraud Schulze (eds), *Aber nicht im Gleichschritt. Zur Entstehung der Freien Deutschen Jugend* (Berlin, 1997), 25–38, 34; Gert Geißler and Ulrich Wiegmann, *Schule und Erziehung in der DDR. Studien und Dokumente* (Neuwied, Berlin, 1995), 199; Karl-Heinz Winstermann, '"Nie wieder Faschismus, nie wieder Krieg"' in Franz-Werner Kersting (ed.), *Jugend vor einer Welt in Trümmern* (Weinheim, 1998), 107–13.
6. Ulrich Mählert and Gerd-Rüdiger Stephan, *Blaue Hemden, rote Fahnen. Die Geschichte der Freien Deutschen Jugend* (Opladen, 1996), 48–49.
7. Zentralrat der FDJ (ed.), *Handbuch des FDJ-Gruppenleiters* (Berlin, 1956), 263ff.
8. 'Untersuchungen an 6 Oberschulen (9.9.1957)', BArch. DR2/781, 20.
9. Peter Hübner, 'Die FDJ als politische Organisation und sozialer Raum' in Gotschlich (ed.), *'Links und links'*, 58–69, 61.
10. Interviews with Hans-Peter D. and Wolfgang V. (1999).
11. 'Lage an den Oberschulen' (1963), StAL IVA-2/9.02/353, 156–57.

12. 'Informationsberichte an ZR der SED' (c. 1963), StAL FDJ 199 (Kiste Nr. 65).
13. 'Umfrage '69', 20.
14. Ibid., 63.
15. 'Entwurf für den Leitartikel des Oberbürgermeisters in die LVZ: Die Stadtverordneten beraten Probleme der Jugend' (c. February 1961), Leipzig Stadtarchiv, StV&RdSt, Nr. 2311, 78.
16. 'Die Aufgaben der weiteren Einschränkung von Jugendkriminalität und Rowdytum (ca.1960)', BArch. SAPMO, DY6/3937.
17. 'Umfrage '69', 19, 23, 90.
18. 'Argumente und Meinungen der FDJler zu den politischen Ereignissen' (1960–62), StAL, FDJ Bezirksleitung Leipzig, 82 (Kiste Nr. 79).
19. West German sociologist Helmut Schelsky referred to similar trends in creating a 'sceptical generation'. Helmut Schelsky, *Die skeptische Generation. Eine Soziologie der deutschen Jugend* (Cologne, 1957), 465–70.
20. 'Beitrag zur Intelligenz-Einschätzung' (11 December 1963), StAL, IV A-2/9.01/341, 106.
21. 'Die Aufgaben der weiteren Einschränkung ...'
22. 'Bericht über die Untersuchung zur politischen Massenarbeit unter der Jugend in den Wohngebieten der Städte Rostock, Jena und Merseburg (26 November 1955)', BArch. SAPMO DY30/JIV2/2J/161.
23. Ernst Wollweber, 'Aus Erinnerungen. Ein Porträt Walter Ulbrichts', *Beiträge zur Geschichte der Arbeiterbewegung* 3 (1990), 350–78, 377.
24. 'Protokolle der 25. Tagung des Zentralkomitees der SED' (24–27 October 1955), BArch. SAPMO IV2/1/152.
25. Ibid.
26. Ibid.
27. Alan McDougall, *Youth Politics in East Germany. The Free German Youth Movement 1946–1968* (Oxford, 2004), 75.
28. Ibid., 68ff.
29. 'Walter Ulbricht auf dem V. Parlament der FDJ in Erfurt: Die Jugend zu guten Patrioten erziehen!', *Junge Welt* (28 May 1955).
30. 'Protokolle der 25. Tagung'.
31. Ibid.
32. Ibid.
33. 'Diskussion um die Probleme der 13–16jährigen. Zusammenfassung einer Diskussion mit 30 Direktoren und stellv. Direktoren in Berlin-Weissensee' (14 April 1961), BArch. DR2/6956, 115.
34. Christine Bartram and Heinz-Hermann Krüger, 'Vom Backfisch zum Teenager – Mädchensozialisation in den 50er Jahren' in Heinz-Hermann Krüger (ed.), *'Die Elvis-Tolle, die hatte ich mir unauffällig wachsen lassen'. Lebensgeschichte und jugendliche Alltagskultur in den fünfziger Jahren* (Opladen, 1985), 84–101, 88–89.
35. Dietrich Mühlberg, 'Haute Couture für Alle? Über Mode und Kulturverständnis' in Dorothea Melis (ed.), *Sibylle. Modefotographie aus drei Jahrzehnten DDR* (Berlin, 1998), 8–19, 11.
36. Bartram and Krüger, 'Vom Backfisch zum Teenager', 92.
37. Erica Carter, 'Alice in Consumer Wonderland: West German Case Studies in Gender and Consumer Culture' in Angela McRobbie and Mica Nava (eds), *Gender and Generation* (London, Basingstoke, 1984), 185–214, 187.
38. Angela McRobbie, 'Settling Accounts with Subcultures: A Feminist Critique' in Angela McRobbie, *Feminism and Youth Culture* (Houndsmills, London, 2nd edn, 2000), 26–43, 39.
39. Brigitte Reimann, *Aber wir schaffen es, verlaß Dich drauf! Briefe an eine Freundin im Westen* (Berlin, 1995), 85–88. She nevertheless managed to outlive the shame and bodily injury caused by an illegal, self-administered abortion, and went on to enjoy a prodigious number of extramarital affairs before being cut short by cancer in 1973 at the age of forty.

40. Volker Ackermann, *Der 'echte' Flüchtling. Deutsche Vertriebene und Flüchtlinge aus der DDR 1945-1961* (Osnabrück, 1995), 238f.
41. Reimann, *Aber wir schaffen es*, 85f.
42. 'Heimliche Kontrolle', *Junge Welt* (7/8 January 1956).
43. Erica Carter, *How German is She? Postwar West German Reconstruction and the Consuming Woman* (Ann Arbor, 1997), 206.
44. *Bravo* 42 (1958) cited in Carter, 'Alice in Consumer Wonderland', 185, 203-4.
45. Bartram and Krüger, 'Vom Backfisch', 93.
46. Carter, 'Alice in Consumer Wonderland', 201.
47. Ibid., 213.
48. 'Die FDJ dankt Erich Honecker', *Junge Welt* (29 May 1955).
49. 'Siegrid Groß, Kreis Zittau: Auch Mädchen sollen ins Schwarz treffen', *Junge Welt* (28 May 1955).
50. Although Ulbricht's speech was made at the end of May, it took nearly three weeks for it to be printed. 'Antwort auf aktuelle Fragen der Jugend. Aus der Rede von Walter Ulbricht auf dem V. Parlament der FDJ am 26. Mai 1955. Aufklärungsarbeit unter der ganzen Jugend verbessern', *Junge Welt* (18/19 June 1955).
51. 'Darf der Lehrling eine Freundin haben?', *Junge Welt* (11/12 June 1955).
52. '"Darf der Lehrling eine Freundin haben?" Warum eigentlich nicht?', *Junge Welt* (17.6.1955).
53. 'Museum, Klubhaus oder Sitzungstempel?', *Junge Welt* (14 June 1955).
54. 'Ein Bürokrat erwischt!', *Junge Welt* (15 June 1955).
55. 'Heraus aus den Büros!', *Junge Welt* (16 June 1955).
56. 'Streifzug durch das III. Gesamtberliner Jugendforum', *Junge Welt* (2 March 1956).
57. *Junge Welt* (16/17 June 1956).
58. 'Ich habe meinen Freund verloren. Eifersucht hat schlimme Folgen. Wer hilft Irma?', *Junge Welt* (23/24 December 1955).
59. 'Wer verschmäht die Dame Perlon? Unsere Leser sagen ihre Meinung und fragen: Was sagt der Handel dazu?', *Junge Welt* (23 June 1955).
60. 'Wie zur Schule?', *Junge Welt* (23/24 December 1955).
61. 'Sind die Zöpfe daran schuld?', *Junge Welt* (17 January 1956).
62. 'Tanz – ohne Tyrannen', *Junge Welt* (11/12 August 1956); 'Sie schaden sich selbst. Wenn Mädchen nicht mit Jungen tanzen wollen', *Junge Welt* (7/8 April 1956).
63. 'Jungen und Mädchen in einem Zelt?', *Junge Welt* (25 May 1956); Rudolf Weise, 'Die Bedeutung des Kollektivs für die sexuelle Erziehung', *Das Aktuelle Traktat* (1956), 41-61.
64. 'Wenn Mädchen unter sich sind ... Ein Forum mit Hilde Benjamin', *Junge Welt* (25 May 1956).
65. 'Gedanken über Jugendliebe von Prof. Dr. Neubert, Jena', *Junge Welt* (2/3 June 1956). The editors of *Junge Welt* introduced Neubert's article with a picture of a girl in a two-piece swimsuit and the caption 'only half hidden by wild oats so that no boy tries to get saucy with you'.
66. 'An euch alle, die ihr jung seid! Zentralrat der FDJ wendet sich an die gesamte Jugend unserer Republik', *Junge Welt* (9 February 1956).
67. 'Jungen waren "ausgewiesen". Erstes Forum der FDJ und des FDJ für Mädchen in Frankenhausen', *Junge Welt* (17 May 1956).
68. Hans Marchwitza, *Roheisen* (Berlin, 1955).
69. Ibid., 78.
70. Ibid., 521.
71. Michael Mitterauer, *A History of Youth* (Oxford, 1992), 224; Wolfgang Müller, 'Jugendverbände und "offene Jugendarbeit"' in Gotschlich et al. (eds.), *Aber nicht im Gleichschritt*, 62-65.
72. Horst Brasch, 'Stenographisches Protokoll der Sitzung der Jugendkommissions des Nationalrates der Nationalen Front des Demokratischen Deutschland am 17. Juli 1959 im Hause des Zentralrats der FDJ', BArch. SAPMO DY6/3949, 20.

73. Ibid., 15.
74. Horst Groschopp, 'Herkommen, Struktur und Verständnis' in Hildegard Bockhorst, Brigitte Prautzsch and Carla Rimbach (eds), *Woher – Wohin? Kinder- und Jugendkulturarbeit in Ostdeutschland* (Remscheid, 1993), 14–30.
75. Ibid., 15.
76. Walter Ulbricht, 'Antwort auf aktuelle Fragen der Jugend', *Junge Welt* (18/19 June 1955).
77. Groschopp, 'Herkommen, Struktur und Verständnis', 16.
78. Hans Szewczyk, 'Zur Psychohygiene des Heranwachsenden. Vortrag gehalten auf der Tagung der Med.-wiss. Gesellschaft für Psychiatrie und Neurologie in Leipzig am 9. Juni 1960', *Zeitschrift für Psychiatrie, Neurologie und medizinische Psychologie* 2 (1961), 55–61, 58.
79. Ibid., 59.
80. Ibid.
81. 'Rowdytum' (c. 1960), StAL, BDVP 24/113, 87, 133.
82. Speech by Jugendfreund Klaus-Dieter Z., 'Protokoll über einen Erfahrungsaustausch über die Arbeit der Jugendklubs in der DDR' (1960), BArch. SAPMO DY24/6724.
83. Walter Ulbricht at the 25th Conference.
84. 'Jugendkriminalität' (1964–66), Landesarchiv Berlin, STA Rep. 303/26.1, Nr. 490, 51–52.
85. 'Aufstellung der negativen Konzentrationen Jugendlicher', Landesarchiv Berlin, STA Rep. 303/26.1, Nr. 483, 52–62.
86. 'Bericht über die Lage der Jugend im Bezirk (9.5.61)', StAL, RdB Volksbildung, 3723.
87. On the problems associated with 'soft policing', see Philip Cohen and David Robins, *Knuckle Sandwich. Growing Up in the Working-class City* (Harmondsworth, 1978), 120–124.
88. 'Analyse über die Lage und der Arbeit mit der Jugend in der Stadt Leipzig (15.2.1965)', StAL IVA-5/01/269, 88.
89. 'Informationsbericht (9.12.1965)', StAL IVA-5/01/269, 227–39.

◊ *Chapter 8* ◊

REMILITARISATION

Militarism is a belief system that is 'based on the assumption that military values and politics are conducive to a secure and orderly society'.[1] Militarism 'manifests the excesses of those characteristics generally referred to as machismo, a term that originally connoted the strength, bravery and responsibility necessary to fulfil male social functions'.[2] A society does not have to be at war to be militaristic. Factors like the extent to which political leaders have military backgrounds; the extent to which military uniforms are a persistent feature of public sphere; and the proportion of national resources that are devoted to military expenditure are just as important in determining whether a society is militaristic.[3] In the late 1940s, the militarism of the GDR stemmed largely from the military experiences of its leaders and the way in which war and struggle dominated their language and concepts for the transformation of society.[4] As Victor Klemperer argued, it was above all in the realm of language, idiom and imagery that the population's ability to comprehend, understand and perceive had been twisted and warped by National Socialism. Such was the pervasiveness of Nazi-influenced language that even victims and enemies could end up speaking it.[5]

Taking part in discussions organised by the FDJ in Dresden after the war, Klemperer was shocked to see how much youth continued to 'cling to Nazi thought processes. They do not realize they are doing it; the remnants of linguistic usage from the preceding epoch confuse and seduce them.' Most problematic were the notions of heroism that young people had received from their schooling. 'Even the girls were thoroughly infatuated with the most dubious notions of heroism.' Klemperer believed that it was 'impossible to have a proper grasp of the true nature of humanitarianism, culture and democracy if one endorsed this kind of conception, or to be more precise misconception, of heroism'. 'As soon as this concept was even touched upon, everything became blurred, and we were adrift once again in the fog of

Nazism.'⁶ And yet it was precisely this fog that the SED's hot air (with its emphasis on the verbal 'annihilation', 'destruction' and 'liquidation' of others) continued to contribute to.⁷

The state-socialist leap into the future was 'an integral part of the political strategy that entwined central direction with voluntarism, the notion that decisive action by an enlightened vanguard would rally the population behind the cause and cow the opposition'.⁸ The communists surrounding Ulbricht believed that they were overcoming and eradicating the historical and structural causes of fascism. But, although in its rhetoric the party leadership emphasised the importance of working-class unity, the reality was internal division and accusations of betrayal. The Stalinists in the GDR attempted to compensate for the fragility of their position with the violence of their language. 'We must bravely and fearlessly track down the enemy agencies and their nests, smash them and reveal them in front of the whole population as centres of enemy Anglo-American monopoly capital.'⁹ Ironically, Horst Sindermann, the man who in 1949 spoke these words, later had his masculinity called into question by the Party Control Commission (the ZPKK). In 1950, he was accused of having fallen apart and become soft during Nazi captivity.¹⁰ Johannes R. Becher was also accused of cowardice. Walter Janka repeated rumours that he tried to commit suicide after losing his nerve and running away from the front during the heroic defence of Stalingrad.¹¹

From 1948 onwards, the regime's anti-militarism became increasingly aggressive and one-sided. While condemning the West German government as a regime composed of warmongers and former Nazis, SED ideologues began emphasising the need to defend peace by force of arms. Hardliners sought to defend, maintain and utilise communist traditions of heroic sacrifice and struggle by creating paramilitary organisations. If their outward justification was to support and bolster the ideology and strength of the state, these organisations also offered an opportunity to preserve and maintain the ideal of tough and, if necessary, violent, proletarian masculinity. They looked to militarised voluntarism as the means to overcome the obstacles ranged against them. The headlong rush to establish a socialist state was marked by the dropping of pacifism in favour of remilitarisation – rearming of the police, the creation of a People's Army and the extension of military training.¹²

Under Honecker, the FDJ played a key role in this remilitarisation. The FDJ was given uniforms and encouraged to practise shooting. At its Fourth Parliament in Leipzig in May 1952, members put on 'decidedly militaristic displays'.¹³ From its initial position as a non-partisan anti-militarist youth organisation, the Free German Youth was transformed into a highly politicised and militarised subsidiary of the party. The military bearing was particularly intense during marching exercises before the First of May and later during the Hans-Beimler military sports competition.¹⁴ From once having been taught to oppose militarism, FDJ members were now encouraged to see violence as a useful tool in the development of socialism. In the face of Christian protests, the FDJ began to propagate violence as a legitimate solution to political problems. During the establishment of state-run department stores (the *Handelsorganisation* or HO), private proprietors were 'encouraged' to shut up shop by applying the pressure of militant, uniformed youth. Although such actions corresponded to the desire of young men to play at 'revolution', for many it was a reminder of the intimidation used by the SA.[15]

The uniforms and ideological training, Manfred Klein suggests, did prove 'psychologically effective' in creating and heightening divisions between 'us' and 'them'.[16] The opportunities for aggressive posturing offered by the attacks on the middle classes and symbolic purges of young Christians were capable of mobilising those in the FDJ who felt hostility towards their more privileged and respectable neighbours.[17] Nevertheless, even atheist workers felt uneasy at the sight of young men once again in uniforms carrying weapons.[18] As one cynical young man who had fled over the border put it, 'it's important not to underestimate the effect of the military apparatus on simple souls. He who goes in a lukewarm communist comes out a convinced SEDler ... The man in question can become an instructor for the firm's Fighting Group or receive some other function that demands little in the way of productive work.' In popular parlance, the National People's Army was a repository for all those born with two left hands and two left feet.[19]

A special paramilitary youth organisation, the Gesellschaft für Sport und Technik (GST), was created in August 1952. It provided members with exceptional opportunities for sport and physical recreation in preparation for future military training.[20] Although the GST also admitted girls, it remained a male-dominated club in which boys became familiar with weapons and military technology and gained experience in shooting and running over obstacle courses. In the summer of 1956 *The Banner* (a newspaper for GST members) produced a series of images of girls with guns. Contrary to expectations, it was reported that the best shot with an air rifle in Prenzlauer Berg was not 'big and strong ... and boyish'.[21] While the pictures emphasised that women could hit the target just as well as men, the captions told a different story, one in which female GST members were rated on their looks and partnership potential. In November 1956 a philosophy student and nubile co-ed from Humboldt University was celebrated for having won a silver medal in shooting. 'And if she also strikes men's hearts with a bull's eye, our reporter would not tell. But ... with such dreamy eyes.'[22] The focus on the shooter's prettiness was perhaps a response to the underlying fear that now that they had access to guns and the skills to use them young women might well turn them round on their male oppressors.[23]

Invoking the communist past allowed the SED leaders to capitalise on their status and experiences as party veterans. They drastically limited the 'political imaginary', keeping it 'encased in the era of coal and steel, armed revolution and hard-fought street battles'.[24] Solidarity and collective strength were seen as essential to the regime's survival and ultimate victory. The Red Front Fighters were held up as invincible warriors. 'What splendid blokes [*prächtige Kerle*] they were!'[25] Young East Germans were educated to know their enemies and to be prepared to use force to defend their state's interests. The communists even created their own rituals of blood, honour and sacrifice. By kissing the red flag (elsewhere described as having been soaked in the blood of fallen workers) young people engaged in a new form of transubstantiation, in which the spirit of antifascism was passed on from generation to generation.[26] According to Erich Honecker, 'The legacy of the heroes of the German working class ... their blood sacrifice in the peasant wars, in the revolutionary, armed struggles of 1848, 1918–23, 1933–45 is also sacred [*heilig*] for members of the German People's Police.'[27] The People's Policemen killed in the line of duty were added to the list of martyrs. Honouring their deaths (through continued service) represented a 'holy obligation' (*heilige Verpflichtung*) on the part of the living.[28] But this rhetorical emphasis on the power of blood as a source of communion and as a stimulus to vengeance unconsciously mirrored the rituals of the SA and the Hitler Youth.[29] Refusing to accept that the KPD was in any way to blame for Hitler's seizure of power, Honecker felt obliged to 'emphasise the historical truth: the KPD was the most determined opponent of Nazism. In the antifascist resistance the Communists always set a shining example, indomitable in the face of Nazi terror, faithful to their convictions unto death.'[30]

For adolescent males, war traditionally conjured up visions of peril and adventure. Believing that young men in the West were being systematically poisoned by means of Wild West novels and the *Landser* (a magazine glorifying Germany's military past), the SED sought to use hero literature and war films on its own youth in order to stimulate a desire to fight for socialism and the GDR. Their own books were little different in emphasising the importance of muscularity and the savage nobility of war.[31] Nevertheless journalists dismissed criticisms about the violence of such literature, arguing that what counted was not whether people were shot or killed but 'who shot and why'.[32] What was important was to link 'natural' aggression in the right direction. Every pupil was required to read *How the Steel was Hardened*.[33] It marked out the path for revolutionary young men to follow. It told the story of Pavel Kortschagin, a rough young man from a very modest Ukrainian working-class background. Set against the background of German occupation, revolution and civil war, it told the story of his development both as a young man and as a communist. It portrayed a violent and tough, but virtuous masculinity. Having been expelled from school, Pavel was forced to grow up quickly. As a kitchen skivvy in the local station restaurant, he received an education in mistreatment and physical violence. The experience made him tougher and harder like the steel in the book's title. Pavel went on to become a soldier and then a cavalryman in the Red Army. He endured dreadful hardships, but constantly stood out through his self-denial and self-sacrifice. The book contrasted the moral and physical superiority of Pavel's rough but virtuous masculinity with the refined cowardice of the 'mother's boy' son of his middle-class neighbours.

In recounting Pavel's experiences, the frequent dangers he faced and his heroism and loyalty in the face of adversity, the book acted as an adventure story for communist boys. What is most remarkable about the novel is the number of unconsciously homoerotic undertones it contains. Everything the revolutionaries struggle for is of grandiose dimensions, demands stiff discipline and unrelenting hardness. One quickly tires of the repeated references to workers' limbs, tools and other attributes being immensely '*kräftig*'. Given its role as an example to young people, it is surprising how prominent a role sexual violence plays in Pavel's story. Women repeatedly figure both as sex objects and as sexual victims. Pavel first experiences sexual exploitation while working as a bottle washer. The kitchen maids are forced by poverty to prostitute themselves to the waiters, who perversely earn more through tips than workers labouring in the factory. Witnessing the sullying of his dear Frossja acts as a rite of passage for Pavel and opens his eyes to the injustices of the world.[34] But, having used the device of non-consensual sex once to draw in the reader and emotionally attach him to Pavel, the writer goes on to use it again and again. There are subsequently no fewer than four incidents of gang rape in the book. In one particular incident, a young women who is about to be raped by the White Russians asks Pavel to take her in order to deprive them of her virginity. Pavel refuses and the girl goes to her fate with silent reproach in her eyes.[35]

Women only had a legitimate existence in the book as active comrades or passive victims. Female communist functionaries are all sexually attractive, but untouchable, wrapped up as they are in the work of the party. Any other position was considered indecent (spin-the-bottle parties) or decadent (his fur coat-wearing, cocaine-sniffing former neighbour). Pavel experiences true love with Tonja, an independent and self-confident young woman, but is forced to leave her because she is incapable of fully renouncing her bourgeois ways.[36] In the end, he marries a victim, a woman he feels sorry for. He encourages her to overcome her difficulties by embracing the party.[37] At the end of the novel, she is frequently away on official business while he is left at home alone, blind and crippled. This reverses the view of woman as passive, powerless and submissive. But it reinforces the importance of the male body. Even his wife is no longer interested in him when he has ceased to be a true man. His is a life spent for communism. The superhuman strength demanded by the party has wrecked his body, but he is happy to have been part of the project of the construction of socialism.

A long tradition of trade union defence of workers' welfare and rights, the opportunities made available to them by the Nazi 'Strength through Joy' movement and, not least, the open border with the West put limits on the degree to which East German workers were prepared to sacrifice themselves in pursuit of the communist leaders' pipe dreams. In the event, the 1953 uprising represented a failure of nerve on the part of the authorities and the defenders of socialism. In the weeks prior to 17 June, the police had been issued with orders to be less authoritarian in their dealings with the public. As a result, when confronted by a revolt by workers, many former proletarians in the police did not know how to react. Special measures had to be introduced in order to restore their 'fighting spirit'. Officers and men were confined to barracks and subjected to hours of Soviet propaganda films (*Steely Fighters, Far from Moscow, Red Banner, Storm over Asia*) interspersed with rousing choruses of *Kampflieder*.[38] In the aftermath of the uprising, the regime formed Fighting Groups of the Working Class to put down any future attempt at a 'fascist putsch'. The workplace-based paramilitary *Kampfgruppen* took over from the Red Front Fighters' League as 'visual representations of idealized revolutionaries as powerful men marching in disciplined formation'.[39] Trained in house-to-house street fighting, the aim was to create a repository of aggressive machismo that could absolutely be relied upon to put down any future unrest.[40] 'Our party has at its disposal, in the form of the Fighting Groups, an army of well-armed, trained fighters, who are ready at any time to eliminate anyone who dares to raise his hand against the Workers' and Peasants' State.'[41]

If the socialist heroes did enjoy some success in the early years, their impact was weakened by symbolic over-representation. While the party continued to emphasise quantity over quality, they were increasingly challenged and undermined by competition from the heroic figures created by capitalist popular culture. From comic book characters like Tarzan and Superman to the inarticulate cowboys of Westerns and suave spies like James Bond, the West bombarded East German youth with its own visions of heroism. The SED tried to present masculine youth as being involved in a great challenge. 'The new socialist epoch demands fearless pioneering achievements of youth, an even greater pioneering spirit than that demanded by the discovery of America.'[42] But the narrowness of life in the closed-in GDR was no match for the wide open frontier. With an image of heroic manhood that was 'toxic, seductive, impure', real Westerns solicited the 'addictive identification' of working-class youth.[43] It was very difficult for the GDR's heroic propaganda, with its heavy bathos, to compete with films like *The Magnificent Seven*.[44] Starring Horst Buchholz, 'Germany's James Dean', who had started out playing a delinquent in the West German film *Die Halbstarken*, the film had a major impact on the imagination of East German youth.[45] 'What impress young people the most are the composure, the casualness, the adventurousness and the expert shooting of the "heroes" together with the outstanding abilities of the actors. Those who watch it hardly realise that the intended effect of the film is to prepare youth for acts of violence and war.'[46]

SED propagandists condemned West Germany's (re)introduction of conscription in 1956 as an aggressive act by a warmongering state and offered those who wanted to refuse military service asylum in the GDR.[47] Nevertheless, regime leaders demanded that 'their' young men 'voluntarily' sign up for service in the National People's Army, which was also founded in 1956.[48] Military service was an enormous imposition on individual freedom and caused great disruption to careers and relationships. As a result, it was fiercely resented and acted as a major cause of *Republikflucht* among young men.[49] Throughout East German society, but particularly in education, the military took an increasingly important role. Everywhere – on facades, in posters, as statues, in films, books and newsprint – revolutionaries were depicted as 'physically powerful men marching in disciplined formation'. Aesthetically, there was little to separate them from the heroic figures of the Third Reich.[50] At times, military training was specifically cited as a way of converting former Nazis to socialism. In 1960, an FDJ leader from Erfurt described how his group had managed to win a young man for socialism by making him leader of the shooting circle. At first he had said, 'My father was a Nazi and you communist swine must be hanged.' But he was an expert at shooting and went every day to shoot water rats at the river. 'I said to him, "What do you think about leading the group? You've got a good eye and can handle a gun." The lad now runs the circle and in a very orderly fashion too.'[51]

Crossovers between the two regimes emerged in other ways too. A report to the Politbüro from September 1957 stated, 'We remember that in 1939 the Communist Party of Germany presented the national standpoint before the whole world and, in the *German People's Newspaper*, [we] condemned most strongly the Anglo-American plans for the division of Germany. Our party and our government are representatives and defenders of the best national traditions of the German people.'[52] In 1959 Willi Stoph, the Minister for Defence, was promoted to the rank of General for his role in helping to form the National People's Army. In 1960 Stoph was forced to resign because an article he had written for his regimental newspaper, while a lieutenant in the *Wehrmacht*, was republished in West Germany. The article stated that taking part in a parade on Hitler's birthday had been 'the greatest experience' of his life.[53] As far as the SED was concerned, what rendered the GDR's military unambiguous and beyond reproach was the fact that it was led by antifascists.

Although those who had been involved in the desperate struggle against fascism became objects of admiration, their experiences of repression and struggle had often left them with violent, explosive tempers. Not only were they 'hard as iron', but they were also often vengeful, intolerant and punitive.[54] The lessons they had learned from their suffering were not about tolerance, but about the importance of maintaining power, keeping others in check and always ensuring their own self-preservation.[55] A jarring contradiction persisted between the SED leadership's support for more modern, youthful and women-friendly aspects of socialism and its continued emphasis on old-fashioned, reactionary-militarist rhetoric. Brigitte Reimann recorded in her diary her shock and feelings of utter defenceless when confronted by the local head of the Stasi, 'this loud, coarse, brutal, shouting, military anachronism [*Landesknecht*]'.[56]

Violence was seen by some in the SED as a natural expression of working-class male identity. But it had to be officially directed, channelled and controlled in order to serve the interests of the state. Brute force and intimidation were frequently encouraged as means for dealing with problem youth. Thus youth club leaders were admonished for shying away from 'talking with their fists', with the comment that 'a punch in the face isn't good, but we shouldn't shrink from it'.[57] During their clashes with the rockers People's Policemen could feel justly proud of themselves for putting gang members in hospital.[58] The police had even called on the services of the national wrestling team (which was fortuitously based at the National Sports Academy in Leipzig) to sort out the gangs. To institutionalise the capacity for violence and to use it against adolescents who failed to conform, the SED created 'order groups' (*Ordnungsgruppen*) in 1959.[59] Specially introduced to combat the gang problem, the order groups essentially constituted the paramilitary wing of the FDJ. Their mission was to police official youth functions (from parades to discotheques) and to bring the fight for conformity to the street, using brute force as the means to quell unruliness by the gangs. The regime was prepared to sanction the use of overt intimidation, humiliation and violence against young people who visibly deviated from party-imposed norms.

Overall, it was proposed to create 4,000 new order groups with a total membership of 30,000 'to tackle the persistence of capitalist immorality among young people'. 'They smash provocateurs and carry out the fight against rowdies, criminal elements, speculators, hoarders and the influence of the class enemy (listening to Western senders, reading of "Dirt and Shame" literature, etc.). They ensure that work-shy elements, do-nothings and parasites engage in steady, honest work and revise their thinking.'[60] Would-be recruits, meanwhile, compared the order groups with the *Volkssturm* (the adolescents sent into battle by Hitler as the Red Army advanced on Berlin).[61] Members of the order groups were to receive special training for their 'fight against provocateurs, rowdies and other hostile influences'.[62] Contact sports and martial arts were seen as particularly useful in increasing 'their political vigilance and combat-readiness'. As 'helpers of the state and security organs of the GDR', the order groups had the task of maintaining 'internal order and security'. For many, however, the order groups were little more than 'organised FDJ gangs'.[63] The response to the call for members was not as enthusiastic as the regime hoped. Prospective members did not fancy their chances without weapons or, at the very least, truncheons. As one young man put it, 'we're not going to let ourselves be beaten up by rowdies'.[64]

From the start, the 'provisions for the creation of order groups' overtly foresaw a gender-specific division of their functions. 'The girls in the order groups see their specific task as being to ensure that order and hygiene as well as a better sales culture exist in shops and pubs, as well as unmasking traffickers, hoarders and speculators. They talk to fiancées and mothers about the winning of young people [i.e. young males] for the armed forces.'[65] The East German media persistently presented the message that, when their men were away performing their duty in defending the state, the role of women was to support them. A photograph published in *Junge Welt* in 1955 showed one heroic young man marching forward with a machine gun. His girlfriend followed one step behind holding a bunch of flowers.[66] Wives and mothers were routinely praised if they 'selflessly and faithfully stood by their husbands and sons while they carried out their difficult service'.[67] Under the rubric 'Wife and Family', *Armee Rundschau* encouraged women to stand by their men. 'I will always be helpful to my husband. One must take responsibility for the other.'[68] Officers' wives were not only encouraged to bring up their families alone in spite of their husbands' frequent absences, but to go out to work.[69] The figure of the sexually frustrated, but self-sacrificing army wife (widowed by her husband's single-minded love for and duty to the military life) became a recognisable character in novels produced by the East German military's own publishing house.[70]

The authorities tolerated and even tacitly encouraged a culture of machismo within the armed forces as long as it was state-supportive. While in society and in production men had at least to pay lip service to gender equality, in the locker-room atmosphere of the police and the armed forces men could be men without fear of contradiction. Machismo was allowed to flourish in such an environment because it served the higher purpose of defending the state. The attitudes and behaviour that so offended SED functionaries when exhibited by rockers were permitted and even encouraged. Hence images of naked women, which were seen as corrupting for ordinary citizens, were deemed acceptable and even beneficial for soldiers.[71] During the late 1950s, women generally appeared clothed in *Armee Rundschau*, but with captions referring to their potential as sexual partners or their 'friendly little breasts'.[72] The cover of the September 1959 issue depicted a pair of National People's Army (NVA) soldiers with their bikini-clad girlfriends at the beach and their uniforms piled up neatly alongside.[73] Editorial attempts to improve soldiers' manners – notably in relation to their 'importunate' behaviour towards girls and their attempts 'to play the muscleman' (*Kraftmeierei*) – sat alongside pictures of pretty girls with risqué captions.[74] One cartoon showed a soldier climbing a ladder to a waiting girl's bedroom. The caption read 'On holiday: preparing for lights out'.[75] Although the military hierarchy was keen to avoid its soldiers committing rape on leave, when incidents occurred in which civilians were harassed and beaten up by groups of drunken off-duty soldiers or transport policemen, they were hushed up.[76] Investigators discovered that even at the FDJ's elite training school, the *Jugendhochschule Wilhelm Pieck*, life was dominated by a '*Landserton*' (squad-room atmosphere). Such attitudes were supposed to belong to the past. But they continued to cause fights between young men, together with the sexual harassment of female trainees.[77]

The German communists never tired of emphasising that theirs was a culture imbued with humanism, which represented all that was progressive in their nation's history. But in the GDR the communists repeatedly made a virtue of their disregard for the suffering of others. Tolerance and understanding appeared hopelessly weak and inconsistent (in other words, helplessly female).[78] Erich Mielke set the tone by arguing that he would rather have a Stasi officer who knew how to 'eradicate the enemy' ('*seine Feind zu vernichten*') than one who knew how to read and write.[79] At times it was as if the veterans were itching for an opportunity to prove their toughness. With no warfare to act as a release for pent-up aggression, they prized the ruthless determination of their soldiers at the border. The border became the one place where East German men could act out frontier masculinity without contradiction. The regime's leaders repeatedly defended and praised the shooting dead of would-be escapers like Peter Fechter.[80] Newspapers like *Visier* and *Der Kämpfer* encouraged servants of the state to be resolute and unflinching in the way in which they dealt with enemies of the state.

Conclusion

Although they talked constantly about fascism, the German communists failed to see that it was connected to masculinity. Communist attempts to foster support and willingness to defend the GDR led them to foster the same masculine ideals and values as those cherished by previous German regimes, not least the Nazis.[81] They sought to use masculinity to generate hegemony. Boys continued to learn that 'traits such as strength, competitiveness, inexpressiveness and aggressiveness' were expected of them as males.[82] Literature and propaganda portrayed images of an idealised masculinity based on strength, courage and willingness to defend socialism. The SED diagnosed the causes of fascism as being social and economic. But it failed to realise (or chose to ignore) the extent to which the notions of gender ascribed to men and women had also played a role in Nazi hegemony.[83] The communists condemned the 'monopolists and militarists' in West Germany for failing to remove corporal punishment (and with it the fascist spirit) from schools. But, in creating paramilitary organisations and emphasising physical confrontation as a means of resolving disputes, they kept alive '*die alten Prügelmethoden*' in their own state.[84] Some of those who became policemen and army officers in the GDR had proved themselves through opposition to the Third Reich. The tragedy of these men was that they were unable to overcome the emotional traumas of the Nazi period. As a result, antifascism served to legitimate a multitude of sins, including militarism, violence and inhumanity to groups classed as other. The state's need to make macho displays of force in order to restore its drooping authority led people to make comparisons between it and the Third Reich.

Notes

1. Betty Reardon, *Sexism and the War System* (New York, 1985), 14.
2. Ibid., 15.
3. David Morgan, 'Theater of War. Combat, the Military, and Masculinities' in Harry Brod and Michael Kaufman (eds), *Theorizing Masculinities* (Thousand Oaks, London, New Delhi, 1994), 165–82.
4. Eric Weitz, *Creating German Communism 1890–1990. From Popular Protests to Socialist State* (Princeton, 1997), 370, 379.
5. Victor Klemperer, *The Language of the Third Reich*, trans. Martin Brady (London, New York, 2000), 20.
6. Ibid., 2.
7. For examples of this kind of language, see Volker Koop, *'Den Gegner vernichten'. Die Grenzsicherung der DDR* (Bonn, 1996); Erich Honecker on the 'Liquidierung der Jungen Gemeinde' (April 1953), BArch. SAPMO DY24/II.895.
8. Weitz, *Creating German Communism*, 367.
9. 'Horst Sindermann Referat (Leipzig, 1.12.1949)', StAL, IV-5/01/003.
10. Catherine Epstein, *The Last Revolutionaries. German Communists and their Century* (Cambridge, MA, London, 2003), 148.
11. Walter Janka, *Schwierigkeiten mit der Wahrheit* (Berlin, Weimar, 1990), 175.
12. Weitz, *Creating German Communism*, 365–66.
13. Corey Ross, 'Protecting the Accomplishments of Socialism? The (Re)militarisation of Life in the German Democratic Republic' in Patrick Major and Jonathan Osmond (eds), *Workers' and Peasants' State. Communism and Society in East Germany under Ulbricht 1945–1971* (Manchester, New York, 2002), 78–93, 83.
14. Jürgen Fuchs and Gerhard Heike, *Dummgeschult? Ein Schüler und sein Lehrer* (Berlin, 1992), 27; Elfie Rembold, '"Dem Eindringen westlicher Dekadenz ist entgegenzuwirken". Jugend und die Kultur des Feindes in der DDR' in Jan Behrends, Thomas Lindenberger and Patrice Poutrus (eds), *Fremd-Sein in der DDR. Zu historischen Ursachen der Fremdenfeindlichkeit in Ostdeutschland* (Berlin, 2003), 167–88.
15. Manfred Klein, *Jugend zwischen den Diktaturen 1945–1956* (Mainz, 1968), 67.
16. Ibid., 79.
17. 'Stimmung und Argumentation zum Kommunique des Politbüros' (15 June 1953), BArch SAPMO, DY24/2301.
18. Frederik Hetmann, *Enteignete Jahre. Junge Leute berichten von drüben* (Munich, 1961), 32.
19. Ibid., 66–67
20. Paul Heider, *Die Gesellschaft für Sport und Technik* (Berlin, 2002).
21. *Das Banner* (11–24 July 1956).
22. 'Verträumte Augen und doch einen scharfen Blick', *Das Banner* (14–27 November 1956).
23. The combination of sexy girls, guns and dodgy captions could still be found as a dominant theme of *Konkret* (the other GST publication) ten years later. See, for example, *Konkret*, April, May 1965, September 1966.

24. Weitz, *Creating German Communism*, 368.
25. Max Zimmering, *Buttje Peter und sein Held* (Berlin, 1951), 159–60.
26. For examples of such flag-kissing rituals, see *Kinder, Kader, Kommandeure*, directed by Wolfgang Kissel and C. Cay Wesnigk (1992); for the flag as an unbroken link between the dead heroes of yesteryear and the modern fighters of today, see Erich Honecker, 'Bereit zur Verteidigung unserer Errungenschaften', *Der Kämpfer* 1 (1957), BArch. SAPMO DY30/2513.
27. 'Erich Honecker: Zum 15. Jahrestag der Gründung der Deutschen Volkspolizei (5.6.1965)', BArch. SAPMO DY30/2512.
28. 'Erich Honecker: Zum 20. Jahrestag der Deutschen Volkspolizei (17.9.1960)', BArch. SAPMO DY30/2512.
29. Alf Lüdtke argues that this mirroring was mutual, with the Nazis appropriating the colour red from the labour movement. Alf Lüdtke, 'The Appeal of Exterminating "Others": German Workers and the Limits of Resistance', *Journal of Modern History* 64 (December 1992), 46–67, 57.
30. Erich Honecker, *From My Life* (Oxford, New York, 1981), 34.
31. Jürgen Fuchs, *Fassonschnitt* (Reinbek, 1984), 278; Günter de Bruyn, *Vierzig Jahre* (Frankfurt am Main, 1996), 15, 75.
32. 'Helfen nur Verbote? Die Berliner Zeitung diskutierte mit ihren Lesern über Jugendliteratur', *Junge Welt* (10 April 1956).
33. Nikolai Ostrowskij, *Wie der Stahl gehärtet wurde* (Berlin, 1947); for a subversively homoerotic interpretation of this novel, see Olaf Brühl, 'Arschficker oder Arschkriecher? Kleines schwules Glossar eines Außenseiters' in Günter Grau (ed.), *Schwulsein 2000: Perspektiven im vereinigten Deutschland* (Hamburg, 2001), 163–206, 196.
34. Ostrowskij, *Wie der Stahl gehärtet wurde*, 22.
35. Ibid., 122. In addition to the prison incident, there are depictions of rapes occurring during the White Russian pogrom (90–91); attempted gang rape by members of a red patrol (181); and the brutal rapes of Walja and Rosa prior to execution (190–92). Elsewhere in the book, a Komsomol functionary, Raswalichin, tries to rape his fellow functionary Lida (345) and a young teacher is tricked into losing her virginity by a cad commissar (401).
36. Ibid., 208.
37. Ibid., 437.
38. 'Konterrevolutionärer Putschversuch 17.6.1953', StAL, BDVP 24/42, 126.
39. Weitz, *Creating German Communism*, 370.
40. Hauptverwaltung Deutsche Volkspolizei, *Programm für die Ausbildung der Kampfgruppen* (Berlin, 1955); Hauptverwaltung Deutsche Volkspolizei, *Programm für die Breitenausbildung der Deutschen Volkspolizei und für die Ausbildung der Kampfgruppen im Jahre 1957. Nur für den Dienstgebrauch!* (Berlin, 1956).
41. 'Redemanuskript von Erich Honecker auf einer Parteiversammlung in Berlin-Köpernick am 29. Nov. 1957', BArch. SAPMO DY30/2183.
42. 'Der Jugend Vertrauen und Verantwortung' in Zentralkomitee der SED, *Jugend von heute. Hausherren von Morgen. Kommuniqué des Politbüros des ZK der SED zu Problemen der Jugend in der DDR* (Berlin, 1963), 1–34, 11.
43. Suzanne Clark, *Cold Warriors. Manliness on Trial in the Rhetoric of the West* (Carbondale, Edwardsville, 2000), 91.
44. *The Magnificent Seven*, directed by John Sturges (USA, 1960).
45. *Die Halbstarken*, directed by Georg Tressler (BRD, 1956).
46. 'Beitrag zur Intelligenz-Einschätzung' (11.12.1963), StAL, IV A-2/9.01/341, 107.
47. Helmut Bohn, *Armee gegen die Freiheit. Ideologie und Aufrüstung in der Sowjetzone* (Cologne, 1956), 133; Committee for German Unity, *West Germany Prepares War of Revenge. Facts on the Rebirth of German Militarism in the Bonn State* (Berlin, 1954); Josef Schwarzer (ed.), *Deutsche Kriegsbrandstifter wieder am Werk. Eine Dokumentation über die Militarisierung Westdeutschlands* (Berlin, 1959).

48. 'Jugendliche fordern Schaffung einer Volksarmee. Schutz unserer Errungenschaften oberstes Gesetz', *Junge Welt* (17 January 1956); 'Wir gehen zur Volksarmee. Jugendliche stimmen dem Beschluß der Volkskammer zu', *Junge Welt* (20 January 1956); Torsten Diedrich and Rüdiger Wenzke, *Die getarnte Armee. Geschichte der kasernierten Volkspolizei der DDR 1952 bis 1956* (Berlin, 2001); Andrew Bickford, 'Command Performance: Militarization, Masculinity and the State in the GDR and Post-unification Germany' (Rutgers University: Ph.D. Thesis, 2002), 25ff.
49. Corey Ross, *Constructing Socialism at the Grass-Roots* (Manchester, 2000), 77; Günther Glaser, '"Niemand von uns wollte wieder eine Uniform anziehen ..." Konflikte in der kasernierten Volkspolizei 1948–1952' in Evemarie Badstübner (ed.), *Befremdlich Anders. Leben in der DDR* (Berlin, 2000), 312–48.
50. Fuchs, *Fassonschnitt*, 185.
51. 'Erfahrungsaustausch über die Arbeit der Jugendklubs in der DDR' (1960), BArch. SAPMO DY24/6724.
52. 'Vorschläge zur Lösung des Problems "Grenzgänger"'.Politbüro des ZK der SED (Protokolle), Sitzung, 10 September 1957. Protokoll Nr. 38/57, BArch. SAPMO DY30/JIV2/2/558. In the spring of 1940 an article had appeared in a KPD-controlled exile newspaper in London under the name of Walter Ulbricht. It claimed that Britain's aggression against Nazi Germany was evidence that it constituted 'the most reactionary power in the world'. Kurt Hiller, *Rote Ritter* (Berlin, 1980), 108.
53. Reinhold Andert and Wolfgang Herzberg, *Der Sturz. Erich Honecker im Kreuzverhör* (Berlin, Weimar, 1990), 265. For examples of other leading military figures in the GDR with *Wehrmacht* and even Condor Legion pasts, see Hans Ehlert and Armin Wagner (eds), *Genosse General. Die Militärelite der DDR in biografischen Skizzen* (Berlin, 2003); Josie McLellan, *Antifascism and Memory in East Germany. Remembering the International Brigades 1945–1989* (Oxford, 2004), 52.
54. Willi Hellmann, *Mein erstes Leben. Ein General der VP erinnert sich* (Berlin, 2001), 57–58.
55. Lutz Niethammer, *Der 'gesäuberte' Antifaschismus. Die SED und die roten Kapos von Buchenwald* (Berlin, 1994), 90f.; Jorge Semprún, *What a Beautiful Sunday!*, trans. Alan Sheridan (London, 1984).
56. Brigitte Reimann, *Ich bedaure nichts: Tagebücher 1955–1963* (Berlin, 2000), 110.
57. 'Protokoll des Berichtes über die Arbeit im Klubhaus Erich Zeigner am 18.9.1953 (3.2.1954)', StAL IV5/01/483.
58. 'BDVP: Bericht über die Presley und 42er Bande (10.12.1958)', StAL BDVP 24/113, 90.
59. Michael Walter, *Die Freie Deutsche Jugend. Ihre Funktionen im politischen System der DDR* (Freiburg, 1997), 151–59; Arnold Freiburg and Christa Mahrad, *FDJ. Der sozialistische Jugendverband der DDR* (Opladen, 1982), 242–48.
60. 'Beschluß über die Ordnungsgruppen der FDJ vom 22. August 1961', BArch. SAPMO, DY 24/3753-1.
61. 'Dienstreise nach Hohenstein' (October 1964), BArch. Berlin DR2/6840, 32.
62. 'Amt für Jugendfragen Protokoll (13.9.1961)', BArch. SAPMO DY6/3937; 'Zusammenarbeit mit der FDJ' (20.6.1959), StAL, BDVP 24/113, 97–98.
63. 'Einsatz an den erw. Oberschulen (19.10.1961)', BArch. DR2/6298, 84.
64. 'Durchführung des Beschlusses des Sekretariats der Bezirksleitung "Zu einigen Fragen der Jugendarbeit und dem Auftreten der Rowdygruppen" vom 13.10.1965', StAL IVA-5/01/269, 226.
65. 'Beschluß über die Ordnungsgruppen der FDJ vom 22. August 1961'.
66. 'Wir schützen unsere Republik', *Junge Welt* (1 May 1955).
67. 'Erich Honecker: Zum 20. Jahrestag der Gründung der Deutschen Volkspolizei (5.6.1965)', BArch. SAPMO DY30/2512; Erich Honecker, 'Erhöht die Bereitschaft zur Arbeit und zur Verteidigung der Heimat', *Junge Welt* (21 April 1955); variations on the phrase 'He stands by his man there and I try to do it here' appeared frequently in the 1950s and 1960s. For example, 'Zeit zwischen den Stühlen', *Neues Leben* 3–4 (1969).

68. *Armee Rundschau*, September 1959.
69. *Armee Rundschau*, March, April 1958.
70. Heinz Kruschel, *Der rote Antares* (Berlin, 1979); Walter Flegel, *Der Regimentskommandeur* (Berlin, 1973).
71. Christine Eifler, '"… es schützt Dich mein Gewehr". Frauenbildern in der NVA Propaganda' in Zentrum für Interdisziplinäre Frauenforschung der Humboldt-Universität zu Berlin (ed.), *Unter Hammer und Zirkel: Frauenbiographien vor dem Hintergrund ostdeutscher Sozialisationserfahrungen* (Pfaffenweiler, 1995), 269–76; Christine Eifler, '"Ewig unreif". Geschlechtsrollenklischees in der Armeerundschau' in Simone Barck, Martina Langermann and Siegfried Lokatis (eds), *Zwischen 'Mosaik' und 'Einheit'. Zeitschriften in der DDR* (Berlin, 1999), 180–88.
72. *Armee Rundschau*, September 1957. In 1960, the magazine printed pin-ups from around the Eastern bloc.
73. *Armee Rundschau*, September 1959.
74. *Armee Rundschau*, April 1958.
75. *Armee Rundschau*, March 1958.
76. 'Wenn Du Ausgang hast', *Armee Rundschau* 1 (1956) warned that attempts to prove what 'big men' they were could easily lead soldiers to catch venereal disease or to commit sexual crimes.
77. 'Erziehungsarbeit an der Jugendhochschule "Wilhelm Pieck" (May/June 1961)', BArch. SAPMO DY 24/ 3844; 'Randalierende Jugendliche in der Innenstadt (Leipzig, 4.9.1961)', StAL, BDVP 24.1/420.
78. Eifler, "Ewig Unreif", 187; 'Zur Lage an der erweiterten Oberschulen' (October 1961), BArch. DR2/6298, 75.
79. 'Erich Mielke über die Anforderungen an MfS-Mitarbeiter, 1953' cited in Jens Gieseke, *Die DDR-Staatssicherheit. Schild und Schwert der Partei* (Bonn, 2000), 20.
80. Werner Sikorski and Rainer Laabs, *Checkpoint Charlie und die Mauer. Ein geteiltes Volk wehrt sich* (Berlin, 1997), 58–62.
81. George Mosse, *The Image of Man. The Creation of Modern Masculinity* (New York, Oxford, 1996), 182.
82. Theodore Cohen, 'Making Men out of them: Male Socialization in Childhood and Adolescence' in Theodore Cohen (ed.) *Men and Masculinity. A Text Reader* (Belmont, 2000), 53–60.
83. Alfons Kenkmann, *Wilde Jugend. Lebenswelt großstädtischer Jugendlicher zwischen Weltwirtschaftskrise, Nationalsozialismus und Währungsreform* (Essen, 1996), 256.
84. The *'alten Prügelmethoden'* refers to the canings, whippings and beatings teachers used to administer as punishments for misbehaviour. 'Argumentation zu Verleumdungen des Schulgesetzes und der Schulordnung durch einige reaktionäre Kirchenkreise' (c. 1959), BArch. DY6/3939.

~ Chapter 9 ~

ROCK 'N' ROLL

Rock 'n' roll was an international phenomenon that transformed expressions of masculinity and femininity throughout Europe.[1] The rocker scene was 'downright macho', but it was a 'modernised form of machismo'.[2] It constituted a rejection of the military ideal, in which boys were expected to dress smartly and to behave in a controlled manly fashion. The new stress on casualness contrasted sharply with the stiff, uniformed masculinity of yesteryear and was marked by an aversion to all that was formal and in uniform. What had once been held up as dashing, smart and brisk (*zackige*) was now dismissed in favour of casualness, which to the younger generation denoted not just a style, but a sense of self-confidence and worldly superiority. Instead of standing stiff and straight, the rockers slouched and scowled, hands in their pockets. Some working-class jazz fans (notably the *Schlurfs* of Vienna) had gone casual during the war.[3] The Anglo-American invasion and occupation of the western half of Germany resulted in a generalisation and legitimisation of casualness among a wide cross-section of German youth. Casual did not denote non-aggressive. Like the working-class culture from which it emerged, rocker culture was decidedly confrontational.[4] 'In the forefront was not a devaluation of physical strength, aggressiveness and violent achievement of interests but dissociation from the military (uniforms, subordination, ordering within an authoritarian system) and from the soldierly-military as the quintessence of masculinity.'[5]

The presence of several hundred thousand American GIs stationed in West Germany (including in 1958 Elvis Presley himself) was a major factor in making rock 'n' roll available to and popular among German youth. With rock 'n' roll, young working-class men staked their own claim to masculinity. The advent of cheap transistor radios transformed young people's lifestyles and experiences by giving them the ability to listen to music collectively whenever and wherever they wanted.[6] Not only did they provide a potent symbol of rebellion, but they also offered a simple and straightforward means of contradicting and disproving the regime's messages and claims. The first transistors or 'box radios' (*Kofferradios*) began to appear under young workers' arms on street corners in 1959.[7]

In the West, the rockers' ambivalent, ambiguous pursuit of sex and beauty, attention and violence led to them being named *Halbstarken* (literally meaning 'half as strong'). The term referred back to groups of youth that had existed at the turn of the century and which had shocked adult authorities with their own precocious desire to act like men.[8] At first, the communists looked on with unconcealed glee as the rockers rioted in West Berlin. *Junge Welt* condemned an 'unprovoked' assault by the police, armed with truncheons, on an 'orderly' and 'disciplined' group of youths who were doing nothing more than standing around peacefully on the street. The newspaper poured scorn on claims in the Western press that such 'depraved youths' needed to undertake military service in order to be educated as 'orderly citizens'.[9] The *Schadenfreude* soon evaporated when young men in their own republic began exhibiting similar behaviour. Nevertheless, SED commentators consciously strove to avoid using the term *Halbstarken* ('we ought to remove it from our vocabulary') and chose instead to label the new forms of rebelliousness with the English derivative *Rowdytum*.[10] This label emphasised that they were new and entirely alien phenomena rather than extensions of earlier traditions of working-class youth nonconformity. 'You won't ever have heard the word "*Halbstarke*" (which is customary in West Germany) from us, the leading comrades of the party and state. We don't recognise this word. We don't know any young people with such a character. We only know young people.'[11]

Racialisation

Not only was the music imported from abroad, but it was also infectious. 'With the music you were contaminated. Those were the phrases they used.'[12] Behind this notion of music being infectious lay racial and sexual stereotypes. Teenagers embraced the Afro-American elements in rock 'n' roll that their parents and elders found strange and shocking.[13] Throughout Europe, adult authorities dismissed rock 'n' roll as being primitive largely because of its origins in the black ghettos. Thus Sir Malcolm Sargent in *The Times* referred to the music as 'an exhibition of primitive tom-tom-thumping … There is nothing new or wonderful about the music. Rock 'n' roll has been played in the jungle for centuries.'[14] In the GDR too, political leaders sought to capitalize on criticisms of rock 'n' roll as a debasement of culture. After a Bill Haley concert in West Berlin ended in a riot, *Neues Deutschland* reported that 'On Sunday evening in the Sports stadium in West Berlin, the dehumanising effect of an anti-music was demonstrated … In a land that produced Bach and Beethoven, today young people are transformed into violent beasts with the help of "music".[15] Another article was headlined 'Orgy of American Non-culture'.[16] The East German authorities firmly believed that young people who were exposed to 'hot' music were at risk of becoming overly sexually charged. In their eyes, the 'inflaming rhythm' of rock 'n' roll stimulated dancers to gyrate their bodies in 'wild contortions' at great risk to their health and morals.[17]

Rock 'n' roll served as a political football and as a means for the SED to try and win influence in the West. Bill Haley's October 1958 tour coincided with elections in West Berlin. *Neues Deutschland* declared the SED as 'the only real way out for West Berlin youth', promising to 'free them from the poison of Western unculture' and loudly declaring 'Ami, go home!'[18] Three years later, in a speech justifying the building of the Berlin Wall, Walter Ulbricht tried to play down the extreme nature of the decision to seal the border, cutting East Germans off from their friends and relations in the West, saying 'a lot less happened than during an average rock 'n' roll concert in the sports stadium in West Berlin'. He went on to say that the GDR would not make the same mistake as the Social Democrats had in 1933 when they surrendered the capital to the Nazis, even though they controlled a police force of over 100,000 men.[19] It seems strange that Ulbricht should, almost in the same breath, link such apparently disconnected events as the Bill Haley concert of 1958 and the Nazi seizure of power of 1933 to justify the decision to imprison the entire East German population. But to Ulbricht there was no contradiction. The Social Democrats had failed to act when the brown shirts and swastikas of the Nazis had stared them in the face. The cold war, in

Figure 1. Wild and uninhibited dancing to rock 'n' roll. Still from *Die Glatzkopfbande*.

contrast, was a war that was fought by subterfuge and sleight of hand. Though more subtle and refined, the methods used by the class enemy were no less dangerous. Socialism had to be defended from fascism, whatever form it took.

The only types of music acceptable in socialism were those with tonal harmonies that made them appear perfect, complete and capable of resolving all tensions – in other words, music that could act as anaesthesia.[20] Instead, rock 'n' roll constituted 'American atonal noise', 'deafening, brutish noises which really have nothing to do with music'.[21] To its critics, the raucous rock 'n' roll was nothing but 'jungle music' and an invitation to indulge in primitive urges. More than Americanisation, the communists objected to the African-Americanisation of German culture.[22] The cold war coloured a music already tainted by its unfamiliar racial undertones. In Leipzig, the rockers sought to utilise the competing rhetorics. When it came to getting Western radio stations to play their requests they presented themselves as poor and needy relations who required special support. Meanwhile, they tried to exploit the authorities' rhetoric by arguing that their support for black culture represented 'solidarity with the repressed'. Unable to resist subtle digs at the police for their ignorance about youth culture, they made out that all rock 'n' roll singers (Elvis Presley and Bill Haley included) were black.[23] For their part, the leaders of the FDJ showed that they had their fingers on the pulse by greeting the emergence of rock 'n' roll with an attack on bebop. Hanns Eisler was wheeled out to argue that 'the crazy limb contortions' (*'die verrückten Gliederverrenkungen'*) exhibited by the rockers had nothing to do with the way real negroes in America danced to 'proper jazz'. Socialists were not against 'well-played jazz', but 'idiotic movements' had 'nothing at all to do with normal people!' Hermann Axen called for *Junge Welt* to produce reports on the 'degeneration and exploitation' of jazz.[24] Professor Eisler obliged by stating that Louis Armstrong had been pressured by his profit-hungry managers, not just to play the trumpet, but to make a clown of himself.[25]

The 'new' youth subcultures contained competing and contrasting cultural forms. Rock 'n' roll represented 'an explosion of male aggression, sexuality and delinquency fused into a kind of raucous urban blues'.[26] The American novelist, fan of bebop and experimenter with drugs Norman Mailer described the hipsters as 'white Negroes' because they lived sensuously and by their wits without concern for the consequences or the future.[27] The hipster, he argued, was a 'philosophical psychopath' possessed of 'a lust for power, a dark, romantic, and yet undeniably dynamic view of existence'.[28] Mailer romanticised the world of 'promiscuity, pimpery, drug addiction, rape, razor-slash, bottle-break', of 'exploitation, cruelty, violence, frustration and lust' that he saw his archetypal 'Negro' as living in and that the hipster aspired to join.[29] 'The Negro's experience appears to be the most universal communication of the West, and the authority of their tortured senses may indeed be passing by the musical states of their artistic expression, *without language, without conscious communication*, into the no doubt equally tortured sense of the wild sensitive spawn of two vast wars.'[30] Black music 'encouraged wild, passionate, and disharmonious movements of the body and stimulated each youth "to do his own thing".' This 'joy in bodily movement and expression, in rhythm and the undisciplined release of feeling was diametrically opposed to the manly qualities' traditionally expected of whites.[31] Mailer was criticised for underestimating the racism inherent in the hipsters' appropriation of what they saw as black culture. 'The white Negro accepts the real Negro not as a human being in his totality, but as the bringer of a highly specified and restricted "cultural dowry" ... In so doing he creates an inverted form of keeping the nigger in his place.'[32]

Nevertheless, the black bohemian and his white imitators, Mailer argued, with their 'passionate instinct about the meaning of life' had a greater hold on truth than the Marxist would-be radicals.[33] In the GDR, intellectuals largely accepted the regime's disdain for unruly, plebeian culture, seeing it as having been responsible for the rise of Nazism. In spite of their appreciation for the difficulties of ordinary workers, they had been shocked by the violence of the June 1953 protests.[34] Although banned for not sufficiently following the authorised version of events, Stefan Heym's novel *Tag X* nevertheless depicted the violence committed by young men as being far from positive and unambiguous. One was said to be wearing a T-shirt depicting 'a lasso-swinging cowboy'. Another had a 'spidery hand, an almost feminine face, but with a brutal mouth'.[35] Christa Wolf, meanwhile, was shocked by the wanton destruction of young demonstrators in Leipzig and their 'wild, unbridled hatred of this state'.[36] She described such groups as having 'something really threatening, something violent from the past about them'.[37] In the regime's attacks on youth subculture, the fans of bebop and their successors the rockers and the beat fans were made to function as racialised others. Despite their claims to oppose fascism and racism, intellectuals in the GDR failed to speak out against the racism inherent in such stereotypes. The closest an East German writer came to identifying with those in the youth subcultures was Brigitte Reimann in her 1961 'youth novel' *Ankunft im Alltag*.[38]

The novel was set in the huge industrial complex of '*Schwarze Pumpe*' (Black Pump) in Hoyerswerda, where Reimann had gone to immerse herself in the 'romantic, sweaty' atmosphere of audacious men as part of the *Bitterfelder Weg*.[39] Venturing as if into an alien culture, Reimann tried to find aspects of life in this other world that she could combine with her idealistic hopes of socialist development.[40] 'In his extremely tight jeans, S. had the rolling gait of those modern delinquents [*Eckensteher*], who in their weary nonchalance desperately try to imitate the Western demi-monde.'[41] Another character in her novel stood on a stool with an imaginary guitar in his hand, his shoulders ecstatically twitching, singing 'Rock Around the Clock', his brain 'swamped by syncopated, hacked to pieces rhythms'.[42] For Reimann, such macho posturing was stupid ('ranting and raving have nothing to do with masculinity') but could be excused when exhibited by the young men who worked hard during the day and who had often lost parents in the war.[43] The boys in her brigade, particularly two with learning difficulties, evoked her feelings of tenderness ('my pity for all those left behind in life'). As a young girl, she had wanted to be a missionary to the savage tribes of Africa ('*wollte ich nicht Negermissionar werden?!*').[44]

Her new life in Hoyerswerda offered opportunities for working among (and trying to convert) the 'white Negroes' closer to home. Working in production allowed her not only to get her hands dirty ('*ich bin negerschwarz zurückgekommen*'), but to mix with the workers. Marvelling at her ability to communicate 'with the so-called ordinary people', those her fellow writers dismissed as 'the uneducated masses', at times she seemed in danger of 'going native'.[45] Friends noticed that she had begun to look like a teenager. A brigade excursion saw her 'rocking to provoke the others'. An evening with the 'culture circle' left her with 'dim memories of wildly dancing rock 'n' roll ... and of a kiss in the middle of our improvised dance floor'.[46] She not only fell in love with her brigadier, who in the novel embodies a true working-class hero, but also with a bulldozer driver, whose '*Negerlippen*' she kissed with abandon and who she succeeded in the end in turning into a writer.[47] Her novel ends with the female character being sexually attacked, not by a real *Halbstarke*, but by a wannabe, the spoilt son of an antifascist fighter.[48]

Figure 2. Mugshot of one of the 'fascist cowboys' involved in the June 1953 uprising.

While their appropriation of black culture may have been implicitly racist, in Europe rock 'n' roll offered young whites an opportunity to break out of the rigid structures of class and gender and at the same time provided them with a tremendous sense of liberation and release. For many teenagers in East and West, rock 'n' roll remained a private transgression, a musical orientation that had to remain closeted. Although their class and/or gender prevented them from publicly demonstrating their affiliation, privately they experienced all the transgression that rock 'n' roll could offer. Yorkshire feminist Sheila Rowbotham described the sense of release created by rock 'n' roll as an 'explosion of pentupness'. Every rock record 'went straight to your cunt and hit the bottom of your spine'.[49] Covert listening to Western music fell within the borders of respectability as long as it was not too loud. But, once young people started to dance (or 'gyrate') to the music, they started to transgress norms and taboos. What distinguished the rocker from the rock 'n' roll fan was the desire to act out the rock 'n' roll attitude in public. In itself, the act of listening to rock 'n' roll had to be a performance, a ritual.[50] It had to be loud and public. 'It wasn't much fun listening to them on your own between four walls.'[51] In the open, they had a better chance of drawing attention to themselves and, they hoped, of attracting girls. They were always in search of a space that was public enough to attract other people's attention, but private enough to avoid the heavy hand of the law. 'We provoked them simply through our presence. For the petit bourgeois it goes without saying, for the socialists twice as much.'[52] Attracting attention to themselves and making people stare at them increased their confidence and self-assurance.

Sexualisation

The most important item in the rocker's wardrobe was a pair of jeans. Still called 'rivet trousers' (*Niethosen*), these were universally black. A slogan popularised by the SED at the time was that 'In every rivet trouser there hides a divot' ('In jede Niethose steckt eine Niete'), playing on the double meaning of *Niete* as rivet and 'dead loss'. At an exchange rate of six East Marks to one West, imported trousers were hugely expensive. To spoil their value, the police would tear off the back pocket or take the badge off the belt. There were also alleged cases of policemen making youngsters publicly remove their 'bullet trousers' (*Geschoßhosen*).[53] To add to their appeal, the boys wore 'James Dean jackets', ideally made of leather, but more often made of an artificial synthetic (*Ölkunstleder*).[54] On their feet, they wore moccasins or winkle-pickers, 'shoes with pointed toes', and even the two-tone, black-and-white shoes favoured by gangsters and spivs.[55] For girls, too, it was the fashion to dress in black, with 'beautiful trousers, pullovers, petticoats and ballerina shoes'. After all, 'you couldn't dance rock 'n' roll with heels on'.[56]

Something that was particularly strange to older generations of male workers was the emphasis would-be toughs (*Halbstarken*) placed on their hair. Perfecting the new haircuts required them to spend as much time in front of the mirror as on the street. To older generations, this concern to preen and beautify was puzzling and perturbing, appearing as it did feminine, almost homosexual. Their hair was unmanly not only because of its length but because it took so much narcissism to perfect. Nevertheless, for the young men concerned, this new attention to fashion reflected an extension and inflation rather than a negation of their machismo. It manifested a heightened sense of themselves as sexual beings and marked their determination to pursue the female into submission through raw and overt displays of masculinity. Playing on adult fears, they clustered around street corners, ignoring adult authority and provoking confrontations and fights by staring back and insulting passers-by.[57] In some ways, the rockers' aggression can be seen as a compensation for their feminised appearance and a warning to any who dared to call them 'pretty boys'. Nevertheless this emphasis on physicality and hard-edged beauty was not without a certain attraction for gay men. One man described how he went from an orphanage to a street gang, all the time hiding his homosexuality behind a mask of machismo. 'I didn't belong at all. Rough and butch on the outside, I longed deep inside to be taken in someone's arms. Hard shell, soft core; maybe a woman could have handled that but not the guys I was running around with ... I always hung around with manly types.'[58]

The police and press in the GDR responded to these developments with a mixture of scandalised fear and aggressive intolerance. Police harassment did little to dampen the fans' ardour for the music. It only increased the lengths to which they had to go to enjoy it. As soon as the police closed one loophole, the rockers would find another, travelling to nearby towns to hear music banned in their own.[59] Rock 'n' roll constituted not just a fundamental attack on the eardrums and sensibilities of older generations, but a new form of dancing apart, which shocked, fascinated, attracted and repelled. Strange as it may seem from today's perspective, by dancing apart rockers were challenging and subverting gender norms and enjoying a sense of sexual freedom. For older generations brought up on the need for rigid restrictions on all sexual urges, the freedom exhibited by rock 'n' roll dancers was indecent and intolerable. Consequently, in FDJ dance halls there were signs on the dance floor stating 'Dancing apart is forbidden'.[60] Unlike the 'closed', 'taught' forms of dancing dominated by mock upper-class conceptions of etiquette and rigidly controlled by notions about what 'the man' and 'the woman' should do, rock 'n' roll, in contrast, seemed like a hedonistic free-for-all, without rules about how, when and why a young person could dance. 'In the homes of individual young people, they celebrate "rock 'n' roll" parties and busy themselves with games [of such a nature] that decency forbids description.'[61] To dance rock 'n' roll was not only to reject tradition but also to challenge decorum with dancers creating a space in which social and gender relations were temporarily suspended. Together with the new forms of clothing and haircut, rock 'n' roll symbolised an attitude of rebelliousness that challenged existing conventions and values.

Hostility to uninhibited forms of dancing was not new. During the Third Reich young people in Leipzig as elsewhere had rebelled against the confines of the Nazi vision by dancing forbidden 'nigger dances' like the samba and the rumba, together with swing jazz.[62] As a music with black origins, rock 'n' roll was also seen to lead to sexual excess.[63] Apart from the explicitly sexual lyrics (which were only partially understandable to East German audiences), the dancing of rock 'n' roll had obvious sexual connotations. Although the male was generally expected to be in command, a female dancer could turn convention on its head by upending her partner and flinging him around the floor. Whoever was in charge, skirts flew, sweat poured and dancers left the floor feeling drained but elated. The images that endure of rock 'n' roll tend to be of the most proficient, acrobatic couples, but little attention has been paid to the nervous 'first time' experiences of dancers making their initial foray out onto the dance floor, a youth cultural space in which girls often had the upper hand.[64] As one male interviewee confided, although he was duty bound to give the appearance of being casual (*lässig*), nonchalant and effortlessly cool, underneath, there was a great fear of failure. Nevertheless, to the victor came the spoils; prowess on the dance floor guaranteed success with the opposite sex.[65]

The elasticity of the rock 'n' roll dancers contrasted sharply with the stiff correctness of their elders. In their body language too, the rockers sought to exhibit their casual cool. 'They tried above all to emulate the unconventional, informal, studied indifference of the figures on the screen.'[66] The apparently effortless masculinity of the young generation of Hollywood actors was taken up and practised by young German men: Marlon Brando with his cool and sexy nonchalance; James Dean, the very embodiment of casualness; Elvis Presley, with his trademark lip curl and pelvic gyrations. The casualness that young Germans strove so hard to emulate represented a rejection of the 'soldierly habitus' of short hair and smart clothes.[67] The rocker style pushed back the boundaries of what constituted acceptable masculine behaviour in other ways too. The new taste for 'colourful and fashionable clothing' contrasted with the German tradition of masculine reserve.[68]

Rock 'n' roll provided the soundtrack for the sexualisation and rebellion of youth. 'This simple, brutal, hard-as-nails, boiling hot, sweat driving stomping rock 'n' roll'.[69] The authorities were used to describing the gangs as a threat to women and as being habitually engaged in 'harassment of passers-by, mostly young women and girls'. For many girls, the '*Halbstarke* milieu was (it has to be said) stupid, scary, blokey and tacky'.[70] But to the authorities' disgust, there were actually girls who enjoyed the rockers' company. When the *Meuten* began to include girls (and still exhibit the same behaviour) the police had to alter the way they defined the problem. In contrast to the women presented as passive victims of rowdy harassment, these gang girls were presented as Jezebels who actively led them astray. Merely by their presence, they provoked the boys into even greater displays of disorderliness. In fact, the position of rocker girls was ambiguous. Within the street culture, as in the traditional working-class culture generally, male sexism was dominant.[71]

U.S. feminist Wini Breines argues that sexism 'in mainstream and alternative cultures constrained and shaped their defiance into forms not easily recognisable by analysts not predisposed to discover gender rebellion. But it was gender rebellion. The stirrings prefigured its full-scale articulation a decade or so later.'[72] Rock 'n' roll was sexually liberating and life-transforming in spite of the ongoing patriarchy and sexism. Breines argues that disaffected girls often became the girlfriends of male dissidents and delinquents because 'girls' identities were inextricably bound up with boys', their acceptance [being] determined by whether or not they belonged to a male'.[73] According to Klaus Renft, 'there were a few girls, but they were mostly spoken for'.[74] Outnumbered 'perhaps ten to one', the role of the girls within the gangs was limited and they were kept subordinate and marginal by the boys' rampant machismo. Here the rockers drew on proletarian sensibilities (or lack of sensitivity). Girls were objectified in an aggressively macho and potentially rapacious world view. On the other hand, as a relatively small minority within the group, rocker girls experienced 'power' in being able to 'pick and choose' between the boys.[75]

Although in no sense 'equal', within the gang, they felt relatively free from the constraints of patriarchy by the standards of the time. 'In love, it worked or it didn't. That's how easy it was,' said Christa, a female member of the Capitol *Meute*.[76] Although a subordinate minority, they were also prized and protected, free to be themselves within a circle of male admirers. Nevertheless, even in the *Meuten*, prevailing conventions continued to emphasise marriage and eventually 'settling down'.[77] Having met one another in the Capitol *Meute*, both Manfred and Christa had each been in different 'steady' relationships (in one case to the point of engagement) before falling in love with one another and getting married. When I spoke to them, they had already enjoyed over forty years of marriage together. The passage of time appeared to have romanticised their views of relations between boys and girls in the gang. The distance from their lives then inevitably coloured how much they were willing to reveal. They were especially keen to play down the potentially violent aspects of rocker culture. But, if Christa chose to remember the boys as being perfect gentlemen, it was because she had no wish to let the authorities' slurs against her friends stick. 'I always felt relaxed with the boys. It was the police who gave me the shits.'[78] The reason why the police made her more uneasy than the rough antics of the boys was that the policemen were dominated by their own macho culture, one mixed with power and politics, which made it far more unstable and unpredictable.

Politicisation

In the East, the struggle over notions of masculinity took on a political colouring. The models for outrageous masculine behaviour in the 1950s were American. This was enough to convince the communist authorities that the changes in youth fashion were entirely new and dangerous alien intrusions that had to be suppressed to prevent the spread of contamination to other parts of the youth population, thereby endangering the project of socialist construction. Rock 'n' roll, the authorities argued, was used by the Western militarists and warmongers to render young people primitive and unscrupulous, 'raw enough' to be directed into any kind of barbarism. In the face of a petty and interfering state, youth's appropriation of alternative symbols of masculinity and desire to be left alone became potent sources of resistance and refusal. The state's adoption of a paternalistic approach towards youth led to it becoming the figure against which young men rebelled.

The communists believed in their own working-class masculinity. But, in the day-to-day administration of their dictatorship, SED leaders oscillated between overt authoritarianism and the smothering attentions of the nanny state. Although at times radiating hope, at others twisted into hate, the most common face of the regime experienced by the population was of hidebound officialdom and of a bureaucracy remote from and uncomprehending of their day-to-day reality. The party's need to establish its authority led to conflict with those in the gangs who disputed that violence by the police was legitimate. Rather than allowing their territories to be overrun and their culture stifled, the young working-class men in the gangs were pushed by machismo and unspoken peer pressure to challenge and oppose the state.

The teenage rebels existed in a twilight zone between conventional conceptions of respectability and criminality. Although to outsiders they all seemed universally 'hostile or even criminally inclined', in reality the subculture constituted an overlapping of styles and cultures.[79] A subculture developed in which those who looked and dressed like juvenile delinquents mingled and mixed with those who actually were. With the rise of rock 'n' roll, the hangers-on became more and more numerous, crystallising around the nucleus of the original gangs to form something quite new and different – an amorphous, structureless in-crowd of music fans and aficionados. Appreciation for and knowledge of the music brought respect and a certain immunity. Rockers could enjoy gang protection without being required to join in. The music acted as a bond between the fans and others who were more interested in traditional gang activities per se. Together, they stood like outlaws on the edges of respectable society. For those who stood on the other side of the line, the rockers were a threat, menacing them with a vision of an uncontrolled, unsafe future.

Dissent and deviance merged with one another as different expressions of a shared rebelliousness. Although older and more respectable people may have felt intimidated by their numbers and behaviour, for the most part, they simply stood around and chatted and were loud and cheeky, activities that even in the GDR did not constitute arrestable offences. As a result, ABVs (volunteer policemen) and the local police patrols (*Schutzpolizei*) had little alternative but to take down their names and addresses for their 'rowdy card file' (*Rowdykartei*) and to try and get them to move along.[80] Given their numerical and physical superiority this was no easy task. Even if they could get the gang to disappear for half an hour, they were bound to be back on their old stomping ground again as soon as the policemen's backs were turned. Repeated run-ins with the local police and ABVs tended to lessen fear and respect for them. Outdated lectures and wagging index fingers were met with sneers, sarcastic comments, feigned naivety, interruptions and other audible and visible jokes as the 'pack members' clustered around the hapless policeman. Gang leaders played an important role in squaring up to and poking fun at authority and yet, at the same time, in making sure that other gang members did not go far enough to get themselves into serious trouble. The authority that the gang leader (in the past known as the *Cliquenbulle*) was able to enjoy rivalled and often outweighed that of 'the cops' (popularly described as *Bullen*).

Figure 3. Still from Berlin – *Ecke Schönhauser* depicting a face-off between a People's Policeman and rowdy teenagers.

'Liquidation' of a Conspiracy to Rock

The police were determined to establish that behind rocker incidents there existed a subversive, conspiratorial organisation. Sinister emphasis was placed on the fact that their 'ringleaders' sought not to draw attention to themselves and that gang members mostly only knew each other by their nicknames. Overexcitement and high jinks were reinterpreted as 'organised' incidences of subversion co-ordinated and controlled by foreign espionage agencies. As the largest and most visible group of rockers, the Capitol *Meute* attracted the most police attention.[81] In addition to their jeans and 'Texas shirts', members of the Capitol *Meute* were reported to wear fascist insignia round their necks in the form of 'the Iron Cross and even the *Ritterkreuz*'.[82] There is a clear discrepancy between the authorities' claims that gang members were dangerous criminals and the fact that they were still at large and not already under arrest. Although it was not unusual for delinquents and young people with convictions for petty crimes to gravitate towards the rebellious clusters, the great majority in the *Meuten* do not seem to have done anything sufficiently serious to justify arresting them.

The local authorities were forced to recognise that 'not all the young people who loaf around on the streets in the evening are bad'. Although 'rowdy-like' (*rowdyhaft*) clothing and haircuts were prevalent among factory workers, it was difficult to argue that those wearing them were delinquent because their employers stated that they worked hard and earned well. 'Even young workers who have received awards from their factories can be found standing around on the corner in the evenings and not knowing what to do with themselves.'[83] Often being a good worker encouraged weekend misbehaviour because with money in their pockets, they 'wanted to draw a bit of attention to themselves'. Local communist functionaries were forced to recognise that there were even a few of them 'whose fathers are members of our party'.[84]

The emphasis the rockers placed on exclusivity and authenticity ensured that they did not respond well to regime attempts to take over and incorporate their culture. In the late 1950s and the mid-1960s, Leipzig saw a number of highly public clashes between members of the *Meuten* and the police. When, having spent so much effort trying to repress their culture, party leaders suddenly decided that they wanted to appear young and popular, members of the *Meuten* were keen to show their own lack of appreciation through loud and vocal 'audience participation'. An incident that sparked a long-running vendetta between rockers and the police in Leipzig occurred at the end of the *Pressefest* organised by the *Leipziger Volkszeitung* in June 1958. Those in the Capitol *Meute* did not think very much of one of the singers and showed their lack of appreciation by booing her. 'We wanted to hear something else and started whistling.' The crowd's mood was not improved by the showing of a film about communists. The People's Police tried to 'restore order' by wading in and indiscriminately flailing their batons.[85]

According to the official police report, 'About 150 to 200 young people organised a disturbance and disrupted dancing in the *Messehalle* with wild rock 'n' roll dancing. As a result, a fight developed. The special commando and five radio patrol cars came into operation. The People's Police energetically asserted their authority. Quite a few hooligans were arrested and the hall was cleared.'[86] The authors of what was now described as a 'planned disturbance' were 'the so-called Banana gang'.[87] The reactions of the police and the state authorities showed what was at stake. Members of the Capitol *Meute* were arrested and charged with riot and defaming the state (*Staatsverleumdung*). A campaign of harassment against the rock 'n' roll youth subculture was instituted at all levels. The 'ringleaders' were to be subjected to 'permanent surveillance' (*laufend überwacht*) and the gangs to be 'eliminated once and for all' (*endgültige Beseitigung*).[88]

Humiliation

Embarrassed by what had happened, the authorities sought revenge on the rockers by subjecting them to public humiliation. Under the headline 'Scarecrows in the Petersstraße', the *LVZ* declared, 'Shirt bright and short – according to the motto: the more tasteless the better. And the trousers? The upper part is kept intentionally so narrow that everyone can see that the youngster wearing them has nothing in his pants.'[89] In fact the figure in the cartoon resembled a bearded jazz fan (or beatnik) rather than a rocker. Nevertheless, the authorities were clearly not only attacking the rockers as lower-class and tasteless, but as only half men. 'What should one do with such scarecrows?' the author asked.

> What's clear is that they have nothing to look for on our streets. Our street picture should be dominated by a clean youth, one determined to perform great things for the work of socialist construction and not by those who believe the career of a trafficker, of a gangster or of a prostitute in West Berlin is the right one for them.[90]

If the authorities' aim had been to make the rowdies submit, they had clearly made a fundamental miscalculation. They had selected the group in society least likely to give in quietly. They had no interest in staying on at school and, in most cases, were already earning money. This gave them such a sense of self-confidence and self-worth that it was very difficult to take away from them. A conception of masculinity emphasising toughness meant that it was more important to prove one's courage and suffer the consequences than to back down and lose face within the group. Far from shying away from negative publicity, the rockers revelled in the attention they were getting. The attempt to humiliate them only served to goad them into further, more overt displays of defiance. 'Because of the "Scarecrows in the Petersstraße" article, which appeared in the *LVZ*, the accused ganged together to form a mob and carried out a so-called protest demonstration. At 21.30 hours, a group of about 30 young people moved in the direction of the market shouting and roaring.'[91] Their intention, it was claimed, was to find the person who had written the article and beat him up. Those involved have a different story to tell. They had been swimming in the afternoon and were on their way back to the centre of town when they began singing a Bill Haley number ('Hey Mambo, the Mambo Rock'). The protest had arisen spontaneously 'aus der Laune heraus'.[92] Asked why they had done it, Manfred said that it was in protest at the attempts to ban their music and to deny their existence. They wanted to show them that they were there – and that they weren't about to go away.[93] The price that he and the others paid for their protest was six months' imprisonment without trial. 'There was never a political background. They'd have loved to have been able to ascribe one to us.'[94] Asked if he had not known that this would happen Manfred just shrugged.

By the time the incident was reported in the local paper, it had taken on much more dramatic proportions.

> These young people moved through the streets singing American songs in their original version. At the same time they spat at passers-by and pulled the trigger of air pistols in front of their faces. They pushed old people from the pavement onto the street. Telephone boxes and benches were smashed up senselessly. But they made no halt even before bigger crimes. Thus five gang members stole no less than 21 cars. Seven others indulged in coarse abuse of the functionaries of our state and, in addition, stole 10 motor scooters.[95]

It must have been quite an evening. Following the 'protest demonstration', the *Leipziger Volkszeitung* published a selection of mugshots of male rockers under the heading 'not a question of fashion, but of politics'. The photograph of 'their haircuts' was juxtaposed against record covers seized in house raids revealing 'their culture' (*ihre Kultur*). Displayed next to the '*Texaskleidung*' (Texas clothing) was a collection of *Schundliteratur* (for the most part Zorro comics), medallions, knuckledusters, knives and pistols. The message was clear, contamination with Western non-culture led to crime as well as political and moral deviancy.

The article went beyond simply deriding their fashion sense and questioning their masculinity. Instead it argued that their activities were to be interpreted as a political act – part of a plot designed to undermine the fabric of the GDR. Rowdyism was a conspiracy orchestrated by western intelligence agencies to infiltrate East Germany with highly structured, criminal gangs whose task it was to gather information on Soviet military installations and cause uproar and provocations against the regime.

> The clothing is the outward feature. Behind it hide proper gangs, rigidly organised according to special articles of association. These statutes include for example that a member of the gang is not allowed to be a member of the FDJ, cannot sing

Eastern songs and instead must sing Western songs loudly in American on the street. A few of these youngsters manifest exactly the picture of moral depravity as is glorified in Western trash literature. Young people get this 'literature' from West Germany. From there they also receive their rock 'n' roll records. From there they get morphine cigarettes and their weapons. These gangs have proper ties to gangs of a similar nature in West Germany and maintain 'exchanges of experiences' with them. In other words, the spiritual fathers sit in West Germany. They're the same ones who deaden West German youth with their brutal non-culture [and] educate them to brutality and desire for murder ... Countless are the attempts by the intelligence agencies in West Germany to smuggle their ideology into our republic in order to weaken it.[96]

Fritz Beier, the First Secretary of the Leipzig party organisation, took it upon himself to counter energetically 'the false conception that the tendency of many young people towards rock 'n' roll, criminal adventure stories and wild haircuts is only a crazy fashion'.

> Behind this fashion lies more. With it is ultimately also tied the question of war or peace. Interrogations by the criminal police have clearly proved that some of these gangs are in contact with West German agencies. These agencies want for our youth to stand outside society so that they will be vulnerable for the imperialistic ideology of killing and aggression.[97]

The *Meuten* were much too amorphous to fit the authorities' paranoid description of 'organised hooliganism' (*organisierte Rowdytum*), inspired and orchestrated by intelligence agencies in West Berlin. Nevertheless, there was a sense in which protests were choreographed by the expectations and self-understandings of those involved. Regime attempts to vilify youth subcultures proved counterproductive because they created an atmosphere of excitement and expectation that would not otherwise have existed. By publicising the rockers' exploits, the authorities provided negative role models for groups of young people who had not yet come into contact with the subculture and examples of how to behave when confronted by the police.

A much vaunted, and subsequently much ridiculed, attempt to wean young people off rock 'n' roll was the Lipsi. In essence, it represented an artificial, safe alternative, a dance step that was compatible with socialism. The Lipsi was the brainchild of a Leipzig trio, René Dubianski and the dance teachers Christine and Helmut Seifert. The 'i' on the end gave the word an American ring, but in actual fact it was a shortening of Lipsia, the roman name for Leipzig, home of the dance step's creators. Couples 'danced it to a faster rhythm, but they avoided any of the dangerous "openness" of dancing apart'.[98] On 15 April 1959, the Wahrener *Meute* showed their appreciation for the authorities' efforts by undertaking a 'protest march' with the aim of 'enlightening the population about their true nature'. In the course of this protest, they 'instigated hatred against state functionaries' and 'glorified Western non-culture' by shouting, 'We don't want no Lipsi and no Alo Koll. We want Elvis Presley with his rock 'n' roll.'[99]

Under the auspices of the National Front, a series of talks were held in different institutions and workplaces in Leipzig with the aim of dissuading young people from engaging in such activities and getting the rest of the population involved in the fight against rowdyism. By drawing attention to them the authorities provided gang members with local notoriety and kudos with their peers. As a result of their 'incomplete school education' they were not in a position to take in what was being said to them.[100] The authorities had a much clearer idea of the sorts of associations they wanted to pin on young people than the sorts of behaviour rowdies were actually involved in (described vaguely as 'such behaviour' and 'such haircuts'). 'Among all these young people there must be two or three for whom it can be proved that they are acting on behalf of one or other Western [secret] service. That should then be published.'[101]

If in the West, the provocative activities associated with adolescence came to be mistaken for delinquency, in the GDR they became interpreted as premeditated acts of treason and as a threat to the state. 'From the experience of those gangs already liquidated, one must conclude that these groups are also involved in carrying out enemy activity in the form of encouraging defection [Abwerbung], smears [Hetze], defamation of the state and other crimes.'[102] The police believed that increased surveillance would allow them to 'grab individual ringleaders through rapid actions'; to 'ban entry to particular streets'; and to 'disperse trouble spots and signal their movement to other parts of town'.[103] But, far from diminishing the problem, increased surveillance served to magnify it. Where previously they had been dealing with four or five main gangs, the authorities discovered the existence of upwards of twenty. By subjecting the gangs to more intensive observation and harassment, the regime succeeded in fulfilling its own prophecy. The gangs became more and more openly rebellious and their attempts to preserve their autonomous cultural space became linked to more general themes of political opposition.

Escalation

In June 1960, a large crowd of young Leipzigers (numbering around a thousand) were looking forward to watching the American film *Trapeze*, starring Burt Lancaster and Tony Curtis. 'The film showing could not, however, begin as arranged at 9 p.m. because the cultural event that was occurring in the same place lasted until 9.45.' The preceding cultural event had the title 'Friendship Games for Friends' and was attended by the Soviet Consul together with leading SED functionaries. The party had clearly offered young people something they wanted (access to a popular American film) in return for what it wanted (feigned support for the duration of the Soviet delegation's visit). Unfortunately poor timekeeping led the crowd that had gathered to see the film to feel that they had been cheated and that the SED was reneging on its side of the bargain. Like their plebeian forebears, the rockers sought restitution through riot. They registered their grievances and sought to restore what they saw as acceptable boundaries by resorting to symbolic disobedience.[104] 'Among the filmgoers, above all among the youth, a negative mood developed, caused by the delay in starting the film. In order to guarantee that the cultural event went off smoothly and that control was exercised over entries and exits, the special unit [*Sonderkommando*] and a radio patrol car [*Funkstreifenwagen*] of

Figure 4. Mugshots used by the Leipzig police to portray the rockers as strange and other.

the local People's Police had to be put into action.'[105] The scheduled demonstration of veneration and gratitude to the Soviet Union was disrupted as the rockers resisted the SED's attempt to instrumentalise popular culture and reclaimed the Clara Zetkin park as their own. They demonstrated the artificial and imposed character of SED ritualisation and demonstrated their loyalty with those they viewed as their true 'friends'.

Although the SED was prepared to explore a number of different potential solutions to the problem of dissident rock 'n' roll youth subculture, in the end it resorted to a 'tried and tested' mixture of wrongful arrest, imprisonment and orchestrated violence. Vigilante attacks were made on the most well-known gangs: 'When the Presley gang again took over the pavement towards the end of 1958, they were thrashed in such a way that some of them had to receive medical treatment. Through this "organised self help" by citizens [or police and Stasi], the 42nd gang was also dissolved at this time.'[106] Those involved were arrested and put on trial for breach of the peace, violent sexual offences, breaking and entering, defamation of the state and wilful damage of property.[107] During the course of 1959, several gang members were convicted of treason and espionage. As far as the GDR authorities were concerned, the transit camps in West Berlin acted as recruitment centres for foreign espionage agencies. Thanks to the GDR's pliant judicial system, if someone was a 'returnee' (in other words someone who had fled the Republic only to return) this alone was sufficient to merit a 'considerable term of imprisonment'.[108]

Even when the 'ringleaders' of the *Meuten* were arrested and given long prison sentences of up to four years for 'spying', other youngsters stepped in to fill their shoes. The authorities were incapable of understanding that youth subcultures were constantly regenerating phenomena. As older members left, usually to settle down in a steady relationship, they were replaced by younger kids. The police believed that if they could round up the ringleaders of the gangs, then the problem would go away. Unfortunately, the gatherings that occurred were highly fluid and unstructured. As a result, police razzias failed to net the whole 'gang membership'. The rockers who met up on the street often knew very little about each other apart from the shared interest in Western music and culture. They developed a shared sense of belonging through their common clothes, haircuts and interests. Again and again, the police claimed to have 'liquidated' a particular gang only to find that a few weeks later young people began to meet up again in the same place. The result of the concerted attacks on the gangs was that by the end of the summer, crowds of as many as 500 to 600 youths were gathering in the Ernst-Thälmann Straße every evening.[109] The excessive punishment meted out to those young people they did succeed in catching is a measure of the authorities' impotence and inability to control the problem.

Far from wiping out an undesired culture, 'liquidation' served to magnify and publicise the gangs, attracting allies together with emulators, who began to identify with the negative image that the regime itself had created. While rock 'n' roll had acted as the stimulus for innate, intuitive forms of rebellion against the stifling and oppressive norms governing appearance and behaviour, it was the overreactions of the authorities that provoked the most embarrassing displays of protest and opposition, undermining the authority of the regime. Although the poses struck by youth nonconformists were more of an attack on older generations' notions of what was respectable and decent than an assault on the state, they undermined the SED's claim to be able to plan, order and control society. Fans of rock 'n' roll were a visible demonstration of failure: 'on the public street they sang Western hits and rocked wildly'. When the authorities sought to crush their culture, the slogan 'Long live Elvis Presley' became accompanied by 'Down with Ulbricht'.[110]

Conclusion

The defiant pursuit of difference by nonconformists not only made local policemen appear foolish and incapable. It also exposed the regime's worst traits. Just as the growth of youth subcultures undermined the SED's claims to be modern, so too did its own wild overreactions contradict its claims to 'civilisation'. In the end, fears about rowdies becoming politicised proved to be self-fulfilling prophecies. Cultural dissidence easily spilled over into political protest, particularly when it was subjected to excessive politicisation by an interfering regime. As long as the SED remained rigidly opposed to the spread of Western youth culture, it remained vulnerable to opposition on the part of young people. The party's attempts to manufacture an image of mass popular support could easily be undermined by the activities of a small group of 'rowdies'. By proclaiming to the whole world that they were going to control male youth and eradicate 'rowdyism', the SED set itself up for a fall. Official attempts to control young people's clothes and haircuts proved much less effective than the more subtle influence of teenage magazine articles and the pressure of commercialisation in the West.[111] The GDR's much more overt attempts to manipulate youth fashion by imposing restrictions on tailors and barbers were hopelessly heavy-handed.[112] The rocker craze came to an end when it ceased to be fashionable. The actions of the authorities played no part in its demise. Just when they believed that they had gained the upper hand, a new style of music came out of Liverpool (via Hamburg) and the conflict began all over again.

    The combination of new fashions and old behaviours was too much for the authorities to cope with. They fought rock 'n' roll as an alien, imperialist intrusion. But in trying to suppress the new youth culture they came into conflict with the macho ethos that the rockers used to define themselves. Conflicts over space and identity snowballed under the combined pressure of publicity and police violence. The local SED leadership's solution to the problem of rock 'n' roll in the Clara Zetkin park was to build a wall around the dance area.¹¹³ Faced with changes in fashion, ideological weakness and decadent dancing, the party reacted by imposing a physical barrier. This was to be the solution that on 13 August 1961 was imposed on the rest of the country in a desperate attempt to stem the flow of Western media influence in and young people out of the Republic. But although SED leaders were able to erect barriers, they found it much more difficult to dismantle the divisions of culture and *Eigensinn* separating parts of the population from the official vision.

According to a report on 'endangered youth' by Leipzig's town council, the number of young people 'who appeared negatively in groups and concentrations' was estimated at around 9 per cent of the youth population.¹¹⁴ In schools, the party was able to force young people to hide their scepticism, disbelief and nonconformity behind feigned support for the regime. On the street, in the park and at the fairground, however, the party's supporters and defenders could find themselves in enemy territory. One Leipzig SED functionary complained that he could not go into the local youth clubhouse without being verbally abused.¹¹⁵ He was not alone in finding a wall of barely concealed hostility, which it was very difficult to breach. Such spaces remained on the fringes, 'wild' and uncontrolled. Ultimately, there were limits to the SED's ability to set parameters on how young people lived their lives.

Notes

1. Günther Kaiser, *Randalierende Jugend: Eine soziologische und kriminologische Studie über die sogenannten 'Halbstarken'* (Heidelberg, 1959), 20.
2. Kaspar Maase, *Bravo Amerika. Erkundungen zur Jugendkultur der Bundesrepublik in den fünfziger Jahren* (Hanover, 1992), 103, 128.
3. Christian Gerbel, Alexander Mejstrik and Reinhard Sieder, 'Die "Schlurfs". Verweigerung und Opposition von Wiener Arbeiterjugendlichen im "Dritten Reich"' in Emmerich Talos, Ernst Hanisch and Wolfgang Neugebauer (eds), *NS-Herrschaft in Österreich 1938–1945* (Vienna, 1988), 243–68.
4. Maase, *Bravo Amerika*, 120.
5. Ibid., 128.
6. 'Koffersuper "Sylvia" kommt demnächst in den Handel. Dieses handliche Kleinkoffer-Batteriegerät. 215DM (ohne Netzteil)', *Junge Welt* (19/20 May 1956).
7. 'Rowdytum und Bandentätigkeit (15.12.59)', StAL BDVP 24/113, 102; 'Stenographisches Protokoll der Sitzung der Jugendkommissions des Nationalrates der Nationalen Front des Demokratischen Deutschland am 17. Juli 1959 im Hause des Zentralrats der FDJ', BArch. SAPMO DY6/3949, 20.
8. Detlev Peukert, 'Die "Halbstarken". Protestverhalten von Arbeiterjugendlichen zwischen Wilhelmischen Kaiserreich und Ära Adenauer', *Zeitschrift für Pädagogik* 30 (1984), 533–48.
9. 'Ausnahmezustand am Wedding. Duensing droht Westberliner Jugendlichen. Knüppelgarde wieder einsatzbereit', *Junge Welt* (27 July 1956).
10. Walter Friedrich, *Flegeljahre? Zur Erziehung 13- bis 16jähriger Jungen* (Berlin, 1964), 17.
11. 'Ihr seid die Schmiede der deutschen Zukunft' in Zentralkomitee der SED, *Jugend von heute. Hausherren von Morgen. Kommuniqué des Politbüros des ZK der SED zu Problemen der Jugend in der DDR* (Berlin, 1963), 67.
12. Interview with Manfred S. (1999).

13. Dick Bradley, *Understanding Rock 'n' Roll. Popular Music in Britain 1955–1964* (Buckingham, 1992), 121.
14. Linda Martin and Kerry Seagrave, *Anti-Rock. The Opposition to Rock 'n' Roll* (Hamden, 1988), 32–35, 47.
15. 'Bill Haley und die NATO', *Neues Deutschland* (29 October 1958).
16. 'Orgie der amerikanischen Unkultur', *Neues Deutschland* (29 October 1958).
17. 'Bekämpfung des Rowdytums. Brennpunkt "Klara-Zetkin-Park"' (14 August 1960), StAL, BDVP 24/113, 91.
18. 'Orgie der amerikanischen Unkultur', *Neues Deutschland* (29 October 1958).
19. Radio address reproduced in Hartwig Bögeholz, *Deutsch-deutsche Zeiten. Eine Chronik. Deutschland von 1945 bis 1995* (Munich, 1996).
20. Jacques Attali, *Noise. The Political Economy of Music*, trans. Brian Massumi (Manchester, 1985), 46.
21. 'Orgie der amerikanische Unkultur'; '"Vogelscheuchen" – und was sagen ihre Eltern?', *LVZ* (31 July 1958).
22. See, for example, 'Veronikas', *Ostsee-Zeitung* (2 September 1954).
23. Interview with Manfred S.
24. 'II. Berliner Jugendforum ... Um den Jazz', *Junge Welt* (28/29 January 1956).
25. 'Diesmal ging es um den Jazz. Ein Wunsch des Berliner Jugendforums wurde erfüllt', *Junge Welt* (7/8 April 1956).
26. Roger Horrocks, *Male Myths and Icons. Masculinity in Popular Culture* (Houndsmills, 1995), 129.
27. Norman Mailer, 'The White Negro. Superficial Reflections on the Hipster' in *Advertisements for Myself* (New York, 1981), 294–345. First published in *Dissent* (Summer 1957).
28. Ibid., 304.
29. Ibid., 310.
30. Ibid., 325.
31. George Mosse, *The Image of Man. The Creation of Modern Masculinity* (New York, Oxford, 1996), 184–85.
32. Mailer, 'White Negro', 330.
33. Ibid., 319.
34. Stefan Heym's unpublished novel, *Der Tag X*, was later published as *5 Tage im Juni* (Munich, 1974).
35. Heym, *5 Tage im Juni*, 198, 200f.
36. Christa Wolf, *Im Dialog: Aktuelle Texte* (Berlin, Weimar, 1990), 36.
37. Ibid., 35–36.
38. Brigitte Reimann, *Ankunft im Alltag* (Berlin, 1961); in his novel *Es geht seinen Gang oder Mühen in unserer Ebene* (Halle, 1977), Erich Loest partially managed to compensate for his earlier, crassly hostile treatment of Western-influenced youth culture in *Die Westmark fällt weiter* (Halle, 1952) by presenting beat fans (of whom his son was one) as harmless and misunderstood.
39. Reimann, *Ankunft im Alltag*, 51.
40. Brigitte Reimann, *Ich bedaure nichts. Tagebücher 1955–1963* (Berlin, 1997), 121.
41. Reimann, *Ankunft im Alltag*, 72.
42. Ibid., 73.
43. Ibid., 112; Reimann, *Ich bedaure nichts*, 145.
44. Reimann, *Ich bedaure nichts*, 123.
45. Ibid., 136, 185.
46. Ibid., 161.
47. Ibid., 139, 158.
48. Reimann, *Ankunft im Alltag*, 209.
49. Sheila Rowbotham, *Woman's Consciousness, Man's World* (Harmondsworth, 1973), 14–15.
50. On the importance of performance and ritual, see Bradley, *Understanding Rock 'n' Roll*, 120ff.
51. Interview with Manfred S.

52. Interview with Klaus Renft (2000).
53. 'Streifzug durch das III. Gesamtberliner Jugendforum', *Junge Welt* (2 March 1956).
54. Interview with Klaus Renft.
55. Interview with Manfred S.
56. Interview with Christa S. (1999).
57. Christine Bartram and Heinz-Hermann Krüger, 'Vom Backfisch zum Teenager – Mädchensozialisation in den 50er Jahren' in Heinz-Hermann Krüger (ed.), *'Die Elvis-Tolle, die hatte ich mir unauffällig wachsen lassen'. Lebensgeschichte und jugendliche Alltagskultur in den fünfziger Jahren* (Opladen, 1985), 84–101, 95.
58. 'Body', worker born in 1947, in John Borneman (ed.), *Gay Voices from East Germany. Interviews by Jürgen Lemke* (Bloomington, Indianapolis, 1991), 115–16.
59. 'Rowdytum (Dec. 1958)', StAL BDVP 24/67, 252.
60. Hans-Dieter Schütt, (ed.), *Klaus Renft. Zwischen Liebe und Zorn* (Berlin, 1997), 51.
61. 'Keine Frage der Mode, sondern der Politik. Was steckt hinter den "Vogelscheuchen"?', *LVZ* (31 July 1958).
62. Alfons Kenkmann, *Wilde Jugend. Lebenswelt großstädtischer Jugendlicher zwischen Weltwirtschaftskrise, Nationalsozialismus und Währungsreform* (Essen, 1996), 286–87; Bernd Polster, 'Treudeutsch, Treudeutsch. Swingheinis unterwandern den Kolonnenzwang' in Bernd Polster (ed.), *'Swing Heil'. Jazz im Nationalsozialismus* (Berlin, 1989), 129–43; 'Jugenderziehung, Jugendverwahrlosung', StAL SD-Berichte.
63. Detlev Peukert, *Inside Nazi Germany*, trans. Richard Deveson (London, 1993), 166–69; Arno Klönne, 'Jugendprotest und Jugendopposition. Von der HJ-Erziehung zum Cliquenwesen der Kriegszeit' in Martin Broszat, Elke Fröhlich and Anton Grossmann (eds), *Bayern in der NS-Zeit* (Munich, 1981), vol. IV, 527–620, 600–3; Uta Poiger, *Jazz, Rock and Rebels. Cold War Politics and American Culture in a Divided Germany* (Berkeley, 2000), 22–29; Maase, *Bravo Amerika*, 60, 97; Bradley, *Understanding Rock 'n' Roll*, 102ff.
64. Simon Frith and Angela McRobbie, 'Rock and Sexuality' in Simon Frith and Andrew Goodwin (eds), *On Record: Rock, Pop and the Written Word* (London, 1990), 371–89.
65. Interview with Hans-Peter D. (1999).
66. Maase, *Bravo Amerika*, Note 5, 120.
67. Ibid., 113–31.
68. Ibid., 121.
69. Chris Hyde, *Rock 'n' Roll Tripper. Stories und Bilder* (Rheinberg, 1983), 9f.
70. Maase, *Bravo America*, 103.
71. Peukert, *Inside Nazi Germany*, Note 24, 268.
72. Wini Breines, *Young, White and Miserable. Growing Up Female in the Fifties* (Boston, 1992), 129–30.
73. Ibid., 143–44.
74. Interview with Klaus Renft.
75. Interview with Christa S.
76. Ibid.
77. Simon Frith, *Sound Effects. Youth, Leisure and the Politics of Rock 'n' Roll* (New York, 1981), 238–39.
78. Interview with Christa S.
79. James Gilbert, *A Cycle of Outrage. America's Reaction to the Juvenile Delinquent of the 1950s* (New York, Oxford, 1986), 17.
80. 'Niederschrift über Fragen der Jugendkriminalität und des Rowdytums (30.10.58)', StAL, BDVP 24/113, 86–89.
81. 'Der Kampf gegen Jugendkriminalität und Rowdytum (ca. 1959)', StAL BDVP 24/113, 111.
82. 'Der Kampf gegen Jugendkriminalität und Rowdytum im Bezirk Leipzig (1960–61)', StAL BDVP 24/113, 218.
83. 'Stenographisches Protokoll', 67.

84. 'Beratung über Fragen der Jugendkriminalität und des Rowdytums (29.10.58)', StAL, BDVP 24/113, 87b.
85. Interview with Manfred and Christa S.
86. 'Information (22.6.1958)', StAL BDVP 24/65, 243b.
87. Ibid.
88. 'Bericht über die Pressley und 42er Bande (10.12.58)', StAL BDVP 24/113, 90-91
89. 'Vogelscheuchen in der Petersstraße', LVZ (23 July 1958).
90. Ibid.
91. 'Zusammenrottung lärmender Jugendlicher am Capitol' (26 July 1958), StAL, BDVP 24/66, 98.
92. Interview with Manfred and Christa S.
93. Ibid.
94. Ibid.
95. '"Vogelscheuchen" – und was sagen ihre Eltern?', LVZ (31 July 1958).
96. 'Keine Frage der Mode, sondern der Politik'.
97. '"Vogelscheuchen" – und was sagen ihre Eltern?'.
98. Poiger, Jazz, Rock and Rebels, 185; Timothy Ryback, Rock around the Bloc: A History of Rock Music in Eastern Europe and the Soviet Union (New York, Oxford, 1990), 29; Wiebke Janssen, '"Heute, tanzen alle jungen Leute, im Lipsi-Schritt, nur noch im Lipsi-Schritt". SED und Jugend in den fünfziger Jahren', Hallische Beiträge zur Zeitgeschichte 6 (1999), 58-74.
99. Alo Koll was a local dance band popular with the regime. 'Der Kampf gegen Jugendkriminalität und Rowdytum im Bezirk Leipzig (ca. 1960-61)', BDVP 24/113, 216; in February 1961, Brigitte Reimann wrote in her diary, 'our deadly boring Lipsi has completely lost'. In Hoyerswerda, 'the party leadership, the intellectuals – they all rocked and rolled through the neighbourhood … It is always a bit strange for me the way comrades can throw off their skins and reveal how weak they are as people.' Reimann, Ich bedaure nichts, 164.
100. 'Niederschrift (30.10.58)', StAL, BDVP 24/113, 87.
101. Ibid., 88a.
102. 'Rowdytum und Bandentätigkeit' (16 December 1959), StAL BDVP 24/113, 102.
103. 'Auswertung der Jahresanalyses der Kreise auf dem Gebiete des Jugendschutzes' (27 January 1958), StAL, RdB Bildung, Kultur und Sport 1723.
104. See E.P. Thompson, 'The Moral Economy of the English Crowd in the Eighteenth Century', Past and Present 50 (1971), 76-136.
105. 'Veranstaltung im Klara Zetkin Park (June 1960)', StAL BDVP 24/73, 235b.
106. 'Bericht über die Pressley und 42er Bande', 90b.
107. In the first quarter of 1959 seventy young people between the ages of seventeen and twenty were arrested and accused of acts of violence against property and females. 'Bekämpfung der Jugendkriminalität und des Rowdytums (11.3.1960)', StAL BDVP 24/113.
108. 'Bekämpfung der Jugendkriminalität' (26 March 1960), StAL BDVP 24/113, 159.
109. 'Bericht über die Entwicklung des Rowdytums und dessen Bekämpfung (21.1.60)', StAL BDVP 24/113, 147; 'Der Kampf gegen Jugendkriminalität und Rowdytum (1960-61)', StAL BDVP 24/113, 216.
110. 'Meldung des Staatssicherheitsdienstes (29.11.59)', BArch SAPMO DY30/IV2/16/230.
111. Maase, Bravo Amerika, 146-75.
112. 'Der Kampf gegen Jugendkriminalität und Rowdytum (ca. 1959)'.
113. 'Kriminalpolizei: Stellungsnahme zur Bekämpfung des Rowdytums – Brennpunkt Klara-Zetkin-Park' (24 August 1960), StAL, BDVP 24/113, 167.
114. Based on an estimate of 1,500 gang members out of a population of 17,101 fourteen- to eighteen-year-olds. 'Teilbericht zur Analyse über Jugendarbeit in der Stadt Leipzig (11.1.1965)', StAL, IVA-5/01/269, 9.
115. 'Informationsbericht über die Durchführung des Beschlusses des Sekretariats der Bezirksleitung "Zu einigen Fragen der Jugendarbeit und dem Auftreten der Rowdygruppen" (13.10.1965)', StAL, IVA-5/01/269, 221.

◌ Chapter 10 ◌

Manufacturing Consent

*T*he building of the wall was the ultimate display of force by a state. The GDR no longer saw any need to disguise its intention to defend itself (if need be by aggression). Members of the *Kampfgruppen* were photographed standing upright and steely-faced at the border (in front of the Brandenburg Gate) stemming by force the flow of bodies and ideas between East and West.¹ Three days after the border was closed, the FDJ issued an appeal to young men in the

Figure 5. Forming a wall in Berlin (13 August 1961).

name of 'the Fatherland' calling on them to volunteer for military service. 'Every real man [*ganzer Kerl*] who has his heart in the right place is now proving his love for the German Democratic Republic ... In these decisive days, every young socialist burns with the desire to master the modern techniques of warfare and to demonstrate courage, stamina and discipline.'[2] The order groups were tasked with the implementation of a 'Blitz against NATO broadcasters' designed to force the population to turn their aerials around and to stop receiving radio and television from the West.[3] The SED showed that it was prepared to use overt intimidation, violence and humiliation against members of the population involved in activities (such as tuning in to Western media) that it had arbitrarily condemned as being 'hostile to the state'.

If, in the West, the closure of the border was presented as the heartless and brutal act of a morally bankrupt communist regime, internal propaganda presented it as a necessary step to counter a real threat. The danger came not so much from the imperialist armies as from capitalist ideology, which threatened to undermine the GDR from within and to drain away its manpower. While the Western powers held back and looked on, it was groups of 'rowdies' who tried to influence and sway those defending the frontier with insults and taunts (offering them cigarettes if they would cross over).[4] While Eastern 'rowdies' defamed the state by protesting against the wall, their like-minded brothers in the West tried to help free them by attacking and tunnelling under the border.[5] If the SED needed any more evidence, this was proof that male youth needed to be brought under control. As Walter Ulbricht told the Politbüro on 22 August 1961, 'If the Fatherland calls, the first duty of youth is to come to its defence.' Anyone who did not was now to be regarded with the utmost suspicion. Ulbricht was not opposed to the machismo of those in the gangs. If they joined the NVA and allowed themselves to be trained as defenders of socialism, he saw great potential for them. But woe betide them if they did not. For those who argued that it was unthinkable for Germans to shoot other Germans, he had a clear message: 'who provokes will be shot'.[6]

After the period of renewed repression that coincided with the building of the wall, the summer of 1964 saw the GDR go on a renewed 'image offensive' designed to present a new, young and modern face to the world.[7] The previous year, the Politbüro had issued a communiqué to young people offering them increased freedom in return for their overt commitment to the building of socialism. Careful planning and skilful rhetoric masked the fact that concretely little about young people's position in the GDR had actually changed. 'Youth', Walter Ulbricht told his image-makeover experts, 'has the task of forming the future of the GDR and of the whole German nation.'[8] As the embodiment of modernity, young people were the key to transforming world opinion about the state behind the wall. The SED could only allow them to fulfil their destiny by 'overcoming the bureaucratism that here and there has become a habit with us. I'm talking about the bureaucratism that begins with the Working Group for Youth in the Central Council of the FDJ and [can be seen] everywhere.'[9] According to Ulbricht, the younger generation had grown up under the conditions of the Workers' and Peasants' State and had no direct experience of the 'fight against capitalism'. As a result, 'a whole series of new educational problems' existed. The major problem was an imbalance in young people's attitudes to work and leisure. According to Horst Schumann, the First Secretary of the FDJ, 'The first thing they all think about is leisure, dancing, fashion, amusing themselves, that is what life means for them. Naturally, they do their work, they study too, but for them it is more or less a necessary evil, that they can't get out of ... [The way they perceive the world is] characterised by letting themselves go and just living for the day.'[10]

Ironically for the SED, rebelliousness among youth was a product not of poverty, but of plenty. Despite the party's best efforts to keep young people's eyes firmly fixed on planned production targets, there were worrying signs of a growth of individualism and hedonism among youth. By removing the spectre of unemployment and poverty from their horizon, the leadership ensured that East German teenagers never again needed to fear for their existence.[11] Unfortunately, this also meant that the 'right to work' became less important than the 'right to party'. If young people were to accomplish the task set out for them by the SED, then it needed to change the way they saw themselves and their reason for existence. 'If your life is to have meaning, then every hour and every day you must engage yourself for socialism.'[12] Youth's supposed idealism seemed to offer the regime its most important resource. If young people could be hooked into cooperation and enthusiastic support by means of symbolic rather than material incentives – acceptance and recognition rather than improvements in wages and the standard of living – then the regime had a chance to break out of the vicious circle of failing incentives and poor productivity.

In the course of the early 1960s, teachers began to play a more important role in the planning of FDJ activities. The FDJ began to become a compulsory extension of the curriculum rather than an alternative to school.[13] Without an unblemished record of full engagement in FDJ activities and other initiatives, it became much more difficult to obtain a place at high school or university. As school and the FDJ became increasingly synonymous, girls increasingly took advantage of the opportunities for participation and leadership in the youth organisation. The fact that teaching posts came to be increasingly filled by women had another unforeseen effect on the character of the youth organisation.[14] It meant, that in spite of its increasing 'militarisation', in the 1960s the FDJ underwent a period of cultural feminisation, becoming more female both in numbers and in character.[15] The more girls were attracted to the youth organisation and the more it became an addition to schooling, the less attractive for working-class boys it became. Instead of the 'girly' activities and prissy uniforms of the FDJ, they sought the homosocial bonding of male-dominated gangs.

A new generation was coming of age that was no longer so politically aware of and marked by experiences of Nazism, total war and defeat. Educated in the GDR, they took certain of its assumptions for granted. This led older people to feel that they lacked alternative criteria with which to compare and order their experiences of socialist society.[16] Young people, however, complained that older generations did not need 'to keep going on about what used to be the case'.[17] A new generation of university-educated intellectuals was emerging that identified with some of the SED's key values but which resented the continued emphasis placed on staid and petit bourgeois notions of morality. Recognising that the system needed firm boundaries if it was to function at all, would-be reformers placed greater importance on softening the edges of socialism in the GDR and thereby making it more liberal, tolerant, flexible and permissive. They claimed their own cultural identity and believed that it was possible to change the GDR into a society that was 'humane and worth living in'.[18] They did not just want the GDR to be 'normal', they wanted it to be at the cutting edge. They demanded more 'fizz' and 'froth' in socialism. Things that to older generations were unimportant (and potentially suspect) like music, fashion, art, cinema and sex were seen as essential. The fashion magazine *Sibylle* started life as just another unsophisticated publication for stolid housewives. It was transformed by the arrival of a generation of young women graduates who saw themselves as spokeswomen for the career woman. They set about creating a magazine that depicted self-confident, believable, emancipated women. 'Optimism was the highest precept. Cheerfulness and zest for life belonged to the official guidelines.'[19]

Ulbricht and other leading members of the SED continued to associate fashion with an ethos of luxury in which women sold themselves through their femininity. In socialism, there were to be no 'fashion dolls' (*Modepüppchen*).[20] They had gained such views in the socialist youth groups of the 1920s. Women were to shine through the naturalness of their healthy bodies and their concrete achievements. Nevertheless, both politicians and social scientists were forced to recognise that consumerism was undermining these old romantic notions and altering the way in which young people perceived the regime and its youth policy. By making everything else appear old and dusty, Walter Friedrich argued, the new possibilities for 'motorbike rides and camping trips' with a soundtrack (and mental horizons) provided by pop songs were changing experiences of what constituted youthful 'romanticism'.[21] At the same time, 'unfashionable' clothes were beginning to pile up and could not be shifted even at giveaway prices. Regime leaders were obliged to recognise that consumers' ideas about fashion might be an important economic (as well as psychological) factor.[22]

By satisfying the new generation's consumer demands and appealing to their modern and progressive outlook, reformers hoped to win them over to the cause of socialism. This meant accepting aspects of mass culture and the concept of choice.[23] The new, more democratic and market-oriented approach fitted in well with the ethos of the youth club – voluntary, loosely organised and with a friendlier and less authoritarian tone.[24] Embracing certain aspects of capitalist consumer culture and giving them a socialist spin does seem to have been a shrewd marketing tool. The youth magazine *Neues Leben* led the way with articles on relationships ('Probleme: Du und ich'), East German actors, sports stars, music and youth fashion.[25] Getting closer to young people often meant addressing their gender differences. For him, there were advertisements for adventure stories and pictures of attractive, occasionally naked women. For her, there were problem pages, fashion tips and adverts for skin cream. The Politbüro's new-found interest in fashion also stemmed from the fact that the pictures that magazines like *Sibylle* and *Neues Leben* presented of life in socialism showed a world that was much more 'harmonious, clean and friendly' than the GDR ever actually succeeded in being.[26]

Modernisation without the Problems of Modernity

For Walter Ulbricht, the transformation of education had been a major achievement, but 'one cannot say that it has been accompanied by a firm orientation in the development of youth's consciousness'. Ulbricht's attention had been caught by a children's TV programme he had seen on East German television.

> We hear on TV that a schoolgirl declares her lifetime goal to be owning a house with five rooms. There shouldn't be more rooms than that because otherwise there would be too much housework! This house should be situated near a lake so that they wouldn't have to build a 'swimming pool'. Those were the very words she used! I'm very clear about this. I only need to hear something like that once [general mirth]. And that at the *Kant-Oberschule* in Berlin of all places. Kant would turn over in his grave if he could hear that.[27]

Such dreams of being a spoilt, idle *Luxusfrau* had no place in Walter Ulbricht's vision of a glorious communist future for the GDR. For Ulbricht, the problem was that, within the administration, 'everyone makes his own youth policy, as he understands it, one from this standpoint, the other from another, one from a cultural position, the other from the position of scientific-technical progress. Is it not necessary to clear up this question?'[28] Although he was officially presented as being the mastermind behind the GDR's educational project, Ulbricht's comments revealed discontent with certain aspects of the new system. Comparing the way young people were being educated in the GDR with the education he had received as a boy in the *Kaiserreich*, there was much that he could find that was wrong with it. 'Back then, in Germany under the Kaiser, at least there was a class teacher.'[29]

Ulbricht's attitudes to education were dominated by his own personal experiences as a pupil at the *Volksschule* and later as a member of the socialist youth organisation. In 1914, along with the other men of his generation, Ulbricht had become a soldier. At the front, he had experienced at first hand the effects of German militarism: 'impassive, lifeless creatures, incapable of resistance, who, in spite of their fear and deafened by shouts of hurrah, run into the waiting arms of death'.[30] Nevertheless although he was a fierce critic of German (and later West German) militarism, throughout his life Ulbricht remained convinced of the value of militant struggle, military organisation and discipline. On his return to Leipzig in 1918, he had taken part in the Spartacus Uprising and had stood 'shoulder to shoulder' at the barricades. After joining the KPD, he came to preside over the permanent military council and was responsible for increasing the fighting strength of the party. His entire career in the KPD had been devoted to trying to implement a Leninist, military-style command structure.[31]

Even when he became the leader of the GDR, Ulbricht's self-image remained very much that of a simple and straightforward man's man. His biographers were keen to emphasise that he had been 'a boy like any other, scrapping with fellow pupils and playing football in the streets'.[32] He was proud of his sporting ability and had been a member of the Acorn Workers' Gymnastics Club since 1907. Although he thought learning was important too, Ulbricht repeatedly emphasised the importance of sport as the key to developing socialist personality characteristics. Even as an old man, he 'used every opportunity to be with young people and to practise sport'.[33] Ulbricht harked back to the beneficial effects of gymnastics in engendering manly qualities. Propaganda pictures depict the GDR's ruler in a variety of sporting poses (skiing, skating, rowing, hunting).[34] But, whether he was doing physical jerks or playing tennis, engaging in volleyball or ping-pong, Ulbricht always had his trousers pulled up over his ample stomach. He was so proud that the Lower Saxon Agriculture Minister had remarked that he still looked 'proper powerful' (*recht kräftig*) that he included this anecdote in his official biography.[35] Nevertheless, rather than increasing support for him, this need for attention and favourable propaganda instead served to undermine his dignity.

The combined effect of all these influences on Ulbricht's personal development was an obsession with order. 'Even in his most democratic-sounding speeches and writings, he could barely avoid lapsing into the rhetoric of order.'[36] He saw the key to control over education as being the creation of a chain of command like the one that existed in the military. When he visited a school or a factory, he expected to be met by someone with responsibility, someone who was in charge and who would take the flak if anything was not right. This was the way it was done in the army. 'When I come to a unit, I receive an accurate report of what the situation is. Woe betide the political officer if he doesn't tell me what kind of a mess his unit

Figure 6. Walter Ulbricht being influenced by stalwart members of the working class as a member of the *Leipzig* Gymnastic Association at the beginning of the century.

is in.' This was also the structure of command Ulbricht had implemented in the economy. 'In industry I have to have a chain of command, don't I? There I have a manager, a general manager and a work leader. Those are the ones I make responsible! But with you lot [in the education system] nobody's responsible. There too, order must be created.'[37] For 'ten years', Ulbricht said, he had been trying to drum it into the education ministry that they needed to implement a similar chain of command. 'In 1958, I raised the issue of the class teacher! Who the hell is actually responsible?' The problem was the new, 'people's democratic order' and the 'sloppiness' that had resulted from it. 'That's the way the whole education system has been mucked up.' But, 'to be polite, I'll say that a "liberalisation" has occurred'. In many ways, though, Ulbricht felt that the new, reformed East German education system was not a patch on the old one.

Figure 7. Man of action Walter Ulbricht demonstrating his continued vigour by playing volleyball with 'the youth'.

Before we had to cram to get marks. But now that's been abolished. That's the difference. Back then, we did gym. When it was still called 'gymnastics', you knew exactly what you were doing. But what's it called now? [Interruption: physical education!] No! That was also too straightforward an education. Where is the novelty? It consists in the fact that one no longer needs to do gym, but that one can play ring-a-ring o' roses during this time. With gym, we marched up in ranks of four, counted off and went 'left-right-march!' to the equipment! After the warm-up we did gymnastics. But, here in the GDR, we no longer do gym. Instead off they go into the heavenly spheres. There everyone can do their ring-a-ring o' roses exactly the way they want.[38]

Ulbricht was clearly worried that the GDR had gone too far in certain areas and was drifting away from its true purpose, as a workers' and peasants' state (with an emphasis on disciplined bodies). Implicitly, he felt that the education system was becoming too feminine. In common with conservatives throughout the world, he felt that an insidious and emasculating intellectualism had encroached on the education system, displacing the importance of discipline and physical education as key components of a young man's spiritual and moral (as well as physical) development. Such an education would not produce the heroes of production or the socialist warriors needed to defend the GDR.

> There are not enough applicants for mining, the blast furnaces as well as for agriculture. What do you think: are our young men too weak for such work in the coal mines, in the steelworks and in the cement industry? Recently on TV I saw how young athletes were being trained as hairdressers and this was how they were demonstrating their strength. I don't know if we need so many young men in the hairdressing salons. I doubt it. I think that it would be better to train girls as hairdressers. This would also be more agreeable for the young men who come to the salon as customers.[39]

What Ulbricht wanted was a return to older values. But, because the SED claimed to be following the 'scientific laws' of Marxism-Leninism, it could not be seen as going backwards and reneging on what had previously been proclaimed as progressive and liberal-minded modernisation. If what Ulbricht intended was a restoration of traditional values (and with them a renewed emphasis on masculinity), the means of achieving this had to appear new and modern. Monika Kaiser has interpreted Ulbricht's decision to implement the youth communiqué as a sign that he was more open-minded and forward-looking than has previously been admitted.[40] But there is a danger of confusing looking to the future with being progressive. Ulbricht was prepared to consider using radical methods to achieve his aims, but he remained completely committed both to the ends and to the means of dictatorship. What he objected to were dictatorial methods that were ineffective. Although the communiqué was widely interpreted as a sign that there would be greater toleration for 'young and modern' ways of thinking, Ulbricht was not at all happy about the new fashions he could see taking hold in his Republic. 'We'll have your teaching seminars inspected,' he threatened the Minister for Education, Alfred Lemmnitz, 'then we'll see how the teachers are trained there. We'll check how many female teachers go to school with make-up and short skirts, etc. to give the children this example. We'll check all of that and we'll see who's to blame for the training teachers are given. That's the question.'[41]

Democratisation was the furthest thing from Ulbricht's mind as he tried to find a solution to the youth problem.

> State apparatus is state apparatus, it isn't a voting association. Votes are held in the Volkskammer in order to advise and conclude laws, but, when the state apparatus has something to carry out, it is to do so exactly. Otherwise, it is impossible to work. And that goes for all areas. But the trick is not to do it in a formalistic, administrative way, but to do it in a way that people will be convinced that their initiatives are being developed.

The 'art' (Kunst) was to dictate a law from above but to make it appear as if it was a response to genuine problems and real discussions. In the final, published version of the Jugendkommuniqué, Ulbricht's cynical attitude to teenagers and their opinions had been transformed into: 'We have thought about your questions openly, truthfully, soberly and critically, as is our way.'[42]

Not only had the whole system become too soft and liberal for Ulbricht, but it was far too top-heavy and bureaucratic. The education ministry had all sorts of think tanks working for it to come up with new names and reforms. The FDJ did a very good job at splitting hairs in drafting laws. But neither organisation seemed to have much of an idea of 'how youth now lives and how the problems will be solved'. In Ulbricht's mind, extra-legal agitation was needed to create the momentum necessary to carry through the reforms. 'The main question, though, is the new presentation of the problems, the changing of working methods, the lively implementation. To do it as if we have no law and won't make any law ... the law is only an assistance to put pressure there where things aren't going normally.'[43] Ulbricht hoped that the communiqué would provide a means of avoiding and removing the contradictions inherent in 'modern' development. He wanted to initiate a drive for modernisation without encouraging the changes in outlook and behaviour so apparent in Western countries. He wanted the improvements in industry, the economy, education and governance that allowing free rein to independence, autonomy, creativity and initiative would bring. But he could not trust the population sufficiently to allow them any real freedom. Faced not only with increasing complexity and diversity but also with the appearance of phenomena that had not been planned or predicted, Ulbricht hoped to impose order from above. As is evident from the way in which the communiqué was received, however, significant sections of East German society still eagerly hoped for and anticipated the very changes that Walter Ulbricht so opposed.

Cultural Revolution: 'Socialism with a Cheeky Face'

The person responsible for spinning the message until it appeared palatable (and plausible) to media-savvy teenagers was Kurt Turba. At the meeting in March 1963, Turba had been praised by Ulbricht for his work as editor of *Forum* magazine. Ulbricht had suggested that 'public treatment' of questions like that of youth criminality should be carried on in the way it had been begun in *Junge Welt* and *Forum* so that there were 'no exaggerations, but the tone should be right. In no way should some exaggerated criticism of youth come out. The enemy should not be provided with ammunition with which to derail the discussions.' Questions were to be handled as matter-of-factly as possible. Ulbricht laid a great deal of importance on the FDJ itself posing the questions 'so that we don't give the impression that we have to intervene or that we have the intention of intervening'.[44] Turba responded to Ulbricht's criticism of the FDJ's bureaucracy and incompetence by suggesting making young people themselves the agents of change. His idea was to harness young people's capacity for idealism and their 'natural' desire for change and to use them as a dynamic force to shake up society. The phrase Turba coined to describe these young revolutionaries was 'impudent socialists': 'es ist unsere Aufgabe, sozialistisch frech zu sein'. Although it referred to them as the 'house masters' (*Hausherren*) of tomorrow rather than as 'impudent socialists', the communiqué embodied many of these ideas about the role young people could play in challenging outdated working practices and acting as a motor for change.

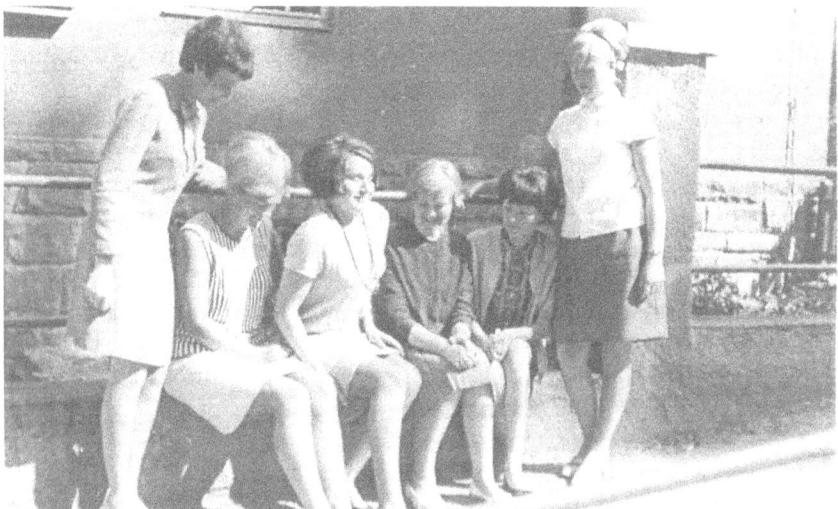

Figure 8. In creating a chronicle for their school, pupils captioned this picture 'That's the power of the working class. Former pupils of, now teachers at our school'.

By speaking directly to young people, the communiqué cut out the layers of middle-ranking bureaucrats and set out what youth's tasks were to be in the transformation of society. They were to be 'creative and self-confident forgers of a happy future'.[45] The communiqué combined the notion that young people were malleable and idealistic with a recognition that they were often poorly treated and misunderstood. *Junge Welt* announced that the communiqué sounded a new melody for youth, a 'joyful optimism' that would overcome 'the soulless administration' and 'remains of dogmatism' in the GDR.[46] One area in which the Politbüro was keen to show itself to be modern and progressive was in relation to sex. Like sport, sex offered a useful potential area of overlap between young people's interests and those of the regime. In the *Jugendkommuniqué*, the Politbüro recognised that 'our youth is maturing earlier'. The changes in education and the youth organisation designed to ensure full equality between boys and girls meant that they came together a lot earlier and a lot closer than in the past. Being secretive, prudish, restrictive or draconian was unlikely to solve problems caused by the onset of adolescence.[47]

The communiqué not only declared young people to be mistreated by older generations, but emphasised that they would soon replace them. 'Only youth are in the position to master the great problems of societal progress.'[48] In the factories, the publicity surrounding the communiqué generated significant alarm among older generations, who feared that they were about to be superseded. Conflicts developed as older, more established workers sought to hold onto positions of power and influence. Control of skilled positions and machinery was a particular source of contention, as these were associated with masculine prowess and acted as a source of hierarchical privilege.[49] Older workers struggled to find arguments for why the younger, fitter, better-educated generation was not up to the task of taking over from them. Ulbricht's intention had been to ensure that any 'modern' changes that occurred in society were rigidly controlled. The consequences of the youth communiqué, however, appear to have had exactly the opposite effect. By embarking on a campaign against bureaucratic inertia, Ulbricht unwittingly unleashed expectations for wide-ranging progressive and democratising reforms.

The communiqué targeted youth. But it had a much more important impact on writers, journalists, artists, musicians and film-makers, who were all highly adept at reading (and writing) between the lines. They saw the matter-of-fact tone of the *Jugendkommuniqué* as a sign that the ice was finally thawing and that opportunities were being opened up for experimentation and free expression within socialism.[50] Ulbricht's actual statements in March 1963 make it clear that he had no intention of unleashing creativity in the cultural sphere. What he wanted was for young people to form a modern, capable workforce and for the education system to achieve this function. What he absolutely did not want were teachers 'who have succumbed to the influence of Western lifestyles' or TV programmes designed to develop young people's fashion sense. 'As if youth is there for fashion designers! Young people should be decently dressed! Our industry should produce decent clothing! The FDJ should say what problems there are! But we were unaware that youth exists for fashion designers. It's the first time we've heard that.'[51] To liberals and reformers within the administration, the rhetoric about ending 'contradictions' and 'bureaucracy' appeared to signal that the regime was now aware of the need for change. What Ulbricht had intended was precisely the opposite: a return to traditional values.

Young Stars: Beat Music in the GDR

During the course of the mid-1960s and coinciding with the brief period of toleration inaugurated by the 1963 *Jugendkommuniqué*, a home-grown beat music 'scene' developed in the GDR. Beat concerts provided young East Germans with a means of letting off steam about their 'discomfort with the uniformity, pressure to conform and inhibited ideas about morality'.[52] The expectations and interests of young people in Leipzig and Liverpool were surprisingly similar in the early 1960s. Both were international cities undergoing prolonged post-war decline. Both had very lively musical scenes, with young working-class male amateur musicians living for their music, spending all their money on equipment and relying on their girlfriends to make clothing for them.[53] The difference was that the youth of Liverpool could travel and escape – even if, at first, only to Hamburg.

Hamburg was the making of the Beatles. After spending two years playing poorly paid and physically demanding gigs to raucous audiences of sailors, criminals and prostitutes, they emerged in 1963 as a 'charismatic powerhouse', something wild at the fringes of British pop. Their success brought undreamed-of riches and enough fame to rival Jesus Christ. Heavily influenced by rock 'n' roll and rhythm and blues records, the key achievement of the Beatles was to make black music acceptable to white audiences.[54] What was new and different about their music was its syncopated rhythm.[55] The consequence of this change in beat was a rushing sense of freedom and release. 'Reviving the Fifties' rock-and-roll rebellion in the mid-Sixties, The Beatles acted as a major conduit of black energy, style and feeling into white culture, helping to restore it to its undernourished senses and thereby forwarding the "permissive" revolution in sexual attitudes.'[56] Young white people discovered a type of dance that went against the puritanism and rigidity of their upbringing. This type of music allowed them a 'resistant response' to the instrumentalism and disciplining of the body. Rather than conserving their energies for work, beat fans expressed their lack of inhibitions and their new-found pleasure in their bodies through dance.[57]

Ian MacDonald characterises the atmosphere of the time in Britain as 'post-Christian nowness', in which 'immediate sexual gratification became the ideal of a society in which church-going was falling in inverse relationship to the rise in television ownership'. The Beatles were perfect models for this change in outlook: 'their early lyrics are careless, streetwise, immediate, sensationalistic – the expression of minds without respect for age or experience, interested only in the thrills, desires and disappointments of the present'.[58] Another key feature of the Beatles' music was their 'breezy unorthodoxy'. 'Lennon and McCartney had a wry disregard for education and training, shunning technical knowledge in the fear that it would kill their spontaneity and tame them into sounding like everyone else.'[59] The fact that the Beatles were all self-taught 'amateurs' who played by ear and who improvised their own songs had a tremendous impact on young people (and especially young men) throughout the Western world. If the Beatles stuck to their own particular style because they did not want to sound like everyone else, very soon everyone else wanted to sound like them.

The SED's new, more liberal attitude to music and dancing was summed up in the phrase, 'Welchen Takt die Jugend wählt, ist ihr überlassen: Hauptsache, sie bleibt taktvoll!'[60] In part, this was a reference to the failure of the Lipsi. However, while it appeared less prescriptive, the clever play on words masked continuing ambivalence. For progressive-minded lower-ranking functionaries, it could appear that young people were now allowed to do what they wanted in their enjoyment of youth culture. The actual meaning was that, although young people would be allowed room for manoeuvre, there were limits and the limits would continue to be set by the party. With their eyes fixed on the 'Germany meeting' (*Deutschlandtreffen*) scheduled for May 1964 (the first all-German meeting of the FDJ and its allies in over a decade) it was important for SED leaders to be able to portray the GDR as being young and dynamic. This meant that functionaries were encouraged to err on the side of liberalism. Although very few had actually read the communiqué, beat fans soon exploited the space opening up within the system for 'independent initiatives' and 'creative expression'.[61]

Before Ulbricht had even conceived of the communiqué, young musicians had already been busy creating a beat music scene that was very literally 'underground'. Taking over communal basements and cellars, young beat fans decorated them with their own collages and posters, turning them into subterranean pieds-à-terre for the enjoyment of beat music. Particularly among the boys, there was a desire to go further than simply dressing like the Beatles, but to start copying their music too. Guitar groups with names like the the Bottels, the Brittels, the Butlers, the Shatters, the Five Stones, the Musik Stones and the Nameless formed in working-class neighbourhoods, quickly winning reputations and status for themselves among local youth. The communiqué increased the scope for young amateur musicians to earn money by putting on performances for larger audiences. Money was important because it allowed amateur musicians to buy better instruments and amplifiers. Much of their equipment had to be cobbled and soldered together because the cost of proper amplifiers and sound desks was much too high.⁶² In addition to the musicians themselves, a beat group would often possess a hinterland of friendly technicians and fixers. This mixed bag of artists and assistants was often joined by former schoolmates, who helped carry their gear, and girlfriends, who provided glamour. Together, they created an aura of something happening around the band. Time not spent playing or practising was usually taken up by drinking, swapping stories and going to other bands' gigs.

Getting a chance to play in public nearly always entailed negotiations with local bureaucrats and a few sleights of hand. The sixty-forty rule on music of Western origin also applied to live concerts and gigs. As a result, it was officially expected that 60 per cent of the songs played would be of socialist production. Had any of the bands actually stuck to the ruling, then they were likely to have been booed off stage and had their equipment smashed to pieces. Fortunately, however, the self-appointed monitors of decorum and good taste were sufficiently recognisable – as tired and disapproving forty-something SED hacks amid a teaming sea of excited teenagers – for the musicians to be able to notice their arrival and deftly switch (often mid-song) from capitalist to socialist musical production. Thanks to the party's sporadic approach to reform, an incoherent jumble of different institutions and organisations were involved in catering for young people's free-time needs. The sheer range of outlets meant that it was impossible for the authorities to exercise all-encompassing surveillance and control. It was always possible to find a work canteen or somewhere on the edge of town where the exercise of political control was more lax.⁶³

Internal reports produced by the police in West Berlin show that they were equally alarmed about the impact of Beatle mania on youth. One such report described boys and girls who had entered a trance-like state of ecstasy during a beat concert in 1965 as primitive and bestial, arguing that they were so hypnotised that they had lost control of their bladders.⁶⁴ The shared sense of complicity that existed between musicians and fans heightened feelings of 'resistant communality' by giving all involved a sense of genuine subversiveness.⁶⁵ The lack of commercialisation in the early GDR beat music scene created a much more intensive bond between fans and musicians, akin to that enjoyed by the Beatles during their early Cavern Club performances. Their audiences were far from simply passive consumers and had a real stake in the way in which the bands developed. As far as the fans were concerned, they had put the musicians where they were and consequently the groups belonged to them. Without their continuing financial support, the bands could not afford to continue to grow and become more successful. In return, they demanded that the musicians gave the concerts everything they had. Musicians made up for what they lacked in sophisticated sound and lighting equipment with powerful, crowd-pleasing stage performances. Through their costumes, their look and

Figure 9. Let's twist again like we did last summer. Proof of Walter Ulbricht's commitment to modern but safe youth activities.

gestures, they imitated the intense emotions of bands like the Beatles and the Stones, playing as if they were performing to full stadiums rather than in a dingy local hall. 'These songs were freer, more exciting, darker, crazier. They were beautiful, kitsch, incomprehensible, seductive. They came from far away.'[66] Musicians and fans fed off one another to create an atmosphere as close as possible to the real thing, thereby transporting themselves far away from the GDR and its mundane reality.

A key component of this imaginary transportation was style. As Dick Hebdige explains,

> The basis of style is the appropriation and reorganisation by the subject of elements in the objective world that would otherwise determine and constrict him. The mod's cry of triumph ... was for a romantic victory, a victory of the imagination; ultimately for an imagined victory. The mod combined previously disparate elements to create himself into a metaphor, the appropriateness of which was apparent only to himself.[67]

In the GDR, youth subcultures represented not just opposition to the imposition of a communist youth organisation and political indoctrination, but a desire to develop and preserve their own lifestyle and identity in the face of official hostility. Much more than had been the case with rock 'n' roll, the style surrounding beat music offered teenagers a genuine alternative lifestyle encompassing a range of different outlooks and expressions. For some, it was an almost philosophical rejection of the dominant hegemony, with attitudes equivalent to those of the beatniks and the early hippies. In the mid-1960s, the most important item in the beat boy's wardrobe was his transistor radio. This was usually accompanied by home-made flares and a parka, but occasionally also a blazer.

Even more than rock 'n' roll, beat fashions provoked older generations by challenging and undermining their notions of masculinity. Covert surveillance pictures show boys with as many as four transistors standing demonstratively in the entrance to a cinema in East Berlin.[68] Girls, who in the meantime were more equally represented in the subculture, stood out as a result of their short skirts. More counterculture than pop culture, and more overtly rock 'n' roll than the Beatles, the Rolling Stones offered a music that was harder and more aggressive.[69] '"Paint it Black" had nothing to do with a poem by Becher or Majakowski ... with phrases, with songs about tanks, national anthems, flag ceremonies and standing straight. It lifted us up and took us away from the stupid routine.'[70] The Stones were particularly popular with the streetwise members of working-class gangs who had come to be labelled 'dropouts' (*Gammler*) by the authorities. While moves towards liberalisation drew musicians into a closer, though still ambivalent, relationship with the regime, those in the gangs continued to pursue self-segregation.

For all its shortcomings, the *Jugendkommuniqué* had nevertheless created unprecedented space for young people. Aided by sympathetic youth club workers, amateur musicians were able to create their own opportunities for activity and expression. One particularly popular venue in Leipzig was the *Kino der Jugend*. According to Dieter, its volunteer manager, the secret of its success was 'to keep it as unpolitical as possible'. Local youngsters were also heavily involved in refurbishing and repainting the cinema. 'We understood how to make something out of nothing. We asked friends and people who came to the *Filmclub*, "Hey mate, do you know someone who can draw and paint?" Then we got them to do posters for us as advertising.' A deal was arranged with the manager of the Capitol cinema whereby a boy on a motorbike would collect film reels straight after they had been shown there and bike them over to the *Kino der Jugend*. Although slightly older, Dieter still had an implicit understanding of the youngsters who visited the cinema. He remembered telling the cultural functionary in charge of film distribution in Leipzig, 'Whatever you do, don't send us a heavy partisan film or something like that.' From experience, he could guess what the likely reaction would be.

Carried away by the cinema's success and the enthusiasm of the youngsters, who came along every week, Dieter let himself be talked into allowing amateur beat bands to perform on stage. 'At first, the bands were there as a prelude to the film, but they proved so popular that in the end it was all music with a bit of film at the end.' Klaus Renft, at the time lead singer of the Butlers, remembered it as being a great venue for gigs. 'The atmosphere was really wild.'[71] For Dieter S., however, it became increasingly difficult to keep the youngsters under control. 'It was absolute bedlam. There were 900 young people in there, starting at twelve and the oldest of them were eighteen. The average was twelve to sixteen. You can imagine the howling and the roaring ... It was always at boiling point. At any moment it could tip over.'[72] The crowd of teenagers became so big that they had to start turning them away at the door and, on occasion, had policemen guarding the side exits. 'What was dangerous was that they were all sat so close together.' They were all packed in so tightly that many a time he feared for his cinema seats, which were 'old in any case'. Nevertheless, it was impossible to prevent the youngsters shifting around to the music. 'Young people want to have their fling, want to dance around ... If you are going to let young people do things themselves then you have to reckon with the occasional mishap.'[73]

Conflicting Conceptions of Modernity

The 1964 *Deutschlandtreffen* (showcasing the GDR for an outside audience) brought Western-inspired youth culture onto the fringes of mainstream, officially orchestrated events for the first time. By letting young people 'do their thing' unhindered, the regime was obviously hoping to avoid embarrassing incidents such as those that had occurred during the late 1950s when its 'bread and circus' shows had been disrupted by unruly youth-cultural dissidents. This time, the regime endeavoured to win favour for itself by ensuring that the view from the outside was of attractive and nubile youth enjoying themselves. As the *Spiegel* reporter Hermann Schreiber put it, the West German delegation was met by a 'crowd of young Saxon girls with bunches of flowers and white nylon blouses, slightly damp from the drizzle'. Nevertheless, the official orchestration did not go entirely without incident. A protest occurred when the beat music was prematurely turned off. Practised in the socialist art of shouting out slogans, the 'young builders of socialism' marched along the Frankfurter Allee shouting 'in part indecent, in part simply rebellious slogans' until they were stopped by a police roadblock and the more vocal among them were arrested.[74]

Once the visitors had gone home, the mood within the administration began to harden against beat. No official announcement was made, but, in the year following the event, there were signs that sections of the administration were moving in different directions, often in complete contradiction to one another. To avoid being swamped by the wave of enthusiasm for beat, FDJ functionaries at first tried to surf on top of it. In the process, they opened up opportunities for amateur beat musicians to perform under their aegis. According to Kurt Turba, this move had been directly encouraged by Erich Honecker, who had advised him: 'either we let the beat wave run its course or we put ourselves at its head and put our stamp on the movement ['mit unseren Stempel aufdrücken']. We have to do the latter.'[75] Meanwhile, bridling at the new-found freedom amateur musicians were enjoying, local cultural functionaries began to increase the pettiness of restrictions on performances. In defending their music and fragile autonomy from such encroachments, the Butlers found support and encouragement from an unusual and unlikely source. *Neues Deutschland*, the 'organ of the SED', weighed in on the side of the young Leipzig musicians, arguing that theirs was the same music as was played on the civil rights march in Selma, Alabama, and that the sacrifices they made for their music were more than compensated for by the pleasure they gave to their fans. The article described 'the unbelievable love' the Butlers showed for their music, noting that they practised almost every day, 'often until two in the morning'. In May 1965, the author, Heinz Stern, and the cultural editor of *Neues Deutschland* were called to a special meeting held by the SED regional authorities.[76] Defending the Butlers against charges from the provincial authorities that they were work-shy, the journalists from Berlin joked that 'The Butlers work so hard to please their public that they should be allowed to sleep in once in a while.' Stern described the campaign by the Leipzig authorities against the Butlers as constituting a 'terror'. Following the meeting, in a move that was interpreted by the Leipzig authorities as 'a deliberate provocation', the Butlers were invited to play at *Neues Deutschland*'s press festival.[77]

Stern had committed ideological heresy in his article by arguing that it was impossible to divide dance music into categories of socialist and capitalist: 'dance music cannot be divided into imperialist and socialist. Give free rein to youth and to their music.'[78] Within the administration, Stern's article sparked a debate about what kind of socialist society the GDR should aim to be. Did everything in it still have to be rigidly controlled or was there instead space for a limited degree of autonomy and 'letting off of steam'? Was Western-inspired youth culture compatible with the development of socialist consciousness or was the survival of the GDR dependent on ensuring that East and West remained rigidly separated? Differences of personality and outlook aside, the SED's leaders were faced with a fundamental contradiction in their stance towards modernity. Ulbricht had hoped to use the communiqué as a means of modernising the economy and society. Yet, while young people were keen to embrace 'modern' developments, what they meant by the word 'modern' was very different from the conceptions of those in the party leadership. For Ulbricht, in particular, modernity was about fulfilling the vision of socialism by lowering the gap between rich and poor and satisfying the population's wants and needs in terms of employment and basic consumption. The only way to achieve this was by means of increased productivity. To overcome the challenges of the future, to produce the much needed technological improvements and innovations and to cope with the demands of increased technocracy and 'scientific' planning, young people needed to possess the appropriate qualifications and an attitude of hard work and determination.

For teenagers, however, being 'modern' was about having 'modern' clothing and haircuts, possessing progressive, forward-looking attitudes and having access to the latest technology and consumer products. 'I am for the long beat cut. It's an expression of a modern young person.'[79] While the SED's conception of 'modernisation' demanded delayed gratification and self-sacrifice in the name of society, young people's ideas about how to be modern placed emphasis on immediate rather than delayed gratification and personal consumption as an expression of individuality and difference. It did not really matter to them what they had to do at work as long as they had the money and the opportunities to do what they wanted in their free time. While the SED could tinker with the edges, there was little they could do to mask the fact that 'in the GDR there is no freedom. Not every citizen can express his opinion freely.'[80]

The 1964 *Deutschlandtreffen* had proved a great success. The GDR had been able to present an open-minded and tolerant face to the world. Western journalists had been impressed by officially organised events where FDJler could be seen twisting in their blue shirts.[81] But, once the summer of 'sun, sex and socialism' was over, East German would-be reformers showed no signs of running out of steam. The GDR's young film-makers and writers had been creatively pushing back the boundaries of what was allowed and exploring uncharted territory by tackling previously taboo subjects.[82] If Ulbricht had hoped to outflank the moderates by stealing their thunder, he had obviously seriously miscalculated. If, on the other hand, it was all just a cynical plot to get certain groups to reveal their true colours, then it had succeeded far beyond his

Figure 10. Photographs of beat fans ('amateur or drop-outs') from Lichtenberg.

original intentions. In August 1964, Paul Fröhlich, First Secretary of the SED in Bezirk Leipzig, received first-hand experience of 'impudent socialism'. He was visited by a member of the FDJ Central Council demanding to know what his administration was doing for youth. A letter was sent to Kurt Turba, whom Ulbricht had made head of a special Politbüro Youth Commission, asking him exactly what the comrade thought he was doing trying to inspect the party apparatus. 'As a consequence of his arrogant and supercilious (cheeky) behaviour, Comrade Fröhlich demanded that he leave the office immediately.'[83]

The runaway success of beat music among East German youth had not been foreseen when the officials were drawing up the youth communiqué. The new music style and the suddenly fashionable clothing and haircuts created a crisis over modernity in the midst of the SED's attempts at re-modernisation. On the one hand, the party presented young people as the vanguard and protean force for the revolutionary transformation of society. On the other, many within the SED (including Ulbricht himself) were deeply suspicious of and hostile to any unplanned, uncontrolled developments. The experiment of 'loosening the reins' that bound youth raised questions and issues that the SED had no way of answering. Most notably: how far could socialism modernise without converging with the West? Ulbricht's hopes of the communiqué magically resolving contradictions in the GDR's socialist development proved hopelessly misguided. The hope of finding a path to contradiction-free development floundered against the 'Janus face of modernity'.

At the beginning of 1965, the Ideological Commission of the Politbüro, led by Kurt Hager, stated that 'the personal interests of young people still stand in the foreground. Contacts with the FDJ become ever more superficial, and the influence of the school ... and the teacher is no longer the most important factor.'[84] The youth communiqué had coincided with a huge wave of energy and enthusiasm. But, instead of being channelled into building socialism by transforming East German industry, it was being dissipated and misspent in the 'mania' surrounding the Beatles. In the power struggle within the administration between those who were in favour of continued liberalisation and reform and those who wanted to revert to an emphasis wholly on indoctrination and control, the rapid upsurge of beat seemed to offer an incontrovertible argument that reform was misguided. Having trumpeted their acceptance of 'modern music, modern clothing, modern haircuts and modern forms of dance', SED functionaries fully expected to be accused of being opposed to modernity if they launched a backlash against beat. To counter such accusations, a memorandum was issued advising them to cease referring to beat music as being 'modern', but instead to describe it as 'recent' (*neuzeitlich*).[85]

The threat that beat posed to the regime was in undermining its rhetoric and self-legitimisation. However much the party sought to dress up its attack on beat, it clearly marked a retrograde step and stood in marked contrast to the SED's pro-modern and pro-youth rhetoric. Pupils at the *Erweiterte Oberschule* Borna argued that 'Modern haircuts shouldn't just be equated with Western ideology. A total ban on such guitar groups would be wrong.'[86] Liberalisation had temporarily brought the local cultural officials out of step with the police and the party leadership. Those in the beat music scene could have difficulty in perceiving who their friends were and who their enemies. Thus it was possible for Klaus Renft to write to Erich Honecker, the person responsible for organising the crackdown on beat music, in the mistaken belief that he might be willing to overrule the narrow-mindedness of local functionaries. In the summer of 1965, a group within the Politbüro led by Honecker began compiling evidence that could be used against the beat groups, their fans and the liberals who had condoned their activities. Youth club leaders, it was reported, were allowing amateur bands with 'American' names and English lyrics to perform gigs in their clubs. FDJ functionaries had not only condoned such activities, but had organised Republic-wide guitar competitions for the most talented up-and-coming groups.[87] One forum had been held under the banner 'Cold War – Hot Hits'.[88] East German media executives had been providing them with recording contracts and airplay. The rot of Western subversion had set so far into East German society that young FDJ apparatchiks could be heard discussing West German TV broadcasts in the corridors of the FDJ headquarters in Berlin.[89]

In December 1965, Horst Schumann criticised the sceptics who 'doubt and deny everything' and the objectivism 'that positions itself between two fronts'.[90] Those who had shown the most enthusiasm and reforming initiative now attracted the most suspicion. The continued emphasis in SED propaganda on youth as the 'house masters of tomorrow' belied the increasing belief within the party that young men's vision into the future was obscured by their long hair. Youth clubs were singled out for particular criticism.

> Many of the youth clubs that were conceived as the nuclei of a new young socialist society have unfortunately become reserves for young people with backward views and habits. From this reservoir a few rowdy gangs have noisily and rudely pushed themselves into the foreground of interest. Admittedly they are not capable of putting the extraordinarily great and positive achievements of our youth in the shadows, but we would fail if we forgot that youth is a sensitive and impressionable material.[91]

Although Ulbricht's impatience with the lumbering momentum of the FDJ had acted as the spur for changes in youth policy, it is clear from his many comments and interjections that the underlying message of the communiqué – that young people could now be free of petty-minded restrictions – was not one that he truly intended. True, he saw it as being necessary for a 'thorough discussion of problems affecting youth' and of the relations between the younger and older generations. But he saw no reason for a let-up in the 'fight against the influences of bourgeois decadence', only for that fight to be more consequential.[92] What had started out as an attempt to foster a new generation of 'impudent socialists' degenerated into a fearful confusing mess, in which the only thing SED functionaries could be sure of was that large numbers of young people cared little for their message but were instead sullenly indifferent and ungrateful. 'Friends who are not yet convinced of the victory of socialism let themselves be led astray by the dazzling facades of capitalism; the high work productivity of West Germany and the U.S.A.; and the particular difficulties that still exist here with us.'[93]

For those in the subcultures, their culture, the 'modern' culture of the English-speaking world, seemed to offer freedom from the narrow-minded constraints prevalent in the GDR. It stood for casual, easy-going attitudes and an emphasis on pleasure and experiences rather than on compulsion and self-discipline. It was in the process of defending their right to make their own decisions that they managed to challenge and undermine societal norms. Ulbricht had never had any time for young men who had 'concluded from some film about robbers they've been to that they don't really need to have a proper job'.[94] With the arrival of the fashion for beat, it was possible to identify 'idlers and lazy bones' not simply through their disrespect for the socialist work ethic but also thanks to their failure to get themselves decent haircuts.

Ironically, the rebellion against middle-class values in the West threatened to do more harm in undermining the communists. In many ways, it was a 'pseudorevolt' (Attali) against the world of pettiness constituted by adults.[95] But, because of the much more starkly politicised conditions and context of everyday life in the GDR, their oppositional stance acquired considerable import and significance. As in the Third Reich, ostensibly non-political forms of youth nonconformity posed a threat because, 'in their sweep, they possessed a relatively wide support among the youth population and, to a certain extent, spread contagiously'.[96] Not only did the state itself perceive the existence of subcultures as political, but state reactions succeeded both in politicising nonconformity and in turning *Eigensinn* into opposition. On several occasions (the most notable being the demonstrations that followed the ban on beat in October 1965), what was ostensibly a diffuse and non-political movement of youth defiance flowed over into political protest. Their stubborn challenges to official notions of culture also became challenges to the political system per se.

Conclusion

Although tolerated for the duration of the 1964 festival of youth, the wave of excitement and interest generated by beat music began to undermine official notions of 'modernity'. The ban on beat music in October 1965 served as a prelude to the wider attack on liberalisation and cultural freedom that took place at the Eleventh Party Plenum in December of that year. The SED found it easier to release young people's desire for change than actually to harness and utilise it. Overtaken by events and by doubts about the validity of the enterprise, party leaders abandoned the risky and uncertain attempt to win young people's trust for the certainties provided by prescription, self-congratulation and hostility to any novelty or nonconformity. Problems were once again 'administratively swept under the carpet'.[97] Recognition that young people might have their own specific consumer and leisure interests was tempered by a failure to accept that they had a right to be interested in Western music. Attempts to satisfy youth's consumer demands did not come with an acceptance of their right to make choices.

There was a failure to recognise the legitimacy of their desire for autonomy and self-determination. Compromises and concessions on fashion and music were soon reneged on in a return to campaigns against Western 'infiltration'. Not only did they expose the ambivalence and contradictions in the SED's project, but they also revealed cleavages within the state hierarchy, with different official agencies championing divergent concepts. Each of the attempts at compromise and co-option (or 'liberalisation' and 'reform') had contained within it the seeds of a possible reconciliation with parts of disbelieving, marginalised youth. More often than not, however, extending the hand of friendship to young people 'standing on the sidelines' constituted yet a further attempt to 'colonise their lifeworlds'.[98] The disingenuousness of some of the reformers, together with the erratic nature of policy shifts, greatly reduced the effectiveness of these periods of toleration. The party's attempts to create a more enlightened and progressive image for itself were rapidly submerged by a return to the same old attitudes of intolerant incomprehension and repression.

In terms of Realpolitik and the long-term stability of the regime, the failure of the state to establish informal spaces for young people also proved harmful. After the state effectively renounced its duty to look after vulnerable youth (following the crackdown on beat music), the Protestant churches stepped in to take its place. With post-revolutionary hindsight, the unintended bringing together of pastors and local disgruntled youth was one of the regime's key failings and a seed of its ultimate collapse. The alliance between the Protestant Church and alienated and dissident youth came about almost by accident. A former member describes how the remnants of the Capitol *Meute* developed into the first 'beat congregation'.

> In the winter of 1967 it was so cold that we began meeting a few metres further down the street in the Thomas Church. We were about as discreet there as a tarantula on a cheesecake. The pastor, who didn't know how to get rid of us and who also had some understanding for our situation, promised to find a room for us. That's how this peculiar first youth congregation came about, which wasn't actually a congregation because we weren't Christians.[99]

In the sanctuary of the church, they 'talked openly about everything that affected us, about the Prague Spring, the student movement in West Germany, the sexual revolution, the Stasi, how to escape from the GDR, about homosexuality and whether or not the system was capable of reform, etc.'[100] Despite accusations from the state that they were 'having orgies' in the church, it continued to provide a safe haven for them and took on many of the youth work functions abdicated by the state. As well as providing safer and more private meeting points, the churches played an important role in politicising and articulating youthful feelings of opposition. Although at times the tight confines of the church could be claustrophobic, in the decades following the invasion of Czechoslovakia in 1968, youth nonconformists were nevertheless welcomed as conscientious objectors to military service (who were forced to serve as *Bausoldaten*). Their similar experiences of intimidation and repression made up for their differences in background and education, and helped to forge a shared outlook and sense of opposition. Together these permanent outcasts formed the cadres of the unofficial peace movement and opened the churches up to a wide range of opposition groups. It was they who were at the forefront of the citizens' rights groups and demonstrations that stimulated the collapse of SED rule.[101]

Notes

1. Werner Sikorski and Rainer Laabs, *Checkpoint Charlie und die Mauer. Ein geteiltes Volk wehrt sich* (Berlin, 1997), 16.
2. 'Aufgebot der FDJ vom 16.8.1961: "Das Vaterland ruft! Schützt die Republik!"', BArch. SAPMO, DY24/3753-I.
3. 'Beschluß des Sekretariats des ZR der FDJ über die Ordnungsgruppen der FDJ (22.8.1961)' BArch. SAPMO DY24/3753-I; Karl Heinz Jahnke et al. (eds), *Geschichte der Freien Deutschen Jugend* (Berlin, 1976), 181; 'Analyse der Entwicklung der Jugendkriminalität im Bezirk Leipzig' (c. 1962), StAL BDVP 24.1/420, 85–86.
4. For the official view, see the film 'Knockout Punch', *Der Kinnhaken*, directed by Heinz Thiel (DEFA, 1962).
5. Sikorski and Laabs, *Checkpoint Charlie*, 70; Kurt Shell, *Bedrohung und Bewährung. Führung und Bevölkerung in der Berlin-Krise* (Cologne, 1965), 353; Corey Ross, *Constructing Socialism at the Grass-roots* (Manchester, 2000), 162.
6. 'Rede des Genossen Walter Ulbricht im Politbüro am 22.8.1961', BArch. SAPMO DY24/3727. Ulbricht ended this speech by stating, 'Also der Kampf geht frisch und fröhlich weiter.'
7. 'Informationen über den Verlauf der Deutschlandtreffen in der Hauptstadt' (1964), Landesarchiv Berlin, C Rep 902, 2121; Hermann Schreiber, 'Sonne, Sex und Sozialismus', *Der Spiegel* 22 (27 May 1964), 33–37.
8. 'Stenografische Niederschrift: Sitzung der Jugendkommission beim Politbüro des ZK und der Regierungskommission für die Ausarbeitung des Jugendgesetzes (29.3.1963)', BArch. SAPMO IV2/2.111/8.
9. Ibid.
10. Ibid.

11. 'Der Jugend Vertrauen und Verantwortung' in Zentralkomittee der SED, *Jugend von heute. Hausherren von Morgen. Kommuniqué des Politbüros des ZK der SED zu Problemen der Jugend in der DDR* (Berlin, 1963), 1–34, 6.
12. Ibid., 10.
13. ZIJ, 'Zur Lage unter der Jugend' (1988), DY30/ IV2/2.039/246, 114.
14. Ina Merkel, *... und Du, Frau an der Werkbank. Die DDR in den 50er Jahren* (Berlin, 1990), 110.
15. Edeltraud Schulze, *DDR-Jugend. Ein statistisches Handbuch* (Berlin, 1995), 227; Dorothee Wierling, *Geboren im Jahr Eins. Der Jahrgang 1949 in der DDR. Versuch einer Kollektivbiographie* (Berlin, 2002), 238; Dorothee Wierling, 'Leitbilder, Vorbilder, Abbilder. Mädchen in der FDJ' in Christina Benninghaus and Kerstin Kohtz (eds), *'Sag' mir, wo die Mädchen sind ...' Beiträge zur Geschlechtergeschichte der Jugend* (Cologne, 1999), 103–26; In later decades the increasing politicisation of the youth organisation together with a relaxation of parental attitudes meant that for girls too the FDJ became less attractive.
16. Walter Friedrich, *Flegeljahre? Zur Erziehung 13- bis 16jähriger Jungen* (Berlin, 1964), 4, 31.
17. 'Verwirklichung der sozialistischen Frauen- und Jugendpolitik' (2 December1964), BArch. SAPMO DY6/3940.
18. Dorothea Melis, 'Mode nach Plan. Oder Erziehung zum Verzicht' in Dorothea Melis (ed.), *Sibylle. Modefotographie aus drei Jahrzehnten DDR* (Berlin, 1998), 48–63, 54.
19. Ibid., 51.
20. Dietrich Mühlberg, 'Haute Couture für Alle? Über Mode und Kulturverständnis' in Melis (ed.), *Sibylle*, 8–19, 10.
21. Friedrich, *Flegeljahre?*, 26.
22. Mühlberg, 'Haute Couture für Alle?', 10–12.
23. Horst Groschopp, 'Herkommen, Struktur und Verständnis' in Hildegard Bockhorst, Brigitte Prautzsch and Carla Rimbach (eds), *Woher – Wohin? Kinder- und Jugendkulturarbeit in Ostdeutschland* (Remscheid, 1993), 14–30, 18.
24. Ibid., 21.
25. Zentralrat der FDJ, *Rhythmen, Späße, Bühnensterne: Magazin der Jugend 'Neues Leben' Jahrbuch 1963* (Berlin, 1963).
26. Melis, 'Mode nach Plan', 63.
27. 'Stenografische Niederschrift ...'
28. Ibid.
29. Ibid.
30. Lieselotte Thoms, Hans Vieillard and Wolfgang Berger, *Walter Ulbricht. Arbeiter, Revolutionär, Staatsmann* (Berlin, 1968), 14.
31. Ibid., 30–33.
32. Ibid., 7.
33. Nationalrat der Nationalen Front, *Walter Ulbricht. Ein Leben für Deutschland* (Leipzig, 1968), 153ff.
34. Ibid.
35. Thoms et al., *Walter Ulbricht*, 144.
36. Eric Weitz, *Creating German Communism 1890–1990. From Popular Protests to Socialist State* (Princeton, 1997), 318.
37. 'Stenografische Niederschrift ...'
38. Ibid.
39. 'Ihr seid die Schmiede der deutschen Zukunft' in Zentralkomittee der SED, *Jugend von heute*, 35–70, 61.
40. Monica Kaiser, *Machtwechsel von Ulbricht zu Honecker. Funktionsmechanismen der SED-Diktatur in Konfliktsituationen 1962 bis 1972* (Berlin, 1997), 134, 169.
41. 'Stenografische Niederschrift ...'
42. 'Der Jugend Vertrauen und Verantwortung', 6.
43. 'Stenografische Niederschrift ...'
44. Ibid.

45. 'Der Jugend Vertrauen und Verantwortung', 10.
46. *Junge Welt* (27 September 1963).
47. 'Der Jugend Vertrauen und Verantwortung', 14, 30.
48. Ibid., 30.
49. 'Einschätzung und Berichte zur Durchsetzung des Jugendkommuniqués (1963-1966)', StAL IV A-2/16/454.
50. Leonore Krenzlin, 'Vom Jugendkommuniqué zur Dichterschelte' in Günter Agde (ed.), *Kahlschlag. Das 11. Plenum des ZK der SED 1965. Studien und Dokumente* (Berlin, 2nd edn, 2000), 154-64, 157.
51. 'Stenografische Niederschrift …'
52. Michael Rauhut, 'DDR-Beatmusik zwischen Engagement und Repression' in Günter Agde (ed.), *Kahlschlag. Das 11. Plenum der SED 1965* (Berlin, 1991), 52-63, 58.
53. Colin Fletcher, 'Beats and Gangs in Merseyside' in Timothy Raison (ed.), *Youth in New Society* (London, 1966), 148-59.
54. Ian MacDonald, *Revolution in the Head. The Beatles' Records and the Sixties* (London, 1995).
55. Dick Bradley, *Understanding Rock 'n' Roll. Popular Music in Britain 1955-1964* (Buckingham, 1992), 112-13.
56. MacDonald, *Revolution in the Head*, 9.
57. Bradley, *Understanding Rock 'n' Roll*, 115-16.
58. MacDonald, *Revolution in the Head*, 19.
59. Ibid.
60. 'Der Jugend Vertrauen und Verantwortung', 29. 'It is up to youth to choose their tack: the main thing is that they remain tactful.'
61. Groschopp, 'Herkommen, Struktur und Verständnis', 17; Ministerium für Kultur, *Die Kulturhäuser zu Volkshäusern entwickeln* (Berlin, 1963).
62. Wierling, *Geboren im Jahr Eins*, 234.
63. Peter Wicke, 'Rock Around Socialism. Jugend und ihre Musik in einer gescheiterten Gesellschaft' in Dieter Baacke (ed.), *Handbuch Jugend und Musik* (Opladen, 1998), 293-305.
64. 'Erfahrungsbericht über den polizeilichen Einsatz anläßlich von Beat-Veranstaltungen in der "Neuen Welt" und im "Europa-Palast" (West Berlin, 23.12.1966)', Landesarchiv Berlin, B Rep 020, Nr. 7812.
65. Bradley, *Understanding Rock 'n' Roll*, 129.
66. Jürgen Fuchs, *Fassonschnitt* (Reinbek, 1984), 281-82.
67. Dick Hebdige, 'The Meaning of Mod' in Stuart Hall and Tony Jefferson (eds), *Resistance through Rituals. Youth Subcultures in Postwar Britain* (London, 1976), 87-96, 91-92.
68. 'Bilddokumentation zu Vorkommnissen mit negativen Jugendlichen' (1964-69), BArch. DO1/38215.
69. Wierling, *Geboren im Jahr Eins*, 233; Fuchs, *Fassonschnitt*, 124.
70. Fuchs, *Fassonschnitt*, 282.
71. Interview with Klaus Renft (2000).
72. Interview with Dieter S. (1999).
73. Ibid. As one of the things the boys liked to do was to jump off the balcony, a mishap of some kind or another was more or less inevitable.
74. Schreiber, 'Sonne, Sex und Sozialismus', 33-37.
75. 'Aussprache beim Genossen Kurt Turba am 5.10.1965', Landesarchiv Berlin, C Rep 902, 2118.
76. Hans-Dieter Schütt (ed.), Klaus Renft, *Zwischen Liebe und Zorn* (Berlin, 1997), 63-64.
77. Ibid., 58-64.
78. Heinz Stern, 'Butlers Boogie', *Neues Deutschland* (4 April 1965).
79. 'Meinungen zum Artikel der LVZ "Dem Mißbrauch der Jugend"' (October 1965), BArch. SAPMO DY30/IVA2/16/68.
80. 'Capitol Meute' (c. 1966), BStU, Ast. Lpz., 348/67, 62.
81. Schreiber, 'Sonne, Sex und Sozialismus', 33-37.

82. Ulrich Mählert and Gerd-Rüdiger Stephan, *Blaue Hemden, rote Fahnen. Die Geschichte der Freien Deutschen Jugend* (Opladen, 1996), 159.
83. 'Leiter der Jugendkommission (22.8.1964)', BArch. SAPMO DY30/IVA2/16/68.
84. Reports to the Politbüro (June-July, 1964), BArch. SAPMO DY 30/IV2/16/50.
85. 'Reaktion der verschiedensten Bevölkerungsschichten auf den Artikel der LVZ "Dem Mißbrauch der Jugend keinen Raum"' (21 October 1965), BArch. SAPMO, DY30/IVA2/16/68.
86. 'Meinungen zum Artikel der LVZ'.
87. Michael Rauhut, *Beat in der Grauzone. DDR-Rock 1964 bis 1972. Politik und Alltag* (Berlin, 1993), 64–95.
88. Groschopp, 'Herkommen, Struktur und Verständnis', 17.
89. Mählert and Stephan, *Blaue Hemden*, Note 184, 168–69.
90. Ibid.
91. 'Der Vater verließ den Saal. Beobachtungen und Notizen bei einem Jugendprozeß', *Neues Deutschland* (19 December 1965).
92. 'Stenografische Niederschrift …'
93. 'Bericht der ideologischen Kommission (14.1.1964)', StAL IVA-2/16/453, 37.
94. 'Ihr seid die Schmiede', 68.
95. Jacques Attali, *Noise. The Political Economy of Music*, trans. Brian Massumi (Manchester, 1985), 110.
96. Arno Klönne, 'Jugendprotest und Jugendopposition. Von der HJ-Erziehung zum Cliquenwesen der Kriegszeit' in Martin Broszat, Elke Fröhlich and Anton Grossmann (eds), *Bayern in der NS-Zeit* (Munich, 1981), vol. IV, 527–620, 620.
97. Helmut Müller cited in Alan McDougall, *Youth Politics in East Germany. The Free German Youth Movement 1946–1968* (Oxford, 2004), 198.
98. Jürgen Habermas, *Legitimation Crisis* (Cambridge, 1988), 48.
99. Ilona, 'Wir lebten von dem, wovor wir uns fürchteten' in C. Remath and R. Schneider (eds), *Haare auf Krawall. Jugendsubkultur in Leipzig 1980 bis 1991* (Leipzig, 1999), 12–23, 15.
100. Ibid.
101. Mary Fulbrook, *Anatomy of a Dictatorship. Inside the GDR. 1949–1989* (Oxford, 1995), 203ff.; 'Bausoldaten' (1970s), BStU, ZA, HA XX AKG 104; 'Friedensbewegung' (1980s), BStU, ZA, HA XX 2544.

⋘ Chapter 11 ⋙

MAKING MEN OUT OF THEM

*T*he building of the Berlin Wall, on 13 August 1961, dramatically increased the scope for militarisation. With the introduction of conscription, in 1962, all eighteen-year-old males now had to submit to military training and discipline.[1] Conscription was designed not only to increase the defensive capability of the GDR, but to establish control over male youth. It provided a year and a half in which the authorities could 'take them firmly in hand, set clear boundaries, apply pressure' and, it was hoped, bind them to the regime.[2] Male youth was to be 'broken in'.[3] 'The leather jackets and flat tops [*Bürstenjonnys*] should be taught to be decent blokes [*anständigen Kerlen*] in the People's Army.' Workers who had already done their military service appreciated the fact that those who had preferred to stand around on street corners (*die Eckensteher*) would now have to fall into line.[4] Military service would provide the short sharp shocks (and haircuts) the party felt that they needed. As in other militarised societies, military service became an important milestone in the passage from boyhood to manhood.[5] Having had mixed success in creating 'socialist personalities', the SED tried instead to create soldierly personalities.[6] The traditional harsh military regime designed to instil unquestioning obedience by physically punishing recruits and pushing them to the limits of exhaustion was combined with an oppressive atmosphere of authoritarianism, intimidation and distrust.[7] Recruits were made to feel that any unguarded critical comments could easily lead to a court martial for treason, subversion or espionage.[8] Even after they had completed their eighteen months of basic training, recruits continued to belong to the military. As reserves, they could be recalled at any time.[9]

If for some boys (usually those from the countryside) military service seemed to promise escape, adventure and success with the ladies, most experienced their arrival in the barracks as disorienting and destabilising. They were immediately confronted with a 'total institution', separated from the outside world and with complete power over them.[10] Every detail of their actions and movements was regulated, denying the individual recruit any privacy or freedom to decide for himself. This sense of powerlessness was reinforced by subjecting new recruits to physical demands that were too much for them. The recruits' ignorance of their new surroundings and of the language and rules of military life increased their vulnerability and sense of being incapable. For officers and older intakes, the new recruits were unmanly weaklings. Discipline and drill demonstrated the power of the collective over the individual and rehearsed the latter's unconditional submission. The military aimed to destroy all spontaneity and to control every movements of the recruits' bodies. Even the gaze was controlled.[11] As in the Prussian army a century earlier, non-commissioned officers in the NVA tolerated and, in some cases, encouraged rituals in which the new recruits were physically abused and tormented.[12] Andrew Bickford has found numerous cases of older recruits taking advantage of younger troops and forcing them to take part in various rituals, which in extreme cases involved being forced to masturbate in public or lick urine out of older soldiers' helmets.[13]

The humiliation and removal of the capacity to make decisions were part of a process of mortification, which destroyed the old identity in order to form a new one. Christian Müller describes it as being almost like giving up citizenship of one country and being initiated into another.[14] Previously firmly held beliefs, convictions and moral values were replaced with new ones. Recruits began to look and talk like soldiers, with their own military-specific vocabulary and canteen manners. Burping and slurping their food helped them not to stand out from the others but were met with incomprehension when they returned home. Exposure to screaming, bellowing superiors and the crude jokes of their fellow soldiers lowered their standards of speech and behaviour. Many found that neat alcohol provided a socially acceptable anaesthetic for loneliness and boredom. Their personalities changed to the point that recruits became strangers not just to their families and friends, but also to themselves.

If military service was never quite accepted as normal by young men, surviving it nevertheless became a significant rite of passage. Not only was it unavoidable, but it marked their transition to manhood and to the adult world. It created new friendships and a spirit of camaraderie. It also imposed new divisions. Military service brought together recruits with very different backgrounds, accents and outlooks. Masculinity became the single most important thing they had in common and the thing they used to judge and assess one another. It came down to 'beard growth, a long cock, a hairy chest, an attractive girlfriend, with as big breasts as possible'.[15] Crammed together like sardines, the recruit's relationship to his own body and sexuality also changed. Although it made privacy impossible, barrack life also brought men into closer, sometimes more intimate, relationships with each other. Although in public the emphasis was on demonstrating heterosexuality, in private homosexual relationships could and did occur.

What was important was what my buddies thought of me. I didn't give a shit about what my superiors thought. We soldiers were in this unique transition phase from boyhood to manhood. Play and seriousness changed like the weather and no one knew exactly if what had just occurred was play or real. Why should we have cared? Most of us had stuck our girlfriend's picture on the inside of our locker door.[16]

Military service in the GDR had a lot to do with making men German. Although it rejected the social order that had underpinned it, the SED nevertheless embraced what it saw as the 'positive aspects' of the Prussian military tradition. Arguing that its own uniforms were more reflective of German military traditions, GDR propaganda condemned *Bundeswehr* soldiers for wearing alien, American-style uniforms.[17] There was something schizophrenic about the antifascist regime clothing its soldiers in traditional German uniforms. Even before the first one had been worn by an East German soldier, teenagers were asking why they resembled those of the Second World War.[18] The fact that the 'colours, cut and hang' of the uniforms were so traditional was meant to 'underline the societal progress in our state and to underline that a new army of the German people and working class has arisen that is free from aggressive goals'.[19] Jürgen Fuchs could find little to differentiate his '*Fassonschnitt*' haircut and the grey uniform of the NVA from what his father had worn in the *Wehrmacht*. His new surroundings in the barracks reminded him of the concentration camps he had seen in films.[20]

Like the Nazis before them, the communists were very worried about 'work-shy' tendencies and 'parasitism' among youth. The tendency of young, unskilled workers to change jobs frequently in order to increase their wages or independence and to avoid employers who did not treat them well merged for the SED with the skiving of young workers who were addicted to alcohol or who had problems ordering and planning their lives. While at certain periods the authorities chose to see the latter as people suffering from problems and who needed the regime's help and supervision to overcome them and live healthy and productive lives, at other times it attacked what it saw as the deliberate refusal of such 'feckless' young people to contribute fully to the project of the construction of socialism.[21] The regime repeatedly embraced draconian, 'common sense', knee-jerk solutions to the problem of youth nonconformity that in their language and methodology closely resembled tactics previously used (to ill effect) by the National Socialists. As Walter Ulbricht told the Politbüro in August 1961, 'Youngsters who don't want to work will learn how to in work camps.'[22]

East German communists were surprisingly keen to embrace petit bourgeois notions of Germanness and to condemn behaviour that was judged according to such criteria as being non-respectable.[23] The Stalinists needed to highlight the indecency of those classed as 'other' in order to be able to see themselves and their own actions as being decent. Thus even young people whose respectability was incontestable (such as young Christians) were accused of being dirty, unhygienic and sexually deviant.[24] Reports on youth subculture in East Germany used similar techniques of exaggeration to those of the tabloid press in the West, laying stereotype on stereotype until they had created a phenomenon that bore little resemblance to the original. They then served as folk devils, or 'visible reminders of what we should not be'.[25] The language and notions used to label and stereotype young people who did not fit into the communists' blueprint for youth often bore a striking resemblance to the language used in the Third Reich to label so-called 'community aliens' (*Gemeinschaftsfremde*).[26] In 1955, local functionaries in Döbeln referred to the problems caused by 'asocial' single-parent families, which had been resettled in the district during the Third Reich. The mothers were described as being 'disorderly, with big mouths, for the most part recipients of welfare'.[27] Particular problem groups were 'work-shy layabouts, drinkers and other asocial elements', who were deemed to be parasitic because they took more from society than they were capable of providing.[28]

Fear of the Other

George Mosse argued that modern masculinity reaffirms and strengthens its image 'in confrontation with its enemies', who represent all that the manly man is not. The citizen-soldiers of the twentieth century had to steel themselves against weakness, not only in themselves, but also in others. These are 'figures constructed largely in direct opposition to the masculine stereotype'. In Germany, the effeminate counter-types traditionally came from already stigmatised groups such as Jews, gypsies, criminals and asocials.[29] But Germans were not alone in creating a sense of difference from – and superiority to – other races.[30] Other Europeans also generated stereotypes (concerning lasciviousness and idleness), which they fastened on to those they colonised and enslaved. The negative attributes they attributed to the 'other' were often a projection of their own unacknowledged desires.[31]

Although the young men involved in the youth subcultures were unquestionably German, their music was not. In creating negative stereotypes about beat and rock 'n' roll fans, the authorities alluded to common racial and sexual stereotypes. The fact that jazz and rock 'n' roll both had specifically black origins was referred to in comments about young people listening to 'ape music' (*Affenmusik*) and wearing 'monkey shirts' (*Affenhemden*).[32] Police reports commonly presented young men who listened to black music as a threat to women and as potential rapists. In films and in cartoons, rockers were depicted as having simian characteristics.[33] Racial connotations were also evident in the argument that gang members were 'primitive' and the charge that they were involved in sexually harassing women and young girls (verbally or by means of wolf whistles). When accompanied by claims that they were whipped into a frenzy by 'hot music', such misbehaviour was racialised to suggest that the 'white Negroes' were potential rapists.

The negative stereotypes about people belonging to the youth subcultures were particularly dangerous for young women. Although according to official policy women belonged in the workplace and not the home, this did not give them the right to roam the streets. East German etiquette books of the 1950s and 1960s are indicative of the official pressure for working-class people to adopt middle-class ways. Given the implicit assumption that men could not help themselves, the key focus for the etiquette books was on controlling the actions of women. Young women were to conduct themselves at all times in a feminine manner. In the factory, they should avoid coarse jokes and improper, unwomanly behaviour.[34] 'At dances women should never approach men, but should wait to be asked to dance. Nor should they initiate conversation; that too remained the prerogative of men. The passive role was considered part of the "natural" character of the female sex.'[35] In sex education manuals too, it was considered the role of the woman to fend off advances by the male. A widely read advice book from 1956 stated, 'The young girl must know that she must keep to the limits. She should not wonder if with too much of a décolleté or too strong an emphasis on her breasts she triggers sexual arousal in the man and that he becomes importunate.'[36]

The police conceived of themselves as the defenders of young women's morals. If in police reports it was common to portray gang members as would-be rapists and as a danger to women, any young woman who willingly consorted with them was perceived as recklessly exposing herself to the risk of infection. As a result, although they claimed to be protecting young women's honour, the authorities responded particularly aggressively to young women who willingly consorted with the gangs. Seeing them as worse than prostitutes, the police rounded stray girls up and forced them to undergo tests for venereal disease. 'In the last few days, eleven young women were arrested in the park grounds, above all on the dance floor, and, of these, five girls had to be taken for medical and in-patient treatment as a result of a sexually transmitted disease.'[37] Girls who were caught up in the round-ups of gang members could expect little respect from the police. 'Usually there was a punch in the face, for the girls too, not to mention the sexist come-ons and the threats.'[38]

In the aftermath of the 1953 uprising, the authorities had printed mugshots of young men who had been involved and had asked the population to judge for themselves.[39] One of the young men singled out as a scapegoat was described as having 'doubtful girls [zweifelhafte Mädchen] on his arm, for whom his boogie-woogie shirts and his bebop haircut, T-shirt [spelt Niggihemd] and stripy socks were just right'.[40] The implication was that youth subcultural style was not respectable and that only girls with impure motives could be drawn to such decadence. Later in the 1950s, female rock 'n' roll fans were said to believe that 'the career of a prostitute in West Berlin was the right one for them' ('die Laufbahn einer Nutte in Westberlin sei das für sie Geeignete').[41] The exercising of freedom in dress and choice of company was equated with debasement and moral depravity.

Stereotypes of female nonconformity depicted aggressive and out-of-control female sexuality. During the campaign against beat music in October 1965, *Neues Deutschland* printed a cartoon caricaturing concerts by beat musicians. In it, a male musician with long hair and high heels bends over backwards, contorting himself to the excitement of his fans.[42] The audience is entirely female and the girls can be seen in various positions of sexual ecstasy, mouths and legs wide open, screaming for more. One protruding fishnetted leg suggests a link to prostitution while another girl is shown simply with her legs in the air. Their faces contorted with aggressive glee, the girls are then shown clambering over one another to grab at the musician. The words 'POP' and 'POWER' are visible on their backsides. The last scene is one of devastation, the hall ruined, the musician half-naked, bald and bruised, both his hair and his instrument gone, the microphone lying flaccidly between his legs. Still visible on his left foot, however, is a 'stripy sock', a stylistic feature that was long out of fashion with East German youth, but that nevertheless served as a convenient reminder for the SED of the link between youth subcultural nonconformity and counter-revolution.

A major problem for the German communists (albeit one that they failed to recognise) was that, whenever they sought to use negative stereotypes and scapegoats, the popular stereotypes available to them had already been used (and shop-soiled) by the Nazis. As a result, in trying to whip up 'moral panics' about young people, the communists had little choice but to reuse labels and images already tainted by association with National Socialism. Although SED denunciation of rock 'n' roll as 'infectious' reflects earlier National Socialist condemnation of swing music, it is important to note that even in liberal democracies like Britain in the 1950s and 1960s it was common to describe youth subculture as being 'like a disease'. 'People are somehow "infected" by delinquency, which "spreads" from person to person, so one has to "cure" the "disease".'[43] The mods and rockers involved in clashes in Margate in 1964 were described by the magistrate sentencing them as vermin and as 'long-haired, mentally unstable, petty little hoodlums … who can only find courage like rats, in hunting in packs'.[44] Nevertheless, there was something deeply unpleasant about the way the East German authorities used the language of filth, infection, vermin and disease to describe the rockers. In one instance, female rockers were described as having hair eaten away by rats.[45]

Although the SED attempted to justify its deep intrusion into the sphere of youth culture by claiming that young people were at risk of fascism, in actual fact, it was the attitudes of the East German authorities to youth nonconformity that most closely resembled those of the Nazis. By embracing the notion that the preservation of social order necessitated cultural purity, hardline supporters of the regime began unconsciously aping Nazi rhetoric. 'We are for a decent dance music, clean clothing and respectable behaviour of all young people.'[46] As an antidote to the 'disease' caused by foreign influences, they suggested a large medicinal dose of good, clean German culture (*saubere Volkstümlichkeit*). 'This epidemic of systematically lost inhibitions is an ideological disease, which if development and young people are left to themselves infects and spreads. Above all young people but also parents, the workplace, the school, entertainment providers not to mention the cultural association should strive for the damming of these aberrations.'[47]

In closed institutions like prisons, mental asylums and barracks, the state's true conception of masculinity was most visible. It was here that the real meaning behind preambles, phrases and stilted words became clear and that the state appeared in its most naked and brutal form. The comrades were able to turn against the deviants, the outsiders, the dissidents who were stigmatised as 'weaklings'.[48] Official instructions provided one set of standards for dealing with suspects and prisoners. The unofficial 'canteen culture' provided another overlapping perspective that had everything to do with preserving masculine pride.[49] The will to dominate, to exploit and to oppress, Pierre Bourdieu argues, stems from the 'fear of losing face and of being excluded from the world of "men" without weakness'. Only by disregarding the suffering of others can they be regarded as tough. Manliness is constructed 'in front of and for other men and against femininity, in a kind of *fear* of the female, firstly in oneself'.[50] Although projected outwards as pride, confidence and strength, machismo is actually driven by fear. The macho's honour is constantly under threat. Any transgression is perceived as an implied insult that it is essential for him to punish if his honour and authority are to be maintained. Fear of the judgements and assessments of other men leads to conformity and the suppression of all characteristics of thought, speech, dress and demeanour that could be seen as weak or feminine.[51] Repressing all feelings of insecurity, machos deny any feelings of understanding or compassion for others. The only emotions that they allow themselves to express are strong, tough ones like anger, jealousy, contempt and hate. Uniform clothing and hairstyles provide safety from ambiguity. They signal and symbolise their belonging to a culture that is incontrovertibly and unambiguously male.

Within young offenders' institutes, like the notorious *Jugendwerkhof Torgau*, a harsh and brutal regime was encouraged. The way in which they were run owed a lot to Prussian traditions of military discipline.[52] Much of the daily routine consisted of compulsory sport (*Zwangssport*), designed to push inmates to the limits of physical exhaustion, together with punishing cleaning details.[53] Mistreatment by prison guards of young offenders

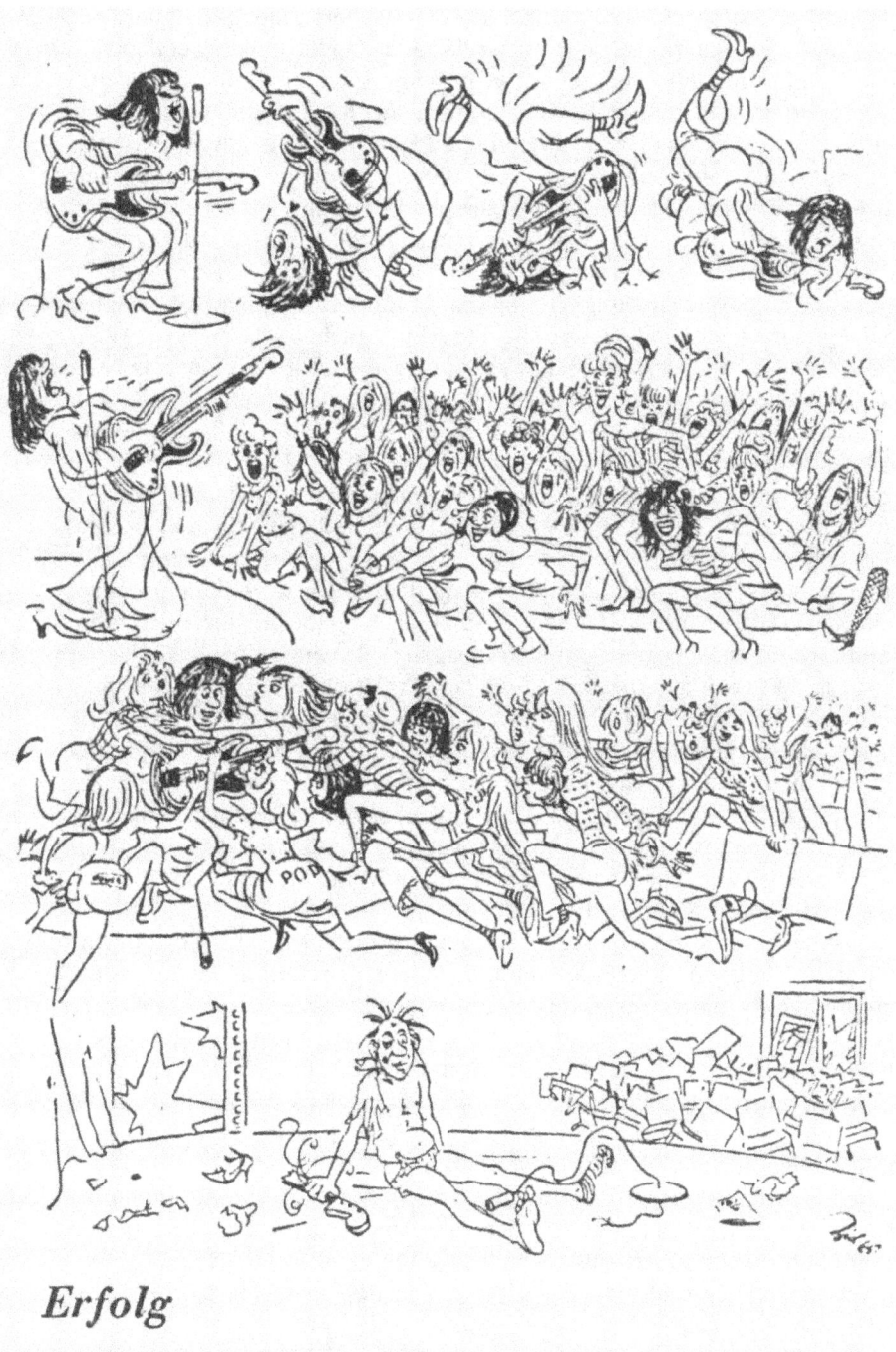

Figure 11. Caricature showing the negative effects of beat music.

(political or otherwise) was routine. The atmosphere among the guards in Torgau was particularly tense in the weeks following the building of the wall. Before being put into the cells, two prisoners were needlessly kicked, knocked to the ground and punched in the head.[54] The hostility of the long-serving prison officers was not directed solely at the inmates. In the hypermasculine atmosphere of the guardroom, even men from within their own ranks could attract their ire by failing to live up to their expectations of toughness and discipline. A party discussion following 13 August 1961 revealed the existence of a clash of cultures.

On one side were the long-serving, hard bitten prison guards. Belonging to the prison service had allowed them to rebuild their shattered lives. 'What did we say after the war? Just get us out of here and we'll work like crazy and eat dry bread the whole year.'[55] They had had no need then for their own opinions. Now the most important things to them were discipline and obedience. Their masculinity and sense of honour had become intimately bound up with their uniforms. Years of keeping juvenile delinquents locked up in Torgau had narrowed the guards' horizons and made them distrustful of anything connected with youth. Their anxieties were expressed in a fear of contamination and pollution. Provoking their anger were the university-trained young educators, who believed that teaching the prisoners was more important than taking part in military exercises. Having selfishly studied at the cost of the workers they had squandered their opportunities by learning nothing about real life or about how to obey orders. Instead of respecting their uniforms and showing that they were worthy of wearing them, they showed their contempt with haircuts that were almost as bad as those of the inmates. 'If he was wearing jeans on the street there would be nothing to distinguish him from the other young layabouts.'[56] With the class enemy at the gates, they were spreading defeatist poison within the citadel itself. 'Such a haircut does not go with the uniform. Here we cut the hair off troublemakers with such haircuts.' The younger men were accused of having forgotten about the sacrifices made by older generations and of being interested only in themselves. Just because they had been to university, they thought that that afforded them the luxury of having their own opinions. If they could not stomach the military side of prison life, then they had no place as prison officers. In language redolent of thoughts of castration, they turned on a young graduate who had fallen asleep during a military exercise and accused him of 'squirming like a worm'.[57]

In July 1963, a prisoner at Torgau managed briefly to escape. When the guards succeeded in recapturing him, they meted out a brutal beating in front of shocked and sickened members of the general public, who openly voiced the opinion that those involved were as bad as the Nazis.

> Lying on the ground, H. received a series of kicks and punches from People's Policemen M. and F. until, bleeding from the face, he was taken to the waiting prison van. Four other People's Policemen were in the yard so no danger of a

renewed escape existed. At the van, Police Superintendent M. sent H. into the back with a kick so that he tripped and stumbled.

In the area where he was captured a crowd of about 30 people formed who expressed their indignation through calls like 'SS and Gestapo methods – we're no longer under the Nazis you know ['wir sind doch nicht mehr bei den Nazis']'.

In the yard of the offenders' institute, once the prisoner had left the van he was immediately grabbed by Lieutenant S. and the teacher P. and beaten with kicks and punches until he reached the iron door. During these punches and kicks, H. fell several times to the ground and was also worked on with fists as he lay on the floor ... In front of the door to the detention cells a pool of blood about 30 cm wide had formed.[58]

The clash between the official, militaristic and new, alternative forms of machismo is reflected in a story by Erik Neutsch.[59] The mayor of a town on the banks of the Saale is in crisis. A hero of the first hour, he had sided with the party at the crucial moment and had recognised that what counted 'was the power of the working class, now or never'. Now he finds himself confronted with an issue that he thought that he would never have to face. Pressure is coming from Berlin for the town's thousand-year-old street plan to be transformed according to the modern, new, concrete vision. In the mayor's mind, the order and tradition he cherishes are suddenly threatened. 'Recently all kinds of thieves and riff-raff [*Diebesgesindel*] have been hanging around the town.' He fears that changes to the town will draw in more strangers, 'like the vultures that descend on a corpse, plundering and robbing and doing all sorts of other immoral things'.[60]

The town is not only menaced by outsiders, but also by an internal enemy. 'The station and the cinemas are under daily surveillance. There, in particular, troops of youngsters gather who do not want to get used to our way of life, law, order and hard work. Their hair is long and getting longer. Their trousers are brightly covered in flowers like women's skirts. And now they've even started stealing.' While more dangerous beasts prowl outside the city walls, inside the packs of scavengers and laughing hyenas wait for their moment to pounce. How different this is from his own youth. In 1945, he came home

> filthy and in rags, skinny like a gnawed bone and saw that the Nazis, those who were guilty for the war, were still sitting in administrative functions. Because nobody else wanted to clear them out, I did it. In spite of the fuss the women made [*Trotz des Weibergeschreis*] ... I understood the necessity of the hour, to complete what was started in 1918. What I did not know was whether it would succeed, whether we were strong enough, but I did not hesitate.[61]

The mayor's impression of the beat fans is not improved by a visit to a cellar one of the groups uses to practise in. 'On the walls they hung pictures of long-haired singer boys, balloon-cheeked, trumpet-blowing Negroes and scantily clad ladies, Bible sayings mixed with statements by capitalist politicians ... In the middle of a collection of naked women hung a traffic sign saying "Warning! Multiple curves".[62] The mayor thinks of his own youth. He and his friends had also hidden themselves away in cellars. But their purpose had been to read Mayakorsky and Gorki, not to dance around to beat. Above all what frightened him was what they did to the girls, whom they enticed down to the cellar with their beat music. This fear led him to inspect the cellar as if it were the hiding place of a gang of drug dealers. In reality what is objectionable about the boys is that they see 'laying girls' as a way of proving their manhood. Conquering the opposite sex makes them 'feel strong, like heroes'. The mayor condemns the boys for doing what he is incapable of doing (but would, if he were honest, desire to do himself) while idealising an artificial and equally male-centred image of femininity.

In the interminable smoke-filled meetings in which the future of the town is discussed, the mayor's mind often wanders to Sigrid, the daughter of his friend Paul, a tram driver. He thinks of her pretty face and her slender hips and of how she spent the summer sweltering in a conductor's uniform in order to save enough money to buy herself a bikini. What would Paul say, the mayor thinks, if he suddenly found out that his daughter went through the black curtains at night and let herself be photographed 'as she is' and her picture pinned to the wall next to the pin-ups with a Bible verse saying, 'Then a whore steals one's bread'. His attraction to the much younger woman is transformed into a fatherly need to protect her from the acquisitive intentions of decadent young men, young men who unlike him have white teeth, suntanned faces and healthy, muscular arms. He converts his envy into righteous indignation at the boys' exploitation of the female form and their readiness to treat girls merely as disposable sex objects.

The focus of his envy is Sigrid's one-time boyfriend Gerhard, the middle-class son of the town's chief architect. The mayor prides himself on having grown up as one of seven children without a breadwinner, his father having died in the first war. His mother had nevertheless brought them up respectably. Gerhard, in contrast, brought up in the lap of luxury, has become selfish and spoilt. Without ever having had to struggle for anything, he can afford the luxury of being rebellious. Nobody gains anything from his childish, self-centred disorderliness. But good, honest working-class girls who knew what it was to work for their money and to skimp and save to buy something nice run a considerable risk of being hurt by his behaviour. He needs 'to learn that life also contains duties'. Poverty was by no means a panacea, the mayor admitted. But it taught responsibility. 'This was his morality in life. This is what he held on to.'[63] The story ends with the discovery that Sigrid had let Gerhard have his way with her only then to dump her for another. For him it was just 'fooling around', but it left her feeling 'dirty and ashamed'. The thought of it made the mayor ball his hands into fists. 'We won't let anyone dance around on our heads, least of all with beat.'[64] This story provides a highly evocative account of the clash of masculinities as seen through the eyes of East Germany's leading producer of idealist 'hero literature'. Today Neutsch regrets the 'unfulfilled and ultimately betrayed ideals', 'this trusting naivety' and 'the shitty party discipline'.[65] But, at the time, he was caught up in the macho fantasy he portrayed.[66]

By the early 1960s the regime had ceased to condemn older generations for their participation in the Third Reich to such an extent that, in 1963, Walter Ulbricht could describe the older generation as 'those who liquidated fascism in the GDR'.[67] The younger generation, meanwhile, had ceased to be untainted, but had instead come to be seen as dangerously exposed to fascism (which had conveniently been reinterpreted as Westernised culture and consumer capitalism). The SED was aware that many of its problems in controlling young people stemmed from the conditions they had grown up in in the aftermath of the war. As Erich Honecker put it,

> We have a few youngsters who grew up in the ruined families of the post-war period, who did not reach the end of the eighth school year, who were unable to take up a proper apprenticeship, who were hardly supervised by the youth organisation, who even stayed away from work and in the end ended up on the wrong path.

But lest this be taken as sympathy or an excuse for their behaviour, he continued: 'Such young people are particularly susceptible in relation to imperialist sexual and criminal propaganda.'[68]

Honecker later claimed that the Eleventh Plenum had dealt with more serious issues than 'the question of how long we should allow skirts to be or the question of décolletés and bikinis'.[69] But the plenum had been one long condemnation of the decadence allegedly caused by the new, 'socialist realist' trends in literature and film. 'We don't need moaning and complaining bystanders, we need revolutionaries who will transform the world ... What matters is bringing the revolutionary heritage of their fathers before young people's eyes, [presenting] their experiences in the class struggle vividly, graphically, excitingly, in a convincing and differentiated fashion.'[70] What was at stake in 'the decisive struggle against the old and the backward' was the fight 'against the influences of capitalist unculture and immorality that find expression in the American sex propaganda and in the glorification of banditry'.[71]

The reference to 'banditry' was an allusion to the film *Spur der Steine*. Unfortunately for Honecker, unlike so many other provocative DEFA films, Frank Beyer's masterpiece could not just be made to disappear silently because it had already premiered (to great applause from the audience at the Worker's Festival in Potsdam).[72] Pre-publicity for the film had emphasised its realism. Newspaper reports had repeatedly stated that it was being filmed in Leuna, the 'young chemical giant in the heart of the republic', where Neutsch had 'collected the material for his novel'. The film crew were studying photographs and archival material in order to capture 'true to life the atmosphere of the first years of the construction of Leuna II'.[73] Real Leuna 'bricklayers, iron workers, carpenters and dumper-truck drivers' were being employed as extras. 'No sacrifice is too great for them ... Next to me someone says, "Krug fits in the role like a fist in the eye" and I think to myself he's not wrong.' Manfred Krug himself was quoted as saying what a pleasure it was to play the role because 'it contains so many features of the worker's life that are natural, authentic and true'.[74] According to one report, he had been seen at various different building sites in the Republic dressed provocatively in a smoking jacket carrying out 'ethnographic studies' [*Volkstudien*].[75]

Saddled with a film that had been endlessly lauded for its realism, but which was no longer politically suitable, the party leadership opted for Stalinist tactics in an attempt to shove the genie forcefully back in the bottle. Although the film continued an unbroken, sell-out run in Halle, screenings in the International in East Berlin and the Capitol cinema in Leipzig were brought to a premature end by agitators brought in to scream the film down.[76] Although their behaviour was worse than that of the Capitol *Meute*, they had been bussed in from a training centre for party ideologues. Following the line set out in *Neues Deutschland*, the film was denounced as presenting a 'distorted picture of our socialist reality, the battle of the working class, its glorious party and the great sacrifices made by its members in their work'. It was proclaimed to be a 'denigration of the party' and an insult to the working class, which was removed from cinemas 'at the request of the workers'.[77]

The writer Werner Bräunig was singled out for particularly harsh condemnation during the Eleventh Plenum. Although he had not yet finished writing the novel *Rummelplatz* (Fairground) an opening chapter had been published in the literary magazine *New German Literature*.[78] Written in the slang of a Wismut miner (*Wismutkumpel*), the story described what happened when young, working-class men drank too much at the Christmas fair. For a few hours they sought recompense for their hard existence in the fairgrounds of the world, in vodka and in the warm skin of a girl. One had a shop assistant as a girlfriend. He was her seventh, but this time the 'right one'. Another had a 'cooked breakfast relationship' (*Bratkartoffelverhältnis*) with a widow, but had caught the clap from her. 'That's namely what they were just talking about.' They sang a song together about a Polish girl, one that the Kaiser's soldiers had already sung before them, one that every third German knew how to sing. At the fair, groups came together and 'often there was a punch-up if someone from one side had a girl who belonged to the other, a hunting outrage [*Jagdfrevel*]'. There was more freedom at the fair, in the milieu of 'the itinerant entertainers, small-time crooks, the crazies and the prostitutes'. Like the main station, it was a demi-monde in which unusual characters like 'Shaky Alfons, a homosexual who lived from black market deals' could be found.[79]

The story was told from the perspective of a boy from the educated middle class who had become one with his drunkard and ruffian colleagues. 'A professor's little boy, if they knew that in the shaft then he'd get sugar blown up his arse by the pound.' He had responded eagerly to the challenge presented by manual labour in extreme conditions and had become 'one of those who went hard at it and who could knuckle down to it'.[80] He had been one of those who had dreamed of being a hero – 'a fighter pilot, a U-Boat commander … he'd read all the adventure stories and war books'. Then without a sound the heroes had all disappeared overnight. They took with them the swastikas from the flags and left behind a 'world without lustre or make-up and also without hope'. Although Bräunig's novel seemed to be taking a path already marked out (and well-trodden in metaphor and cliché) by Erik Neutsch and Brigitte Reimann, what was new and radically different was the degree of unconcealed anger his characters expressed towards the offensive hypocrisy surrounding them. The voluntary policeman of the Nazi era (*der Blockwart*) found new functions and a monopoly on ration coupons. The Hitler Youth gymnastics teacher crossed over to the Antifascist Youth (*Antifa-Jugend*) and bossed people about with the official slogan '*bau-auf-bau-auf*'. The young Siegfried, meanwhile, found himself demoted and degraded to a shit eater (*Dreckfresser*), 'one of last customers in the great German closing-down sale'. An epidemic of piety (*Frömmigkeit*) had broken out, causing the impotents nearly to die with joy. They searched the godless heavens and the stolen horizon for adventure. In reality, they were searching for a Fatherland.[81]

Wrapped up as they were in the myths they had created about antifascism, SED leaders found it easy to see youth subcultural nonconformists as 'fascist spawn'.[82] Not only were they unsympathetic to the plight of many of these supposed delinquents, but they were prepared to imprison them and eradicate their culture – 'to eradicate the seeds of evil, whatever wind they are brought to us by' – with a clear conscience.[83] Young people had once been presented as the great hope for the future because they were the one section of German society (aside from the SED leadership) untainted by National Socialism. But, in the autumn and winter of 1965, this privileged, untainted position in relation to the past was once and for all revoked. They were no longer seen as safer but as more dangerous because they lacked direct exposure to Nazism.[84] Unlike those who had fought for their country (and Hitler), the younger generation knew nothing of poverty, of sacrifice and struggle, of building a new life on the ruins of the old one. But above all it was their casual clothing and long hair – indicative of their lack of a soldierly habitus – that engendered feelings of hostility among older workers and regime officials.[85] Because the GDR was 'a clean state' (*ein sauberer Staat*), it could not tolerate the existence of dirty, unkempt and unhygienically promiscuous rebels.[86]

To underline the seriousness of these claims, members of the Central Committee were treated to a report on the activities of a delegation of students from the Technical University in Dresden during the potato harvest in Gustävel,

Kreis Sternberg. The students engaged in all kinds of unsocialist activities – lazing about, drinking to excess, complaining about the food, insulting the women who worked in the collective kitchen and generally being ungrateful and uncooperative (one said he could not go to work because a local witch had cursed him). During the celebration to mark their departure the students stretched the local hospitality to breaking point. Three drunken students clapped out 'the rhythm' as one after another they took turns with a seventeen-year-old farmer's daughter. They left her lying naked and unconscious on her bed. 'To the cynical laughter' of the others, the ringleader had poured beer over her. They left for their own beds, each taking a girl with him.[87] This and other reports was part of a special folder, marked 'top secret', that could only be read within the reading room of the Central Committee building. As Mitter and Wolle suggest, 'It is not without a certain frisson to imagine how members and candidates of the Central Committee swayed back and forth between voyeurism and moral indignation as they read these and similar papers.'[88]

Although they came at the problem from very different ideological angles, hardliners within the SED found themselves in agreement with conservative and Catholic critics of American culture in West Germany.[89] Although adults distrusted many of the regime's claims and resisted its encroachments on their own and their families' freedoms, there was a groundswell of support for the regime's tough approach to rebellious youth. In spite (or perhaps because) of their much more direct and complicit experiences of war and Nazism older generations were eager to point an accusatory finger at young people. Long hair was not only an affront to their conceptions of masculinity, but also to processes of self-justification in which they believed that, following the war, they had 'paid for' their own mistakes through self-denial. By rejecting their values and self-conceptions, young people were seen to be mocking their sacrifices.

The 1965 clampdown on beat music marked a widening of the security forces' reach and an intensification of the militarisation of society. Under the direct supervision of Erich Honecker (who in August 1961 had overseen the building of the Berlin Wall), the police and Stasi made preparations to stage a counter-demonstration of force to crush what they saw as signs of anarchy and 'beat fanaticism'. Reports on police preparations show that they were armed for a major insurrection with machine pistols and truncheons in addition to water cannons and police dogs.[90] Their function was part of a demonstration of absolute state authority and, with it, a ritualised enactment of masculine force. The People's Police painted their conflict with the beat fans as a heroic struggle against dropouts armed with 'pistols, knives and knuckledusters'. They also saw it as a chance to assert their superiority, saying that they had been taunted with the slogans 'We'll beat the People's Police!' and 'The People's Police tremble before us!'[91] Dozens of the 267 young men arrested were sent straight to be re-educated in the coal mines. As soon as they arrived, they were forcibly shorn. The conditions in which they were held were unhygienic and highly demeaning.⁹² They were forced to spend the next week wearing only the clothes they had been arrested in. Forced to carry out hard labour, they were denied access to proper toilets or washroom facilities.

The *Leipziger Volkszeitung* justified the official measures by publishing a picture of the Beatles carrying weapons. The picture was supposed to link beat excesses to war crimes and genocide in Vietnam.

> For those of you who don't recognise it, this is a picture of the Beatles, carrying not guitars, but weapons. These are the same types of weapons used by the Americans – with the support of the British government – to propagate war crimes and genocide in Vietnam.
> Today beat – tomorrow sub-machine guns ...
> Today brutalization – tomorrow war against a peace-loving country.
> This is the imperialistic policy, driving the feelings of young people in false and dangerous directions, manipulating them for their class aims [*Klaßenziele*].
> The imperialist powers use the Beatles to propagate their psychological warfare, by suggesting the Lone Ranger model to young people. It is no accident that this picture was found in the possession of young Leipzigers. This picture shows the absurdity of the oft-repeated claims about the peaceful and harmless nature of the Western way of life.⁹³

The attacks on the Beatles were particularly ironic given previous attempts by communists to emphasise their proletarian origins. The Beatles' playful irreverence (and subsequent experimentation with eastern mysticism) sat uneasily with attempts to depict them as being representatives of a Wild West ethos. Even if it had been their intention to do so, the angry beat fans had no chance of unseating the regime. Although power was clearly weighted against them, the beat fans could feel that in October 1965 they had achieved a moral and a symbolic victory. 'We are young. You can't change that. Before there was applause and nothing happened. Today it's time to boo and hiss. Old people just don't understand. What happened on the Karl-Marx-Platz, that was something sensational.'⁹⁴

SED leaders were unable to see a contradiction between antifascism and continued militarism. For veteran communists, there was nothing strange or unusual about holding military manoeuvres at the site of a concentration camp. In October 1965, representatives of the armies of the GDR, Poland, Czechoslovakia and the Soviet Union met at Buchenwald to pay their respects and to demonstrate their readiness to use force against the enemies of socialism.⁹⁵ Somewhat incongruously, the GST magazine *Konkret* proclaimed, 'Ten thousand line the streets – grown-ups, young people and children. Their greatest pleasure: the autograph of a soldier. Not from hit singers or film actors, no, from soldiers.'⁹⁶ In a speech marking the contribution of the People's Police to the Warsaw Pact military manoeuvres at Buchenwald, Comrade Major General Dahl, the Chief of Police, spoke of how they had found work for the criminal and work-shy elements who had protested against the ban on beat.

> It is also the task of the People's Police to put a stop to these elements ... We are strong enough to educate them as respectable people ... They thought that they could use our clubhouses or our dance halls to smash up the furniture there and other things besides. We have ensured that we very quickly restored order and hygiene and, together with the population, we will enforce order for the reputation of our town and so that we can say: *Jawohl*, in Leipzig it's possible to live respectably, nice and quiet![97]

Major General Dahl went on to say that

> We had them examined and it was found that precisely these dropouts – who can never belong to our youth and can never be the idol of hard-working youth – were so dirty and filthy that we first had to hose them down and shave off their hair. Only then could we call the doctors because we had detected that various of them were sexually diseased.[98]

Those who approved of such measures often betrayed far from progressive notions about what to do with nonconformist youth, together with traits of altogether authoritarian, not to say fascist, personalities:

> The only thing that would help would be a few sturdy men, armed with truncheons, washing powder and brushes to give them a decent scrubbing on the spot and then give them a good punch in the belly. If one of them were to insult me, I'd smack his head in, even if it meant myself having to go to prison. Discussion serves no further purpose.[99]

The sight of young men with long hair made their blood boil. In part, the violence of this type of reaction was provoked by the fear that tolerance of the overt effeminacy of another might possibly be seen to reveal latent homosexuality in oneself.[100] Rank-and-file communists wanted to get their hands on these young people, but only, as they made clear, in order to break their limbs.

Conclusion

In the aftermath of the demonstration, the 'antifascist veteran' and Minister for State Security, Erich Mielke, drew up a new set of guidelines for dealing 'systematically' with nonconformist groups by means of sustained surveillance and infiltration.

> The imperialist threat, in particular the measures of the West German imperialists for the preparation of a concealed war against the GDR, forces us to be more energetic in putting an end to the occurrence of such groups and above all to ensure that such herds do not arise in the future. This is all the more urgently necessary because the appearance of such groups can easily be used by the enemy as a means of feigning 'resistance'.[101]

All sorts of nonconformist behaviour now came under the Stasi's remit, accelerating its expansion into society. In schools, new structures of reporting and surveillance were implemented. Margot Honecker was determined to overcome scepticism and inner conflict with renewed emphasis on indoctrination and pressure to conform. The implicit support given by many young people to the Prague Spring led to a further tightening of the screw. Stasi, school and military now formed a tight net to catch and punish the disobedient and potentially subversive. Steps were also taken to ensure that, in future, unpolitical youth would never again have the upper hand in the youth clubs.[102]

Describing his time as an army recruit in the aftermath of the 1968 Warsaw Pact invasion of Czechoslovakia, Jürgen Fuchs kept coming back to the image of the beat fan at the mercy of the army. In his dream-like vision, recruits are forced to sacrifice their hair before arriving at the barracks for basic training or risk incurring the wrath of the military men. One young man refuses and is made to serve as an example. He is he made to stand with a guitar around his neck confronting the other recruits as they stand naked in line waiting for their medical inspections.[103] He has to stand in front of the lectern and the flag as the 'opposite of the soldier, as a provocation, unmanly, musical, without hatred'.[104] For a man to wear his hair long was 'to look like a Beatle, like a *Gammler*, a pig, an asocial, a Westerner ... every word a swear word ... bastards, renegades,

Figure 12. Photograph allegedly 'proving the threat' posed by Western non-culture. The Beatles with guns.

dissidents and Anglo-American hippies, who hang around on the streets, listen to loud music and lie in bed all week with full-breasted women' because they are too lazy and cowardly to defend freedom.[105] While the authorities began frothing at the mouth at the thought of young men with long hair, older generations responded to the military *Fassonschnitt* with respect and approval. Fuchs describes the contagious militarism that surrounds their send-off at the station. A few fathers are walking around with their stomachs in and chests out. 'They look at the officers with a smile and a wink as if to say "Let them have it, it won't do them any harm." We men know what's what and these little sprogs have everything to learn.'[106] The act of teaching youngsters a lesson brought the communists closer to those who had fought for the fascists. Whatever had previously divided them, the older generation shared an appreciation of discipline and military aesthetics.

Notes

1. Walter Jablonsky and Wolfgang Wünsche (eds), *Im Gleichschritt? Zur Geschichte der NVA* (Berlin, 2001); Rüdiger Wenzke, *Die NVA und der Prager Frühling 1968* (Berlin, 1995); Otto Wenzel, *Kriegsbereit. Der Nationale Verteidigungsrat der DDR 1960 bis 1989* (Cologne, 1995); Manfred Backerra (ed.), *NVA. Ein Rückblick für die Zukunft. Zeitzeugen berichten über ein Stück deutscher Militärgeschichte* (Cologne, 1992).
2. Jürgen Fuchs, *Fassonschnitt* (Reinbek, 1984), 117.
3. Ibid., 339.
4. 'Presseinformation' (September 1961), StAL FDJ Bezirksleitung Leipzig 82 (Kiste Nr. 79).
5. Pierre Bourdieu, *Masculine Domination*, trans. Richard Nice (Cambridge, 2001), 25.
6. Hauptredaktion Propaganda- und Agitationsschriften, *Vom Sinn des Soldatenseins. Ein Ratgeber für den Soldaten* (Berlin, 1968). Not to be confused with Friedrich von Rabenau, *Vom Sinn des Soldatentums* (Cologne, 1941).
7. Christian Müller, *Tausend Tage bei der 'Asche'. Unteroffiziere in der NVA. Untersuchungen zu Alltag und Binnenstruktur einer 'sozialistischen' Armee* (Berlin, 2003), 166.
8. Fuchs, *Fassonschnitt*, 20, 143.
9. Hans-Dieter Schütt, (ed.), *Klaus Renft. Zwischen Liebe und Zorn* (Berlin, 1997), 75.
10. Müller, *Tausend Tage*, 155.
11. Fuchs, *Fassonschnitt*, 57, 147.
12. Thomas Rohkrämer, *Der Militarismus der 'kleinen Leute'. Die Kriegervereine im Deutschen Kaiserreich 1871–1914* (Munich, 1990), 162.
13. BArch. Militärarchiv DVW1 55657, 140, cited in Andrew Bickford, 'Command Performance: Militarization, Masculinity and the State in the GDR and Post-unification Germany' (Rutgers University: Ph.D. Thesis, 2002), 53.
14. Müller, *Tausend Tage*, 156ff.
15. Fuchs, Fassonschnitt, 145.
16. Joseph (born 1944) in John Borneman (ed.), *Gay Voices from East Germany. Interviews by Jürgen Lemke* (Bloomington, Indianapolis, 1991), 124.
17. Bickford, 'Command Performance', 25.
18. 'Streifzug durch das III. Gesamtberliner Jugendforum', *Junge Welt* (2 March 1956).
19. 'Uniformen der Nationalen Volksarmee', *Das Banner* (January–February 1956).
20. Fuchs, *Fassonschnitt*, 383, 220, 136.
21. Thomas Lindenberger, 'Das Fremde im Eigenen des Staatssozialismus. Klassendiskurs und Exklusion am Beispiel der Konstruktion des "asozialen Verhaltens"' in Jan Behrends, Thomas

Lindenberger and Patrice Poutrus (eds), *Fremd-Sein in der DDR. Zu historischen Ursachen der Fremdenfeindlichkeit in Ostdeutschland* (Berlin, 2003), 153–65.
22. 'Rede des Genossen Walter Ulbricht im Politbüro am 22.8.1961', BArch. SAPMO DY24/3727.
23. Catherine Epstein, *The Last Revolutionaries. German Communists and their Century* (Cambridge, MA, London, 2003), 122.
24. '"Junge Gemeinde" – Tarnorganisation im USA-Auftrag', *Leipziger Volkszeitung* (19 April 1953).
25. Stanley Cohen, *Folk Devils and Moral Panics* (London, New York, 3rd edn, 2002), 25.
26. Robert Gellately and Nathan Stoltzfus (eds), *Social Outsiders in Nazi Germany* (Princeton, Oxford, 2001).
27. 'Jugendhilfe – Heimerziehung' (4 Januray 1955), StAL RdB Bildung, Kultur und Sport: 1723, 89.
28. 'Ergebnisse im Zusammenhang der Regierungsmaßnahmen von 13.8.61', StAL BDVP 24.1/201, 63.
29. George Mosse, *The Image of Man. The Creation of Modern Masculinity* (New York, Oxford, 1996), 12–13.
30. Michael Roper and John Tosh (eds), *Manful Assertions: Masculinities in Britain since 1800* (London, New York, 1991), 13.
31. Ibid., 14.
32. 'Protokoll des Berichtes über die Arbeit im Klubhaus Erich Zeigner am 18.9.1953 (3.2.1954)', StAL IV5/01/483.
33. The dance scenes were accompanied by grunting noises. *Die Glatzkopfbande*, directed by Richard Groschopp (DEFA, 1963).
34. Anna-Sabine Ernst, 'Vom "Du" zum "Sie": Die Rezeption der bürgerlichen Anstandsregeln in der DDR der 50er Jahre' (ms., 1992), 17–21, cited in Eric Weitz, *Creating German Communism 1890–1990. From Popular Protests to Socialist State* (Princeton, 1997), Note 89, 378.
35. Weitz, *Creating German Communism*, 378.
36. Wolfgang Bretschneider, *Sexuell Aufklären rechtzeitig und richtig* (Leipzig, Jena, 1956), 154.
37. 'Stellungsnahme zur Bekämpfung des Rowdytums – Brennpunkt Klara-Zetkin-Park (24.8.1960)', StAL BDVP 24/113, 167–175, 172.
38. Ilona, 'Wir lebten von dem, wovor wir uns fürchteten' in C. Remath and R. Schneider (eds), *Haare auf Krawall. Jugendsubkultur in Leipzig 1980 bis 1991* (Leipzig, 1999), 12–23, 14.
39. 'Urteilt selbst!', *LVZ* (24 June1953), 3.
40. 'Diebe, Straßenräuber, Brandstifter – das sind die "Ritter der abendländischen Kultur"', *Neues Deutschland* (1 July 1953).
41. 'Vogelscheuchen in der Peterstraße', *LVZ* (23 July 1958).
42. Cartoon in *Neues Deutschland* (24 October 1965), 6.
43. Cohen, *Folk Devils*, 46.
44. Ibid., 88.
45. 'Vogelscheuchen in der Peterstraße'.
46. 'Meinungen zum Artikel der LVZ "Dem Mißbrauch der Jugend"' (October 1965), BArch. SAPMO DY30/IVA2/16/68.
47. Ibid.
48. Jürgen Fuchs and Gerhard Hieke, *Dummgeschult? Ein Schüler und sein Lehrer* (Berlin, 1992), 5; Anette Horn, 'An End to Conformity: Jürgen Fuchs' Experience of the Army in *Fassonschnitt* (Crewcut) and *Das Ende einer Feigheit* (An End to Cowardice)' in Peter Monteath and Frederic Zuckerman (eds), *Modern Europe. Histories and Identities* (Adelaide, 1998), 291–98.
49. James Messerschmidt, *Masculinities and Crime. Critique and Reconceptualisation of Theory* (Lanham, 1993), 174ff.
50. Bourdieu, *Masculine Domination*, 52.
51. Michael Kimmel, 'Masculinity as Homophobia. Fear, Shame and Silence in the Construction of Gender Identity' in Theodore Cohen (ed.) *Men and Masculinity* (Belmont, 2000), 29–41.
52. 'Prussian' was also how political prisoners described the system of soulless military

discipline instituted in the notorious Bautzen II prison. Karl Wilhelm Fricke and Silke Klewin, *Bautzen II. Sonderhaftanstalt unter MfS-Kontrolle 1956 bis 1989* (Leipzig, 2001), 77, 83, 91.
53. Brigitte Oleschinski et al., 'Der Geschlossene Jugendwerkhof Torgau' in *Einweisung nach Torgau. Texte und Dokumente zur autoritären Jugendfürsorge in der DDR* (Berlin, 1997), 121–24.
54. 'Bericht über den praktischen Einsatz des Offizierlehrganges (SV) vom 24.8.61 bis 26.8.61 in der STVA Torgau', StAL, BDVP 24/1/956, 20.
55. Ibid.
56. 'Bericht über den praktischen Einsatz'.
57. 'Jugendhaus Torgau: Protokoll der Dienstversammlung' (30 August1961), StAL, BDVP 24/1/956, 22–24.
58. 'Sachstandsbericht über die Körperverletzung durch VP-Angehörige des Jugendhauses Torgau (Torgau, 12.7.63)', StAL BDVP 24/1/956, 254–57.
59. Erik Neutsch, 'Drei Tage unseres Lebens', in *Helden-Berichte* (Berlin, 1976), 72–109.
60. Ibid., 76.
61. Ibid., 82.
62. Ibid., 93.
63. Ibid., 95.
64. Ibid., 95.
65. Volker Müller, 'Moralist im Niemandsland. Erik Neutsch wird heute siebzig Jahre alt', *Berliner Zeitung* (21 June 2001).
66. Jürgen Fuchs recorded his disappointment at seeing a picture of Neutsch in an army newspaper. The writer was aiming through the sights of a heavy machine gun. Jürgen Fuchs, *Das Ende einer Feigheit* (Reinbek, 1988), 58.
67. 'Ihr seid die Schmiede der deutschen Zukunft' in Zentralkomitee der SED, *Jugend von heute. Hausherren von Morgen. Kommuniqué des Politbüros des ZK der SED zu Problemen der Jugend in der DDR* (Berlin, 1963), 35–70, 49.
68. 'Der Vater verließ den Saal. Beobachtungen und Notizen bei einem Jugendprozeß', *Neues Deutschland* (19 December 1965).
69. 'Rede E.H. in Auswertung der 11. Tagung des ZK der SED und Vorbereitung des 20. Jahrestages der DDR (31.1.1966)', BArch. SAPMO DY30/2150.
70. 'Bericht des Politbüros an die 11. Tagung des Zentralkomitees der SED (15.-18.12.1965)', BArch. SAPMO DY30/2067, 158.
71. Ibid.
72. Volker Müller, 'Nach 23 Jahren: Premiere für "Spur der Steine". Balla oder Die späte Ankunft eines Kunstwerkes in der Wirklichkeit. Notizen über zwei Begegnungen mit dem Regisseur Frank Beyer', *Neues Deutschland* (21 November 1989).
73. 'Manfred Krug als Balla. Vorbereitungen zur Verfilmung der "Spur der Steine"', *Thüringische Landeszeitung* (30 April 1965); 'Blende auf für "Balla"-Film', *Junge Welt* (24 June 1965).
74. 'In Leuna ist der "Balla" los. Leuna II Schauplatz der Dreharbeiten auch um Mitternacht. Der "Krug" sitzt auf der Rolle wie die Faust auf dem Auge', *Lausitzer Rundschau* (17 July 1965).
75. 'Auf Ballas Spuren', *Freie Erde Neustrelitz* (17 July 1965).
76. 'Die Spur der Steine und die Last der Erinnerung. Interview mit Frank Beyer', *Junge Welt* (23 November 1989); Felicitas Knöfler, 'Mit Vaterlandsliebe und Mutterwitz. Fast ein Vierteljahrhundert unter Verschluß, jetzt wieder im Kino: Frank Beyers DEFA-Film "Spur der Steine"', *Tribüne* (27 November 1989).
77. 'Hans Braunseis, 'Ende des großen Verbots. Wie bewältigen wir die aktuell wirkenden, aber allzu spät zur Auseinandersetzung kommenden Kunstwerke?', *Der Morgen* (2 December 1989); Karl Knietzsch, 'Die Spur der "Spur der Steine". Gedanken zur Wiederaufführung eines ehemals verfemten Films', *Die Union* (6 March 1990); 'Wohin die Spur der Steine führt ... Verbotene DEFA-Filme kommen wieder', *Neue Zeit* (28 November 1989).
78. Werner Bräunig, 'Rummelplatz', *Neue Deutsche Literatur* 10 (1965), 7–29.
79. Ibid., 20.

80. Ibid., 11.
81. Ibid., 15.
82. *Vorwärts* (22 June 1953), 3.
83. 'Der Vater verließ den Saal ...'
84. Ibid.
85. Dorothee Wierling, 'Die Jugend als innere Feind. Konflikte in der Erziehungsdiktatur der sechziger Jahre' in Hartmut Kaelbe, Jürgen Kocka and Hartmut Zwahr (eds), *Sozialgeschichte der DDR* (Stuttgart, 1994), 404–25, 410–11.
86. 'Bericht des Politbüros', 158.
87. 'Information über den Studenteneinsatz der TU Dresden im VEG Gustävel, Kreis Sternberg' reproduced in Armin Mitter and Stefan Wolle, *Untergang auf Raten. Unbekannte Kapitel der DDR-Geschichte* (Munich, 1993), 389ff.
88. Ibid., 391.
89. Uta Poiger, *Jazz, Rock and Rebels. Cold War Politics and American Culture in a Divided Germany* (Berkeley, 2000), 46.
90. Police preparations for countering the beat demonstration (28 October–5 November 1965), StAL, BDVP 24.1/236.
91. Report to the Politbüro: 'Information über Vorfälle in der Stadt Leipzig (6.11.1965)', BArch. SAPMO DY30/JIV2/2J/1540.
92. 'Ich war sechzehn ... Erinnerungen von Jürgen Wede', *Freitag* 48 (23 November 1990).
93. 'Beatles, Ledernacken, Aggression', *LVZ* (5 November 1965).
94. Pupils from the 9th class of the 34th *Oberschule*, 'Meinungen zum Artikel'.
95. 'Der Schwur von Buchenwald. Gedanken zum feierlichen Meeting der am Manöver "Oktobersturm" teilnehmenden Truppen und der Weimarer Bevölkerung', *Neues Deutschland* (20 October 1965).
96. 'Herzen in eigener Sache', *Konkret* (March/1966).
97. 'Stenografisches Protokoll: Jugendaussprache "Die Jugend und der Oktobersturm" am Mittwoch, dem 3.11.1965 in der Kongreßhalle Leipzig', StAL, IVA-5/01/269, 146–83.
98. Ibid.
99. 'Reaktion der verschiedensten Bevölkerungsschichten auf den Artikel der LVZ "Dem Mißbrauch der Jugend keinen Raum"' (21 October 1965), BArch. SAPMO, DY30/IVA2/16/68.
100. Kimmel, 'Masculinity as Homophobia'.
101. Erich Mielke, 'Dienstanweisung Nr. 4/66, Verschlußsache Nr. 365/66 "Zur politisch-operativen Bekämpfung der politisch-ideologischen Diversion und Untergrundtätigkeit unter jugendlichen Personenkreisen in der DDR" (15.5.1966)' cited in Armin Huttenlocher, 'Zurück oder vorwärts, du mußt dich entschließen ...' in Klaus Behnke and Jürgen Wolf (eds), *Stasi auf dem Schulhof. Der Mißbrauch von Kindern und Jugendlichen durch das Ministerium für Staatssicherheit* (Berlin, 1998), 78–102, 79f.
102. Hendrik Rahn, 'Für jeden etwas – ist das richtig?', *Mitteilungen des Zentralhauses für Kulturarbeit der DDR, Leipzig* 4:4 (1966); Hans Dilßner, 'Eigenverantwortung und Selbsttätigkeit der Jugend – Voraussetzungen für eine gute Jugendklubarbeit', *Auf neuen Wegen. Methodische Hinweise und Materialien für die Klubarbeit* 127 (1966).
103. Fuchs, *Fassonschnitt*, 65–66.
104. Ibid., 68.
105. Ibid., 67.
106. Ibid., 20.

Chapter 12

PREDATORY MALES

After deposing Ulbricht, Erich Honecker was at pains to emphasise how different he was from the older man. Having built his career on opposition to reform, he nevertheless initiated a period of liberalisation and limited toleration, coinciding with the 1973 international student games (*Weltfestspiele*). A film to mark the occasion shows Honecker distributing very large flagpoles to slim, long-legged blondes with FDJ shirts and miniskirts. He is then filmed passionately embracing a symbolic (and uniformed) female veteran of the North Vietnamese Army (while the translator looks on with a mixture of bemusement and alarm). Elsewhere delegates of all races and peoples can be seen flirting and cavorting to a soundtrack provided by (West German leftist guitar band) Floh de Cologne. One gangly young FDJler can be seen evidently enjoying playing a kissing game with a giggling *señorita* from South America. The real stars of the show, however, were the would-be student revolutionaries from the Third World. For her part, Angela Davis single-handedly managed to inject dignity and coolness to the worldwide movement for socialism, human rights and an end to war. Coupled with an Afro, her rendition of the clenched fist salute gave it new power and meaning.[1]

True to form, however, Honecker's apparent conversion to artistic and other freedoms was disingenuous and brief. More than twenty thousand 'critical' and 'potentially criminal' people were warned not to even think about visiting Berlin during the games. In order to ensure the 'unbroken cleanliness of streets and squares' two thousand more citizens, who had arbitrarily been classed as 'asocials', were arrested. Several hundred were held in psychiatric clinics for the duration.[2] Subcultures did not disappear as a result of such measures, but the regime tried to avoid overt confrontations through increased use of surveillance and infiltration. The massive extension of the Stasi surveillance apparatus seemed to offer improved possibilities for nipping protest in the bud. The 1970s still saw intimidating clusters of aggressive-looking young men dressed in leather jackets hanging around doing nothing on particular street corners. But by this stage they were more likely to belong to the Stasi.³ Nevertheless, despite ongoing harassment by the authorities, large numbers of long-haired hippies continued to hitchhike across the country to appear en masse at rock and blues concerts in the provinces. They dressed eclectically, wearing Levi's jeans, military parkas or Thälmann-style leather coats, blue-and-white striped butchers' shirts and sandals or hiking boots. With their 'slovenly, unkempt, dirty and neglected appearance', their 'uncultivated, loutish behaviour' and their 'sexual misconduct', they disturbed and perturbed.⁴ Some even adopted elements of 1970s socialist revolutionary chic, with berets, Mao jackets and Che Guevara beards.⁵ Although they constituted a colourful mixture of different types and outlooks, working-class male adolescents continued to make up the core of participants.⁶

In March 1975, Klaus Renft's combo was again banned, this time for defaming the security forces. Frontman 'Monster' had announced at a concert in Karl-Marx-Stadt that it was being held under the motto 'The Germans, a nation of thinkers and barbarians'.⁷ In 1976 Altenburg, a town near Leipzig, celebrated its thousand-year anniversary. Two and a half

Bild 1

o9.3o Uhr - Gammlertruppe auf der Freilichtbühne der NVA.

Figure 13. A *'Gammler* troop' lounging on the stage of the NVA at the 1973 World Youth Festival Photographs of beat fans ('amateur or drop-outs') from Lichtenberg.

thousand *Gammler* and 'young people of decadent appearance' turned up to attend a rock concert organised as part of the celebrations. More than ten years after the beat demonstration in Leipzig, the slogan 'the state is powerless' once again raised its head. The crowd insulted the People's Police, calling them 'bulls' (*Bullen*) and 'Nazi pigs' (*Nazischweine*).[8] On 7 October 1977, a tragedy occurred during a rock concert on the Berlin Alexanderplatz. Fans who had climbed onto a ventilation shaft to get a better view were too heavy and fell through the metal grate into the space below. The police decided that it would help the paramedics to reach the accident if they beat their way with truncheons through a crowd numbering several thousands. A riot ensued, in which sixty-six policemen were injured, and the crowd shouted political slogans like 'Down with the bull pack', 'Murderers' and 'Nazis'.[9]

There was a clear feeling that the state, in its love for order and conformity, had taken on fascist tendencies. Nevertheless, by the end of the 1980s, youth nonconformists were praising the Nazis and boasting pride in those aspects of life in the GDR that fitted in with the National Socialist vision. The alarming rise of right-wing extremism after 1989 and the horrific attacks on foreigners (leading to several deaths) did much to tarnish the achievement of unification and to raise fears abroad about the new Germany.[10] Although the period after the *Wende* saw a rise in right-wing extremism and racist attacks in both halves of Germany, attention was particularly focused on the East.[11] Violent xenophobia and overt expressions of appreciation for fascism were all the more shocking because they appeared to contradict everything that the communist regime had stood for. The GDR conceived of itself as being an antifascist state. Yet out of it emerged significant numbers of young people with extreme right-wing attitudes. How can such a contradiction be explained and what does it mean?

Following the regime's collapse, the GDR's 'founding myth' as an antifascist state came under serious and sustained attack, both in academic works and in political and journalistic critiques.[12] Revelations about the scale of spying for the Stasi coincided with reports of an alarming rise in attacks by right-wing extremists born and brought up in the GDR.[13] These developments bolstered criticisms of the 'regimented' and 'totalitarian' nature of East German education. In some cases, the GDR education system was presented as being essentially similar to that of the Third Reich. Indicative of this trend was Hermann Ottensmeier's book, published in 1991 and entitled *Fascist Education System in Germany between 1933 and 1989: Continuity between the Third Reich and the GDR*.[14] Not only had Communism been seen to have failed, but there was now nothing to distinguish it from National Socialism.[15] Although the education young people received in the GDR was important, it was less influential in causing racist and right-wing extremist violence than machismo. It was extreme performances of masculinity (or deviant machismo) that led to racist, chauvinistic, xenophobic, homophobic and other forms of supremacist violence. Although Germany is far from alone in possessing such forms of extremism, the fact that in the Third Reich they had previously led to the concentration camps, racial war and the annihilation of groups viewed as inferior meant that the re-emergence of such attitudes was viewed as particularly abhorrent.

Problems with Antifascist Education

One of the most contentious and divisive issues in assessing the impact of education and other attempts to influence youth in the GDR concerns the effects of efforts to educate young people as 'antifascists'. Antifascism was a fundamental component of the GDR's 'founding myth' and an essential part of transforming young people into future citizens. The SED pointed to its early and thorough denazification of the education system of the GDR as evidence of its claims to be the better Germany. Opposition to fascism was correctly perceived as being the single most important factor capable of uniting the East German population in recognition of the state's right to exist and the population's duty to support and defend it. The belief that they once belonged to an antifascist state still represents an important part of the East German psyche.[16] There was much about the officially 'prescribed' version of antifascism that was contrived and self-serving.[17] Nevertheless, in criticising the official image and mythologisation, it is important not to negate the reality that lay underneath it and was, in large part, obscured by it.[18]

SED propaganda favoured a 'regimented' image highly reminiscent of Nazi manipulation and mass orchestration. Militaristic ceremonies, rituals and forms of organisation were maintained and positively encouraged. Young people were repeatedly depicted wearing uniforms, marching, engaging in communal gymnastics and carrying weapons.[19] Many of those educating and leading them had formerly belonged to Nazi organisations. As Stefan Heym argued, the SED had no alternative but to use former Nazis. 'Who were the workers in the factories? Former Nazis. Who were the low- and also the high-level functionaries? Former Nazis. Who else could one build socialism in Germany with?'[20] Pro-military education started in Kindergarten. As early as they could learn to read and write, children were introduced to agitation and propaganda. Child agitators were not only taught that socialism was superior, but that capitalism was 'parasitic and rotten'. Their teachers were taught that 'We decide the subject and do not let ourselves be pushed into the defensive. The right and the necessity to do so stems from the fact that we alone possess a scientific world view, Marxism-Leninism.'[21] In *Streitgespräche*, children were taught to hate imperialists and to love the GDR. While they were still at the age of playing cops and robbers and cowboys and Indians, the regime deliberately tried to transmit to them an image of the enemy. Bombarded from an early age with pro-military propaganda and tales of the heroic struggle against fascism, children were confronted with concepts and ideas that they were often much too young fully to comprehend. The teachers at one nursery in Leipzig were horrified to find that one of their young charges had decorated the puppet theatre with a swastika. Luckily for them, he was able to justify his actions to the education inspectors by saying that he had wanted to represent the 'bad people' so that he could shoot at them with his toy gun.[22]

Antifascist education in the GDR has been criticised on a number of levels: for its 'prescribed' nature; its self-serving distortion of the truth; its militarism; its authoritarianism (from collective potty training onwards); and its failure to challenge 'traditional German' values and norms. The repetitive and overly convoluted references to fascism in history and civics classes tended to weaken and dilute the message. From the start there was a tendency to underplay the importance of the Holocaust and to present the Jews and other groups targeted by the National Socialists as passive victims in contrast to the heroic activism of the communist *Kämpfer*.[23] The destruction of European Jewry was sidelined as a result of the more pressing need to create a usable national culture. In 1953 the VVN, which represented 'the interests of too broad an array of vocal Nazi victims, including Jewish survivors of the Holocaust', had been replaced by the 'Committee of Antifascist Resistance Fighters in the GDR'. 'This emphasis on fighting not only underscored the SED's quest for political legitimacy through a combative antifascism, but also reiterated the gendered militancy of the SED's past and present antifascist struggle.'[24] Given the authoritarian and militaristic nature of East German education, it is legitimate to ask if this encouraged the development of right-wing extremist attitudes. Could the emphasis on love of Fatherland, military know-how and fighting capability not have resulted just as easily in an affinity for Nazism? Could 'education to hatred' of the capitalist, imperialist West not turn to hatred of all outsiders?

The great majority of young people reacted with abhorrence to fascism. Eighty-four per cent of those surveyed said that they would do everything in their power so that fascism could never be repeated.[25] When pupils were directly confronted with the crimes of the Nazis (in visits to concentration camps or talks by veterans), the SED could usually count on an emotional response.[26] As one youngster described,

> The visit to Buchenwald was very upsetting for me. I was moved and deeply shaken. For the first time I had a profound insight into the life of the prisoners. From this time I have a great respect for all antifascist resistance fighters and feel a deep hatred against the imperialist forces that were and are the authors of such wretched misery.[27]

But the deliberate blurring of National Socialism with Western 'imperialism' undermined the positive aspects of the regime's emphasis on antifascism. That Great Britain and the U.S.A. had also fought against Hitler was rarely heard.[28] The fact that Leipzig had been liberated by the Americans, not the Russians, was not mentioned at all.

By the end of the 1980s, references to the Second World War and to the Holocaust had become so abstract and vague that even those who responded well in other settings admitted that in history lessons they experienced 'relatively little'.[29] In contrast to the official message transmitted by formal education, the often more ambivalent accounts of National Socialism passed on by family socialisation had a much more direct emotional impact. Unlike the peaks of emotion created by special one-off talks and visits, the impact of the family was sustained and self-reinforcing. As early as 1961, a teacher had written to the party leadership warning that, although young people had, in general, a better and clearer view of history than most adults educated under capitalism, 'whether we like it or not, this false view of history seeps through the adults into our young people'.[30] In 1962 in Altenburg the children of leading local educators were involved in an incident in which they proclaimed support for the recently executed Adolf Eichmann and hatred for his victims. 'The Jews are un-German and must be exterminated' read one slogan. 'One is dead, but thousands more will continue his work' read another.[31] A similar incident occurred at the *Humboldt Oberschule* in Magdeburg in 1961. There the

Figure 14. 'Young revolutionaries, from our school follow with interest the account of a former concentration camp prisoner'. School chronicle.

son of a leading education functionary said it was a pity that Hitler had not killed more Jews.[32]

Complete identification was only one possible reaction to the antifascist myth. More often, young people felt an affinity with the antifascists and respect for their suffering. But it was tempered by resentment at the ways in which, despite its claims to have extirpated National Socialism, the GDR relied on forms of repression and authoritarianism that should have had no place in an antifascist state. Ambivalence about the way in which the regime dealt with the Nazi past was often expressed through the scribbling of swastikas. Frequently when young people used fascist rhetoric and symbols they did so ironically in order to draw attention to the similarities between the two systems or instrumentally as a means of goading a reaction. The best way pupils of a Leipzig *Oberschule* could find to draw attention to their civics teacher's unfriendly and overly authoritarian teaching style was by answering the obligatory FDJ greeting of 'Friendship!' at the beginning of the lesson with the words 'Heil Hitler!'[33] Mostly the swastika was simply used as the most powerful means of taunting the regime. Rather than manifesting a seriously held position, it served as a means of drawing attention and of showing daring. The swastika and other attributes of Nazism could also be used as a form of mockery, emphasising the perceived similarities between Communist and Nazi dictatorial rule. Confronted with military-style FDJ membership books – in which they were asked to list their party affiliations and the decorations they had received – secondary-school pupils made explicit comparisons with Nazism and filled in Iron Crosses and 'Member of the NSDAP'.[34]

The striking shape of the swastika together with its omnipresent (almost parodic) function as the symbol of supreme evil continued to exercise fascination over young people, luring even small children into attempts to copy it. By rendering Nazi symbols and ideology taboo the SED ensured that they came to act as a powerful source of fascination and tempting curiosity. The same rebellious urge that led teenagers to aim their air rifles at the portraits of regime leaders during FDJ target practice could also lead them to celebrate Hitler's birthday as a joke.[35] For some, however, the conflicting messages they received and the lack of genuine debate about the past served to undermine and dilute the official message of antifascism. In the same 1989 survey, as many as 15 per cent agreed with the statement that 'fascism also had its good sides'. Among urban apprentices the figure was as high as 21 per cent.[36] Asked to describe how they would react on finding out that a grandfather had been a member of the Nazi Party, their responses revealed a significant degree of confusion, equivocation and even overt identification.

> 'First of all I think of the horrific acts of the fascists (concentration camps, murder, transportations) that makes me a bit sad because this period also had its good sides ...'
>
> ' ... continually to hack away at it, I find, makes no sense ...'

'These people perhaps saw their ideals realised in these associations ...'
'If he [my grandfather] joined out of conviction (not like with the FDJ) and also stood by it right up to the end, then I would be proud of him ...'
'The era of Hitler-fascism was a great moment in German history ...'
'Hitler thought progressively, but he miscalculated ...'
'Such people could be as convinced as members of our party [SED] are today. He too had only done what he thought was right (according to his conceptions).'
'I experience a certain pride in relation to the followers and defenders of fascism. Basically, they also fought for what they believed was a just and worthy ideal.'

While in the West the student revolt of the 1960s provoked earnest discussions about the implications of the past not just in the media and the education system, but also between parents and children, the effects of the changes in education in the East were to increase the gap between what young people learned formally in schools and what they picked up informally at home. The one-sided history taught in schools contradicted but failed to destroy the continued ambivalence to Nazi rule among many in the older generations. Undermining the official message of antifascism were comments and statements by parents and grandparents suggesting an alternative view of the Third Reich that presented it as being 'not that bad really ...' Although young people had initially been encouraged to confront the views and memories of their elders, as the regime matured and sought stability, it increasingly allowed a veil of silence to fall on the complicity (whether as perpetrators or bystanders) of large sections of its own population in support for National Socialism.

Not only was the official picture presented of antifascism ambivalent, but young people were denied opportunities to discuss, analyse and assess their responses freely and openly. Prescribed responses were learned by rote. Instead of provoking discussion and debate, civics lessons served to stifle and suppress genuine understanding. Denying people freedom of speech meant that 'ideas and misconceptions that might have been weakened by the give and take of a more fluid public discussion were contrarily protected from wider scrutiny'.[37] The consequences were confused and ambivalent attitudes to Nazism. The 1960s and 1970s saw numerous incidents involving Nazi rhetoric and symbols. Russian propaganda films, in particular, could spark opposition with strong racist and anti-Semitic overtones.[38] Here young men responded to the ambivalence by identifying with the enemy.

Deviant Machismo

In the preceding chapters, we have seen how machismo could lead young men to stand up to and defy the regime. The potential always existed, however, for those in subcultures to turn their frustration and anger not just against the intolerant and violent state but also against 'others'. Masculine posturing was often a blunt and inarticulate form of protest. The pursuit of acceptance and approval through the adoption of an exaggerated sense of toughness could also lead to serious delinquency and, in some cases, to lives of crime. Youth subcultures presented 'an inchoate and unconscious rebellion' against the values and ethos of both state socialist and liberal, capitalist societies. Rampant machismo was a challenge to bourgeois respectability. But, just because such rebellion is 'anti-bourgeois', this does not necessarily mean that it is 'progressive' or liberating. After all, 'anti-bourgeois ideas' were also used by fascism.[39] Although it was important for the authorities to have overt symbols and labels with which to stamp youth nonconformists as being 'other', not all the pro-fascist elements attributed to them were fictitious. In its deviant variety, machismo could result in veneration of Nazism and contempt for the victims of Nazi tyranny. The emphasis on masculinity (as opposed to politics and ideology) not only produced male chauvinism, but other forms of chauvinism as well.[40] The stress on strength and violence led not only to clashes with the authorities, but to attacks on groups and individuals seen as 'weak' or 'other'. A persistent claim made against the gangs was that they were involved in 'queer bashing'. Homosexuals sought out the same obscure, marginal and liminal spaces as the gangs, but used them for cruising and cottaging rather than for macho self-presentation. The gangs could see them as weak and exploitable, even using attractive young men as 'honey traps' to lure hapless gay men, only then to rob and extort them under threat of violence and blackmail.[41]

For some men, violence (and hurting people) could function as a panacea for individual shortcomings, as a source of erotic fulfilment and as a way of establishing superiority over others. In the GDR as elsewhere, there were groups of men who, in their contempt for women, believed they could rape them with impunity.[42] In 1964, members of the 'Al Capone' gang in Leipzig, led by a young man whose nickname was 'Ape', renamed themselves the Adolf Hitler Club. They planned to use Second World War weapons to rob a bank, but had only succeeded in gang-raping two girls, one of whom was beaten and burned with cigarettes.[43] The authorities frequently used fictitious accusations of criminal behaviour in order to persecute those in the subcultures, but there was a hard core of young men for whom masculinity meant criminality. While for most young men the prospect of spending time in juvenile detention or prison was a strong deterrent, for some it was accepted as an inevitable part of living the life they wished to lead and also a way of proving manhood and obtaining status among their peers.

There is a long history of romantic identification with the figure of the outlaw.[44] From Jesse James to Ned Kelly, such figures have inspired respect for their resilience, humour and refusal to obey. Nevertheless, there is a point beyond which no amount of humour can mask the brutality of their hypermasculinity and violence, no amount of wit can transform them from villains to 'lovable rogues'. As Norman Mailer was forced to recognise, 'since the hipster lives with his hatred ... many of them are the material for an elite of storm troopers ready to follow the first truly magnetic leader whose view of mass murder is phrased in a language which reaches their emotions'.[45] Mailer was criticised for overestimating the radical potential of the hipsters (good only for 'a small home-made pogrom').[46] Rebellious heroes of the type he celebrated have often been dismissed as merely representing the petit bourgeoisie of tomorrow.[47]

The rockers resented anything that entailed uniforms, *Zackigkeit* and submission to authority. In 1959, one high-school rebel (with a motorbike and leather jacket) disrupted a sports festival of the GST by calling for them to sing SA songs.[48] Rockers called for the abolition of the armed forces, the border police and the special task forces (*Kampfgruppen*).[49] But although they were capable of challenging the regime and poking it in places where it was vulnerable, the sense of rebellious defiance that underlay youth subcultures also made them extremely volatile and unstable. There was always a latent propensity in the subcultures to use violence regressively as well as subversively. The lads in the *Meuten* may well have been 'exemplary', as former gang member Christa would have it, but, in a culture that prized strength and ridiculed weakness, the potential was always there for the posturing to turn ugly. Photographs seized by the police frequently revealed gang members acting out scenes of sadism and violence.[50] Fights that turned nasty, rapes, muggings and attacks on homosexuals were a potential companion to more laudable expressions of rebellious protest. East German youth was no better or worse than that of other countries in this respect.

Until the closure of the border, the French Foreign Legion offered another opportunity for young men to establish and prove their ruthlessness. Conjuring up images of exotic travel and adventure, it was an abiding source of fascination for young German men.[51] The freedom those joining the legion desired was very different from liberal freedom. It involved sexual licence and the opportunity to kill for money. The war in Indochina was particularly attractive to German recruits, offering them the chance not only to act out being brutal and heartless, but to engage in a no-holds-barred combat with the communists. According to one ex-legionary, 'the rape, beating, burning and torture of harmless farmers in the course of punitive actions' was an everyday occurrence in Indochina.[52] In popular legend, the legion promised a safe haven from pursuing authorities and a chance to make a fresh start by freeing themselves from their inner demons and submitting to its rigid regimentation and structure of discipline. The hardships endured during training together, with the emphasis in the many rites and myths on the glorious tradition of the legion, reinforced the sense that they belonged to an elite.[53] In addition to the glamour and status that came with being a legionary, there was the self-belief that they were the ultimate in men. Eckard Michels argues that, if anything, young men from the GDR were probably under-represented among those accepted as recruits because Foreign Legion commanders were sceptical about taking them in case they were communist agents. Nevertheless, the legion seemed like a viable option to many refugees who could not find their feet in the West.[54]

Negative Identification

By taking a public stand against particular youth styles, the SED repeatedly succeeded in turning the disputed stylistic feature into a symbol of opposition and rebellion. In a case involving young people from Karl-Marx-Stadt, a gang was reported to have attached hypodermic needles to their jacket lapels as a mark of identification. 'The fashion was copied by a number of young people because they found it "chic" despite not being members of the gang and indeed being completely against the idea of it. Although the People's Police said that the wearing of hypodermic needles was unhygienic, this argument met with complete incomprehension on the part of youth.'[55] As Stanley Cohen showed in relation to the moral panic surrounding the mods and the rockers in Britain, hostile press reporting served to alter and magnify the problem posed by rebellious youth subcultures by simplifying and standardising them.[56] There was a persistent tendency on the part of East German male youth to react to the moral panics orchestrated by the authorities by embracing the negative stereotype. Often the negative behaviour they copied was harmless (like the wearing of needles or other badges) and, in the case of the *Schwerter zu Pflugscharen* symbol, pacific. But, in other cases, their desire to emulate and identify with whatever the authorities found objectionable led them to activities that were potentially dangerous, both for themselves and for others.

An example of the way in which moral panics succeeded in increasing rather than decreasing deviance among youth can be found in the case of a 'leather jacket gang' that developed in a village in the Saxon countryside. H. was (and still is) very much a backwater, with little more than a bus stop where young people could congregate. The village was dominated, however, by the presence of a teacher training college, which imposed an unusual degree of 'redness' (or ideological conformity) on the local inhabitants.[57] In the absence of other forms of entertainment, the male youth of H. developed their own, a peculiar mixture of the traditional (singing songs with altered lyrics; serenading the girls living in a dormitory for female apprentices) and the modern (listening to Western music on their transistors, and posing on their motorbikes and in their leather jackets). In both cases, a high degree of performance was evident in their stylised enactments of gender. If most of the gang were only playing at being men, for Siegfried N., the dominant figure and leading voice in the group, being a German man was a much more serious business. For him, standing above and dominating others (through physicality, strength of will and a commanding tone of voice) was a family tradition. His grandfather on his mother's side was a Prussian military man (expelled from Silesia after the war). Because he had been born out of wedlock and his mother had gone on to marry a high-ranking officer in the NVA, he ended up being brought up 'Prussian fashion' by the grandfather.[58] He ordered the others around in an autocratic fashion and called any who did not want to participate 'cowardly pigs'.[59]

In this highly contained, claustrophobic world (which was subsequently described and documented in detail by the Stasi), there was too little space to do anything without being observed. With little other opportunity to relieve the pressures created by their rapidly expanding egos, the boys turned to alcohol to let off steam. Although they were not major music fans, the media campaign targeting beat fans in the aftermath of the beat demonstration in Leipzig had made a major impact on them. In photographs printed in the local newspaper, the *Leipziger Volkszeitung*, they could see male youths very much like themselves depicted in highly rebellious poses with captions describing them as being filthy, frenzied and fascist. The most impact seems to have been made by the reproductions of tattoos found on juvenile delinquents in Leipzig. Ranging from the dollar symbol to death's heads, the young men portrayed as dangerous deviants had had no qualms about 'inscribing Western unculture into their bodies'. But, far from encouraging the boys of H. to see the light and to renounce their wicked, Western-inspired ways, instead the official press campaign encouraged them to experiment (using needles and ink) with their own home-made tattoos. These included a desert island with Hawaii written under it, a laughing cow, an anchor, a snake and dagger and a dollar symbol.[60] Siegfried N. tried to force the others to take part by calling them 'scaredy-cats' (*Angsthase*) and saying, 'If you don't have a tattoo done, then you're not a real German.'[61]

> After the gathering of beat fans in October 1965, I saw a photo in the *Leipziger Volkszeitung* showing a tattoo found on the body of such a person. Though I didn't read the accompanying article, I liked the tattoo that had the words 'U.S.A.', 'True' and 'Money', which corresponded to my attitude as a result of the influence of Western broadcasts; and, in order to make an impression on other youngsters, I made the same tattoo on my lower arm, using needles and ink.[62]

Armed with leather jackets, sunglasses, motorbikes and jeans, they could 'terrorise' the locals. Older men in the village looked forward to the day when they would be called up for military service, warning them that, if they wanted to make it through basic training, they would have to be obedient. 'We always laughed when we replied "Yes, that's what we'll do, Herr E." because he's a pompous idiot who doesn't realise when we take the piss out of him.'[63] Becoming more and more emboldened by their displays of defiance and fuelled by alcohol, they sought a showdown with their sworn enemies, the students from the alien and imposed training institute for children's home employees. While those in the gang were already earning wages and were waiting for their call-up papers, the students were 'lazy conceited pigs', sheltered from the demands of manual labour but obliged to display meek obedience to party dictates.[64] A further bone of contention was the fact that the institute held dances to which the village boys were not admitted, leaving them outside – allegedly in the bushes spying through the windows in the hope of seeing the girls undress.[65] In a similar fashion, they 'sought to provoke the female students' by appearing naked when they went bathing.[66]

Because the forms that had traditionally been used by the working class for rebellious assertions of their aloofness and 'otherness' had been so effectively appropriated and taken over by the regime, it was not surprising that, in reaction, working-class youths frequently appropriated some of the symbols, songs and customs of its discredited nemesis. In the case of the boys from H., they took the forbidden soldier songs 'Grüß mir die Heimat, Karin mein Glück' and 'Wir fahren gegen England', altering the words to add lines about Ulbricht and Khrushchev, transposing them onto the tune of songs they had learned in school like the workers' fighting song 'Spaniens Himmel breitet seine Sterne'.[67] Having seen a programme about the mercenary 'Congo Müller', Siegfried N. marvelled at what an 'efficient killer' he was, 'what a man', and spoke about how 'he'd clean up real quick if he was in Vietnam'.[68]

The specific trigger to the chain of events that led to their imprisonment was a pub visit five weeks before, in which one of the students had tried to prevent the gang from singing the anthem of the Foreign Legion.[69] The gang decided to get their revenge by waiting for the students outside the entrance to the pub, which also doubled as the village cinema. Ironically, the main feature was *The Man with the Golden Arm*, the story of a Western heroin addict who injected himself with needles. Having consumed several crates of beer, the boys were in no fit state to appreciate such details. They had been celebrating the news that one of their number had become a father (news that only served to reinforce their sense of manly superiority vis-à-vis the subservient students). Standing at the entrance to the room where the film was being shown, they sought to provoke the students by showering the males with insults and the females with beer.

Inside the cinema, Siegfried N. made a nuisance of himself while the others pretended to be shocked and called him a *Halbstarke*.[70] In an inebriated state, Peter K. threw his identity papers against the wall shouting 'Verdammte Zonenpass'. In his interrogation, he said that the alcohol had made him feel strong and that he did not want 'to be seen as an outsider'.[71] The other boys expressed their frustration by raising their arms and shouting '*Sieg Heil*'.[72] When the students left the cinema, the gang chased them back to their institute shouting 'Jewish swine, communist swine, we're going to finish you off, the day of reckoning is coming, then Ulbricht's neck will be broken'.[73] One of the students lost his glasses in the scuffle and, as he was running away from his pursuers, accidentally knocked over an old lady, who expressed indignation about him not looking where he was going. For the local party leadership, however, there was nothing remotely amusing about the incident. The gang members were arrested and interrogated by the Stasi. They were charged and sentenced with 'endangering the state through the spreading of lies and propaganda'.

Skinheads

Deviant masculinity could be even more destructive. In the summer of 1962, a gang of leather-clad bikers supposedly terrorised a holiday resort on the Baltic island of Rügen. In so doing they demonstrated their lack of respect for respectability, order, wisdom and authority. Led by a former Foreign Legionary called King, whom they rigidly obeyed, they made their own law and left a trail of dead and broken bodies behind them. Influenced by the 'Wild West' ethos of Western psychological warfare, they decided to copy Yul Brynner and shave their heads. 'Why is Yul Brynner a great actor?' asked King. 'Because he looks demonic. And why does he look demonic? Because he has no hair.' 'The girls love demonic' ('Auf dämonisch stehen die Bienen'), chorused one of the gang enthusiastically. Although supposedly based on real events, the scenes depicted in the 1963 DEFA film *Die Glatzkopfbande* were entirely fictional.[74] By adding manslaughter to the gang's alleged crimes, the film-makers hoped to paint the delinquent protagonists (who in reality had merely been rockers on holiday) in such a harsh light that nobody could identify with them. Ironically, although the film was later banned, the vision of ruthless, brutal, unrepentantly deviant machos with shaved heads was to come back to haunt the regime.[75]

Although by the end of the 1980s skinheads had become synonymous with neo-Nazis, when they first emerged at the beginning of the decade, they were simply the latest in a series of subcultures to come to East Germany from Britain via West Germany. The skinhead look took off very quickly among football fans and hooligans. Overnight a number of punks, who were tired of the demands of looking and behaving asocial, became skins.[76] With their shaven heads and overt aggressiveness, the skinheads took the traditional nonconformist stance to a new extreme. Many of the initial converts were drawn first to the look. Only subsequently did they attach meaning and justification to their style, telling the authorities that the word 'skinhead' meant 'young worker'.[77] Football matches acted as a focus around which the early skinhead scene could develop.[78] Isolated in their day-to-day lives, this was an opportunity for the skinheads to network and to begin appearing in strength. 'When the opportunity presents itself, they occasionally also beat up the skins of opposing clubs.' Grounds for such a conflict were normally provided by the north-south divide that existed

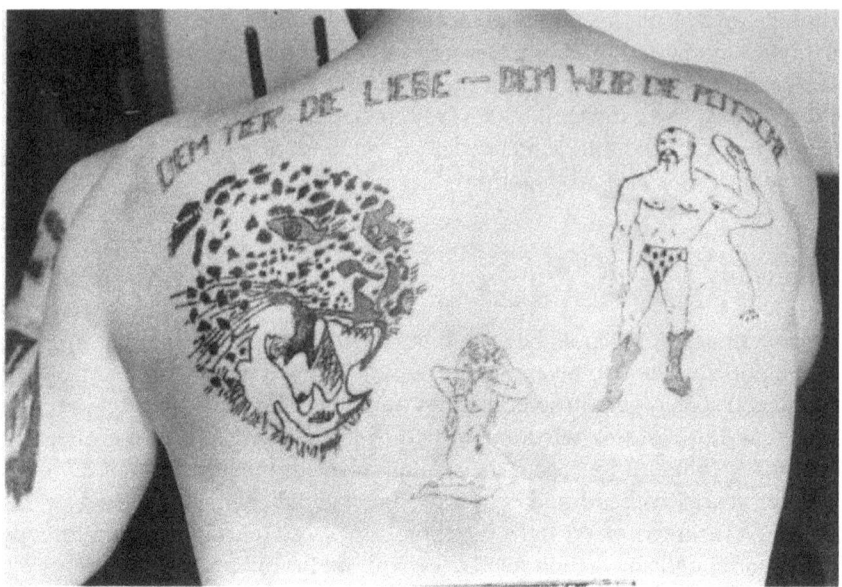

Figure 15. Wild man tattoos. 'For the animal the love, for the woman the whip'. Tattoos found on the back of a rowdy arrested by the police.

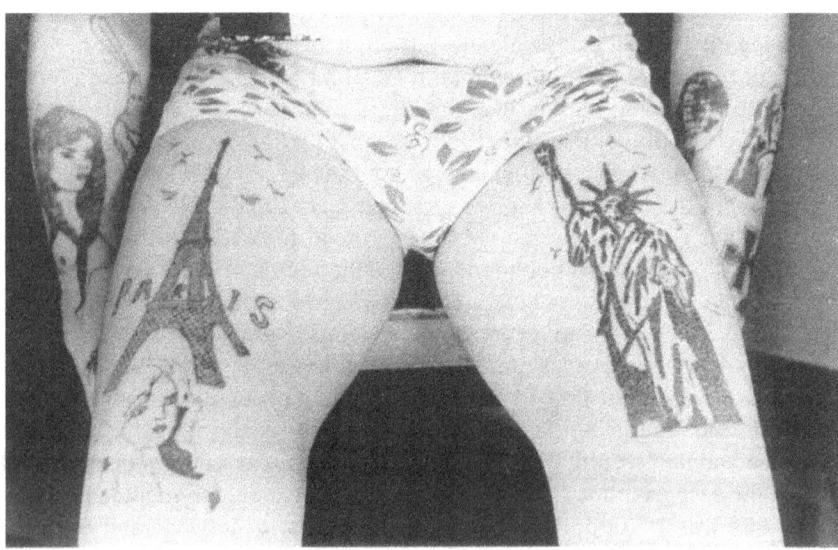

Figure 16. Identification with the imperialist enemies. Tattoos depicting Paris, New York and the Iron Cross. A masked man can just be seen on the suspect's inner right arm.

between the 'Prussians' and the 'Saxons'. In the main, however, their victims were 'foreigners [*Kanaken*], punks and long-hairs [*Müslis*]'.[79] Matches between Dresden, Leipzig and Berlin were important in developing the respective scenes. Local derbies and matches involving Dynamo, the Sports Association of the Protection and Security Organs, could also provide interesting clashes.[80]

What distinguished skinheads from those in other subcultures in the early 1980s was their propensity to use violence and the conservative and petit bourgeois nature of much of their outlook.[81] Violence was an important part of the skinheads' sense of self. It was meted out to dark-skinned foreigners, punks and homosexuals. Their readiness to use violence set them apart from others and reinforced their sense of belonging. In its skinhead variant, violence ceased to be a potential side-effect of subculture and became the *raison d'être*. While punks rejected work as pointless and exploitative, skinheads could embrace it as a means of affirming their manly capability as providers. The authorities were used to emphasising the parasitic, idle and work-shy tendencies of nonconformists. Skinheads, whose employers described them as hard-working and orderly, were therefore a conundrum. Such an ambivalent mixture of violence and conservatism could be confusing because it overlapped with many of the values that the regime held dear. At times, officials despaired that, but for their ill discipline and propensity for right-wing extremism, such young men might have made excellent citizens and soldiers. Officials blindly believed that it would be possible to wean them off fascist beliefs by making them take part in additional military training in the GST or calling them up to serve in the military. And yet a number of would-be brutal thugs had already been through the official paramilitary organisations on their passage towards right-wing extremism as a form of macho fulfilment.[82]

Although it only became a mass phenomenon with the development of the skinhead scene, problems with racism, xenophobia and support for National Socialism had already begun to emerge in the 1960s. Already in 1963 the Stasi noted that those with affinities for Nazism demonstrated an enthusiasm for military affairs from childhood onwards and this acted as a 'breeding ground' for extremist ideas, which if 'incorrectly channelled' could turn into enthusiasm for the fascist *Wehrmacht*.[83] As the emphasis on pre-military training intensified, the number of young men who went radically off target increased. While sections of East German youth were protesting at Biermann's expulsion in 1975, others were attacking Algerian apprentices in *Schwarze Pumpe*.[84] Not only did the authorities fail to bridge the gap between the official ideology and older generations' memories of National Socialism, but they prevented the population from generating genuine contacts and links with the foreigners living in the GDR. Although the numbers of foreign 'guest workers' were far lower in the GDR than in the FRG, significant xenophobia did exist.[85] In a society with full employment, resentment was not so much centred on foreigners taking Germans' jobs, as their taking up resources (like housing and consumer goods) that could otherwise go to Germans. Poles, in particular, were accused of bleeding the East German economy dry by speculatively buying up scarce resources. In addition, they could be presented as lazy for taking part in the Solidarity strike movement. Another flashpoint, particularly among the younger generation, concerned girls in bars and nightclubs. Here it was Algerians who were seen as constituting a particular problem. Sent over by their government to receive training, they were young single men far from home and used to different sorts of restrictions on their behaviour. While the authorities worried about the development of 'intimate relationships' between them and local girls, the skinheads were upset by their preparedness to defend themselves by carrying knives.[86]

While one set of young men responded to the officially sanctioned, aggressive and intolerant machismo by becoming pacifists and refusing to take part in military service, another sought to outdo the regime by becoming even more violent and macho. There was a basic problem with communist emphasis on male heroism. Although in many ways it unconsciously emulated the fascist emphasis on force and the heroic male body, communism was never more than a pale imitation and substitute for the real thing.[87] Although it did allow opportunities for macho posturing, communism was nevertheless always dominated, limited and tamed by demands for submission to party dictates and the overriding goal of the transformation of society. For those who were more interested in violence than ideology, the nihilism of National Socialism was far more attractive. Why devote your manly essence to building something up when you can destroy it? Submission to a charismatic Führer was far more acceptable, particularly as it entailed limitless power for the Nazi warrior to persecute and annihilate subjugated, inferior peoples. Although most young people regarded such acts as abhorrent, the male adolescents in the bottom set were less able to empathise with the victims and more likely to identify with the perpetrators.

In March 1977, 255 eighth-class pupils from the Ho Chi Minh *Oberschule* were taken to see the film *Naked Among Wolves* at the Lindenfels cinema in Leipzig in preparation for their *Jugendweihe* excursion to Buchenwald. Based on Apitz's antifascist epic, the film was supposed to teach them about the moral dilemmas faced by those imprisoned in the concentration camp.[88] Instead, the darkness of the cinema gave them a chance to run amok. 'The discipline of the pupils was catastrophic. When, for example, the SS attacked prisoners in Buchenwald, it was greeted with applause and loud calls of "chase them through the chimney, kick the Jewish swine dead", etc. ... Employees of the cinema tried to get hold of the biggest trouble-makers and were called witch, "Jew-sow" and other insults.'[89] Their response to the communists' struggle for humanity was to laugh in their faces. In their

Figure 17. Still from *Die Glatzkopfbande* showing former Foreign Legionary and gang leader 'King' receiving a pedicure from a blond admirer.

Figure 18. Still from *Die Glatzkopfbande* showing the gang after they had undergone a metamorphosis from annoying to evil by shaving their heads.

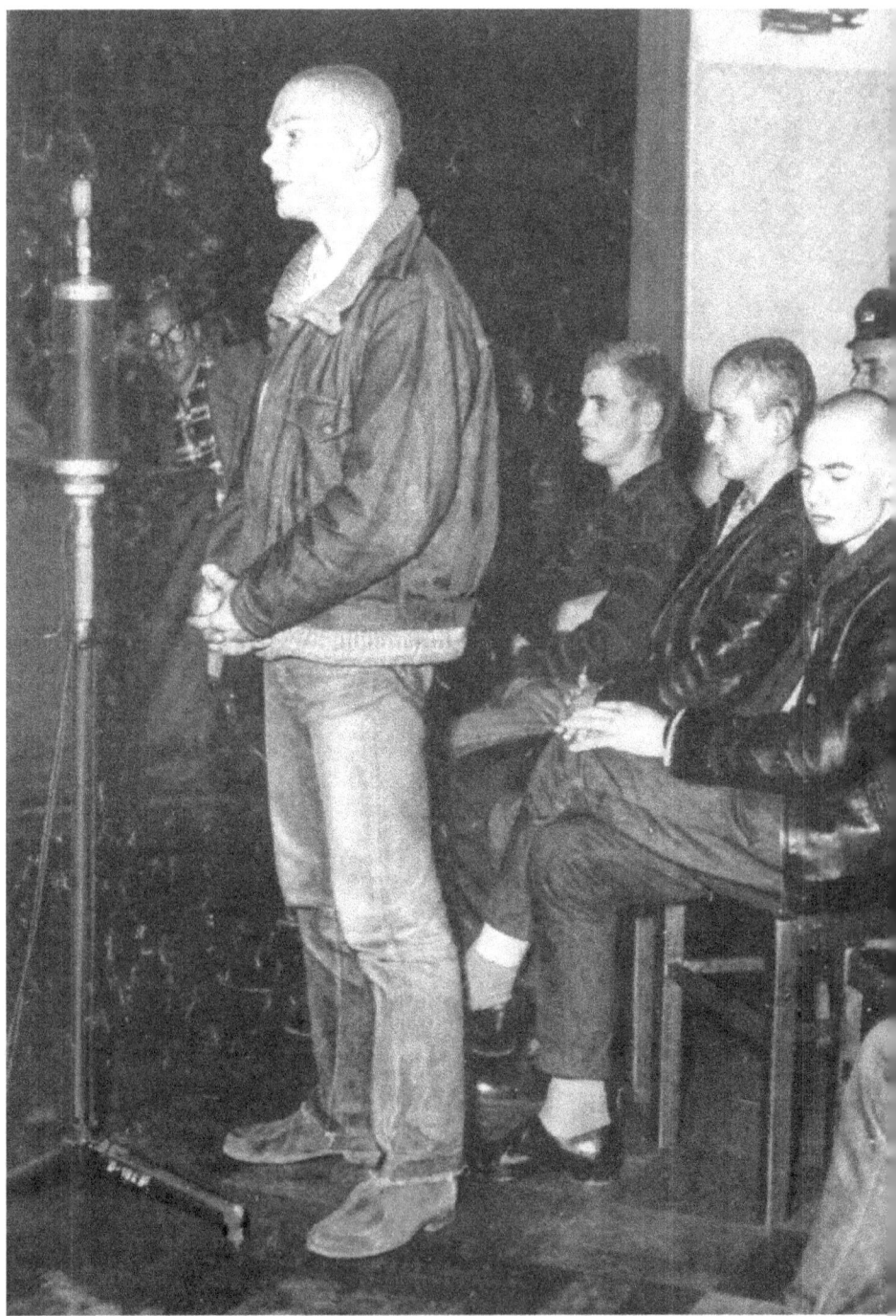

Figure 19. Members of the real *Glatzkopfbande* at their show trial in 1961.

toughness and abhorrence of weakness, the boys showed that they were ready to outdo them.

For all its epic qualities, there was an ambivalence in *Nackt unter Wölfen* that these pupils had obviously picked up on. Propaganda works by establishing an unbridgeable gulf between 'us' and 'them'. But, when young East Germans were confronted with propaganda about the Second World War, it was not always entirely clear to them who was supposed to be 'us' and who 'them'. Leading communists may have fought on the side of the heroic Soviet Union (which had its own ambivalent period between 1939 and 1941), but the boys growing up in East Germany knew very well that their own families had not. 'We are the sons of the enemy. Everything is doubly crazy and upside down: against Hitler and for Stalin ... One's own father was a German and they're the ones being shot at ... Should we be pleased if our fathers are killed?'[90] If the film's depiction of the need for 'iron-hard discipline' in the face of unrelenting and sadistic cruelty was ambivalent, the novel on which it was based was even more so. Not only do the perpetrators succeed at the end of the novel in getting away with their crimes, but the most vicious and nasty amongst them even manages to get the girl – and not just any girl but one with 'full breasts' and 'tight pullovers' who 'willingly lets herself be felt all over'. According to Apitz, the reason Hortense gave herself so willingly to the evil Kluttig is that, unlike her 'limp-dick husband', he at least was a 'real man'.[91]

A major weakness in the GDR's emphasis on antifascism (and a problem that continues to plague teachers in Germany today) was that, perversely, the importance placed on opposition to fascism could have the opposite and undesired effect of making Nazis and Nazism seem forbidden and daring. The conflicting pressures on adolescents were such that it was possible for them to play with Nazi slogans at the same time as believing the concrete actions and effects of the Nazis to be profoundly abhorrent and wrong. Unfortunately, for many young Germans, Nazism functioned as a mood-enhancing joke. Breaking such an important taboo produced its own rush of excitement and adrenaline. Among older Germans, in contrast, Nazi utterances tended to occur as a side-effect of inebriation. The singing of fascist songs, in particular, occurred particularly after extended stays in pubs.[92] Use of the Hitler salute, anti-Semitic insults, demands for a 'Germany with the borders of 1937', the putting up of fascist symbols and slogans, the carrying out of celebrations on Hitler's birthday and use of racist statements against foreigners were all worrying signs. While some such uses of fascist statements and symbols were interpreted as attempts 'to provoke or to cause a sensation, occasionally such actions occurred as a result of neo-Nazi views'.[93] The problem for the authorities was that instances of provocation using swastikas and other Nazi elements were so common that, when genuinely pro-fascist activities did occur, they were difficult to identify and could get lost amid the stack of other cases. Although there was pressure to investigate each and every incidence of unacceptable behaviour, the official taboos that surrounded neo-Nazi sentiments and incidents in the GDR ensured that they could not be discussed in public. As a result the development of a widespread trend of neo-Nazi incidents could only be officially identified and discussed when it was already too late and extreme right-wing ideology had already become established among sections of youth.

By this time, these were young men who were not merely teasing or baiting the authorities, but genuinely believed in the rhetoric and ideals of National Socialism. In May 1977 the headmistress of the Leibniz *Oberschule* found a piece of paper stuck to her chair. 'All teachers are thick as pigshit,' it said. 'The best thing to do is to gas the arseholes! The men will be castrated, the women fucked to death. Apart from the [headmistress], that whore – you'd get the clap from her. Germany lives!'[94] The extreme inhumanity and brutality of the Nazis were abhorrent to most young people, particularly to those with intelligence and sensitivity. But by no means all young people were sensitive or intelligent. Particularly for those whose lack of academic success left them marginal, Nazism could increase their sense of power. The Nazi elite formations had attracted significant numbers of young men from lower working-class backgrounds who appreciated the opportunity to clothe themselves in the uniform of invincibility. Given the importance to young male adolescents of emphasising their lack of weakness, identifying with SS men and Nazis enabled them to present themselves alongside the ultimate in inhumanity.

> Yeah they call me Adolf Hitler and all the Jews go weak,
> when fearsome as a tiger through the gas chamber I sneak,
> As the machine gun begins to clatter and the Jews are overcome,
> they start to cry and I find that real dumb.[95]

Ironically, right-wing extremism in the GDR developed in areas that should have been the most watched and controlled – in the tower blocks surrounding the Stasi headquarters in Lichtenberg and among the supporters of Erich Mielke's own personal football club, the BFC.[96] Constantly under surveillance and surrounded by the attributes, the culture and ethos of Stasi power, the skinheads felt that the only way they could beat and outdo the forces of order was to go to the other extreme. The security services had the entire power of the state, the military and the Soviet Union behind them and demonstrated a readiness to use violence and intimidation against those they identified as enemy or other. Given the fact that so many people in the local community were fanatically and aggressively left-wing, the skinheads later argued that they had little alternative but to become right-wing extremists.[97] The communists always blamed Western media for turning youth sour. Psychological warfare designed to corrupt and brutalise youth was the oft-repeated claim. But the reasons why particular individuals became not just rebellious but deviant usually lay closer to home.

Authoritarian upbringing, emotional distance and respect for military virtues were factors that particularly encouraged the development of right-wing extremist attitudes. In a number of cases, paternal involvement with the party, state or security forces increased the degree and violence of reaction against the ideology and practice of socialism in the GDR. Parents who overdid or were hypocritical in their conformity could inspire enormous contempt in their children – not just for themselves, but for the whole system. A particularly strong link seems to have existed between having an ambivalence to fascism and a father in the security forces. Not only were such fathers strict and authoritarian, but they were also often too preoccupied with work to concentrate on their families. "'All strength for socialism", that does not leave much time for the family.'[98] The absence of or breakdown of meaningful communication with the father allowed harmful right-wing extremist attitudes to develop unchecked. Their hardness and willingness to make sacrifices were held up as moral examples to their sons, but they also became sources of pain and reproach. While some boys sought to rebel against their fathers (and the father state) by growing their hair long, the skins sought to antagonise and outdo theirs by becoming even more extreme, violent and macho.[99]

As far as the authorities were concerned, there was at first little to distinguish between 'skinheads', 'punks' and 'heavy metal' fans. All were seen as groups of rowdies who were guilty of annoying, disquieting and brutally attacking citizens. Occasional instances of veneration of fascism and of neo-Nazi ideas were reported, but they were not identified with any one particular group.[100] After skinheads attacked punks in the *Zionskirche* on 17 October 1987, it was no longer possible for the GDR authorities to hide the fact that a small, but nevertheless significant, minority of young people had adopted racist and anti-Semitic attitudes completely at odds with the ethos of the regime.[101] In the years prior to the *Wende*, they were eagerly courted by West German neo-Nazi groups, keen to use their 'ethnically healthy, Spartan living, sportive and militarily schooled potential' for Germany in the 'final struggle' against inferior races.[102] The East German skinheads combined popular hostility to foreigners in the GDR with phrases copied straight from the West. Interestingly, anti-Turkish sentiments existed among East German skinheads prior to any real contacts with actual Turks.[103] This reveals the extent to which hostility to and scapegoating of foreigners represented an attempt to contrast one's Germanness with the negative stereotype of the 'other' rather than a real confrontation over jobs and resources. The skinheads went to great lengths to indulge their deviant machismo, from making their own baseball bats to spending years in prison.[104]

Prior to the *Zionskirche* incident, neo-Nazis and skinheads were overlapping but by no means identical groups. This high-profile attack served to focus attention on the phenomenon and to link skinheads and

Nazis both in the public imagination and in the minds of the skinheads themselves. The increased press attention acted not only as a challenge for existing skinheads to be more radical and outspoken in their opposition to the state. It also caused others to be attracted by the negative image itself. The security services' remarkable failure to prevent or to intervene during the coordinated assault, which targeted regime opponents, led to suggestions that the Stasi might even have facilitated the *Zionskirche* attack. After *Zionskirche*, the GDR authorities began targeting and demonising skinheads. The system of surveillance and control (from ABVs to *Ordnungsgruppen*), backed up by the system of incarceration (from juvenile detention centres to work camps and Stasi prison), ensured that they were marginalised and harassed, but it proved impossible to convert them or to make them disappear. Far from defeating the right-wing extremists, by the mid-1980s, draconian punishments and repeated incarcerations only served to harden their resolve.[105] All the bad publicity only served to increase the popularity of the skinheads among sections of alienated and disgruntled East German youth.

Neo-Nazism had formed in the shadow of the antifascist state. After the *Wende*, it came to overshadow it. Demonstrating how the tables had turned, the neo-Nazis used the massive statue of Ernst Thälmann with his clenched fist as the backdrop for their demonstration on May Day 1991.[106] Those attacked in the *Zionskirche* incident criticised the 'latent propensity towards fascist thought (xenophobia, hatred of others, scapegoating instead of analysis) of the population as a whole. The same way as in the 1930s, a people is fleeing into the historical cul-de-sac of irrationalism'.[107] As if to fulfil this prophecy, in 1992 the would-be pogrom mob in Rostock paraded their stupidity and inadequacy in front of the national and international press while spouting anachronistic and out-of-place claims to superior German values of order, discipline and cleanliness. Particularly ill-placed was Harald Ewald's demand that foreigners 'should behave themselves in a respectable fashion' after he had been photographed with his arm outstretched in the Nazi salute, his tracksuit bottoms clearly soaked in piss.[108]

Images of a residence for foreign workers in flames flashed around the world to universal despair. It was ironic that the group of foreigners that the mob nearly succeeded in burning to death were Vietnamese. The ire of local residents had originally been raised by Romanian gypsies, who, unable to gain access to accommodation for asylum seekers, had camped outside in the open. Even educated East Germans condemned the gypsies for their inability to adapt and conform and for their lack of belonging to any particular state.[109] The Vietnamese, in contrast, were widely recognised as being the least intrusive and threatening of foreigners. Overnight, however, their presence shifted from being invisible to unbearable. As if the decades of war that had been waged in their homeland by the competing cold war powers, the succeeding imposition of communism and the decline of their domestic economy forcing them to accept contracts as guest workers in the GDR were not enough, the baying mob sought to perpetrate their own version of the My Lai massacre. To bolster their status in the new Germany, they attacked those with no status.

The way in which the communist regime instrumentalised the Third World led to representatives from formerly communist allied states being seen as 'symbols of socialist domination' rather than people with whom one could develop genuine relationships of solidarity or friendship.[110] The regime made a great fuss of foreign visitors but the fanfares and propaganda served to create an association between foreigners and puppets of the state. Large amounts of cash were spent on solidarity drives, education and training, both in the Third World and in East Germany. But the role of educator and benefactor (dispensing wisdom and largesse) tended to reinforce an implicit sense of superiority. Despite the party's claims to have cured the population of such ills, racism and xenophobia remained latent within East German society.[111] Although the SED professed understanding of and solidarity with the Third World, at home this only applied to those who had attained what the German communists saw as the appropriate level of 'civilisation'. Even political refugees could only be accepted if they were prepared to give up their idiosyncrasies, their strange and peculiar ways and embrace a German way of life that was implicitly seen as superior.[112]

The collapse of police authority following the regime's implosion created a vacuum that right-wing extremists from East and West were able to exploit. The fragile balance of power had been held in place in the GDR by disproportionate and excessive use of force. Once that force was taken away there was nothing to hold back a flood tide of racism and xenophobic violence. Law and order suffered as those with a taste for lawlessness and disorder found that they were no longer as closely watched and that the threat of arbitrary arrest and imprisonment had been taken away. The real heroes of autumn 1989 were the men and women who went onto the streets armed only with their consciences, fully conscious that they ran the risk of being massacred in their thousands like the students of Tiananmen Square. In the end, the power of the state crumbled before it could unleash vengeance. The *Kampfgruppen*, stylised as bastions of invincible working-class masculinity, simply evaporated in October 1989. Like naughty schoolchildren, their members feigned illness and failed to turn up for duty.[113]

Although they readily took advantage of the freedoms won by the pro-democracy demonstrations, the neo-Nazis had nothing but contempt for the principle of toleration and non-violence that had underpinned them. Well-meaning youth workers – often Lutheran volunteers – had the almost impossible task of trying to breach the shell-like armour of ideology and macho violence in order to reach what they saw as the young men with problems beneath.[114] One analysis was that East Germans became baseball-bat wielding skinheads because they missed the security and community provided by the FDJ. Others argued that it was a form of protest reaction against the social and economic turbulence East Germany was experiencing as a consequence of unification. But the main reason why young men took part in right-wing extremist politics and violence against foreigners and 'others' was that it was exciting and fun and because it made them feel powerful and important.

Conclusion

The rise of xenophobia and racist violence was a manifestation of unresolved contradictions in the SED's project. With its strong polarisation of 'us' and 'them' and its encouragement of young people to express hatred to enemy outsiders, the SED had a significant degree of responsibility for what happened after its demise. The regime persistently presented the GDR as a pure and morally superior space that was only polluted by evil coming from outside. It had spent forty years blaming the West for fascism. The complicity of its own population in National Socialism was whitewashed and airbrushed. The short-sighted and blinkered vision of antifascism served to blind it to problems within, to shield it from new ways of looking at the problem of fascism and yet it failed to prevent neo-Nazis getting their message across to potential recruits in the East.

As much as the SED is to blame, however, the masculinist chauvinism that prevailed in working-class youth subcultures also played a major role in rendering neo-Nazism attractive in the late 1980s. In previous decades, the authorities' claims about deviant youth seem to have been more mythical than real. The claims made by the police and the Stasi often had a tenuous relationship to the truth. But, by the late 1980s, the fears about rampaging mobs of brutal and fascist 'rowdies' had become a self-fulfilling prophecy. For certain types of young men, there was considerable kudos to be had by playing on official fears. 'Gentle' violence was no longer enough to control them and the prospect of real violence (whether or not any political or ideological significance was attached to it) excited them. What was most shocking to the macho defenders of antifascism was that among the neo-Nazis were some of their own sons. Even more alarming for outsiders was the fact that outwardly there was little to distinguish between the two.

Notes

1. *Wer die Erde liebt*, directed by Jürgen Böttcher and Joachim Hellwig (DEFA, 1973).

2. Sonja Süß, *Politisch mißbraucht? Psychiatrie und Staatssicherheit in der DDR* (Berlin, 1998), 523–34; 'Bekämpfung der Asozialität' (c. 1973)', BArch. Berlin DO1/050/43168; for the preparations in Leipzig, see 'Ministerium des Innern: politische Massenarbeit' (c. 1973), StAL, BDVP 24.1/226; 'Woodstock des Ostens', *Der Spiegel* 35 (26 August 1996), 68–69.
3. Günter de Bruyn, *Vierzig Jahre* (Frankfurt am Main, 1996), 163, 217
4. Michael Rauhut, *Rock in der DDR* (Bonn, 2002), 66–68, 77, 81.
5. 'Rowdytum, Gruppierungen' (Leipzig, 14 February1975), StAL, BDVP 24.1/420.
6. Thomas Kochan, *Den Blues haben. Momente einer jugendlichen Subkultur in der DDR* (Münster, Hamburg, 2002); Rauhut, *Rock in der DDR*, 77.
7. 'Vorkommnisse beim Auftreten der Renft-Combo in Jugendveranstaltungen in Karl-Marx-Stadt im März 1975', SAPMO DY30/18017.
8. Rauhut, *Rock in der DDR*, 70–71.
9. Ibid. 73.
10. Jochen Schmidt, *Politische Brandstiftung. Warum 1992 in Rostock das Ausländerwohnheim in Flammen aufging* (Berlin, 2002).
11. *The Truth Lies in Rostock*, produced and directed by Siobhan Cleary and Mark Saunders (Channel 4, 1993).
12. For a very critical account of this approach to East German antifascism, see Detlef Joseph, *Nazis in der DDR. Die deutschen Staatsdiener nach 1945 – woher kamen sie?* (Berlin, 2002).
13. Notably the account of Ingo Hasselbach, co-written with Winfried Bonengel, *Die Abrechnung: Ein Neonazi steigt aus* (Berlin, Weimar, 1993); *Führer Ex*, directed by Winfried Bonengel (Germany, 2002).
14. Hermann Ottensmeier, *Faschistisches Bildungssystem in Deutschland zwischen 1933 und 1989. Kontinuität zwischen Drittem Reich und DDR* (Hamburg, 1991).
15. This is the view presented by Hermann Weber, 'Die Jugendpolitik der SED 1945 bis 1989. Forschungsfragen, Quellenlage und wissenschaftliche Erwartungen' in Helga Gotschlich (ed.), *'Links und links und Schritt gehalten ...'. Die FDJ: Konzepte – Abläufe – Grenzen* (Berlin, 1994), 20–31, 29–30.
16. Bernd Faulenbach, 'Acht Jahre deutsch-deutsche Vergangenheitsdebatte' in Christoph Kleßmann, Hans Misselwitz and Günter Wichert (eds), *Deutsche Vergangenheiten – eine gemeinsame Herausforderung: Der schwierige Umgang mit der doppelten Nachkriegsgeschichte* (Berlin, 1999), 15–34, 24; Annette Leo and Peter Reif-Spirek, 'Plädoyer für den genauen Blick' in Annette Leo and Peter Reif-Spirek (eds), *Helden, Täter und Verräter. Studien zum DDR-Antifaschismus* (Berlin, 1999), 7–12.
17. 'Der verordnete Antifaschismus. Ein Wort zum Thema "NS-Erbe und DDR"' in Ralph Giordano, *Die zweite Schuld oder von der Last Deutscher zu sein* (Hamburg, 1998), 209–18; Sigrid Meuschel, *Legitimation und Parteiherrschaft. Zum Paradox von Stabilität und Revolution in der DDR 1945–1989* (Frankfurt am Main, 1992), 39–40; Konrad Jarausch, 'The Failure of East German Antifascism: Some Ironies of History as Politics', *German Studies Review* 14 (February 1991), 85–102.
18. Thomas Flierl (ed.), *Mythos Antifaschismus. Ein Traditionskabinett wird kommentiert* (Berlin, 1992); Joseph, *Nazis in der DDR*, 15.
19. For propaganda films, see *Kinder, Kader, Kommandeure*, directed by Wolfgang Kissel and C. Cay Wesnigk (Germany, 1992).
20. '"Ich habe auch geschossen". Der Schriftsteller Stefan Heym über sein Leben als Oppositioneller in drei deutschen Staaten', *Der Spiegel* 53 (1998), 142–47, 145.
21. Zentralrat der FDJ, *Erfahrungen bei der Gestaltung des aktuell-politischen Gesprächs in Pionierkollektiven. Stäbe Junger Agitatoren* (Berlin, 1977), 5.
22. 'Hakenkreuz' (29 October 1976), Leipzig Stadtarchiv St.u.R.(2), Volksbildung, 1680 Band 2, 87.
23. Christopher Hölscher, *NS-Verfolgte im 'antifaschistischen Staat'. Vereinnahmung und Ausgrenzung in der ostdeutschen Wiedergutmachung 1945–1989* (Berlin, 2002).

24. Catherine Epstein, *The Last Revolutionaries. German Communists and their Century* (Cambridge, MA, London, 2003), 156.
25. Wilfried Schubarth, 'Forschungen zum Geschichtsbewußtsein' in Walter Friedrich, Peter Förster and Kurt Starke (eds), *Das Zentralinstitut für Jugendforschung Leipzig 1966-1990. Geschichte, Methoden, Erkenntnisse* (Berlin, 1999), 206-24.
26. *Jugendweihe* ceremonies often included visits to Sachsenhausen or Buchenwald concentration camp.
27. 'Der Rote Oktober und die jungen Revolutionäre unserer Heimat. Schulschrift der Oberschule Ehrenburg, 1969', Saxon School Museum Leipzig B8-143-2900, 150.
28. Jürgen Fuchs, *Fassonschnitt* (Reinbek, 1984), 272.
29. Schubarth, 'Forschungen zum Geschichtsbewußtsein', 110.
30. Letter from Otto S. (5 April 1961), BArch. SAPMO, DY30/ IV2/905/35, 397.
31. 'Information über Friedrich-Engels-Oberschule Altenburg' (June 1962), BArch. SAPMO DY30/ IV2/905/27, 136ff.
32. 'Konzentration von Erscheinungen' (October 1961), BArch. DR2/6298.
33. 'Kurt-Kress OS, Leipzig Südwest', (23 May 1973), StAL, Bt&RdB, 24312, 65-67.
34. 'Nikolai-Ostrowski-Oberschule Torgau' (26 February 1975), StAL, BT&RdB Leipzig, 24788.
35. 'Dr. Sorge Oberschule, pol. Provokation' (20 April 1976), Leipzig Stadtarchiv, Stv&RdSt Leipzig (2) 1680 Band 2, 25.
36. Schubarth, 'Forschungen zum Geschichtsbewußtsein', 67, 97.
37. Jeffrey Brooks, *Thank you, Comrade Stalin! Soviet Public Culture from Revolution to Cold War* (Princeton, 2000), xiv.
38. 'Provokatorische Handlungen während der Vorführung des sowjetischen Films "Blockade" (1975)', BArch. SAPMO DY30/18017.
39. Roger Horrocks, *Male Myths and Icons. Masculinity in Popular Culture* (Houndsmills, 1995), 110.
40. 'Bericht über zwei realisierte Ermittlungsakten zur Bekämpfung des Rowdytums (5.10.1960)', BDVP 24/113, 178-84.
41. BStU, ZA, HA IX 1894. This case is complicated by the fact that the gang was also alleged to have attacked a known member of the MfS.
42. Siegrun Steppuhn, 'Gewaltsame Unzucht und Notzucht als Einzel- und Gruppendelikt' (Humboldt Universität: Ph.D. Thesis, 1970).
43. BDVP response to a request from the Ministry of the Interior for information about youth crime (21 May 1964), StAL, BDVP 24.1/420, 129-32.
44. Eric Hobsbawm, *Primitive Rebels* (Manchester, 1959).
45. Norman Mailer, 'The White Negro. Superficial Reflections on the Hipster' in *Advertisements for Myself* (New York, 1981), 294-345, 316-17.
46. Ibid., 322.
47. Winfried Sträter, '"Das konnte ein Erwachsener nicht mit ruhigen Augen beobachten." Die Halbstarken' in Berliner Geschichtswerkstatt (ed.), *Vom Lagerfeuer zur Musikbox. Jugendkulturen 1900-1960* (Berlin, 1985), 137-70, 165-69.
48. '"Presley-Bande" an der erweiterten Oberschule Pößneck' (c. November 1959), BArch. Berlin DR2/4814.
49. 'Beratung über Fragen der Jugendkriminalität und des Rowdytums (29.10.1958)', StAL, BDVP 24/113, 86.
50. 'Bilddokumentation zu Vorkommnissen mit negativen Jugendlichen' (1964-69), BArch. DO1/38215.
51. Eckard Michels, *Deutsche in der Fremdenlegion 1870-1965. Mythen und Realitäten* (Paderborn, 1999), 197ff; Swedish reporter Hans Axel Holm encountered two men near Rostock. The older man had been in the SS and later in the Foreign Legion. While he viewed the war with ambivalence, his young friend was wholly enthusiastic, dreaming of following in his footsteps. Hans Axel Holm, *The Other Germans. Report from an East German Town*, trans. Thomas Teal (New York, 1970).

52. Michels, *Deutsche in der Fremdenlegion*, 213.
53. Ibid., 211.
54. Ibid., 199–200; '48 sagten: Nie wieder! Viele Bataillone der Fremdenlegion zu 90 Prozent Deutsche', *Junge Welt* (15 May 1956).
55. 'Nationalrat der Nationalen Front: Bericht' (20 March 1963), BArch. SAPMO DY6/3940.
56. Stanley Cohen, *Folk Devils and Moral Panics* (London, New York, 3rd edn, 2002), 66–67.
57. 'Vorkommnisse in H.' (5 April 1967), StAL, IV A-2/9.02/353.
58. Interview with Peter K. Names and location changed to protect anonymity.
59. BStU, Ast. Lpz., AU 762/67, Band IV, 50.
60. BStU, Ast. Lpz., AU 762/67.
61. BStU, Ast. Lpz., AU 762/67, Band III, 39.
62. BStU, Ast. Lpz., AU 762/67, Band II, 38.
63. BStU, Ast. Lpz., AU 762/67, Band I, 120–21.
64. BStU, Ast. Lpz., AU 762/67.
65. BStU, Ast. Lpz., AU 762/67, Band IV, 53.
66. BStU, Ast. Lpz., AU 762/67, Band II, 69.
67. BStU, Ast. Lpz., AU 762/67, Band I, 16. Other songs included 'Schwarzbraun ist die Haselnuß', 'Schwarzbraunes Mädel, Du bleibst zu Haus', 'In einem Polenstädtchen' and 'Wir lagen vor Madagaskar'.
68. Ibid., 160.
69. Ibid., 61, 139.
70. Ibid., 126.
71. BStU, Ast. Lpz., AU 762/67, Band III, 58ff.
72. Under interrogation, they said that they had learnt such Nazi rituals from DEFA films like *Du und mancher Kamerad*, *Kampf um Deutschland* and *Ernst Thälmann*. Ibid., 130.
73. 'H.' (Apr. 1967), StAL, SED IVA2/16/464, 219f.
74. *Die Glatzkopfbande*, directed by Richard Groschopp (DEFA, 1963).
75. Another DEFA film from this period depicted a gang of *Halbstarken*, who inflict a brutal beating on a communist headmaster. The place chosen for the ambush was a Nazi monument known as the 'Pig-opolis (*Saukropolis*)'. *Denk bloss nicht ich heule*, directed by Manfred Freitag (DEFA, 1965). Joshua Feinstein, *The Triumph of the Ordinary. Depictions of Daily Life in East German Cinema, 1949–1989* (Chapel Hill, London, 2002), 178.
76. Klaus Farin and Harald Hauswald, *Die dritte Halbzeit – Hooligans in Berlin-Ost* (Berlin, 2002), 112ff.
77. 'IM Thomas' (c. 1987), BStU, Ast. Lpz., AIM 4971/92, 49.
78. Farin and Hauswald, *Die dritte Halbzeit*, 84ff.; 'Abschrift des vom Informationsbüro der Zionskirche herausgegebenen Materials zur Berliner Skinheadszene - Miasmen im politischen Sumpf der Gegenwart. Die Ostberliner Skinszene (5.5.1988)', BStU, ZA, HA XX 898.
79. Informationsbüro der Zionskirche: Material zur Berliner Skinheadszene'.
80. 'Rowdyhafte Ausschreitungen und andere provokatorische Handlungen durch Personen aus Leipzig beim Fußball-Ligapunktspiel der SG Dynamo Eisleben gegen die BSG Chemie Leipzig am 30.3.1975 in Eisleben', BStU, ZA, ZAIG 2398.
81. Manfred Stock and Philipp Mühlberg, *Die Szene von innen. Skinheads, Grufties, Heavy Metals, Punks* (Berlin, 1990); C. Remath and R. Schneider (eds), *Haare auf Krawall. Jugendsubkultur in Leipzig 1980 bis 1991* (Leipzig, 1999), 164–79; Harry Waibel, *Rechtsextremismus in der DDR bis 1989* (Cologne, 1996); Walter Süss, *Zu Wahrnehmung und Interpretation des Rechtsextremismus in der DDR durch das MfS* (Bonn, 1993).
82. 'IM Thomas'.
83. 'Untersuchungen gegen Untergrundgruppen' (18 March 1963), BStU, ZA, HA IX 11884.
84. 'Unterschriftensammlung durch eine Oberschülerin im Zusammenhang mit dem Einsatz algerischer Werktätiger im Kombinat Leuna' (29 January 1976), BStU, ZA, ZAIG 2474; 'Besondere Vorkommnisse' (1970–73), BArch. SAPMO DY30/18017.

85. Dennis Kuck, '"Für den sozialistischen Aufbau ihrer Heimat"? Ausländische Vertragsarbeitskräfte in der DDR' in Jan Behrends, Thomas Lindenberger and Patrice Poutrus (eds), *Fremd-Sein in der DDR. Zu historischen Ursachen der Fremdenfeindlichkeit in Ostdeutschland* (Berlin, 2003), 245–55; BStU, ZA, ZAIG 2474.
86. Almut Riedel, *Erfahrungen algerischer Arbeitsmigranten in der DDR* (Opladen, 1994).
87. Martin Straub, '"Die Abenteuer des Werner Holt" oder die Sehnsucht nach dem "gefährlichen Leben"' in Annette Leo and Peter Reif-Spirek (eds), *Helden, Täter und Verräter. Studien zum DDR-Antifaschismus* (Berlin, 1999), 211–31, 224ff.
88. Alan Nothnagle, *Building the East German Myth. Historical Mythology and Youth Propaganda in the German Democratic Republic, 1945–1989* (Ann Arbor, 1999), 57.
89. '15.3.77–SB Südwest, Ho-Chi-Minh-OS' in Leipzig Stadtarchiv, StV&RdSt Leipzig (2), 1682 Band 4.
90. Fuchs, *Fassonschnitt*, 294.
91. Bruno Apitz, *Nackt unter Wölfen* (Halle, 1959), 259–60, 436, 538.
92. 'Oberste Gericht: Öffentliche Herabwürdigung' (January 1989), BArch. SAPMO IV2/2.039/217, 144–49.
93. Ibid.
94. 'Leibniz-Oberschule (6.5.77)', Leipzig Stadtarchiv, StV&RdSt Leipzig (2), Volksbildung 1682, Band 4.
95. 'Leibniz-Oberschule (14.6.77)'.
96. Andreas Gläser, *Der BFC war schuld am Mauerbau. Ein stolzer Sohn des Proletariats erzählt* (Berlin, 2003); Waibel, *Rechtsextremismus in der DDR*, 212; Hasselbach and Bonengel, *Die Abrechnung*, 16–18; Burkhard Schröder, *Rechte Kerle. Skinheads, Faschos, Hooligans* (Reinbek, 1992).
97. Wolfgang Brück, 'Skinheads als Vorboten der Systemkrise. Die Entwicklung des Skinhead-Phänomens bis zum Untergang der DDR' in Karl-Heinz Heinemann and Wilfried Schubarth (eds), *Der antifaschistische Staat entläßt seine Kinder. Jugend und Rechtsextremismus in Ostdeutschland* (Cologne, 1992), 47–63, 55.
98. Hasselbach and Bonengel, *Die Abrechnung*, 16.
99. Hasselbach writes the book as a letter to his father, who was 'a high-level functionary'. Ibid., 33.
100. 'Entwicklung und Bekämpfung der Straftaten im Jahre 1987', BArch. SAPMO IV2/2.039/217, 85–90.
101. Waibel, *Rechtsextremismus in der DDR*, 56, 216, 226; 'Jugendanalysen' (c. 1982), BStU, ZA, HAXX/AKG1487; 'Operativer Materialien zu Personen mit neofaschistischen, antisemitischen bzw. ausländerfeindlichen Positionen' (9 February 1989), BStU, ZA, HAIX10712.
102. Joachim Oertel claims to have heard this praise for the GDR in West Berlin skinhead circles. Joachim Oertel, *Die DDR-Mafia. Gangster, Maoisten und Neonazis im SED-Staat* (Böblingen, 1988), 84.
103. 'Monatliche Berichterstattung' (1989), BStU, Ast. Lpz., Abt. IX 00199/01.
104. Hasselbach and Bonengel, *Die Abrechnung*, 137.
105. Ibid., 22ff.
106. Ibid., 127–29.
107. 'Informationsbüro der Zionskirche: Material zur Berliner Skinheadszene'.
108. Klaus Bittermann, 'Die Gespensterwelt der Ossis' in Henryk Broder et al., *Der rasende Mob. Die Ossis zwischen Selbstmitleid und Barberei* (Berlin, 1993), 104–38, 127.
109. Gabriele Goettle, 'Herr und Frau Mob' in Broder et al., *Der rasende Mob*, 55–64, 62.
110. Jan Behrends, Dennis Kuck and Patrice Poutrus, 'Thesenpapier: Historische Ursachen der Fremdenfeindlichkeit in den Neuen Bundesländern' in Behrends, Lindenberger and Poutrus (eds), *Fremd-Sein in der DDR*, 301–7, 301.
111. Damian Mac con Uladh, 'Guests of the Socialist Nation? Foreign Students and Workers in the GDR, 1949–1990' (University College London: Ph.D. Thesis, 2005), 183f.

112. Patrice Poutros, 'Mit strengem Blick. Die sogenannten Polit. Emigranten in den Berichten des MfS' in Behrends, Lindenberger and Poutrus (eds), *Fremd-Sein in der DDR*, 205–24; *Isabel auf der Treppe*, directed by Hannelore Unterberg (DEFA, 1984), deals with the unhappy experiences of a Chilean family, unassimilated, despised and ignored.
113. Interview with Leipzig *Kampfgruppen* member, Hans-Peter D. (1999).
114. Karl-Heinz Heinemann, '"Ihr wollt nicht wissen, wer wir sind, also wundert Euch nicht, wie wir sind!" Interview mit Christine Günther, Sozialarbeiterin in Halle/S' in Heinemann and Schubarth (eds), *Der antifaschistische Staat*, 126–31.

⚜ Chapter 13 ⚜

Conclusion

The date 9 November 1989 marked not only the fall of the Berlin Wall, but also the premiere of the GDR's first and only gay feature film. The key moment in the film is when Philipp, a young teacher having difficulties accepting his own sexuality, is given a talking to by the elderly homosexual, Walter. Played by Werner Dissel with his deep, chain-smoker's voice, his serious, worn-out face and bloodshot, heavy-drinker's eyes, Walter was the image of the communist old fighter.

> Only once did I experience true love ... that was fifty years ago. His name was Karl. I was twenty, he was eight years older. To this day I don't know who denounced us. We were pulled out of the tent, arrested, taken away to Berlin, to the Gestapo. Karl and I were locked up, put in isolation, in solitary confinement. I was put in a concentration camp, Sachsenhausen, pink triangle, scum of the earth. But then I joined the Communist Party. The comrades saved me. Then I was an activist of the first hour. We worked like fanatics and put an end to exploitation. We didn't give a shit if the person working next to us was a Jew or whatever else. Only the queers, we forgot about them.[1]

In 1984 lower-level functionaries began to respond to the growing pressure of people applying to leave the GDR with the propagandistic formula (believed to stem from former concentration camp inmate Hermann Axen) that 'We will have nothing to do with all those who have a false relationship to our state, to work and to the opposite sex.' All of a sudden homosexuals, lesbians and 'asocials' became lumped together in the same category of 'parasites'. For many homosexuals, inside and outside the party, this was the last straw.[2] Fed up with the various forms of suspicion and discrimination to which they were subject, they 'came out' as overt opponents of the regime.[3] Heiner Carow made *Coming Out* on the verge of the East German revolution as a plea for tolerance not only for gays and lesbians, but for all minorities in the GDR including *Andersdenkende* (those who thought differently).[4] Werner Dissel's performance as the homosexual veteran Walter was lent additional poignancy by the fact that, in the 1950s and 1960s, he had appeared in films like *Ernst Thälmann – Sohn seiner Klasse* and *Nackt unter Wölfen*. From 1937 to 1939, he himself had been imprisoned by the Gestapo as a result of antifascist activities.[5]

Coming Out broke moulds not only in addressing the long-suppressed issue of homosexuality, but also in tackling the reality of widespread xenophobia and the open occurrence of neo-fascist attacks in East Berlin. It depicted a state riddled with contradictions and coming apart at the seams. The scenes in the gay bar had echoes of Weimar decadence about them shortly before the Nazis seized power. But above all it manifested the hopeless contradiction between the vision of utopian equality for all and an emphasis on macho superiority that continued to exclude racialised and gendered others. 'More than a story of a single man's coming out, it came to represent the "coming out" of a whole society – not to homosexuality per se, but to having the courage to be "one who thinks differently".'[6]

Attitudes to teenage sexuality (which related to styles of clothing and dancing as well as to petting and intercourse) changed over the decades. At times (such as in 1955, 1963 and 1968), reformers sought to encourage greater tolerance and understanding for more modern attitudes and ways of interacting. At other times (notably in 1965), regime leaders were more than willing to deploy petit bourgeois arguments in order to condemn 'problematic' adolescent behaviours as being alien and other. For a state that placed so much emphasis on achieving gender equality, the attitudes revealed by senior figures (and lower-level functionaries) in response to Western-inspired youth cultures demonstrated the limits of their abilities to conceive and grasp alternative perspectives. Fear of uncertainty (in terms of gender and sexuality) was a characteristic of the cold war in both East and West. It led to a continued use of binary notions of gender in spite of rhetoric about equality.

In the beginning, SED leaders had tried to use male heroes as a means of drawing attention away from their regime's shortcomings and its inherent lack of legitimacy (as a Soviet imposition). Later, when popular support failed to materialise among youth, they sought to use violence against nonconformists in order to re-establish their authority. The army served to dampen the dreams of adolescence and acted as a counter to the individualising trends in modern society.[7] When neo-Nazism raised its ugly shaven head, regime leaders were shocked to see how much it mirrored and reflected the idealised image they had of working-class male youth: strong, powerful, steadfast, resolute and committed, steeled for victory and purged of weakness and all non-German influences. Gripped by their own, idiosyncratic vision of the future, East Germany's communist leaders had remained wedded to a masculine image from the past. 'How does a revolutionary behave in relation to the opposite sex?' was a question they posed of youth, but the possibility that a homosexual could also be a revolutionary or that men did not need to be 'steely hard' to be true socialists was not considered.⁸ As a result, the communists remained part of a history of exclusion and repression of all that was defined as unmanly. Like the Nazis before them, they demanded courage, bravery, discipline, obedience, order and self-control.⁹ Military service remained the crucial test of the true man. Heroic literature encouraged the shielding of 'weak' emotions behind 'hard as steel' exteriors. Those who failed to fit the vision of soldierly manhood were presented as lesser men, as cowards, weaklings and shirkers.

Ironically, the premiere of *Coming Out* was attended by Margot Honecker. With the possible exception of Erich Mielke, she had done more than anyone else to corrupt the GDR's humanistic, antifascist vision. After the regime's collapse, the former Minister for Education was forced to recognise the SED's failure to co-opt young people.

> I see it as a great weakness that we did not succeed in penetrating [sic] the huge sphere of free time and leisure. We provided more material than could be discussed in a school day or a school week, let alone an hour-long lesson. Youth needed not just to be spoon-fed, but to be active in their free time, to be a real part of something. As they became more educated and more emancipated, such a need could only increase.¹⁰

Despite repeated noises from on high, no concrete action was taken. In the end, as a consequence of the changes unleashed by Gorbachev, the system began to unravel.

The inability to make the youth organisation genuinely attractive or to develop an adequate system of youth clubs to replace it can be seen as one of the key failings of the attempt to construct socialism in the GDR. From a socialist standpoint, it was a failure to address the needs of young people who were potentially violent and criminal, but who were also vulnerable and excluded. In 1955, Albert Norden had warned that, if the FDJ was not capable of revising its youth work, then it risked creating 'a murderous pit in young people's hearts'.¹¹ Over thirty years of indifference and inactivity later, the pit of hatred had become bottomless. Neo-Nazis spawned by the regime were more than ready to dance on the graves of the antifascists at Buchenwald.¹² The authorities had shown how good they were at walling problems in. But, for the most part, they had failed to establish the basis for a relationship of mutual respect, genuine admiration, tolerance and love.¹³

Bebop, rock 'n' roll and beat fans were all perceived as threats to order and conformity. The perpetual rejuvenation of the youth subcultural scene made it a recurring thorn in the SED's side. But, for many of those involved, it was no more than a passing phase. A common refrain among former 'rowdies' was that in their day it was all completely different from the way it is nowadays. The passage of time has tended to blur their memories and to lend them a more romantic tone. Their gangs were 'not really' gangs in the way they are today. Seen from the vantage point of respectability and middle age, it is difficult for them to identify with how they might once have thought and acted. Most of the one-time rebels are now indistinguishable from their fellow citizens. They share the same anxieties about young people becoming involved in drugs and crime. Not only was their rebellious phase short-lived, but, in the same way as for the Edelweiss Pirates who went before them, it did not provide them with a lasting immunity.[14]

For the most part, the impulse to embrace the 'exciting ritual and resistant elements' provided by rock 'n' roll gave way to 'retreat into an apathetic, private, domesticated existence' as soon as they had a serious relationship and family commitments.[15] For some former members, however, the gang provided a stepping stone to much more serious deviance, with terms of imprisonment bringing them into contact with hardened career criminals and the temptations of a life of crime. More rarely, gang members could even swap sides and go over to the former enemy. In autumn 1989, not far from the Capitol Cinema where they used to annoy passers-by, Manfred came face to face with 'the Dortmunder', who had once been in the *Meute* with him. To his shock and surprise, his one-time friend had not mellowed with age, but was wearing the uniform of the People's Police.[16]

Their shared appreciation for rock 'n' roll and beat led young people in the 1950s and 1960s into struggles with the state over definitions of culture and modernity. How far they expressed their opposition to the official discourses in terms of defiance rather than immunity depended on their class, gender and (lack of) education. The SED responded to both the inner distance and the overt rejection of many teenagers by increasing its control over education and trying to militarise male youth. Exploiting the weak, the marginal and the vulnerable (together with the vain, the shallow and the greedy), the Stasi reached ever further into society, seeing schoolchildren and those in children's homes as being particularly susceptible to influence.[17] Those who failed to conform became permanently marginalised. Belonging to a subculture ceased to be a temporary phase of wild, irresponsible release before settling down to a life of boredom, sensible consumption and rational, timid choices. As lepers living on the edge of society, their only hope of reintegration was to agree to spy on their fellow nonconformists. All healthy outlets for questioning and expressing independence were systematically closed off, leaving the inevitable feelings of resentment and anger to stew and fester. Meanwhile the irony of an antifascist regime seemingly obsessed with clothing itself in the image of Prussian militarism became steadily more macabre. Parents could only look on as the options for their children were progressively narrowed in order to fit the increasingly outdated dreams of an elderly leadership. For those with vision and a conscience, the warping of society to fit an outdated vision of steeled will and uniform behaviour induced nausea and cries of protest.[18]

SED spokesmen had long justified the repression of Western-influenced youth culture on the grounds that those involved were either culturally inferior or fascist. At the same time, however, in seeking to define and exclude the beat fans, they used notions of German hygiene and 'quality work', which had previously been used to justify the inferiority of foreign forced labourers (*Fremdarbeiter*).¹⁹ The skinheads undermined this message both by embracing a vision of traditional, homogeneous (and racially pure) German culture as superior and in identifying with the Nazi storm-troopers. But, while there are uncomfortable similarities between the machismo of the extreme left (represented by the Stasi) and that of the extreme right (formed by the neo-Nazis), it is important not to neglect the fact that, for the great majority of the population, neither of these positions applied. Most men succeeded in developing healthier and saner forms of masculinity than either the self-styled '*Tschekisten*' or the skinheads were capable. The development of a distinctive secular-rational approach to sexuality and the body (with advice literature encouraging nudism, equal partnership and a pragmatic, 'learning by doing' approach to sex) helped to soften the edges, but could not disguise the continuing contradictions and inequalities (even) in socialism.

Notes

1. *Coming Out*, directed by Heiner Carow (DEFA, 1989).
2. Interview with Klaus Laabs in Jean Jacques Soukup (ed.), *Die DDR. Die Schwulen. Der Aufbruch* (Göttingen, 1990), 78, 120ff.
3. On the discriminations faced by homosexuals, see Kurt Starke, *Schwuler Osten. Homosexuelle Männer in der DDR* (Berlin, 1994), 195ff.
4. Dennis Sweet, 'Die DEFA und ihre "anderen": Heiner Carows "Coming Out" als coming out der "anderen"', trans. Bernd Sahling, *Film und Fernsehen* 1 (1998), 42–47.
5. Frank-Burkhard Habel and Volker Wachter, *Das grosse Lexicon der DDR-Stars* (Berlin, 2002), 69f.
6. 'About Heiner Carow, Coming Out and Being Gay in East Germany', www.icestorm-video.com/carow_interview (accessed 1 May 2004).
7. See Mario Erdheim, *Die gesellschaftliche Produktion von Unbewußtheit* (Frankfurt am Main, 1984), 67, 296.
8. Olaf Brühl, 'Arschficker oder Arschkriecher? Kleines schwules Glossar eines Außenseiters' in Günter Grau (ed.), *Schwulsein 2000. Perspektiven im vereinigten Deutschland* (Hamburg, 2001), 163–206, 196.
9. 'I swear to be a truthful, brave, disciplined and alert soldier, to give absolute obedience to military superiors, to carry out orders with complete determination and always to protect military and state secrets.' Fahneneid der Nationalen Volksarmee in Hauptredaktion Propaganda- und Agitationsschriften, *Vom Sinn des Soldatenseins. Ein Ratgeber für den Soldaten* (Berlin, 1968), 14–15.
10. Reinhold Andert and Wolfgang Herzberg, *Der Sturz. Erich Honecker im Kreuzverhör* (Berlin, Weimar, 1990), 306.
11. 'Protokoll der 25. Tagung des Zentralkomitees der SED' (24–27 October 1955), BArch. SAPMO IV2/1/152.
12. Manfred Overesch, *Buchenwald und die DDR oder die Suche nach Selbstlegitimation* (Göttingen, 1995), 15–16.
13. There were some belated movements in this direction. From 1987 onwards, activists began organising clubs for 'gay FDJler'. Horst Groschopp, 'Herkommen, Struktur und Verständnis'

in Hildegard Bockhorst, Brigitte Prautzsch and Carla Rimbach (eds), *Woher – Wohin? Kinder-und Jugendkulturarbeit in Ostdeutschland* (Remscheid, 1993), 14–30, 21.
14. Alfons Kenkmann, *Wilde Jugend. Lebenswelt großstädtischer Jugendlicher zwischen Weltwirtschaftskrise, Nationalsozialismus und Währungsreform* (Essen, 1996), 256ff.
15. Dick Bradley, *Understanding Rock 'n' Roll. Popular Music in Britain 1955–1964* (Buckingham, 1992), 126–29.
16. Interview with Manfred S. (1999).
17. Irene Kukutz and Katja Havemann, *Geschützte Quelle: Gespräche mit Monika H., alias Karin Lenz* (Berlin, 1990); Klaus Behnke and Jürgen Wolf (eds), *Stasi auf dem Schulhof. Der Mißbrauch von Kindern und Jugendlichen durch das Ministerium für Staatssicherheit* (Berlin, 1998).
18. Jürgen Fuchs, *Fassonschnitt* (Reinbek, 1984), 220; Reiner Kunze, *Die Wunderbaren Jahre* (Frankfurt am Main, 1976), 15, 27–29, 61-63.
19. Alf Lüdtke, 'The Appeal of Exterminating "Others": German Workers and the Limits of Resistance', *Journal of Modern History* 64 (December 1992), 46–67, 63.

Postscript: Where Are They Now?

Manfred and Christa have been happily married for over forty years since meeting in the Capitol *Meute*. They live with his mother and a big dog in the house Manfred grew up in. They continue to enjoy rock 'n' roll although they also listen to country music. Manfred was less bitter about having been imprisoned for six months than the fact that the Stasi wiped his prized collection of original rock 'n' roll recordings. The digitally remastered versions available on CD are no replacement for the originals that he taped from AFN. He remains a passionate collector. In recent years his interest has shifted from beer bottle labels (which are not as available now that most of the East German breweries have closed down) to gas lanterns. Despite his broken nose, Peter K. denied having been a 'notorious fighter'. Although, in his youth he had thought Christianity to be as illusory as Marxism-Leninism, middle age and fatherhood have tempered him and he has found religion. Klaus Renft still lives the rock 'n' roll lifestyle, though these days he expresses himself more through art than through music.

Dieter S., the one-time head of the *Kino der Jugend*, lives in a new estate on the edge of town. He keeps the house tidy, takes the dog for walks, surfs the net and waits for his wife to come home from work. After the turbulence of his youth – which included being accused of treason for shooting at a portrait of Wilhelm Pieck and six years in prison on a charge of espionage for fleeing the Republic and then getting homesick and going back – he finally seems to have found some peace and tranquillity. Having spent nearly twenty years in West Germany, X. returned to Saxony after the *Wende*. As the head of a gun club, he is 'not allowed to be political', but this does not seem to prevent him from holding extreme right-wing views. Ironically, given that he was arrested in 1965 for smashing up a tram, he is now a strong proponent of law and order. That, he said, 'was the one good thing about the GDR'. Vandals and other youths who run wild, he believes, should be locked up in a stadium and made to perform hard labour.

Bibliography

Archives

Bibliothek für Bildungsgeschichtliche Forschung Berlin (BBF)
Brandenburgisches Landeshauptarchiv
Bundesarchiv Berlin (BArch.)
Bundesbeauftragter für die Unterlagen der Staatssicherheit (BStU)
Landesarchiv Berlin
Leipzig School Museum
Leipzig Stadtarchiv
Sächsisches Staatsarchiv Leipzig (StAL)
Stiftung Archiv der Parteien und Massenorganisationen der DDR im Bundesarchiv (BArch. SAPMO)

GDR Newspapers

Armee Rundschau, Soldatenmagazin
Das Banner, Organ des Zentralvorstandes der Gesellschaft für Sport und Technik
Forum
Freie Erde Neustrelitz
Freiheit Halle
Freitag
Junge Welt
Der Kämpfer, Organ der Kampfgruppen der Arbeiterklasse
Konkret, Zeitschrift des Zentralvorstandes der GST für Funktionäre und Ausbilder
Lausitzer Rundschau
Leipziger Volkszeitung (LVZ)
Das Magazin
Der Morgen
Neue Zeit
Neues Deutschland
Neues Leben
Ostsee-Zeitung
Sibylle
Thüringische Landeszeitung

Tribüne
Die Union
Vorwärts

Films

The Blackboard Jungle, directed by Richard Brooks (U.S.A., 1955)
The Challenge of Ideas, produced by the U.S. Army (U.S.A., 1961)
Coming Out, directed by Heiner Carow (DEFA, 1989)
Da habt ihr mein Leben/Marieluise – Kind von Golzow, directed by Barbara Junge and Winfried Junge (Germany, 1996)
Denk bloss nicht ich heule, directed by Manfred Freitag (DEFA, 1965)
Ernst Thälmann – Führer seiner Klasse, directed by Kurt Maetzig (DEFA, 1954)
Ernst Thälmann – Sohn seiner Klasse, directed by Kurt Maetzig (DEFA, 1953)
Führer Ex, directed by Winfried Bonengel (Germany, 2002)
Der Geteilte Himmel, directed by Konrad Wolf (DEFA, 1964)
Die Glatzkopfbande, directed by Richard Groschopp (DEFA, 1963)
Goodbye Lenin!, directed by Wolfgang Becker (Germany, 2003)
Die Halbstarken, directed by Georg Tressler (BRD, 1956)
Isabel auf der Treppe, directed by Hannelore Unterberg (DEFA, 1984)
Kinder, Kader, Kommandeure, directed by Wolfgang Kissel and C. Cay Wesnigk (Germany, 1992)
Der Kinnhaken, directed by Heinz Thiel (DEFA, 1962)
The Magnificent Seven, directed by John Sturges (USA, 1960)
Nackt unter Wölfen, directed by Frank Beyer (DEFA, 1963)
Rebel Without A Cause, directed by Nicholas Ray (USA, 1955)
Red Nightmare, produced by Warner Bros. for the U.S. Department of Defense (U.S.A., 1962)
Rock Around The Clock, directed by Fred Sears (USA, 1956)
Sonst wären wir verloren ... Buchenwaldkinder berichten, directed by Peter Rocha (DEFA, 1982)
Spur der Steine, directed by Frank Beyer (DEFA, 1966)
The Truth Lies in Rostock, produced and directed by Siobhan Cleary and Mark Saunders (Channel 4, 1993)
Wer die Erde liebt, directed by Jürgen Böttcher and Joachim Hellwig (DEFA, 1973)
The Wild One, directed by Laslo Benedek (U.S.A., 1953)

GDR and Soviet Novels

Apitz, Bruno, *Nackt unter Wölfen* (Halle, 1959)
Bräunig, Werner, 'Rummelplatz', *Neue Deutsche Literatur* 10 (1965), 7–29
Bredel, Willi, *Die Prüfung* (Berlin, 1950)
———, *Ernst Thälmann. Sohn seiner Klasse* (Berlin, 1954)
Fadejew, Alexander, *Die Junge Garde* (Berlin, 1950)
Flegel, Walter, *Der Regimentskommandeur* (Berlin, 1973)
Fuchs, Jürgen, *Fassonschnitt* (Reinbek, 1984)

———, *Das Ende einer Feigheit* (Reinbek, 1988)
Heym, Stefan, *Der Tag X/5 Tage im Juni* (Munich, 1974)
Kosmodemjanskaja, Ljubov, *Soja und Schura* (Berlin, 1952)
Kruschel, Heinz, *Der rote Antares* (Berlin, 1979)
Kunze, Reiner, *Die Wunderbaren Jahre* (Frankfurt am Main, 1976)
Loest, Erich, *Die Westmark fällt weiter* (Halle, 1952)
———, *Es geht seinen Gang oder Mühen in unserer Ebene* (Halle, 1977)
———, *Pistole mit Sechzehn* (Hamburg, 1979)
Marchwitza, Hans, *Sturm auf Essen* (Berlin, 1931/1953)
———, *Roheisen* (Berlin, 1955)
Neutsch, Erik, *Spur der Steine* (Halle, 1964)
———, *Helden-Berichte* (Berlin, 1976)
Ostrowskij, Nikolai, *Wie der Stahl gehärtet wurde* (Berlin, 1947)
Plenzdorf, Ulrich, *Die neuen Leiden des jungen W.* (Frankfurt am Main, 1976)
Pludra, Benno, *Haik und Paul* (Berlin, 1957)
Reimann, Brigitte, *Ankunft im Alltag* (Berlin, 1961)
———, *Die Geschwister* (Berlin, 1963)
———, *Franziska Linkerhand* (Berlin, 1974).
Uhse, Bodo, *Die Patrioten* (Berlin, Weimar, 1954)
Wolf, Christa, *Der geteilte Himmel* (Halle, 1963)
Zimmering, Max, *Buttje Peter und sein Held* (Berlin, 1951)

Books and Articles

Abrams, Lynn, *Workers' Culture in Imperial Germany* (London, New York, 1992)
Ackermann, Anton, 'Gibt es einen besonderen deutschen Weg zum Sozialismus?' *Einheit* 1 (February 1946), 23–42
Ackermann, Volker, *Der 'echte' Flüchtling. Deutsche Vertriebene und Flüchtlinge aus der DDR 1945–1961* (Osnabrück, 1995)
Aly, Götz and Susanne Heim, *Architects of Annihilation. Auschwitz and the Logic of Destruction*, trans. A.G. Blunden (London, 2002)
Andersen, Arne, *Der Traum vom guten Leben. Alltags- und Konsumgeschichte vom Wirtschaftswunder bis heute* (Frankfurt am Main, 1997)
Andert, Reinhold and Wolfgang Herzberg, *Der Sturz. Erich Honecker im Kreuzverhör* (Berlin, Weimar, 1990)
Attali, Jacques, *Noise. The Political Economy of Music*, trans. Brian Massumi (Manchester, 1985)
Bach, Kurt, 'Erfahrungen aus den Zusammenarbeit von Schule, Elternhaus, Betrieb und Jugendorganisation bei der geschlechtlichen Erziehung', *Pädagogik Beiheft* 2 (1962), 57–59
Backerra, Manfred (ed.), *NVA. Ein Rückblick für die Zukunft. Zeitzeugen berichten über ein Stück deutscher Militärgeschichte* (Cologne, 1992)
Bakhtin, Mikhail, *The Dialogic Imagination* (Austin, 1981)
———, *Rabelais and his World* (Bloomington, 1987)
Barclay, David and Eric Weitz (eds), *Between Reform and Revolution. German Socialism and Communism from 1840 to 1990* (New York, Oxford, 1998)
Barthel, Horst, 'Die Sozialpolitik bei der Schaffung der Grundlagen des Sozialismus

(1949 bis 1960)' in Gunnar Winkler (ed.), *Geschichte der Sozialpolitik der DDR, 1945-1985* (Berlin, 1989), 70-101

Bartov, Omer, 'The Missing Years: German Workers, German Soldiers', *German History* 8:1 (1990), 49-65

Bartram, Christine and Heinz-Hermann Krüger, 'Vom Backfisch zum Teenager – Mädchensozialisation in den 50er Jahren' in Heinz-Hermann Krüger (ed.), *'Die Elvis-Tolle, die hatte ich mir unauffällig wachsen lassen'. Lebensgeschichte und jugendliche Alltagskultur in den fünfziger Jahren* (Opladen, 1985), 84-101

Basso, Matthew, Laura McCall and Dee Garceau (eds), *Across the Great Divide. Cultures of Manhood in the West* (New York, London, 2001)

Bathrick, David, *The Powers of Speech. The Politics of Culture in the GDR* (Lincoln, 1995)

Bauman, Zygmunt, *Modernity and the Holocaust* (Ithaca, 1989)

Becher, Johannes R., *Verteidigung der Poesie* (Berlin, 1952)

Bednarik, Karl, *Der junge Arbeiter von heute: Ein neuer Typ* (Stuttgart, 1953)

Behnke, Klaus and Jürgen Wolf (eds), *Stasi auf dem Schulhof. Der Mißbrauch von Kindern und Jugendlichen durch das Ministerium für Staatssicherheit* (Berlin, 1998)

Behrends, Jan, Dennis Kuck and Patrice Poutrus, 'Thesenpapier: Historische Ursachen der Fremdenfeindlichkeit in den Neuen Bundesländern' in Jan Behrends, Thomas Lindenberger and Patrice Poutrus (eds), *Fremd-Sein in der DDR. Zu historischen Ursachen der Fremdenfeindlichkeit in Ostdeutschland* (Berlin, 2003), 301-7

Benjamin, Hilde, *Vorschläge zum neuen deutschen Familienrecht* (Berlin, 1949)

_____ , 'Familie und Familienrecht in der Deutschen Demokratischen Republik', *Einheit* 10 (1955), 448-57

Bertram, Barbara, Walter Friedrich and Otmar Kabat vel Job, *Adam und Eva heute* (Leipzig, 1988)

Bessel, Richard, 'Was bleibt vom Krieg? Deutsche Nachkriegsgeschichte(n) aus geschlechtergeschichtlicher Perspektive – Eine Einführung', *Militärgeschichtliche Zeitschrift* 60:2 (2001), 297-305

Betts, Paul, 'The Politics of Post-Fascist Aesthetics. 1950s West and East German Industrial Designs' in Richard Bessel and Dirk Schumann (eds), *Life after Death. Approaches to a Cultural and Social History of Europe during the 1940s and 1950s* (Washington, DC, Cambridge, 2003), 291-321

Biess, Frank, '"Pioneers of a New Germany". Returning POWs from the Soviet Union and the Making of East German Citizens 1945-1950', *Central European History* 32 (1999), 143-80

_____ , 'Männer des Wiederaufbaus – Wiederaufbau der Männer. Kriegsheimkehrer in Ost- und Westdeutschland, 1945-1955' in Karen Hagemann and Stefanie Schüler-Springorum (eds), *Heimat-Front. Militär und Geschlechterverhältnisse im Zeitalter der Weltkriege* (Frankfurt, New York, 2002), 345-65

Bigsby, C.W.E. (ed.), *Superculture: American Popular Culture and Europe* (London, 1975)

Bittermann, Klaus, 'Die Gespensterwelt der Ossis' in Klaus Bittermann, Henryk Broder (eds), *Der rasende Mob. Die Ossis zwischen Selbstmitleid und Barberei* (Berlin, 1993), 104-38

Blanning, Timothy, *The Culture of Power and the Power of Culture. Old Regime Europe 1660-1789* (Oxford, 2002)

Bogdal, Klaus-Michael, 'Hard-Cold-Fast. Imagining Masculinity in the German Academy, Literature and the Media' in Roy Jerome (ed.), *Conceptions of Postwar German Masculinity* (Albany, 2001), 13-42

Bögeholz, Hartwig, *Deutsch-deutsche Zeiten. Eine Chronik. Deutschland von 1945 bis 1995* (Munich, 1996)

Bohn, Helmut, *Armee gegen die Freiheit. Ideologie und Aufrüstung in der Sowjetzone* (Cologne, 1956)

Borneman, John (ed.), *Gay Voices from East Germany. Interviews by Jürgen Lemke* (Bloomington, Indianapolis, 1991)

Borrmann, Rolf, 'Die mittelbare, indirekte Teilnahme des Lehrers an der sexuellen Bildung und Erziehung', *Pädagogik Beiheft* 2 (1962), 24–28

——, *Jugend und Liebe. Die Beziehungen der Jugendlichen zum anderen Geschlecht* (Leipzig, 1966)

——, 'Sozialistische Persönlichkeitsentwicklung und Sexualerziehung', *Pädagogik Beiheft* 30:1 (1975), 1–6

Bourdieu, Pierre, *Masculine Domination*, trans. Richard Nice (Cambridge, 2001)

Bradley, Dick, *Understanding Rock 'n' Roll. Popular Music in Britain 1955–1964* (Buckingham, 1992)

Breines, Wini, *Young, White and Miserable. Growing Up Female in the Fifties* (Boston, 1992)

Bretschneider, Wolfgang, *Sexuell aufklären rechtzeitig und richtig* (Leipzig, Jena, 1956)

Breyvogel, Wilfried and Inge Seemann, 'Aus der Not keine Tugend. Jungen und Mädchen zusammen und doch getrennt 1945–1957' in Wilfried Breyvogel (ed.), *Mädchenbildung in Deutschland* (Essen, 1996), 175–188

Brooker, Will, *Cultural Studies* (London, 1998)

Brooks, Jeffrey, *Thank you, Comrade Stalin! Soviet Public Culture from Revolution to Cold War* (Princeton, 2000)

Browning, Christopher, *Ordinary Men: Reserve Police Battalion 101 and the Final Solution in Poland* (New York, 1992)

Brück, Wolfgang, 'Skinheads als Vorboten der Systemkrise. Die Entwicklung des Skinhead-Phänomens bis zum Untergang der DDR' in Karl-Heinz Heinemann and Wilfried Schubarth (eds), *Der antifaschistische Staat entläßt seine Kinder* (Cologne, 1992), 47–63

Brühl, Olaf, 'Arschficker oder Arschkriecher? Kleines schwules Glossar eines Außenseiters' in Günter Grau (ed.), *Schwulsein 2000. Perspektiven im vereinigten Deutschland* (Hamburg, 2001), 163–206

Budde, Gunilla-Friederike, 'Wettkampf um Gerechtigkeit. Frauenförderung und Arbeiterkinder in den Hochschulreformdebatten in Ost und West', *Jahrbuch für Universitätsgeschichte* 8 (2005), 123–42

Buddrus, Michael, 'A Generation Twice Betrayed: Youth Policy in the Transition from the Third Reich to the Soviet Zone of Occupation (1945–1946)' in Mark Roseman (ed.), *Generations in Conflict: Youth Revolt and Generation Formation in Germany, 1770–1968* (Cambridge, 1995), 247–68

Bundesministerium für gesamtdeutsche Fragen, *Der Volksaufstand vom 17. Juni 1953 in der sowjetischen Besatzungszone und in Ostberlin* (Bonn, 1953)

Capuzzo, Paolo, 'Youth Cultures and Consumption in Contemporary Europe', *Contemporary European History* 10:1 (2001), 155–70

Carter, Erica, 'Alice in Consumer Wonderland: West German Case Studies in Gender and Consumer Culture' in Angela McRobbie and Mica Nava (eds), *Gender and Generation* (London, Basingstoke, 1984), 185–214

——, *How German is She? Postwar West German Reconstruction and the Consuming Woman* (Ann Arbor, 1997)

Chambers, Ian, *Urban Rhythms. Pop Music and Popular Culture* (Basingstoke, 1985)
Clark, Suzanne, *Cold Warriors. Manliness on Trial in the Rhetoric of the West* (Carbondale, Edwardsville, 2000)
Clarke, John, 'The Skinheads and the Magical Recovery of Community' in Stuart Hall and Tony Jefferson (eds), *Resistance through Rituals. Youth Subcultures in Postwar Britain* (London, 1976), 99–102
——, 'Style' in Stuart Hall and Tony Jefferson (eds), *Resistance through Rituals. Youth Subcultures in Postwar Britain* (London, 1976), 175–91
Clarke, John, Stuart Hall, Tony Jefferson and Brian Roberts, 'Subcultures, Cultures and Class' in Stuart Hall and Tony Jefferson (eds), *Resistance through Rituals. Youth Subcultures in Postwar Britain* (London, 1976), 9–74
Cohan, Steve, *Masked Men. Masculinity and the Movies in the Fifties* (Bloomington, Indianapolis, 1997)
Cohen, Philip and David Robins, *Knuckle Sandwich. Growing up in the Working-class City* (Harmondsworth, 1978)
Cohen, Stanley, *Folk Devils and Moral Panics* (London, New York, 3rd edn, 2002)
Cohen, Theodore, 'Making Men out of them: Male Socialization in Childhood and Adolescence' in Theodore Cohen (ed.) *Men and Masculinity. A Text Reader* (Belmont, 2000), 53–60
Cohn, Carol, 'Sex and Death in the Rational World of Defense Intellectuals', *SIGNS* 12:4 (1987), 687–718
——, 'Wars, Wimps, and Women: Talking Gender and Thinking War' in Miriam Cooke and Angela Woolacott (eds), *Gendering War Talk* (Princeton, 1993), 227–46
Combs, William, *The Voice of the SS: A History of the SS Journal 'Das Schwarze Korps'* (New York, 1986)
Committee for German Unity, *West Germany Prepares War of Revenge. Facts on the Rebirth of German Militarism in the Bonn State* (Berlin, 1954)
Corber, Robert, *Homosexuality in Cold War America: Resistance and the Crisis of Masculinity* (Durham, 1997)
Costigliola, Frank, '"Unceasing Pressure for Penetration": Gender, Pathology, and Emotion in George Kennan's Formation of the Cold War', *Journal of American History* 83:4 (March 1997), 1309–39
Crew, David, '*Alltagsgeschichte*: A New Social History from Below?', *Central European History* 22:3/4 (1989), 394–407
Cuordileone, K.A., '"Politics in an Age of Anxiety": Cold War Political Culture and the Crisis in American Masculinity, 1949–1960', *Journal of American History* 87:2 (September 2000), 515–45
Davidson, Michael, *Guys Like Us. Citing Masculinity in Cold War Poetics* (Chicago, 2003)
Davis, Natalie Zemon, 'The Reason of Misrule: Youth Groups and Charivaris in Sixteenth-Century France', *Past and Present* 50 (February 1971), 41–75
Dean, Robert, 'Masculinity as Ideology: John F. Kennedy and the Domestic Politics of Foreign Policy', *Diplomatic History* 22:1 (Winter 1998), 29–62
——, *Imperial Brotherhood, Gender and the Making of Cold War Foreign Policy* (Amherst, 2001)
de Bruyn, Günter, *Vierzig Jahre* (Frankfurt am Main, 1996)
D'Emilio, John, 'The Homosexual Menace: The Politics of Sexuality in Cold War America' in John D'Emilio (ed.), *Making Trouble: Essays on Gay History, Politics and the University* (New York, 1992), 57–73

Dennis, Mike, *German Democratic Republic. Politics, Economics and Society* (London, New York, 1988)
Diedrich, Torsten and Rüdiger Wenzke, *Die getarnte Armee. Geschichte der kasernierten Volkspolizei der DDR 1952 bis 1956* (Berlin, 2001)
Dietzsch, Ina, 'Deutsch-deutscher Gabentausch' in Ina Merkel and Felix Mühlberg (eds), *Wunderwirtschaft. DDR-Konsumkultur in den 60er Jahren* (Cologne, 1996), 204–13
Dilßner, Hans, 'Eigenverantwortung und Selbsttätigkeit der Jugend – Voraussetzungen für eine gute Jugendklubarbeit', *Auf neuen Wegen. Methodische Hinweise und Materialien für die Klubarbeit* 127 (1966)
Dirks, Nicholas, Geoff Eley and Sherry Ortner (eds), *Culture/Power/History. A Reader in Contemporary Social Theory* (Princeton, 1994)
Dölling, Irene, 'Gespaltenes Bewußtsein. Frauen- und Männerbilder in der DDR' in Hildegard Maria Nickel and Gisela Helwig (eds), *Frauen in Deutschland, 1945–1992* (Bonn, 1993), 23–52
Dübel, Siegfried, *Deutsche Jugend im Wirkungsfeld Sowjetischer Pädagogik* (Bonn, 1953)
Edele, Mark, 'Strange Young Men in Stalin's Moscow: The Birth and Life of the Stiliagi, 1945–1953', *Jahrbücher für Geschichte Osteuropas* 50:1 (2002), 37–61
Eghigian, Greg, 'Psychologization of the Socialist Self: East German Forensic Psychology and its Deviants, 1945–1973', *German History* 22:2 (2004), 181–205
Ehlert, Hans and Armin Wagner (eds), *Genosse General. Die Militärelite der DDR in biografischen Skizzen* (Berlin, 2003)
Eifler, Christine, '"… es schützt Dich mein Gewehr". Frauenbildern in der NVA Propaganda' in Zentrum für Interdisziplinäre Frauenforschung der Humboldt-Universität zu Berlin (ed.), *Unter Hammer und Zirkel: Frauenbiographien vor dem Hintergrund ostdeutscher Sozialisationserfahrungen* (Pfaffenweiler, 1995), 269–76
——— , '"Ewig unreif". Geschlechtsrollenklischees in der Armeerundschau' in Simone Barck, Martina Langermann and Siegfried Lokatis (eds), *Zwischen 'Mosaik' und 'Einheit'. Zeitschriften in der DDR* (Berlin, 1999), 180–88
Eley, Geoff, 'Labor History, Social History, *Alltagsgeschichte*: Experience, Culture and the Politics of the Everyday – A New Direction for German Social History?', *Journal of Modern History* 61:2 (1989), 297–343
Ellerbrock, Wolfgang, *Paul Oestreich. Porträt eines politische Pädagogen* (Weinheim, Munich, 1992)
Enloe, Cynthia, *The Morning After: Sexual Politics at the End of the Cold War* (Berkeley, 1993)
Epstein, Catherine, *The Last Revolutionaries. German Communists and their Century* (Cambridge, MA, London, 2003)
Erdheim, Mario, *Die gesellschaftliche Produktion von Unbewußtheit* (Frankfurt am Main, 1984)
Ernst, Anna-Sabine, 'The Politics of Culture and the Culture of Daily Life in the DDR in the 1950s' in David Barclay and Eric Weitz (eds), *Between Reform and Revolution. German Socialism and Communism from 1840 to 1990* (New York, Oxford, 1998), 489–506
Evans, Jennifer, 'Constructing Borders: Image and Identity in Die Frau von Heute, 1946–1948' in Hilary Sy-Quia and Susanne Baackmann (eds), *Conquering Women: Women and War in the German Cultural Imagination* (Berkeley, 2000), 40–61

_____, 'Bahnhof Boys: Policing Male Prostitution in Post-Nazi Berlin', *Journal of the History of Sexuality* 12:4 (2003), 605-36

_____, 'The Moral State: Men, Mining, and Masculinity in the Early GDR', *German History* 23:3 (2005), 355-70

Evans, Richard J., *Proletarians and Politics. Socialism, Protest and the Working Class in Germany before the First World War* (New York, 1990)

Farin, Klaus and Harald Hauswald, *Die dritte Halbzeit – Hooligans in Berlin-Ost* (Berlin, 2002)

Faulenbach, Bernd, 'Acht Jahre deutsch-deutsche Vergangenheitsdebatte' in Christoph Kleßmann, Hans Misselwitz and Günter Wichert (eds), *Deutsche Vergangenheiten – eine gemeinsame Herausforderung: Der schwierige Umgang mit der doppelten Nachkriegsgeschichte* (Berlin, 1999), 15-34

Fehrenbach, Heide, *Cinema in Democratizing Germany. Reconstructing National Identity after Hitler* (Chapel Hill, 1995)

_____, *Race after Hitler. Black Occupation Children in Postwar Germany and America* (Princeton, 2005)

Feinstein, Joshua, *The Triumph of the Ordinary. Depictions of Daily Life in East German Cinema, 1949-1989* (Chapel Hill, London, 2002)

Fenemore, Mark, 'Saints and Devils: Youth in the SBZ/GDR, 1945-1953' in Eleonore Breuning, Jill Lewis and Gareth Pritchard (eds), *Power and the People. A Social History of Central European Politics, 1945-1953* (Manchester, 2005), 168-81

Finch, Lynette, 'On the Streets: Working Class Youth Culture in the Nineteenth Century' in Rob White (ed.), *Youth Subcultures. Theory, History and the Australian Experience* (Hobart, 1993)

Fletcher, Colin, 'Beats and Gangs in Merseyside' in Timothy Raison (ed.), *Youth in New Society* (London, 1966), 148-59

Flierl, Thomas (ed.), *Mythos Antifaschismus. Ein Traditionskabinett wird kommentiert* (Berlin, 1992)

Freiburg, Arnold and Christa Mahrad, *FDJ. Der sozialistische Jugendverband der DDR* (Opladen, 1982)

Fricke, Karl Wilhelm and Silke Klewin, *Bautzen II. Sonderhaftanstalt unter MfS-Kontrolle 1956 bis 1989* (Leipzig, 2001)

Friedrich, Walter and Adolf Kossakowski, *Zur Psychologie des Jugendalters* (Berlin, 1962)

Friedrich, Walter, *Flegeljahre? Zur Erziehung 13- bis 16jähriger Jungen* (Berlin, 1964)

_____, (Geschichte des Zentralinstituts für Jugendforschung) in Walter Friedrich, Peter Förster and Kurt Starke (eds), *Das Zentralinstitut für Jugendforschung Leipzig 1966-1990. Geschichte, Methoden, Erkenntnisse* (Berlin, 1999), 13-69

Frith, Simon, *Sound Effects. Youth, Leisure and the Politics of Rock 'n' Roll* (New York, 1981)

Frith, Simon and Angela McRobbie, 'Rock and Sexuality' in Simon Frith and Andrew Goodwin (eds), *On Record: Rock, Pop and the Written Word* (London, 1990), 371-89

Fuchs, Jürgen and Gerhard Hieke, *Dummgeschult? Ein Schüler und sein Lehrer* (Berlin, 1992)

Fulbrook, Mary, *Anatomy of a Dictatorship. Inside the GDR. 1949-1989* (Oxford, 1995)

_____, *Interpretations of the Two Germanies* (Basingstoke, 2000)

Fursenko, Aleksandr and Timothy Naftali, *'One Hell of a Gamble'. Khrushchev, Castro and Kennedy, 1958-1964* (New York, London, 1997)

Fürst, Juliane, 'Prisoners of the Soviet Self? Political Youth Opposition in Late Stalinism', *Europe-Asia Studies* 54:3 (May 2002), 353-76

Geertz, Clifford, *The Interpretation of Cultures* (London, 1993)

Geißler, Gert, 'Zäsuren in der Schulpolitik der SBZ und der DDR 1945-1965' in Dietrich Hoffmann and Karl Neumann (eds), *Erziehung und Erziehungswissenschaft in der BRD und der DDR*, vol. I, *Die Teilung der Pädagogik, 1945-1965* (Weinheim, 1994), 41-55

Geißler, Gert and Ulrich Wiegmann, *Schule und Erziehung in der DDR. Studien und Dokumente* (Neuwied, Berlin, 1995)

Gellately, Robert and Nathan Stoltzfus (eds), *Social Outsiders in Nazi Germany* (Princeton, Oxford, 2001)

Gerbel, Christian, Alexander Mejstrik and Reinhard Sieder, 'Die "Schlurfs". Verweigerung und Opposition von Wiener Arbeiterjugendlichen im "Dritten Reich"' in Emmerich Talos, Ernst Hanisch and Wolfgang Neugebauer (eds), *NS-Herrschaft in Österreich 1938-1945* (Vienna, 1988), 243-68

Gerhard, Ute, 'Die staatlich institutionalisierte "Lösung" der Frauenfrage. Zur Geschichte der Geschlechterverhältnisse in der DDR' in Hartmut Kaelbe, Jürgen Kocka and Hartmut Zwahr (eds), *Sozialgeschichte der DDR* (Stuttgart, 1994), 383-403

Gieseke, Jens, *Die DDR-Staatssicherheit. Schild und Schwert der Partei* (Bonn, 2000)

Gilbert, James, *A Cycle of Outrage. America's Reaction to the Juvenile Delinquent of the 1950s* (New York, Oxford, 1986)

Giordano, Ralph, *Die zweite Schuld oder von der Last Deutscher zu sein* (Hamburg, 1998)

Gläser, Andreas, *Der BFC war schuld am Mauerbau. Ein stolzer Sohn des Proletariats erzählt* (Berlin, 2002)

Glaser, Günther, '"Niemand von uns wollte wieder eine Uniform anziehen ..." Konflikte in der kasernierten Volkspolizei 1948-1952' in Evemarie Badstübner (ed.), *Befremdlich Anders. Leben in der DDR* (Berlin, 2000), 312-48

Goettle, Gabriele, 'Herr und Frau Mob' in Klaus Bittermann, Henryk Broder (eds), *Der rasende Mob. Die Ossis zwischen Selbstmitleid und Barberei* (Berlin, 1993), 55-64

Gotschlich, Helga, 'Die Gründung der FDJ in der SBZ' in Helga Gotschlich, Katharina Lange and Edeltraud Schulze (eds), *Aber nicht im Gleichschritt. Zur Entstehung der Freien Deutschen Jugend* (Berlin, 1997), 25-38

Gramsci, Antonio, *Selections from the Prison Notebooks* (London, 1971)

Grassel, Heinz, 'Stand und Probleme der Sexualerziehung' in Heinz Grassel (ed.), *Psychologische und pädagogische Probleme der sexuellen Bildung und Erziehung* (Rostock, 1972), 12-50

Grau, Günter, 'Return to the Past: the Policy of the SED and the Laws against Homosexuality in Eastern Germany between 1946 and 1968', *Journal of Homosexuality* 37 (1999), 1-21

Grele, Ronald, 'Movement without Aim. Methodological and Theoretical Problems in Oral History' in Robert Perks and Alistair Thomson (eds), *The Oral History Reader* (London, 1998), 38-52

Grieder, Peter, *The East German leadership, 1946-1973. Conflict and Crisis* (Manchester, 1999)

Groschopp, Horst, 'Herkommen, Struktur und Verständnis' in Hildegard Bockhorst, Brigitte Prautzsch and Carla Rimbach (eds), *Woher – Wohin? Kinder- und Jugendkulturarbeit in Ostdeutschland* (Remscheid, 1993), 14-30

Grose, Peter, *Operation Rollback. America's Secret War behind the Iron Curtain* (Boston, 2000)
Gruchmann, Lothar, 'Jugendopposition und Justiz im Dritten Reich. Die Probleme bei der Verfolgung der "Leipziger Meuten" durch die Gerichte' in Wolfgang Benz (ed.), *Miscellanea. Festschrift für Helmut Krausnick zum 75. Geburtstag* (Stuttgart, 1980), 103–30
Habel, Frank-Burkhard and Volker Wachter, *Das grosse Lexicon der DDR-Stars* (Berlin, 2002)
Habermas, Jürgen, *Legitimation Crisis* (Cambridge, 1988)
Häder, Sonja, 'Mytholigisierung der "Arbeiterkinder"? Mentalitäten – Handlungsmuster – Bildungswege von Kinder aus einem traditionellen Ost-Berliner Arbeiterbezirk (1945-1958)' in Peter Hübner and Klaus Tenfelde (eds), *Arbeiter in der SBZ-DDR* (Essen, 1999), 691–708
Halfeld, Adolf, *Amerika und Amerikanismus* (Jena, 1927)
Hall, Stuart and Tony Jefferson (eds), *Resistance through Rituals. Youth Subcultures in Postwar Britain* (London, 1976)
Hall, Stuart, 'Cultural Studies and its Theoretical Legacies' in Simon During (ed.), *The Cultural Studies Reader* (London, New York, 2nd edn, 1999), 97–109
Harich, Wolfgang, *Keine Schwierigkeiten mit der Wahrheit. Zur nationalkommunistischen Opposition 1956 in der DDR* (Berlin, 1993)
Harsch, Donna, 'Society, the State, and Abortion in East Germany, 1950-1972', *American Historical Review* 102:1 (February 1997), 53–84
———, 'Approach/Avoidance: Communists and Women in East Germany, 1945-9', *Social History*, 25:2 (May 2000), 156–82
Härtel, Christian and Petra Kabus, 'Zwischen Gummibärchen und "Playboy". Ein innerdeutscher Dialog' in Christian Härtel and Petra Kabus (eds), *Das Westpaket. Geschenksendung, keine Handelsware* (Berlin, 2000) 9–22
Hasselbach, Ingo and Winfried Bonengel, *Die Abrechnung: Ein Neonazi steigt aus* (Berlin, Weimar, 1993)
Hauptredaktion Propaganda- und Agitationsschriften, *Vom Sinn des Soldatenseins. Ein Ratgeber für den Soldaten* (Berlin, 1968)
Hauptverwaltung Deutsche Volkspolizei, *Programm für die Ausbildung der Kampfgruppen* (Berlin, 1955)
———, *Programm für die Breitenausbildung der Deutschen Volkspolizei und für die Ausbildung der Kampfgruppen im Jahre 1957. Nur für den Dienstgebrauch!* (Berlin, 1956)
Hebdige, Dick, 'The Meaning of Mod' in Stuart Hall and Tony Jefferson (eds), *Resistance through Rituals. Youth Subcultures in Postwar Britain* (London, 1976), 87–96
———, *Subculture: The Meaning of Style* (London, 1979)
———, *Hiding in the Light. On Images and Things* (London, 1988)
Heider, Paul, *Die Gesellschaft für Sport und Technik* (Berlin, 2002)
Heineman, Elizabeth, *What Difference does a Husband Make? Women and Marital Status in Nazi and Postwar Germany* (Berkeley, Los Angeles, London, 1999)
Heinemann, Karl-Heinz, '"Ihr wollt nicht wissen, wer wir sind, also wundert Euch nicht, wie wir sind!" Interview mit Christine Günther, Sozialarbeiterin in Halle/S' in Karl-Heinz Heinemann and Wilfried Schubarth (eds), *Der antifaschistische Staat entläßt seine Kinder* (Cologne, 1992), 126–31

Hell, Julia, 'At the Center an Absence. Foundationalist Narratives of the GDR and the Legitimatory Discourse of Antifascism', *Monatshefte* 84:1 (1992), 23-25
―――, *Post-Fascist Fantasies. Psychoanalysis, History and the Literature of East Germany* (Durham, NC, 1997)
Hellmann, Willi, *Mein erstes Leben. Ein General der VP erinnert sich* (Berlin, 2001)
Helwig, Gisela, *Jugend und Familie in der DDR. Leitbild und Alltag im Widerspruch* (Cologne, 1984)
Hennig, Reinhold, *Leipzig, Schaufenster der Welt* (Berlin, 1959)
Hensel, Jana, *Zonenkinder* (Reinbek bei Hamburg, 2002)
Herde, Klaus and Wilfried Weidner (eds), *Pioniere voran* (Berlin, 1961)
Herf Jeffrey, *Divided Memory. The Nazi Past in the Two Germanys* (Cambridge, MA, London, 1997)
Herrnstadt, Rudolf, *Das Herrnstadt-Dokument. Das Politbüro der SED und die Geschichte des 17. Juni 1953*, edited by Nadja Stulz-Herrnstadt (Reinbek bei Hamburg, 1991)
Hertwig, Manfred, 'Deformationen. Die Rebellion der Intellektuellen in der DDR' in Reinhard Crusius and Manfred Wilke (eds), *Entstalinisierung. Der XX. Parteitag der KPdSU und seine Folgen* (Frankfurt, 1977), 477-84
Herzog, Dagmar, *Sex after Fascism. Memory and Morality in Twentieth-Century Germany* (Princeton, 2005)
Hesse, Peter (ed.), *Sexuologie*, 3 vols (Leipzig, 1979)
Hetmann, Frederik, *Enteignete Jahre. Junge Leute berichten von drüben* (Munich, 1961)
Hiller, Kurt, *Rote Ritter* (Berlin, 1980)
Hinrichs, Reimer, 'Krankheit ohne Leidensdruck. Psychogramm des Angeklagten', *Kursbuch* 111 (February 1993), 71-86
Hite, Shere, *The Hite Report. A Nationwide Study on Female Sexuality* (New York, 1976)
Hixson, Walter, *Parting the Curtain: Propaganda, Culture, and the Cold War* (New York, 1997)
Hobsbawm, Eric, *Primitive Rebels* (Manchester, 1959)
Hoeft, Brigitte (ed.), *Der Prozeß gegen Walter Janka und andere. Eine Dokumentation* (Reinbek bei Hamburg, 1990)
Hofmann, Michael, 'Die Leipziger Metallarbeiter. Etappen sozialer Erfahrungsgeschichte. Milieubiographie eines Arbeitermilieus in Leipzig' in Michael Vester, Michael Hofmann and Irene Zierke (eds), *Soziale Milieus in Ostdeutschland. Gesellschaftliche Strukturen zwischen Zerfall und Neubildung* (Cologne, 1995), 136-92
Höhn, Maria, *GIs and Fräuleins. The German-American Encounter in 1950s West Germany* (Chapel Hill, London, 2002)
Hollitscher, Walter, *Der überanstrengte Sexus. Die sogenannte sexuelle Emanzipation im heutigen Kapitalismus* (Berlin, 1975)
Holm, Hans Axel, *The Other Germans. Report from an East German Town*, trans. Thomas Teal (New York, 1970)
Hölscher, Christopher, *NS-Verfolgte im 'antifaschistischen Staat'. Vereinnahmung und Ausgrenzung in der ostdeutschen Wiedergutmachung 1945-1989* (Berlin, 2002)
Honecker, Erich, *Unsere Kampfkraft stärken und sicher vorwärtsschreiten zum Wohl des ganzen Volkes* (Berlin, 1973)
―――, *From My Life* (Oxford, New York, 1981)
―――, *Zu dramatischen Ereignissen* (Hamburg, 1992)

Horn, Anette, 'An End to Conformity: Jürgen Fuchs' Experience of the Army in *Fassonschnitt* (Crewcut) and *Das Ende einer Feigheit* (An End to Cowardice)' in Peter Monteath and Frederic Zuckerman (eds), *Modern Europe. Histories and Identities* (Adelaide, 1998), 291–98

Horrocks, Roger, *Male Myths and Icons. Masculinity in Popular Culture* (Houndsmills, 1995)

Horváth, Sándor, 'Pubs and "Hooligans" in a Socialist City in Hungary: the Public Sphere and Youth in Stalintown' in Axel Schildt and Detlef Siegfried (eds), *European Cities, Youth and the Public Sphere in the Twentieth Century* (Aldershot, 2005), 80–89

Hörz, Helga, *Die Frau als Persönlichkeit* (Berlin, 1968)

Hradil, Stefan, 'Die "objektive" und die "subjektive" Modernisierung. Der Wandel der westdeutschen Sozialstruktur und die Wiedervereinigung', *Aus Politik und Zeitgeschichte* 29–30 (1992), 3–14

Hübner, Peter, 'Die FDJ als politische Organisation und sozialer Raum' in Helga Gotschlich (ed.), *'Links und links und Schritt gehalten ...'. Die FDJ: Konzepte – Abläufe – Grenzen* (Berlin, 1994), 58–69

———, 'Arbeiterklasse als Inszenierung? Arbeiter und Gesellschaftspolitik in der SBZ/DDR' in Richard Bessel and Ralph Jessen (eds), *Die Grenzen der Diktatur: Staat und Gesellschaft in der DDR* (Göttingen, 1996), 199–223

Humphries, Stephen, *Hooligans or Rebels? An Oral History of Working-class Childhood and Youth 1889–1939* (Oxford, 1981)

Huttenlocher, Armin, 'Zurück oder vorwärts, du mußt dich entschließen ...' in Klaus Behnke and Jürgen Wolf (eds), *Stasi auf dem Schulhof. Der Mißbrauch von Kindern und Jugendlichen durch das Ministerium für Staatssicherheit* (Berlin, 1998), 78–102

Hyde, Chris, *Rock 'n' Roll Tripper. Stories und Bilder* (Rheinberg, 1983)

Ilona, 'Wir lebten von dem, wovor wir uns fürchteten' in C. Remath and R. Schneider (eds), *Haare auf Krawall. Jugendsubkultur in Leipzig 1980 bis 1991* (Leipzig, 1999), 12–23

Irmscher, Gerlinde, 'Der Westen im Ost-Alltag' in Ina Merkel and Felix Mühlberg (eds), *Wunderwirtschaft. DDR-Konsumkultur in den 60er Jahren* (Cologne, 1996), 185–93

Jablonsky, Walter and Wolfgang Wünsche (eds), *Im Gleichschritt? Zur Geschichte der NVA* (Berlin, 2001)

Jäger, Manfred, *Kultur und Politik in der DDR, 1945–1990* (Cologne, 1995)

Jahnke, Karl Heinz (ed.), *Geschichte der Freien Deutschen Jugend* (Berlin, 1976)

Janka, Walter, *Schwierigkeiten mit der Wahrheit* (Berlin, Weimar, 1990)

Janssen, Wiebke, '"Heute, tanzen alle jungen Leute, im Lipsi-Schritt, nur noch im Lipsi-Schritt". SED und Jugend in den fünfziger Jahren', *Hallische Beiträge zur Zeitgeschichte* 6 (1999), 58–74

Jarausch, Konrad, 'The Failure of East German Antifascism: Some Ironies of History as Politics', *German Studies Review* 14 (February 1991), 85–102.

———, *Dictatorship as Experience. Towards a Socio-cultural History of the GDR* (New York, Oxford, 1999)

Jerome, Roy (ed.), *Conceptions of Postwar German Masculinity* (Albany, 2001)

Joseph, Detlef, *Nazis in der DDR. Die deutschen Staatsdiener nach 1945 – woher kamen sie?* (Berlin, 2002)

Kaes, Anton, 'German Cultural History and the Study of Film', *New German Critique* 65 (Spring/Summer, 1995), 49–56

Kaiser, Günther, *Randalierende Jugend: Eine soziologische und kriminologische Studie über die sogenannten 'Halbstarken'* (Heidelberg, 1959)

Kaiser, Monica, *Machtwechsel von Ulbricht zu Honecker. Funktionsmechanismen der SED-Diktatur in Konfliktsituationen 1962 bis 1972* (Berlin, 1997)

Kenkmann, Alfons, *Wilde Jugend. Lebenswelt großstädtischer Jugendlicher zwischen Weltwirtschaftskrise, Nationalsozialismus und Währungsreform* (Essen, 1996)

Kimmel, Michael, 'Masculinity as Homophobia. Fear, Shame and Silence in the Construction of Gender Identity' in Theodore Cohen (ed.) *Men and Masculinity* (Belmont, 2000), 29–41

Klein, Manfred, *Jugend zwischen den Diktaturen 1945–1956* (Mainz, 1968)

Klemm, Peter, 'Sexualität im Sozialismus' in Peter Hesse. (ed.), *Sexuologie*, vol. 3 (Leipzig, 1979), 200–13

Klemperer, Victor, *The Language of the Third Reich*, trans. Martin Brady (London, New York, 2000)

Klönne, Arno, 'Jugendprotest und Jugendopposition. Von der HJ-Erziehung zum Cliquenwesen der Kriegszeit' in Martin Broszat, Elke Fröhlich and Anton Grossmann (eds), *Bayern in der NS-Zeit* (Munich, 1981), vol. IV, 527–620

———, *Umerziehung, Aufbau und Kulturkonflikt: Zur Geschichte der Jugend im geteilten Deutschland von 1945 bis in die fünfziger Jahre* (Hagen, 1998)

———, *Jugend im Dritten Reich: die Hitler-Jugend und ihre Gegner* (Cologne, 1999)

Kochan, Thomas, *Den Blues haben. Momente einer jugendlichen Subkultur in der DDR* (Münster, Hamburg, Berlin, London, 2002)

Koonz, Claudia, 'Competition for Women's *Lebensraum*, 1928–1934' in Renate Bridenthal, Atina Grossmann and Marion Kaplan (eds), *When Biology became Destiny: Women in Weimar and Nazi Germany* (New York, 1984), 199–236

Koop, Volker, *'Den Gegner vernichten'. Die Grenzsicherung der DDR* (Bonn, 1996)

Kopstein, Jeffrey, *The Politics of Economic Decline in East Germany, 1945–1989* (Chapel Hill, London, 1997)

Kossakowski, Adolf, *Über die psychischen Veränderungen in der Pubertät. Bedingungsanalyse* (Berlin, 1965)

Kotkin, Stephen, *Magnetic Mountain. Stalinism as a Civilisation* (Berkeley, London, 1995)

Krenzlin, Leonore, 'Vom Jugendkommuniqué zur Dichterschelte' in Günter Agde (ed.), *Kahlschlag. Das 11. Plenum des ZK der SED 1965* (Berlin, 2nd edn, 2000), 154–64

Kuck, Dennis, '"Für den sozialistischen Aufbau ihrer Heimat"? Ausländische Vertragsarbeitskräfte in der DDR' in Jan Behrends, Thomas Lindenberger and Patrice Poutrus (eds), *Fremd-Sein in der DDR. Zu historischen Ursachen der Fremdenfeindlichkeit in Ostdeutschland* (Berlin, 2003), 245–55

Kuhn, Annette, 'Der Refamilialisierungsdiskurs nach '45', *Beiträge zur Geschichte der Arbeiterbewegung* 33:5 (1991), 593–606

Kühne, Thomas, *Männergeschichte, Geschlechtergeschichte. Männlichkeit im Wandel der Moderne* (New York, 1996)

Kühnel, Wolfgang, 'Der Lebenszusammenhang DDR-Jugendlicher im Spannungsfeld von institutioneller Verregelung und alltagskultureller Modernisierung', *Zeitschrift für Sozialisationsforschung und Erziehungssoziologie* 1 (1990), 105–13

Kuhnert, Peter and Ute Ackermann, 'Jenseits von Lust und Liebe? Jugendsexualität in den 50er Jahren' in Heinz-Hermann Krüger (ed.), *'Die Elvis-Tolle, die hatte ich mir unauffällig wachsen lassen'. Lebensgeschichte und jugendliche Alltagskultur in den fünfziger Jahren* (Opladen, 1985), 43–83

Kukutz, Irene and Katja Havemann, *Geschützte Quelle: Gespräche mit Monika H., alias Karin Lenz* (Berlin, 1990)

Kunze, Reiner, *Deckname 'Lyrik'. Eine Dokumentation* (Frankfurt am Main, 1990)

Lambrecht, Christine, *Männerbekanntschaften. Freimütige Protokolle* (Leipzig, 1986)

Landsman, Mark, 'The Consumer Supply Lobby – Did it Exist? State and Consumption in East Germany in the 1950s', *Central European History* 35:4 (2002), 477–512

Langer, Hermann, *'Wollt ihr den totalen Tanz?' Streiflichter zur imperialistischen Manipulierung der Jugend* (Berlin, 1985)

Lemke, Jürgen, *Ganz normal anders. Auskünfte schwuler Männer aus der DDR* (Berlin, Weimar, 1989)

Leo, Annette and Peter Reif-Spirek (eds), *Helden, Täter und Verräter. Studien zum DDR-Antifaschismus* (Berlin, 1999)

Lindenberger, Thomas (ed.), *Herrschaft und Eigen-Sinn in der Diktatur. Studien zur Gesellschaftsgeschichte der DDR* (Cologne, 1999)

———, 'Sonnenallee – ein Farbfilm über die Diktatur der Grenze(n)', *Werkstattgeschichte* 26 (2000), 87–96

———, 'Everyday History: New Approaches to the History of the Post-War Germanies' in Christoph Kleßmann (ed.), *Divided Past: Rewriting Post-War German History* (Oxford, New York, 2001), 43–67

———, 'Das Fremde im Eigenen des Staatssozialismus. Klassendiskurs und Exklusion am Beispiel der Konstruktion des "asozialen Verhaltens"' in Jan Behrends, Thomas Lindenberger and Patrice Poutrus (eds), *Fremd-Sein in der DDR. Zu historischen Ursachen der Fremdenfeindlichkeit in Ostdeutschland* (Berlin, 2003), 179–91

———, 'Review of Joshua Feinstein, The Triumph of the Ordinary: Depictions of Daily Life in the East German Cinema, 1949–1989', H-Net Reviews (March, 2004), http://www.h-net.org/reviews/

———, *Volkspolizei: Herschaftspraxis und öffentliche Ordnung im SED-Staat, 1952–1968* (Cologne, Weimar, Vienna, 2003)

Lucas, Scott, *Freedom's War. The US Crusade against the Soviet Union 1945–56* (Manchester, 1999)

Lüdtke, Alf, 'Cash, Coffee-breaks, Horseplay: *Eigensinn* and Politics among Factory Workers in Germany circa 1900' in Michael Hanagan and Charles Stephenson (eds), *Confrontation, Class Consciousness and the Labour Process* (New York, 1986), 65–95

———, '"Deutsche Qualitätsarbeit", "Spielereien" am Arbeitsplatz und "Fliehen" aus der Fabrik: Industrielle Arbeitsprozesse und Arbeitsverhalten in den 1920er Jahren – Aspekte eines offenen Forschungsfeldes' in Friedhelm Boll (ed.), *Arbeiterkulturen zwischen Alltag und Politik* (Vienna, 1986), 155–97

———, 'What Happened to the "Fiery Red Glow"? Workers' Experiences and German Fascism' in Alf Lüdtke (ed.), *The History of Everyday Life. Reconstructing Historical Experiences and Ways of Life* (Princeton, 1989), 198–251

———, (ed.), *The History of Everyday Life. Reconstructing Historical Experiences and Ways of Life* (Princeton, 1989)

———, 'The Appeal of Exterminating "Others": German Workers and the Limits of Resistance', *Journal of Modern History* 64 (December 1992), 46–67

———, *Eigen-Sinn. Fabrikalltag, Arbeitererfahrungen und Politik vom Kaiserreich bis in den Faschismus* (Hamburg, 1993)

Lüdtke, Alf, Inge Marssolek and Adelheid von Saldern (eds), *Amerikanisierung: Traum und Alptraum im Deutschland des 20. Jahrhunderts* (Stuttgart, 1996)
Maase, Kaspar, *Bravo Amerika. Erkundungen zur Jugendkultur der Bundesrepublik in den fünfziger Jahren* (Hanover, 1992)
McDaniel, Patricia, 'Shrinking Violets and Caspar Milquetoasts: Shyness and Heterosexuality from the Roles of the Fifties to The Rules of the Nineties', *Journal of Social History* 34:3 (2001), 547–68
MacDonald, Ian, *Revolution in the Head. The Beatles' Records and the Sixties* (London, 1995)
McDougall, Alan, *Youth Politics in East Germany. The Free German Youth Movement 1946–1968* (Oxford, 2004)
McLellan, Josie, *Antifascism and Memory in East Germany. Remembering the International Brigades 1945–1989* (Oxford, 2004)
McRobbie, Angela, *Feminism and Youth Culture* (Houndsmills, London, 2nd edn., 2000)
——— , 'Settling Accounts with Subcultures: A Feminist Critique' in Angela McRobbie, *Feminism and Youth Culture* (Houndsmills, London, 2nd edn, 2000), 26–43
McRobbie, Angela and Jenny Garber, 'Girls and Subcultures' in Stuart Hall and Tony Jefferson (eds), *Resistance through Rituals. Youth Subcultures in Postwar Britain* (London, 1976), 209–22
Madarász, Jeanette, *Conflict and Compromise in East Germany, 1971–1989* (Basingstoke, 2003)
Mählert, Ulrich and Gerd-Rüdiger Stephan, *Blaue Hemden, rote Fahnen. Die Geschichte der Freien Deutschen Jugend* (Opladen, 1996)
Mailer, Norman, 'The White Negro. Superficial Reflections on the Hipster' in *Advertisements for Myself* (New York, 1981), 294–345
Major, Patrick, 'Going West: the Open Border and the Problem of Republikflucht' in Patrick Major and Jonathan Osmond (eds), *Workers' and Peasants' State. Communism and Society in East Germany under Ulbricht, 1945–71* (Manchester, 2002), 190–208
Marschner, Paul, 'Die Körpererziehung als Faktor sozialistischer Persönlichkeitsentwicklung' in Akademie der Pädagogischen Wissenschaften (ed.), *Erziehung sozialistischer Persönlichkeiten* (Berlin, 1976), 241–46
Martin, Linda and Kerry Seagrave, *Anti-Rock. The Opposition to Rock 'n' Roll* (Hamden, 1988)
Marx, Karl and Frederick Engels, 'Manifesto of the Communist Party' in *Marx and Engels Selected Works* (London, 1968), 35–62
Mazower, Mark, 'Military Violence and the National Socialist Consensus: The Wehrmacht in Greece, 1941–44' in Hannes Heer and Klaus Naumann (eds), *War of Extermination: The German Military in World War II, 1941–1944* (New York, 2000), 146–74
Meckel, Christoph, *Image for Investigation. About My Father* (London, 1987)
Mehlan, Karl-Heinz, *Wunschkinder? Familienplanung, Antikonzeption und Abortbekämpfung in unserer Zeit* (Rudolstadt, 1970)
Melis, Dorothea, 'Mode nach Plan. Oder Erziehung zum Verzicht' in Dorothea Melis (ed.), *Sibylle. Modefotographie aus drei Jahrzehnten DDR* (Berlin, 1998), 48–63
Merkel, Ina, *... und Du, Frau an der Werkbank. Die DDR in den 50er Jahren* (Berlin, 1990)
——— , 'Leitbilder und Lebenswesen von Frauen in der DDR' in Hartmut Kaelbe, Jürgen Kocka and Hartmut Zwahr (eds), *Sozialgeschichte der DDR* (Stuttgart, 1994), 359–62

Merkel, Ina and Felix Mühlberg (eds), *Wunderwirtschaft. DDR-Konsumkultur in den 60er Jahren* (Cologne, 1996)
Merkel, Ina, 'Working People and Consumption under Really-existing Socialism: Perspectives from the German Democratic Republic', *International Labor and Working-Class History* 55 (Spring 1999), 92-111
_____, 'Sex and Gender in the Divided Germany: Approaches to History from a Cultural Point of View' in Christoph Kleßmann (ed.), *The Divided Past. Rewriting Post-War German History* (Oxford, New York, 2001), 91-104
Messerschmidt, James, *Masculinities and Crime. Critique and Reconceptualisation of Theory* (Lanham, 1993)
Meuschel, Sigrid, *Legitimation und Parteiherrschaft. Zum Paradox von Stabilität und Revolution in der DDR 1945-1989* (Frankfurt am Main, 1992)
Michels, Eckard, *Deutsche in der Fremdenlegion 1870-1965. Mythen und Realitäten* (Paderborn, 1999)
Ministerium für Kultur, *Die Kulturhäuser zu Volkshäusern entwickeln* (Berlin, 1963)
Mitrovich, Gregory, *Undermining the Kremlin: America's Strategy to Subvert the Soviet Bloc, 1947-1956* (Ithaca, London, 2000)
Mitscherlich, Alexander, 'Der unsichtbare Vater: Ein Problem für Psychoanalyse und Soziologie', *Kölner Zeitschrift für Soziologie und Sozialpsychologie* 7 (1955), 188-201
Mitter, Armin and Stefan Wolle, *Untergang auf Raten. Unbekannte Kapitel der DDR-Geschichte* (Munich, 1993)
Mitter, Rana and Patrick Major (eds), *Across the Blocs. Cold War Cultural and Social History* (London, Portland, 2004)
Mitterauer, Michael, *A History of Youth* (Oxford, 1992)
Moeller, Robert, *Protecting Motherhood. Women and the Family in the Politics of Postwar West Germany* (Berkeley, Los Angeles, London, 1993)
_____, 'Heimkehr ins Vaterland: Die Remaskulinisierung Westdeutschlands in den fünfziger Jahren', *Militärgeschichtliche Zeitschrift* 60:2 (2001), 403-36
_____, *War Stories. The Search for a Usable Past in the Federal Republic of Germany* (Berkeley, Los Angeles, London, 2003)
Morgan, David, 'Theater of War. Combat, the Military, and Masculinities' in Harry Brod and Michael Kaufman (eds), *Theorizing Masculinities* (Thousand Oaks, London, New Delhi, 1994), 165-82
Mosse, George, *The Image of Man. The Creation of Modern Masculinity* (New York, Oxford, 1996)
Mühlberg, Dietrich, 'Haute Couture für Alle? Über Mode und Kulturverständnis' in Dorothea Melis (ed.), *Sibylle. Modefotographie aus drei Jahrzehnten DDR* (Berlin, 1998), 8-19
Müller, Christian, *Tausend Tage bei der 'Asche'. Unteroffiziere in der NVA. Untersuchungen zu Alltag und Binnenstruktur einer 'sozialistischen' Armee* (Berlin, 2003)
Müller, Christine, *Männerprotokolle* (Berlin, 1985)
_____, *James Dean lernt kochen: Männer in der DDR, Protokolle* (Darmstadt, 1986)
Müller, Wolfgang, 'Jugendverbände und "offene Jugendarbeit"' in Helga Gotschlich, Katharina Lange and Edeltraud Schulze (eds), *Aber nicht im Gleichschritt. Zur Entstehung der Freien Deutschen Jugend* (Berlin, 1997), 62-65
Naimark, Norman, *The Russians in Germany. A History of the Soviet Zone of Occupation, 1945-1949* (Cambridge, MA, 1995)
Nationalrat der Nationalen Front, *Walter Ulbricht. Ein Leben für Deutschland* (Leipzig, 1968)

Neubert, Rudolf, 'Gedanken zum Problem der Sexualpädagogik' in Rudolf Neubert and Rudolf Weise, *Das Sexuelle Problem in der Jugenderziehung* (Rudolstadt, 1956), 7-38
———, *Mein Arztleben. Erinnerungen* (Rudolstadt, 1974)
Neumann, Günter, *Die Insulaner* (Berlin, 1955)
Neutsch, C., 'Zur Zusammenarbeit von Jugendarzt und Schule auf dem Gebiet der sexuellen Aufklärung und Erziehung', *Pädagogik Beiheft* 2 (1962), 30-31
Nickel, Hildegard Maria, 'Ein perfektes Drehbuch. Geschlechtertrennung durch Arbeit und Sozialisation' in Gislinde Schwarz and Christine Zenner (eds), *Wir wollen mehr als ein 'Vaterland'!* (Hamburg, 1990), 73-89
———, 'Geschlechtertrennung durch Arbeitsteilung', *Feministische Studien* 8 (1990), 10-19
Niethammer, Lutz, *Der 'gesäuberte' Antifaschismus. Die SED und die roten Kapos von Buchenwald* (Berlin, 1994)
———, 'Zeroing In on Change – In Search of Popular Experience in the Industrial Province of the GDR' in Alf Lüdtke (ed.), *The History of Everyday Life. Reconstructing Historical Experiences and Ways of Life* (Princeton, 1989), 252-311
Niethammer, Lutz, Alexander von Plato and Dorothee Wierling (eds), *Die Volkseigene Erfahrung. Eine Archäologie des Lebens in der Industrieprovinz der DDR* (Berlin, 1991)
Nothnagle, Alan, *Building the East German Myth. Historical Mythology and Youth Propaganda in the German Democratic Republic, 1945-1989* (Ann Arbor, 1999)
Oehme, Ursula (ed.), *Alltag in Ruinen. Leipzig 1945-1949* (Altenburg, 1995)
Oertel, Joachim, *Die DDR-Mafia. Gangster, Maoisten und Neonazis im SED-Staat* (Böblingen, 1988)
Oleschinski, Brigitte, 'Der Geschlossene Jugendwerkhof Torgau', in Ministerium für Bildung, Jugend und Sport des Landes Brandenburg (ed.), *Einweisung nach Torgau. Texte und Dokumente zur autoritären Jugendfürsorge in der DDR* (Berlin, 1997)
Ostermann, Christian, 'This is not a Politburo, but a Madhouse: The Post-Stalin Succession Struggle, Soviet Deutschlandpolitik and the SED. New Evidence from Russian, German and Hungarian Archives', *CWIHP Bulletin* 10 (March 1998), 61-110
Ostow, Robin, 'Die volkseigene Familienromanze. Arbeitende Mütter und entrechtete Väter in der Deutschen Demokratischen Republik, 1949-1989' in Dagmar Reese, Eve Rosenhaft, Carola Sachse and Tilla Siegel (eds), *Rationale Beziehungen? Geschlechterverhältnisse im Rationalisierungsprozeß* (Frankfurt am Main, 1993), 344-62
Ottensmeier, Hermann, *Faschistisches Bildungssystem in Deutschland zwischen 1933 und 1989. Kontinuität zwischen Drittem Reich und DDR* (Hamburg, 1991)
Otto, Karlheinz, *Disziplin bei Mädchen und Jungen. Ein Beitrag zur Gleichberechtigung der Geschlechter aus psychologischer, pädagogischer, soziologischer und historischer Sicht* (Berlin, 1970)
Overesch, Manfred, *Buchenwald und die DDR oder die Suche nach Selbstlegitimation* (Göttingen, 1995)
Pence, Katherine, 'Labours of Consumption: Gendered Consumers in Post-War East and West German Reconstruction' in Lynn Abrams and Elizabeth Harvey (eds), *Gender Relations in German History: Power, Agency and Experience from the Sixteenth to the Twentieth Century* (Durham, NC, 1997), 211-38

——, '"You as a Woman Will Understand": Consumption, Gender and the Relationship between State and Citizenry in the GDR's Crisis of 17 June 1953', *German History* 19:2 (February 2001), 218-52

——, 'The Myth of a Suspended Present: Prosperity's Painful Shadow in 1950s East Germany' in Paul Betts and Greg Eghigian (eds), *Pain and Prosperity. Reconsidering Twentieth-Century German History* (Stanford, 2003), 137-59

Pendergrast, Mark, *For God, Country and Coca-Cola* (Oxford, 1993)

Petrick, Fritz, *Zur sozialen Lage der Arbeiterjugend im Deutschland 1933 bis 1939* (East Berlin, 1974)

Peukert, Detlev, 'Die "Wilden Cliquen" in den zwanziger Jahren' in Wilfried Breyvogel (ed.), *Autonomie und Widerstand. Zur Theorie und Geschichte des Jugendprotestes* (Essen, 1983), 66-77

——, 'Die "Halbstarken". Protestverhalten von Arbeiterjugendlichen zwischen Wilhelmischen Kaiserreich und Ära Adenauer', *Zeitschrift für Pädagogik* 30 (1984), 533-48

——, *Grenzen der Sozial-Disziplinierung. Aufstieg und Krise der Deutschen Jugendfürsorge, 1878-1932* (Cologne, 1986)

——, *Jugend zwischen Krieg und Krise. Lebenswelten von Arbeiterjungen in der Weimarer Republik* (Cologne, 1987)

——, *Inside Nazi Germany. Conformity, Opposition and Racism*, trans. Richard Deveson (London, 1993)

Pilkington, Hilary, *Russia's Youth and its Culture: a Nation's Constructors and Constructed* (London, 1994)

Plath, Dieter, 'Über Kriminalität und innere Sicherheit' in Günter Agde (ed.), *Kahlschlag. Das 11. Plenum der SED 1965* (Berlin, 1991), 32-38

Podewin, Norbert and Walter Ulbricht. *Eineneue Biographie* (Berlin, 1995)

——, *Albert Norden. Der Rabiner-Sohn im Politbüro* (Berlin, 2001)

Poiger, Uta, 'Rebels with a Cause? American Popular Culture, the 1956 Youth Riots and New Conceptions of Masculinity in East and West Germany' in Reiner Pommerhin (ed.), *The American Impact on Postwar Germany* (Providence, New York, 1995), 92-124

——, 'A New, "Western" Hero? Reconstructing German Masculinity in the 1950s', *SIGNS* 24:1 (Autumn 1998), 147-69

——, *Jazz, Rock & Rebels. Cold War Politics and American Culture in a Divided Germany* (Berkeley, 2000)

——, 'A New, "Western" Hero? Reconstructing German Masculinity in the 1950s' in Hanna Schissler (ed.), *The Miracle Years. A Cultural History of West Germany, 1949-1968* (Princeton, Oxford, 2001), 412-27

Polster, Bernd, 'Treudeutsch, Treudeutsch. Swingheinis unterwandern den Kolonnenzwang' in Bernd Polster (ed.), *'Swing Heil'. Jazz im Nationalsozialismus* (Berlin, 1989), 129-43

Poutros, Patrice, 'Mit strengem Blick. Die sogenannten Polit. Emigranten in den Berichten des MfS' in Jan Behrends, Thomas Lindenberger and Patrice Poutrus (eds), *Fremd-Sein in der DDR. Zu historischen Ursachen der Fremdenfeindlichkeit in Ostdeutschland* (Berlin, 2003), 205-24

Rahn, Hendrik, 'Für jeden etwas – ist das richtig?', *Mitteilungen des Zentralhauses für Kulturarbeit der DDR*, Leipzig 4:4 (1966)

Rauhut, Michael, 'DDR-Beatmusik zwischen Engagement und Repression' in Günter Agde (ed.), *Kahlschlag. Das 11. Plenum der SED 1965* (Berlin, 1991), 52-63

———, *Beat in der Grauzone. DDR-Rock 1964 bis 1972. Politik und Alltag* (Berlin, 1993)
———, *Rock in der DDR* (Bonn, 2002)
Reardon, Betty, *Sexism and the War System* (New York, 1985)
Reimann, Brigitte, *Aber wir schaffen es, verlaß Dich drauf! Briefe an eine Freundin im Westen* (Berlin, 1995)
———, *Ich bedaure nichts. Tagebücher 1955-1963* (Berlin, 2000)
Reinhold, Gerd, Guido Pallak and Helmut Heim (eds), *Pädagogik-Lexikon* (Munich, Vienna, 1999)
Remath, C. and R. Schneider (eds), *Haare auf Krawall. Jugendsubkultur in Leipzig 1980 bis 1991* (Leipzig, 1999)
Rembold, Elfie, '"Dem Eindringen westlicher Dekadenz ist entgegenzuwirken". Jugend und die Kultur des Feindes in der DDR' in Jan Behrends, Thomas Lindenberger and Patrice Poutrus (eds), *Fremd-Sein in der DDR. Zu historischen Ursachen der Fremdenfeindlichkeit in Ostdeutschland* (Berlin, 2003), 167-88
Riedel, Almut, *Erfahrungen algerischer Arbeitsmigranten in der DDR* (Opladen, 1994)
Rink, Dieter, 'Das Leipziger Alternativmilieu zwischen alten und neuen Eliten' in Michael Vester, Michael Hofmann, Irene Zierke (eds), *Soziale Milieus in Ostdeutschland. Gesellschaftliche Strukturen zwischen Zerfall und Neubildung* (Cologne, 1995), 193-229
Roeling, Rob, 'Arbeiter im Uranbergbau: Zwang, Verlockungen und soziale Umstände (1945-1952)' in Rainer Karlsch and Harm Schröter (eds), *'Strahlende Vergangenheit'. Studien zur Geschichte des Uranbergbaus der Wismut* (St. Katharinen, 1996), 99-133
Rohkrämer, Thomas, *Der Militarismus der 'kleinen Leute'. Die Kriegervereine im Deutschen Kaiserreich 1871-1914* (Munich, 1990)
Roper, Michael and John Tosh (eds), *Manful Assertions: Masculinities in Britain since 1800* (London, New York, 1991)
Rosenberg, Emily, '"Foreign Affairs" after World War II: Connecting Sexual and International Politics', *Diplomatic History* (Winter, 1994), 307-37
———, 'Review Article', *Journal of American History* 84:4 (March 1998), 20
Rosenhaft, Eve, 'Working-class Life and Working-class Politics: Communists, Nazis and the State in the Battle for the Streets, Berlin 1928-1932' in Richard Bessel and E.J. Feuchtwanger (eds), *Social Change and Political Development in Weimar Germany* (London, 1981), 207-40
———, 'Organising the "Lumpenproletariat": Cliques and Communists in Berlin during the Weimar Republic' in Richard J. Evans (ed.), *German Working Class 1888-1933. The Politics of Everyday Life* (London, 1982), 174-219
———, *Beating the Fascists? The German Communists and Political Violence, 1929-1933* (Cambridge, 1983)
Ross, Corey, *Constructing Socialism at the Grass-roots* (Manchester, 2000)
———, 'Protecting the Accomplishments of Socialism? The (re)militarisation of Life in the German Democratic Republic' in Patrick Major and Jonathan Osmond (eds), *The Workers' and Peasants' State. Communism and Society in East Germany under Ulbricht 1945-1971* (Manchester, New York, 2002), 78-93
Roth-Ey, Kristin, '"Loose Girls" on the Loose? Sex, Propaganda and the 1957 Youth Festival' in Melanie Ilic, Susan Reid and Lynne Atwood (eds), *Women in the Khrushchev Era* (Houndsmills, New York, 2004), 75-95
Rowbotham, Sheila, *Woman's Consciousness, Man's World* (Harmondsworth, 1973)

Rudloff, Michael (ed.), 'Solche Schädlinge gibt es auch in Leipzig'. Sozialdemokraten und die SED (Frankfurt am Main, 1997)
Rudloff, Michael and Thomas Adam (eds), Leipzig – Wiege der Deutschen Sozialdemokratie (Berlin, 1996)
Rudorf, Reginald, Jazz in der Zone (Cologne, Berlin, 1964)
Rusch, Claudia, Meine Freie Deutsche Jugend (Frankfurt am Main, 2003)
Ryback, Timothy, Rock around the Bloc: A History of Rock Music in Eastern Europe and the Soviet Union (New York, Oxford, 1990)
Satjukow, Silke and Rainer Gries (eds), Sozialistische Helden. Ein Kulturgeschichte von Propagandafiguren in Osteuropa und der DDR (Berlin, 2002)
Savran, David, Communists, Cowboys and Queers. The Politics of Masculinity (Minneapolis, 1992)
Scheibe, Wolfgang, Die reformpädagogische Bewegung, 1900–1932 (Weinheim, 1977)
Schelsky, Helmut, Die skeptische Generation. Eine Soziologie der deutschen Jugend (Cologne, 1957)
Schildt, Axel, 'Von der Not der Jugend zur Teenager-Kultur: Aufwachsen in den 50er Jahren' in Axel Schildt and Arnold Sywottek (eds), Modernisierung im Wiederaufbau. Die westdeutsche Gesellschaft der 50er Jahren (Bonn, 1993), 335–48
_____ , Moderne Zeiten. Freizeit, Massenmedien und 'Zeitgeist' in der Bundesrepublik der 50er Jahre (Hamburg, 1995)
Schindler, Norbert, 'Guardians of Disorder: Rituals of Youthful Culture at the Dawn of the Modern Age' in Giovanni Levi and Jean-Claude Schmitt (eds), Stormy Evolution. A History of Young People in the West (Cambridge, MA, 1997), vol. I, 240–82
Schirdewan, Karl, Aufstand gegen Ulbricht. Im Kampf um politische Kurskorrektur, gegen stalinistische, dogmatische Politik (Berlin, 1994)
_____ , Ein Jahrhundert Leben. Erinnerungen und Visionen. Autobiographie (Berlin, 1998)
Schissler, Hanna, '"Normalization" as Project. Some Thoughts on Gender Relations in West Germany during the 1950s' in Hanna Schissler (ed.), The Miracle Years. A Cultural History of West Germany, 1949–1968 (Princeton, Oxford, 2001), 359–75
Schmidt, Jochen, Politische Brandstiftung. Warum 1992 in Rostock das Ausländerwohnheim in Flammen aufging (Berlin, 2002)
Schmolling, Armin, 'Zur Frage der sittlichen Gefährdung des Lehrers', Pädagogik Beiheft 2 (1962), 34–35
Schnabl, Siegfried, Mann und Frau Intim: Fragen des gesunden und des gestörten Geschlechtslebens (Rudolstadt, 1969)
_____ , Intimverhalten, Sexualstörungen, Persönlichkeit (Berlin, 1973)
_____ , Plädoyer für die Liebe (Leipzig, 1978)
Schneider, Norbert, Familie und private Lebensführung in West- und Ostdeutschland. Eine vergleichende Analyse des Familienlebens 1970 bis 1992 (Stuttgart, 1994)
Schottke, Susanne, 'Zur Entstehung und Entwicklung des Tauchscher. Ein Volksfest und seine Wandlungen' in Katrin Keller (ed.), Feste und Feiern. Zum Wandel Städtischer Festkultur in Leipzig (Leipzig, 1994), 103–16
Schreiber, Hermann, 'Sonne, Sex und Sozialismus', Der Spiegel 22 (27 May 1964), 33–37.
Schröder, Burkhard, Rechte Kerle. Skinheads, Faschos, Hooligans (Reinbek, 1992)
Schubarth, Wilfried, 'Forschungen zum Geschichtsbewußtsein' in Walter Friedrich, Peter Förster and Kurt Starke (eds), Das Zentralinstitut für Jugendforschung Leipzig 1966–1990. Geschichte, Methoden, Erkenntnisse (Berlin, 1999), 206–24

Schulze, Edeltraud, *DDR-Jugend. Ein statistisches Handbuch* (Berlin, 1995)
Schuster, Beate and Angelika Traub, 'Single Mothers in East Germany' in Eva Kolinsky and Hildegard Maria Nickel (eds), *Reinventing Gender. Women in Eastern Germany since Unification* (London, Portland, 2003), 151-71
Schütt, Hans-Dieter (ed.), *Klaus Renft. Zwischen Liebe und Zorn* (Berlin, 1997)
Schwarzer, Josef (ed.), *Deutsche Kriegsbrandstifter wieder am Werk. Eine Dokumentation über die Militarisierung Westdeutschlands* (Berlin, 1959)
Semprún, Jorge, *What a Beautiful Sunday!*, trans. Alan Sheridan (London, 1984)
Sereny, Gitta, *Into that Darkness. From Mercy Killing to Mass Murder* (London, 1974)
Shell, Kurt, *Bedrohung und Bewährung. Führung und Bevölkerung in der Berlin-Krise* (Cologne, 1965)
Sikorski, Werner and Rainer Laabs, *Checkpoint Charlie und die Mauer. Ein geteiltes Volk wehrt sich* (Berlin, 1997)
Sillge, Ursula, *Un-Sichtbare Frauen. Lesben und ihre Emanzipation in der DDR* (Berlin, 1991)
Simon, Annette, 'Ich und sie: Versuch, mir und anderen über meine ostdeutsche Moral zu erklären,' *Kursbuch* 111 (February 1993)
Simpson, Christopher, *Blowback. America's Recruitment of Nazis and its Effects on the Cold War* (New York, 1988)
Smith, Geoffrey, 'National Security and Personal Isolation: Sex, Gender, and Disease in the Cold-war United States', *International History Review* 14 (1992), 307-37
Smith, Ken, *Mental Hygiene. Classroom Films, 1945-1970* (New York, 1999)
Soukup, Jean Jacques (ed.), *Die DDR. Die Schwulen. Der Aufbruch* (Göttingen, 1990)
Stallybrass, Peter and Allon White, 'Bourgeois Hysteria and the Carnivalesque' in Simon During (ed.), *The Cultural Studies Reader* (London, New York, 2nd edn, 1999), 382-88
Stargardt, Nicholas, 'Male Bonding and the Class Struggle in Imperial Germany', *Historical Journal* 38:1 (March 1995), 175-93
Starke, Kurt and Walter Friedrich (eds), *Liebe und Sexualität bis 30* (Berlin, 1984)
Starke, Kurt, *Junge Partner. Tatsachen über Liebesbeziehungen im Jugendalter* (Leipzig, Jena, Berlin, 1980)
―――, *Schwuler Osten. Homosexuelle Männer in der DDR* (Berlin, 1994)
―――, '... ein romantisches Ideal' in Ute Kolano, *Nackter Osten. Erotik zwischen Oben und Unten* (Frankfurt an der Oder, 1995), 77-104
Stock, Manfred and Philipp Mühlberg, *Die Szene von innen. Skinheads, Grufties, Heavy Metals, Punks* (Berlin, 1990)
Stone, I.F., 'Machismo in Washington', *New York Review of Books* (18 May 1972), 13-14
Sträter, Winfried, '"Das konnte ein Erwachsener nicht mit ruhigen Augen beobachten." Die Halbstarken' in Berliner Geschichtswerkstatt (ed.), *Vom Lagerfeuer zur Musikbox. Jugendkulturen 1900-1960* (Berlin, 1985), 137-70
Straub, Martin, '"Die Abenteuer des Werner Holt" oder die Sehnsucht nach dem "gefährlichen Leben"' in Annette Leo and Peter Reif-Spirek (eds), *Helden, Täter und Verräter. Studien zum DDR-Antifaschismus* (Berlin, 1999), 211-31
Streit, Josef, 'Die nächsten Aufgaben der Staatsanwaltschaft', *Neue Justiz* (1966), 65
Strien, Renate (ed.), *Mädchenerziehung und -sozialisation in der Zeit des Nationalsozialismus und ihre lebensgeschichtliche Bedeutung* (Opladen, 2000)
Stumpfe, Mario, 'DDR - Historische Gegenwart. Eine Reflexion' in Stadt Eisenhüttenstadt/Dokumentationszentrum Alltagskultur der DDR (ed.),

Tempolinsen und P2. Eine Sammlung zur Alltagskultur der DDR entsteht (Berlin-Brandenburg, 1996), 142–45

Süß, Sonja, *Politisch mißbraucht? Psychiatrie und Staatssicherheit in der DDR* (Berlin, 1998)

Süss, Walter, *Zu Wahrnehmung und Interpretation des Rechtsextremismus in der DDR durch das MfS* (Bonn, 1993)

Sweet, Dennis, 'Die DEFA und ihre "anderen": Heiner Carows "Coming Out" als coming out der "anderen"', trans. Bernd Sahling, *Film und Fernsehen* 1 (1998), 42–47

Sywottek, Arnold, 'The Americanization of Everyday Life? Early Trends in Consumer and Leisure-time Behaviour', in Michael Ermarth (ed.), *America and the Shaping of German Society, 1945–1955* (Providence, Oxford, 1993), 132–52

Szewczyk, Hans, 'Zur Psychohygiene des Heranwachsenden. Vortrag gehalten auf der Tagung der Med.-wiss. Gesellschaft für Psychiatrie und Neurologie in Leipzig am 9. Juni 1960', *Zeitschrift für Psychiatrie, Neurologie und medizinische Psychologie* 2 (1961), 55–61

Thompson, E.P., 'The Moral Economy of the English Crowd in the Eighteenth Century', *Past and Present* 50 (1971), 76–136

Thompson, Mark, 'Reluctant Revolutionaries: Anti-Fascism and the East German Opposition', *German Politics* 8:1 (1999), 40–65

Thompson, Paul, *The Voice of the Past. Oral History* (Oxford, 3rd edn, 2000)

Thoms, Lieselotte, Hans Vieillard and Wolfgang Berger, *Walter Ulbricht. Arbeiter, Revolutionär, Staatsmann* (Berlin, 1968)

Tietze, Gerhard, 'Die Sozialpolitik beim umfassenden Aufbau des Sozialismus (1961 bis 1970)' in Gunnar Winkler (ed.), *Geschichte der Sozialpolitik der DDR, 1945–1985* (Berlin, 1989), 102–52

Tubbesing, Jürgen, *Nationalkomitee 'Freies Deutschland' – Antifaschistischer Block – Einheitspartei. Aspekte der Geschichte der antifaschistischen Bewegung in Leipzig* (Beucha, 1996)

Tyler May, Elaine, *Homeward Bound. American Families in the Cold War Era* (New York, 1988)

Uhlig, Christa, 'Gleichheit als Bildungsanspruch. Gedanken zum Bildungssystem der DDR' in Klaus Himmelstein and Wolfgang Keim (eds), *Gleichheit und Ungleichheit in der Pädagogik* (Frankfurt am Main, 2001), 149–67

Uhlmann, Irene (ed.), *Die Frau* (Leipzig, 9th edn., 1973)

U.S. Congress, Senate Committee on the Judiciary, *Comic Books and Juvenile Delinquency* (Washington, DC, 1955)

U.S. Senate, *Employment of Homosexuals and Other Sex Perverts in Government* (Washington, DC, 1950)

Verband der Deutschen Journalisten (ed.), *RIAS und SFB im Spionagedschungel Westberlin* (East Berlin, 1962)

von Flocken, Jan and Michael Scholz, *Ernst Wollweber: Saboteur - Minister - Unperson* (Berlin, 1994)

von Rabenau, Friedrich, *Vom Sinn des Soldatentums* (Cologne, 1941)

von Wensierski, Hans-Jürgen, '"Die anderen nannten uns Halbstarke" – Jugendsubkultur in den 50er Jahren' in Heinz-Hermann Krüger (ed.), *'Die Elvis-Tolle, die hatte ich mir unauffällig wachsen lassen' Lebensgeschichte und jugendliche Alltagskultur in den fünfziger Jahren'* (Opladen, 1985), 103–28

Wagnleitner, Reinhold, *Coca-Colonization and the Cold War: The Cultural Mission of the United States in Austria after the Second World War* (Chapel Hill, London, 1994)
Waibel, Harry, *Rechtsextremismus in der DDR bis 1989* (Cologne, 1996)
Walter, Michael, *Die Freie Deutsche Jugend. Ihre Funktionen im politischen System der DDR* (Freiburg, 1997)
Weber, Hermann, *Die DDR 1945-1990* (Munich, 1993)
───── , 'Die Jugendpolitik der SED 1945 bis 1989. Forschungsfragen, Quellenlage und wissenschaftliche Erwartungen' in Helga Gotschlich (ed.), *'Links und links und Schritt gehalten ...'. Die FDJ: Konzepte - Abläufe - Grenzen* (Berlin, 1994), 20-31
Weise, Rudolf, 'Die Bedeutung des Kollektivs für die sexuelle Erziehung', *Das Aktuelle Traktat* (1956), 41-61
Weitz, Eric, *Creating German Communism 1890-1990. From Popular Protests to Socialist State* (Princeton, 1997)
Wenzel, Otto, *Kriegsbereit. Der Nationale Verteidigungsrat der DDR 1960 bis 1989* (Cologne, 1995)
Wenzke, Rüdiger, *Die NVA und der Prager Frühling 1968* (Berlin, 1995)
Wheen, Francis, *Karl Marx* (London, 1999)
Wicke, Peter, 'Rock Around Socialism. Jugend und ihre Musik in einer gescheiterten Gesellschaft' in Dieter Baacke (ed.), *Handbuch Jugend und Musik* (Opladen, 1998), 293-305
Wierling, Dorothee, 'Die Jugend als innere Feind. Konflikte in der Erziehungsdiktatur der sechziger Jahre' in Hartmut Kaelbe, Jürgen Kocka and Hartmut Zwahr (eds), *Sozialgeschichte der DDR* (Stuttgart, 1994), 404-25
───── , 'Leitbilder, Vorbilder, Abbilder. Mädchen in der FDJ' in Christina Benninghaus and Kerstin Kohtz (eds), *'Sag' mir, wo die Mädchen sind ...' Beiträge zur Geschlechtergeschichte der Jugend* (Cologne, 1999), 103-26
───── , 'Opposition und Generation in Nachkriegsdeutschland. Achtundsechziger in der DDR und in der Bundesrepublik' in Christoph Kleßmann, Hans Misselwitz and Günter Wichert (eds), *Deutsche Vergangenheiten - eine gemeinsame Herausforderung. Der schwierige Umgang mit der doppelten Nachkriegsgeschichte* (Berlin, 1999) 238-252
───── , 'Mission to Happiness. The Cohort of 1949 and the Making of East and West Germans' in Hanna Schissler (ed.), *The Miracle Years. A Cultural History of West Germany, 1949-1968* (Princeton, Oxford, 2001), 110-25
───── , *Geboren im Jahr Eins. Der Jahrgang 1949 in der DDR. Versuch einer Kollektivbiographie* (Berlin, 2002)
Willis, Paul, *Learning to Labour. How Working Class Kids Get Working Class Jobs* (Farnborough, 1977)
Wilms, Günter, 'Gleiche Bildungsmöglichkeiten für alle: Bildung in der DDR' in Günter Manz, Ekkehard Sachse and Gunnar Winkler (eds), *Sozialpolitik in der DDR. Ziele und Wirklichkeit* (Berlin, 2001), 243-62
Winstermann, Karl-Heinz, '"Nie wieder Faschismus, nie wieder Krieg"' in Franz-Werner Kersting (ed.), *Jugend vor einer Welt in Trümmern* (Weinheim, 1998), 107-13
Wischnewski, Klaus, 'Die zornigen jungen Männer von Babelsberg' in Günter Agde (ed.), *Kahlschlag. Das 11. Plenum der SED 1965* (Berlin, 1991), 171-88
Wolf, Christa, *Im Dialog: Aktuelle Texte* (Berlin, Weimar, 1990)
Wolle, Stefan, *Die heile Welt der Diktatur. Alltag und Herrschaft in der DDR 1971-1989* (Berlin, 1998)

Wollweber, Ernst, 'Aus Erinnerungen. Ein Porträt Walter Ulbrichts', *Beiträge zur Geschichte der Arbeiterbewegung* 32:3 (1990), 350–78
Wyn, Joanna and Rob White, *Rethinking Youth* (London, 1997)
Zentralen Ausschuß für Jugendweihe in der DDR (ed.), *Jugendstunde. Themenplan zur Vorbereitung auf die Jugendweihe* (Berlin, 1955/56)
Zentralinstitut für Jugendforschung, 'Zur Lage unter der Jugend' (Leipzig, 1988)
Zentralkomitee der SED, *Jugend von heute. Hausherren von Morgen. Kommuniqué des Politbüros des ZK der SED zu Problemen der Jugend in der DDR* (Berlin, 1963)
Zentralleitung der Pionierorganisation Ernst Thälmann, *Thälmann ist niemals gefallen. Geschichten und Berichte* (Berlin, 1961)
Zentralrat der FDJ (ed.), *Handbuch des FDJ-Gruppenleiters* (Berlin, 1956)
_____ , *Rhythmen, Späße, Bühnensterne: Magazin der Jugend 'Neues Leben' Jahrbuch 1963* (Berlin, 1963)
_____ , *Erfahrungen bei der Gestaltung des aktuell-politischen Gesprächs in Pionierkollektiven. Stäbe Junger Agitatoren* (Berlin, 1977)

Unpublished Theses

Bickford, Andrew, 'Command Performance: Militarization, Masculinity and the State in the GDR and Post-unification Germany' (Rutgers University: Ph.D. Thesis, 2002)
Carney, Amy Beth, '"As Blond as Hitler": Positive Eugenics and Fatherhood in the Third Reich' (Florida State University: MA Dissertation, 2005)
Mac con Uladh, Damian, 'Guests of the Socialist Nation? Foreign Students and Workers in the GDR, 1949–1990' (University College London: Ph.D. Thesis, 2005)
McLellan, Josie, 'Remembering Spain. The Contested History of the International Brigades in the GDR' (Oxford University: D.Phil. Thesis, 2001)
Poiger, Uta, 'Taming the Wild West: American Popular Culture and the Cold War Battles over East and West German Identities, 1949–1961' (Brown University: Ph.D. Thesis, 1995)
Steppuhn, Siegrun, 'Gewaltsame Unzucht und Notzucht als Einzel- und Gruppendelikt' (Humboldt Universität: Ph.D. Thesis, 1970)
Wagner, B., 'Geschlechtsspezifische Verhaltensweisen über Rollenspiele' (Jena Institute for Psychology: Diplomarbeit, 1967)

INDEX

A

abortion, 31, 115n39
Abschnittsbevollmächtigter (ABV), 143, 228
Ackermann, Anton, 27
Adenauer, Konrad, 4, 44
advice literature, 3, 24–25, 33, 108, 188, 241
alcohol, 23, 35, 62, 86, 185–6, 217–8
Algerians, 221–2
Altenburg, 207, 211
Americanisation, 72, 81, 135
antifascism, 47–48, 87, 121, 128, 197, 199, 209–13, 225, 230
Apitz, Bruno, 222, 225
Arbeitsbummelei, 77
Armee Rundschau, 24, 126
asocial, 5, 35, 187, 201, 206, 219, 237
authority, 11, 14, 22, 24, 27, 44–47, 59–60, 69–70, 91, 94–95, 112–3, 128, 139, 142–5, 151, 190, 198, 215, 219, 229, 238
Axen, Hermann, 27, 135, 237

B

Bachmann, Heinz, 30
Beat, 32, 77, 136, 153n38, 168–80, 187, 189, 191, 193–4, 198–201, 208, 217, 239–40

Beatles, The, 77, 168–72, 199, 201
mania, 32, 170, 176
bebop, 23, 70, 92, 135–6, 188, 239
Becher, Johannes R., 49, 58, 119, 172
bedroom culture, 11, 105
Beimler, Hans, 48, 119
Benjamin, Hilde, 19, 29, 109
Berlin Wall, 5, 14, 31, 74, 76, 78, 114, 134, 156–7, 184, 192, 198, 237, 239
Bitterfelder Weg, 91, 136
black culture, 133–6, 138, 140, 168, 187
bodies, 24–25, 34, 134, 156, 159, 164, 168, 185, 217
Borrmann, Rolf, 22–23, 57
bourgeois, 12, 24, 60, 74, 90–4, 104, 122, 178, 214
petit, 24, 26, 80, 88, 106, 138, 159, 186, 215, 221, 238
Brando, Marlon, 71, 140
Bräunig, Werner, 4, 196–7
Buchenwald, 26, 199, 210, 222, 239
bureaucratism, 31, 101, 103, 107–8, 142, 157, 165–8
Butlers, The, 34, 169, 173–4

C

capitalism, 2, 62, 73, 108, 158, 178, 195, 209, 211

Capitol Meute, 86, 141, 144–5, 179, 196, 240, 243
capri pants, 106–8
carnival, 35, 93–6
casualness, 25, 32, 71, 123, 132, 140, 178, 197
Central Institute for Youth Research (ZIJ), 7, 32, 63, 78
Centre for Contemporary Cultural Studies (CCCS), 9–10
checked shirts, 70, 81n6, 89, 96
children's homes, 23, 35–36, 218, 240
chores, 20–21, 35, 59, 64
church, 61
  and youth gangs, 179–80
cinema, 4, 59, 76, 105, 159, 196, 222
  as a space to congregate, 73, 86–87, 172, 193, 218, 240
  Kino der Jugend, 172–3
Clara-Zetkin Park, 34, 150–1, 188
cleanliness, 22–23, 35, 42n143, 75, 96, 105, 109, 145, 160, 190, 197, 206, 228
clothing, 13, 29, 58, 72, 76, 79, 86, 89, 106, 110, 140, 144, 146, 168, 175–6, 186, 190, 197, 238
co-education, 55, 57, 109
cold war, 1–3, 29, 47–48, 75, 93, 135, 177, 238
comic books, 58, 71–72, 75–76, 79, 89, 123, 146
concentration camps, 46, 50, 186, 199, 209–12, 222, 237
conscription, 31, 124, 184
conservatives, 12, 22, 32, 164
consumerism, 1, 29, 32, 36, 41n120, 71, 74, 79, 86, 102, 104, 159–60, 170, 175, 179, 195
contamination, 24, 27, 75, 92, 142, 146, 192
cowboy, 3–4, 95, 108, 123, 136
crime, criminality, 3, 75, 77, 86, 100, 142–8, 166, 214, 219
cultural studies, 9–12, 17n75

culture, 6, 10, 14, 30, 49, 73, 75, 91, 96, 110, 127, 190, 210, 240–1
  political, 3, 19
  popular, 2, 32, 72, 76, 78, 89–91, 123, 135, 150
  street, 85–90, 92, 110, 141
  working-class, 60–62, 64, 87, 89, 91, 132, 136, 141
  youth, 69–81, 85, 89–90, 92–93, 102, 105, 108, 135, 151, 169, 173–4, 189, 238, 240

D

dancing, 22–23, 71, 80, 90, 92, 103, 108, 138, 140, 145, 152, 158, 168–9, 173–4, 176, 238
  apart, 25, 90, 134–5, 139
  formal, 91, 108, 139, 188
Davis, Angela, 206
Dean, James, 71, 123, 138, 140
decadence, 22–23, 32, 77, 107, 122, 152, 178, 189, 194–5, 208, 238
DEFA, 4, 74, 195, 219, 233n72, 233n75
defiance, 14, 141, 145, 178, 215, 217, 240
democracy, 27, 44, 100, 118, 229
denazification, 55, 209
de-Stalinisation, 29, 114
Deutschlandtreffen (1964), 169, 173–5
deviance, 32, 142, 216, 240
divorce, 33
domesticity, 3, 21, 24, 26, 34, 42n138, 44–45, 107, 240
double burden, 19, 21, 26, 34
Dresden, 25, 91, 118, 197, 221

E

East Berlin, 35, 64, 93, 108, 160, 172, 174, 177, 196, 206, 208, 221, 238

Edelweiss Pirates, 87, 98n22, 240
education, 31, 54–65, 77, 101, 124, 160–5, 240
 antifascist, 208–13
 gender differences in, 54–60
 Ministry of, 55, 61, 63, 163, 165, 239
 reforms to, 31, 55–57
effeminacy, 23–24, 81n4, 187, 200
Eigensinn, 12, 47, 59, 85, 92, 152, 178
Eisler, Hanns, 108, 135
Eleventh Party Plenum, 32, 179, 195–6
emancipation, 21, 29, 60, 64, 159, 239
espionage, 74, 77, 144, 150, 184, 208, 243

F

fairgrounds, 73, 93, 95–96, 152, 196
false comradeship, 63
 consciousness, 73, 211
 romanticism, 61
family, 1, 11, 19–22, 26, 28, 34, 43–45, 47, 60, 105–7, 109, 126, 211, 227, 240
 Family Code (1965), 21, 31
fan clubs, 77, 79–80
fashion, 6, 23–24, 28, 58, 69, 71–72, 76, 79–80, 89, 102, 104, 106–8, 138–42, 146–7, 151–2, 158–60, 164, 168, 172, 176, 179, 189, 216
Fatherland, 4, 31, 58, 157, 197, 210
fathers, 21, 25, 43–45, 61, 186, 195, 202, 225, 227
FDGB, 91, 110
FDJ, 28, 63, 70, 77, 80, 88, 93–94, 100–105, 107–10, 113, 118–20, 124, 127, 135, 139, 146, 156–8, 165–9, 173, 175–7, 206, 212–3, 230, 239, 242n13
 Order Group, 23, 125

femininity, 22, 24–25, 107, 132, 159, 190, 194
feminism, 10, 14, 25, 34, 138, 141
film-makers, 32, 167, 175, 219
films, 3–5, 49–50, 71–72, 74–75, 86–87, 121, 123–4, 144, 148–9, 172–3, 178, 187, 195–6, 199, 206, 213, 218–9, 222, 225, 237
football hooliganism, 219, 226
Foreign Legion, 215–6, 218–9
freedom, 2, 13, 27, 29, 34, 43, 75, 93, 124, 139, 157, 165, 168, 174–5, 178, 185, 189, 196, 198, 202, 206, 213, 215, 229
Friedrich, Walter, 8, 32–33, 159
Fröhlich, Paul, 176
Fuchs, Jürgen, 186, 201–2, 204n66
functionaries, 23, 26–27, 31, 61–62, 74, 88, 90, 95, 101, 103, 105, 107–8, 113, 122, 126, 144, 146–8, 152, 169, 172–4, 176–8, 187, 209, 212, 237–8

G

Gammler, 77, 172, 201, 208
gang rape, 32, 122, 214–5
gangs, 85–96, 111, 113, 125, 140–2, 145–8, 150, 157–8, 172, 177, 188, 214, 239
gender, 2, 19–26, 28–33, 49, 54–57, 61, 64, 69, 78, 88, 105–6, 108–9, 126–7, 138–41, 160–1, 210, 216, 238
generation, 20, 48, 55, 58–59, 62, 64, 69, 72–73, 80, 86, 101, 121, 132, 139, 151, 158–9, 161, 167, 172, 177–8, 192, 195, 197–8, 202, 213, 221–2
girls, 3, 6, 10, 11, 21–24, 29, 50, 54–59, 63–64, 78–80, 85, 87, 91, 105–9, 118, 120, 126, 138, 140–1, 158, 160, 167–8, 172,

188–9, 194, 196, 198, 214, 216, 218–9, 222,
Gramsci, Antonio, 10–11, 92
Grenzgänger, 76
GST, 120, 199, 215, 221

H

Hager, Kurt, 176
haircuts, 7, 13, 70, 89, 92–93, 103, 110, 139–40, 144, 146–8, 150–1, 175–8, 184, 186, 188, 192
Halbstarken, 123, 133, 137, 139–40, 218, 233n75
Haley, Bill, 133–35, 146
hardliners, 119, 198
Hebdige, Dick, 79, 171
hedonism, 32, 34, 92, 106, 139, 158
hegemony, 7, 10, 11–12, 81, 127, 172
Heimat, 58, 81
Hennecke, Adolf, 47
heroes, heroism, 2–5, 43, 45–50, 54, 95, 109, 118–9, 121–4, 164, 193–5, 197–8, 210, 222, 229, 238–9
  anti-heroes, 71
heroes of labour, 46–48
Herrnstadt, Rudolf, 27–28
Heym, Stefan, 136, 209
Hitler, Adolf, 121, 124–5, 197, 211–4, 225–6
Hitler Youth, 85, 101, 121, 197
Hodann, Max, 28
Hollywood, 2–3, 140
Holocaust, 27, 44, 210–11
homoeroticism, 33, 122
homosexuality, 3, 28, 31, 33, 139, 180, 185, 196, 200, 214–5, 221, 237–8
Honecker, Erich, 27–32, 35–36, 46, 50, 103–4, 107, 119, 121, 174, 177, 195, 198, 206
Honecker, Margot, 63, 201, 239

Humboldt University, 30, 120
Hungarian Uprising, 30, 110–1, 114
husbands, 19–22, 24–25, 44, 126

I

immunity, 12, 29, 69, 73–74, 91, 240
'impudent socialists', 166, 176, 178
infection, 3, 133, 188–9
intellectuals, 32, 91, 136, 159, 164
intelligence agencies, 27, 75, 77, 92, 146–7

J

Janka, Walter, 29,
jazz, 22, 30, 92, 132, 135, 140, 145, 187
jeans, 71, 79–80, 89, 136, 138, 144, 192, 207, 217
Jews, 26, 27, 187, 210–2, 218, 222, 226, 237
Jugendkommuniqué (1963), 165, 167–8, 172
Jugendweihe, 23, 222
Junge Welt, 28, 76, 107–9, 126, 133, 135, 166–7
juvenile delinquency, 3, 86–87, 100, 112, 142, 192, 217

K

Kaiser, Jakob, 93
Kampfgruppen, 30–31, 123, 156, 215, 229
Karl-Marx-Stadt, 90, 207, 216
Khrushchev, Nikita, 1–2, 29, 103, 114, 218
Kinder von Golzow, 34
Klein, Manfred, 120
Klemperer, Victor, 118
knuckledusters, 79, 89, 146, 198
KPD, 19, 26, 49, 87, 121, 130n52, 161

Krug, Manfred, 4–5, 196
KVP, 29, 107

L

Lambrecht, Christine, 21, 34
Law for the Democratisation of German Schools (1946), 55
Law on the Integrated System of Education (1965), 31
Law on the Protection of Mother and Child (1950), 19
League of German Girls, 50
legitimacy, 14, 210, 238
Leipzig, 5–6, 30, 34, 85–86, 93–94, 111–2, 119, 125, 135–6, 140, 144, 146–8, 152, 161, 168, 172, 174, 176, 196, 199–200, 208, 211–2, 214, 217, 221–2
Leipziger Volkszeitung, 83n43, 93, 144, 146, 199, 217
leisure, 20, 29, 62, 71–74, 78, 94, 100–3, 114, 158, 179, 239
Lemmnitz, Alfred, 165
Leuna, 4, 195–6
liberalisation, 29, 32, 112, 163, 172, 176–9, 206
lifestyle, 6, 13, 58, 72, 74, 77, 80, 132, 168, 171–2, 243
Lipsi, 147, 155n99, 169
Loest, Erich, 8, 93, 153n38
lumpen, 87–90, 96

M

machismo, 4, 10, 14, 56, 60, 85–86, 89, 128, 132, 137, 141, 151, 190, 195, 214, 219, 221–2, 227, 230, 238
Magazin, Das, 28
magazines, 21, 24–25, 33, 45, 71–72, 77–78, 106, 121, 151, 159–60, 166, 196, 199
Magdeburg, 104, 212

Mailer, Norman, 135–6, 215
Marchwitza, Hans, 49, 109
masculinity, 1–3, 9–10, 23, 43–49, 59–60, 85–87, 119, 121–2, 127, 132, 137–42, 145–6, 164, 172, 185, 187, 190, 192, 198, 209, 214–5, 219, 229, 241
  aggressive, 1, 10, 47, 59, 71, 87, 120–1, 123, 127, 132, 135, 139, 141, 147, 172, 188, 219, 222, 226
  frontier, 4–5, 95, 123, 127
  laddish, 10, 58–59, 215
  performance of, 61, 86, 138–9, 208–9, 216
mass media, 2–3, 11–12, 33, 54, 69–81, 102, 105, 126, 152, 157, 166, 177, 213, 217, 226
mass organisations, 30, 101, 103
Meuten, 85–89, 98n23, 140–1, 144–150, 179, 215, 240, 243
middle-class, 3, 6, 54, 56, 61, 63, 72, 92, 98n37, 120, 122, 178, 188, 197
Mielke, Erich, 29, 35, 127, 200, 226, 239
milieux, 6, 12, 35, 55, 63–64, 140, 196
militarism, 45, 48, 118–20, 128, 161, 199, 202, 210, 240
misrule, 93–96, 113
modern, 13, 29, 58, 61, 64, 69, 72, 78, 80, 88, 94, 101, 103, 107–10, 125, 132, 136, 151, 157, 159–67, 173–8, 187, 193, 216, 238, 240
Modrow, Hans, 108
Monroe, Marilyn, 72, 76
moral panics, 12, 71, 75, 189, 216
Moscow, 2, 27–28, 35, 123
Müller, Christine, 21, 34
music, 6–7, 10, 23–24, 34, 61, 69, 71–72, 75–77, 80–81, 86, 92–93, 101, 104, 112–3, 132–42, 146, 150–1, 159–60, 167–79, 187–90, 194, 198, 201–2, 216–7, 243

musicians, 8, 32, 34, 167–74, 189

N

National Front
  (GB), 10;
  (GDR), 91, 93, 110, 148
National Socialism, 6–7, 54–55, 93, 118, 189, 197, 208, 210–13, 221–2, 226, 230
neo-Nazis, 219, 225–30, 238–9, 241
Neubert, Rudolf, 21, 25–26, 39n65, 57, 109, 116n65
Neues Deutschland, 28, 92, 133–4, 174, 189, 196
Neues Leben, 160
Neutsch, Erik, 4–5, 91, 193–5, 197, 204n66
nonconformity, 6–8, 70, 133, 152, 178–9, 186, 189–90
Norden, Albert, 29, 103–4, 239
nudism, 29–30, 33, 35, 241
NVA, 48, 126, 157, 185–6, 217

O

Oberschule, 60, 90, 160, 177, 212, 222, 226
opposition, 11, 13, 26–27, 29–30, 59, 61, 70, 87, 93, 95, 119, 128, 148, 151, 171, 178, 180, 209, 213, 216, 225, 228, 240
oral history, 7–9, 17n60
'orgies', 23, 38n47, 134, 180
otherness, 8, 146, 218
Otto, Karlheinz, 56, 64
outlaws, 5, 95, 142, 214

P

paramilitary organisations, 30, 119–20, 123, 125, 127, 221
parents, 34, 56–57, 59, 69–70, 72–75, 105, 133, 137, 190, 213, 227, 240
authoritarian, 13, 106
failure of, 21, 62, 64
parties, 23, 77, 80, 122, 139
Pieck, Wilhelm, 27, 127, 243
police, 4, 9, 14, 23, 28–29, 35–36, 46–48, 72, 75, 85, 89, 92, 94–96, 111–13, 119, 121–8, 133–5, 138–51, 170, 173, 177, 187–8, 192–3, 197–200, 208, 215–6, 229–30, 240
Politbüro, 27–29, 36, 49, 78, 103–4, 124, 157, 160, 167, 176–7, 186
  Communiqué to Youth, 114, 167
  Youth Commission, 176
popular culture, 2–3, 32, 72, 76, 78, 89–91, 96, 123, 150
Prague Spring, 180, 201
Presley, Elvis, 23, 72, 77, 80, 94, 132, 135, 140, 147, 150–1
prisoners, 190–3
  concentration camp, 210, 222
prisoners of war (POWs), 4, 44
promiscuity, 23, 135, 197
propaganda, 2, 4, 19, 24, 32, 45, 73, 81n4, 95, 123, 127, 157, 161, 177, 186, 195, 209–10, 213, 219, 225, 229
prostitution, 23, 35, 86, 122, 145, 188–9, 196
protest, 13, 30, 106, 120, 136, 146–7, 151, 157, 173, 178, 199, 206, 214–5, 221, 230, 240
psychological warfare, 74–78, 95, 199, 219, 226
puberty, 24, 105
punks, 219, 221, 227

R

racism, 10, 136, 138, 208–9, 213, 221, 225, 227, 229–30
radio, 12, 72–80, 135, 157

Radio Luxemburg, 23, 77–78
  transistor, 102, 132–3, 172
reconstruction, socialist, 4, 43, 91, 100, 109
Red Front, 49, 121, 123
re-education, 45, 54–65, 111
reform, 30–32, 103, 108–10, 114, 159, 165, 167–8, 170, 175–7, 179–80, 238
  education, 55, 163
  gender, 21, 23
  social reformers, 92
Reimann, Brigitte, 4, 91, 106, 125, 136–7, 197
Renft, Klaus, 8, 13, 80, 89, 141, 173, 177, 207, 243
Republikflucht, 103, 124
resistance, 10, 13, 29, 92–93, 106, 142, 200
  antifascist, 12, 46, 49–50, 121, 210
  passive, 81
respectability, 22–23, 25, 35, 86, 88–92, 120, 142–3, 151, 186, 189–90, 200, 228
revisionists, 29
RIAS, 77
riot, 71, 77, 93, 133, 145, 149, 208
rockers, 125–6, 132–51, 187, 189, 215–6, 219
rock 'n' roll, 13, 23, 34, 71, 80, 94, 132–52, 168, 171–2, 187, 189, 239–40, 243
Rolling Stones, The, 172
Rostock, 80, 228
rowdies, rowdyism, 4–5, 9, 23, 57–58, 92, 95, 125–6, 133, 141, 143–8, 151, 157, 177, 227, 230, 239
Rudorf, Reginald, 30

S

samba, 70, 93, 140

Schirdewan, Karl, 28–30, 103–4, 110
Schmidt, Elli, 27–28
schools, 34, 55–65, 69, 74, 106, 109, 118, 127, 152, 158, 165, 176, 201, 213, 218, 239
Schumann, Horst, 158, 177
science, 20, 31, 56, 59, 104
Second World War, 3, 43, 48, 72, 186, 211, 214, 225
secularism, 25, 31, 241
self-determination, 13, 87, 179
sex education, 31, 57, 188
sexism, 26, 60, 141
sexuality, 2–3, 9, 13, 22–26, 28–29, 31–33, 57, 105–9, 135, 139, 180, 185, 189, 237–8, 241
shame, 22–23, 34, 90, 106–7, 125, 194
Sindermann, Horst, 27, 119
skinheads, 10, 219–30, 241
Social Democrats, 26–27, 29, 55, 88, 91, 96, 134
Soviet Union, 2–3, 23, 27–28, 31, 44, 46–47, 75, 78, 94, 123, 146, 148, 150, 199, 225–6, 238
Spanish Civil War, 48–49, 87
sport, 35, 46, 48, 54, 58, 61–62, 101, 119–20, 125, 160–1, 167, 190, 221, 227
Spur der Steine, 4–5, 195–6
SS, 45, 88, 222, 233n51
Stalinism, 6, 26–27, 29, 47, 94, 103, 114, 119, 186, 196
Stasi (MfS), 9, 35–36, 80, 125, 127, 150, 180, 198, 201, 206–8, 217, 219, 221, 226, 228, 230, 240–1, 243
stereotypes, 95, 187–9, 216, 227
  gender, 2, 21, 25, 54, 56–57, 81n4
  racial, 12, 133, 136
  simian, 187
Stern, Heinz, 174
Stoph, Willi, 124

street, 11, 23, 25, 49, 59, 61, 73, 100, 105–6, 113, 121, 125, 133, 139, 144–52, 179, 184, 188, 192–3, 199, 202, 206–7, 229
   culture, 85–96, 110–12, 141
   -wise, 86, 113, 169, 172
subcultures, 8–13, 29, 79, 87, 89, 92, 135–6, 142, 145–7, 150–1, 171–2, 178, 187–9, 206, 213–6, 219, 221, 230, 240
subversion, 24, 74–77, 144, 177, 184
swastikas, 197, 210, 212, 225
Szewczyk, Hans, 111

T

Tauchscher, 93–96
teachers, 6, 11, 24, 35, 55–57, 60, 63, 72–73, 80, 101, 113, 131n84, 158, 160, 163, 165, 167, 176, 193, 197, 209–12, 225–6, 237
technology, 20, 56, 70, 104, 120, 175
teenage, 3, 11, 69–81, 88, 100–2, 105–8, 111, 133, 137–8, 142, 151, 158, 165–6, 170–5, 186, 212, 238, 240
television, 2, 56, 59, 61, 71–72, 74, 76–78, 80, 157, 160, 169
territoriality, 10, 85, 87, 142
Thälmann, Ernst, 46, 49, 86, 89, 107, 150, 207, 228, 237
Torgau, 190, 192
transistor radios, 102, 132–3, 172, 216
trash literature, 62, 70–71, 75, 77, 147
Turba, Kurt, 166, 173, 176
Twentieth Party Congress (1956), 29

U

Ulbricht, Walter, 2, 4, 6, 26–32, 61, 64, 66n31, 70, 94, 98n37, 103–5, 107, 109–10, 112, 119, 134, 151, 157–69, 174–8, 186, 195, 206, 218
upbringing, 21, 43, 54, 64, 105, 109, 111, 168, 227
uprising, 1953, 27–28, 46–47, 70, 92–93, 123, 188
U.S.A., 1–2, 9, 11, 70, 72, 75, 211, 217
utopia, 2, 5, 30, 35, 94, 109, 238

V

veterans, 19, 26–27, 102, 120, 127, 199–200, 210, 237
Vietnam, 1, 199, 206, 218, 228
violence, 5, 10, 44, 55, 75, 86–87, 106, 108–9, 119–25, 128, 132–6, 141–2, 150–1, 157, 200, 208–9, 214–5, 221–2, 226–30, 238–9
VVN, 27, 210

W

Wandervogel, 100, 105
Wayne, John, 3, 95
Wehrmacht, 124, 186, 221
Weimar Republic, 26, 47–48, 55, 58, 98n22, 238
Weltfestspiele, 206
West Berlin, 12, 29, 73–76, 105, 108, 133–4, 145, 147, 150, 170, 189
West Germany, 22, 33, 43–44, 55, 71, 73, 75–77, 79, 89, 96, 105–6, 124, 127, 132–3, 147, 178, 180, 198, 219, 221, 243
Westerns, 3, 5, 86, 95, 123
'white Negroes', 135–7, 188
Willis, Paul, 10, 59
Wismut, 4, 91, 196
Wolf, Christa, 50, 91, 98n43, 136
Wollweber, Ernst, 29, 103
women, 44, 49, 54–56, 88, 109, 122, 126, 140, 158, 160, 187, 214, 226
   career, 19–20, 25, 59, 159

loose, 7, 14, 23, 34
mothers, 19–22, 24
wives, 19–22
young, 7, 14, 24, 32, 36, 59, 81n4, 105–8, 120, 159, 188
workers, 4–5, 7, 12, 27–28, 46–49, 56, 59, 62, 64–65, 88, 90–91, 120–3, 136–7, 139, 167, 184, 192, 196–7, 209
female, 22, 59, 109
guest, 221, 228–9
male, 4–5, 19, 47
young, 56, 60, 73, 79, 85, 92–96, 103, 133, 144, 186, 219
working-class
culture, 10, 62, 85, 87, 89–92, 96, 110, 141, 188
movement, 23, 47, 54, 61, 88

neighbourhoods, 6, 88–89, 169
parents, 60, 64
writers, 8, 32–33, 106, 122, 136–7, 167, 175, 196, 204n66

Y

young Christians (*Junge Gemeinde*), 28, 69, 120, 179, 187
youth
clubs, 90, 101, 108–14, 125, 152, 160, 172, 177, 200–1, 239, 242n13
culture, 12, 70–76, 78–81, 85, 89–93, 102, 105, 108, 135, 151, 169, 173–4, 189, 238, 240
policy, 30, 100, 103–4, 159–60, 177
workers, 111, 113, 230

www.ingramcontent.com/pod-product-compliance
Lightning Source LLC
Chambersburg PA
CBHW071223080526
44587CB00013BA/1475